JAVA™

Developer's Resource

A TUTORIAL AND ON-LINE SUPPLEMENT

Elliotte Rusty Harold

Prentice Hall PTR
Upper Saddle River, NJ   07458
http://www.prenhall.com

Library of Congress Cataloging-in-Publication Data
Harold, Elliotte Rusty,
    Java developer's resource : a tutorial and on-line supplement /
Elliotte Rusty Harold.
        p.   cm.
    Includes index.
    ISBN 0-13-570789-7 (alk. paper)
    1. Java (computer program language)   I. Title.
    QA76.73.J38H37   1996
    005.13`3--dc20
                                                    96-26213
                                                    CIP

Editorial/Production Supervision: Craig Little
Acquisitions Editor: Mary Franz
Editorial Assistant: Noreen Regina
Buyer: Alexis R. Heydt
Cover Design: Anthony Gemmellaro
Cover Design Direction: Jerry Votta
Art Director: Gail Cocker-Bogusz
Series Design: Meg VanArsdale

© 1997 Prentice Hall PTR
Prentice-Hall, Inc.
A Simon & Schuster Company
Upper Saddle River, NJ 07458

The publisher offers discounts on this book when ordered in bulk quantities.
For more information, contact

    Corporate Sales Department,
    Prentice Hall PTR
    One Lake Street
    Upper Saddle River, NJ 07458
    Phone: 800-382-3419; FAX: 201-236-7141
    E-mail (Internet): `corpsales@prenhall.com`

Printed in the United States of America

10 9 8 7 6 5 4 3 2 1

ISBN 0-13-570789-7

Prentice-Hall International (UK) Limited, *London*
Prentice-Hall of Australia Pty. Limited, *Sydney*
Prentice-Hall Canada Inc., *Toronto*
Prentice-Hall Hispanoamericana, S.A., *Mexico*
Prentice-Hall of India Private Limited, *New Delhi*
Prentice-Hall of Japan, Inc., *Tokyo*
Simon & Schuster Asia Pte. Ltd., *Singapore*
Editora Prentice-Hall do Brasil, Ltda., *Rio de Janeiro*

To my wife, Beth

Trademarks

CONTENTS

JAVA DEVELOPER'S RESOURCE

PREFACE

Hello world. Welcome to the Java Developer's Resource. I hope you like it.

Java has caused more excitement than any development on the Internet since Mosaic. Internet newsgroups and mailing lists dedicated to Java generate hundreds of messages a day. Thousand-seat Java classes fill up within hours of announcement. Everyone, it seems, is talking about Java. Unfortunately, very few people seem to know anything about it. This book is designed to change that.

Who You Are

This is a book for serious programmers. If Jolt Cola flows in your veins and you think John Von Neumann, Alan Turing, and Grace Hopper are some of the most important figures of this century, then this book is for you. I've never been fond of books that talked down to me, so I hope I've managed to avoid that flaw here.

Nonetheless, it's impossible for authors to know exactly where every one of their readers will be coming from. Some of you, I'm sure, write super-efficient hash table algorithms in C++ on napkins at breakfast while others may be spending their days writing button handlers in HyperTalk. Some of you are spectacular Macintosh programmers while others think graphical user interfaces are a waste of CPU cycles. Therefore, I try not to assume any particular knowledge in this book. Most especially, I do not assume that you have programmed in C or C++, that you have written software for GUI environments, or that you are familiar with object-oriented programming.

On the other hand, I do hope you have some prior experience with programming. There's no question that the more experience you have with programming, the easier it will be for you to learn Java. While I don't assume that you know what the syntax of a for loop is in C, I do assume that you know what a loop is. Similarly, I assume you know what an algorithm is and how you might go about constructing one to solve a given problem. These are concepts that should be common to all programmers, regardless of the languages or systems they're accustomed to working with. There is a certain way of thinking, of planning an attack on a problem, that comes with being a programmer, just as there is a way of thinking that comes with being an artist or a journalist or a scientist; and it is this style of thinking that I assume.

If this isn't true, if you have no prior programming experience at all, I can still promise you that Java is an easier language to teach and learn than most, and you could certainly do worse than trying to learn the skill of programming with Java and this book. Intelligent people have certainly mastered programming beginning with far worse books and infinitely more complex languages. Nonetheless, programming is a skill that's difficult to teach without direct, personal interaction between human beings. I certainly would never have learned to program without teachers to help me over the initial rough spots. If you have no prior programming experience at all, I recommend taking a short course in Java programming to get up and running on the basics of writing and debugging programs, and, more importantly, to learn how programmers think.

Beyond programming skills, this book assumes that you are familiar with the Internet and the World Wide Web and have at least a rudimentary knowledge of HTML. You don't need to be an HTML expert, but you should be able to create a basic web page including links, style tags, and images. If your HTML needs some brushing up, I recommend Larry Aronson's *The HTML 3 Manual of Style* (Ziff-Davis, 1995).

This book also assumes familiarity with high-school-level math. Do you remember asking your teacher what algebra was good for? Computer programming (in any language, not just Java) is one of the things it's good for. It's impossible to teach programming without some familiarity with basic math. However, the math used here is fairly elementary and should not be a large burden for most people.

Using This Book

This book is designed to be read pretty much from start to finish. While it is occasionally possible to read chapters out of order (for example, Chapter 18 on Exceptions can be read any time after Chapter 9), I think you'll get the most out of this book if you read it in the intended order.

Some readers, especially those with a great deal of experience in C++, may find a few of the sections overly obvious, particularly Chapters 6 and 7, which introduce object-oriented concepts for the first time. While I've tried to spice things up for everyone with a few well-placed anecdotes, you should feel free to skip ahead once you understand the syntax and purpose of a particular Java feature.

Chapter Enders

You will find five sections at the end of each chapter. First is a Q&A section with some more detailed questions that may have arisen in the minds of more experienced readers or those of you with particular backgrounds. Then there's a quiz. Everyone should consider the quiz questions. Most of which are a little on the devious side. I hope you'll find them enjoyable and not a little challenging. Third is a series of exercises. For the most part, these range from very simple to quite complex. You may pick those that seem most interesting to you, but it is important that you at least attempt some of them. You can only learn programming by writing programs, not just by reading a book. Then I give you a brief summary of what you should have gleaned from the chapter, a preview of what's coming up, and finally some suggestions for further reading.

Style

A few notes about the style. I've used a source code coloring editor to delineate different parts of Java programs. Java keywords are in bold. Comments are in italic. When entering programs, you do not need to use this formatting. The compiler cares only about the text. It does not concern itself with the formatting.

The appropriate grammar for a book about programming is always a little questionable, especially in a case-sensitive language like Java.

When the rules of English have conflicted with the rules of Java, I have regrettably let English be the loser. You will note that on occasion sentences do not always begin with capital letters. It has sometimes been necessary to begin a sentence with a Java word or phrase that simply does not mean the same thing when capitalized. Most of the time this should be obvious from the context and the formatting.

Conversely, Java tends to capitalize names of classes; and many words that you may not normally think of as proper nouns, like Component and String, are in fact proper nouns in the context of Java. Therefore, they have been capitalized when they are used to refer to their specific use in Java rather than their more generic meaning.

Similarly, it may appear that spaces are missing in a word like LayoutManager. Again, this is because that word needs to fit into Java's rules for naming classes before it fits into the Queen's English. Most of this should be obvious from the context.

Cross-Platform Issues

I am quite to pleased to report that almost all the programs in this book have been tested on Solaris, Windows 95, and the Macintosh. At least for simple programs of the sort used for teaching, Java's claims of cross-platform compatibility seem to be accurate. You will note that screen shots alternate between all three platforms.

In fact the largest problem I encountered in trying to make this book platform-neutral was accounting for different terminologies on different platforms, a problem endemic to any cross-platform book. For the record, Mac users should read folder wherever they see the word directory, and Windows and UNIX mavens should reverse this.

Additional Resources

When I started work on this book many months ago, I posted some of my notes on a web site called Café Au Lait, which currently resides at http://sunsite.unc.edu/javafaq/. As preliminary and incomplete as those notes were, they attracted the attention of Mary Franz at Prentice Hall and led to the book you have in front of you. I hope I know a little more about Java now, and I hope I'm able to impart some of that knowledge to you.

The original Café Au Lait web site is still active and has continued to grow, and I encourage you to visit (http://sunsite.unc.edu/javafaq). Among other things, it now includes the source code from this book and answers to the various exercises and quizzes. It also includes a preliminary version of this book, a Java FAQ list, breaking news about Java, a list of Java user groups, and the usual collection of links to other sites.

As well as the web site, I also run a low-volume mailing list called Café Au Lait which includes various of my musings about Java and other matters. To subscribe, send email to listproc@educom.unc.edu with the following text in the body of the message:

```
subscribe cafeaulait Your_Full_Name_Here
```

To unsubscribe repeat these instructions but replace "subscribe" with "unsubscribe." This is a low-volume, one-way mailing list that should not clog anyone's mailbox. Back issues are available on the Café Au Lait web site.

I am interested in hearing from readers. You can correspond with me directly via email to elharo@sunsite.unc.edu. I am especially interested in hearing about mistakes in this book, and parts you may find less than clear. The more interesting queries may be answered in my newsletter, or in future editions of this or other books. However, please realize that I get several hundred email messages a day; and I cannot and will not respond to personal requests for help. If you have a question about Java, I recommend posting to the appropriate comp.lang.java newsgroup, where it will be seen by thousands of people able to help you.

Acknowledgements

Many people were involved in the production of this book. Donald Ball of sunsite.unc.edu gave the original Web version of this book a home where it could be spotted by my publisher. My acquisitions editor, Mary Franz, got this book rolling; and my agent, David Rogelberg convinced me it was possible to make a living writing computer books. My development editor, Thomas Powell, provided many helpful comments that substantially improved the book. My production editor, Craig Little, put up with my insane attempt to write a book in ClarisWorks. All these people deserve much thanks and credit. Finally, I'd like to save my largest thanks for my wife, Beth, without whose support and assistance this book would never have happened.

Elliotte Rusty Harold
elharo@sunsite.unc.edu
June 24, 1996

PART ONE

Getting Started with Java

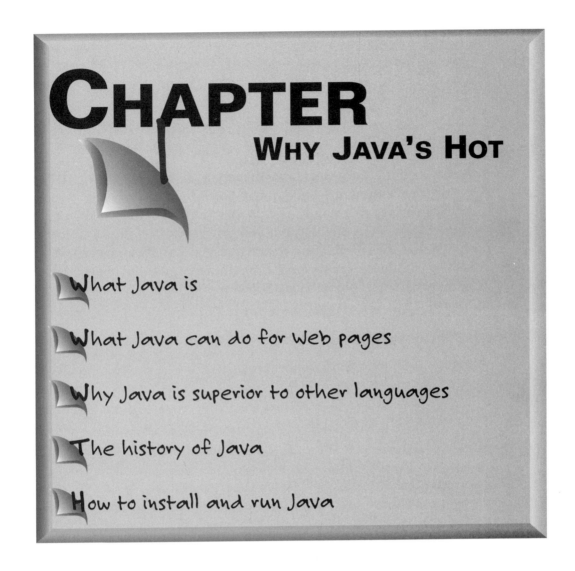

CHAPTER

WHY JAVA'S HOT

- What Java is

- What Java can do for Web pages

- Why Java is superior to other languages

- The history of Java

- How to install and run Java

This first chapter explains why Java is so exciting. You'll find out a few of the things Java can do for Web pages and why Java is a superior language for normal applications too. Then you'll download Java from the Internet, install it, and run your first applet.

What Java Is

Java (with a capital J) is a programming language like C, Fortran, or Basic. You can use Java to write computer applications that crunch numbers, process words, play games, store data, or do any of the thousands of other things computer software can do.

Compared to other programming languages, Java is most similar to C. However, although Java shares much of C's syntax, it is not C. Knowing how to program in C or, better yet, C++, will certainly help you learn Java more quickly, but you don't need to know C to learn Java. Unlike C++, Java is not a superset of C. A Java compiler won't compile C code, and most large C programs need to be changed substantially before they can become Java programs.

Technical Term: Compiler

Occasionally I'm going to use sidebars like this one to explain some techno-babble like "compiler" that most programmers probably already know but novices may find a little confusing.

Computers neither speak nor understand English, French, Arabic, or any other language familiar to the carbon-based life forms known as "human beings." Instead computers understand languages that look like this:

```
FFFF0000 00000010 00000008 00000000 00000000
00000000 00000000 00000000 00000000 00000000
4E560000   422DFDD6   34EBA0BA   84EBA0160
4E5E4E75 846D6169 6E000000 4E560000 6E005E20
```

This is called machine code. To make matters worse, just as different people use different languages, so too do different computers use different machine languages. Therefore the same program may be expressed in completely different ways on different kinds of computers.

In the early days (the 1950s) human beings had no choice but to learn to speak machine language because the computers were far too stupid to learn to speak human. Fifty years later computers still aren't smart enough to speak English, but humans have taught them to speak certain quasi-human languages like C and Java. The programs that translate these specialized programming languages into machine language are called **compilers**.

Compilers translate an entire program into machine language before it is run. Certain languages, most commonly Basic, are translated into machine language line by line as they are run. The programs that do this line-by-line translation are called **interpreters**, and the languages that use them are called interpreted languages. Languages that are compiled (C is one) are called compiled languages. In general compiled programs are about an order of magnitude faster than the equivalent interpreted program and use substantially less memory, especially for small programs.

So which is Java: interpreted or compiled? Actually it's both. It's a little complicated and will be discussed further below.

What's most special about Java in relation to other programming languages is that it lets you write special programs called **applets** that can be downloaded from the Internet and played safely within a Web browser. Traditional computer programs have far too much access to your system to be downloaded and executed willy-nilly. Although you generally trust the maintainers of various ftp archives and bulletin boards to do basic virus checking and not to post destructive software, a lot still slips through the cracks. Even more dangerous software would be promulgated if any Web page you visited could run programs on your system. You have no way of checking these programs for bugs or for out-and-out malicious behavior before downloading and running them.

Java solves this problem by severely restricting what an applet can do. A Java applet cannot write to your hard disk without your permission. It cannot write to arbitrary addresses in memory and thereby introduce a virus into your computer. It cannot crash your system.

Hype Alert In theory, an applet can't crash your system. In practice, Java 1.0.2 has not quite achieved this level of reliability yet. The inability to crash the system is heavily dependent on the crash-proofing of the system itself. Solaris seems quite resistant to crashing and Windows NT is almost as crash-proof. Windows 95 and the Mac, however, are relatively easy to crash. Nonetheless all these systems are becoming more stable with each new release of Java, and the day is not too far in the future when you can stop worrying about buggy code bringing down your entire computer.

There's another problem with distributing executable programs from Web pages. Computer programs are very closely tied to the specific hardware and operating system they run. A Windows program will not run on a computer that runs only DOS. A Mac application can't run on a Unix workstation. VMS code can't be executed on an IBM mainframe, and so on. Therefore, major commercial applications like Microsoft Word or Netscape have to be written almost independently for all the different platforms they run on. Netscape is one of the most cross-platform of major applications, and it still only runs on a minority of platforms.

Java solves the problem of platform independence by using **byte code**. The Java compiler does not produce native executable code for a particular machine as a C compiler would. Instead it produces a special format called Java byte code. Java byte code looks like this:

```
CA FE BA BE 00 03 00 2D 00 3E 08 00 3B 08 00 01 08
00 20 08
```

Where's the CD?

Java's evolving so fast that what we could put on a CD today would be out of date tomorrow.

Instead, we've integrated the book with an On-Line Supplement: an up-to-the-minute Web site with a Java Newsletter direct from the author, answers to the problems in this book, Brewing Java tutorial, code from the book, the Java FAQ, Java challenges, and links to key Java sites.

Point your browser to

http://www.prenhall.com/developers_resource_series

> ## Technical Term: Platform
>
> A platform is a loosely defined computer industry buzzword that typically means some combination of hardware and operating system that will mostly run all the same software. For instance, PowerMacs running System 7.5 are one platform. DEC Alphas running Windows NT are another.

This looks a lot like machine language; but, unlike machine language, Java byte code is exactly the same on every platform. This byte code fragment means the same thing on a Solaris workstation as it does on a Macintosh PowerBook.

Java programs that have been compiled into byte code still need an interpreter to execute them on any given platform. The interpreter reads the byte code and translates it into the platform's native language on the fly. The most common such interpreter is Sun's program java (with a little j). Since the byte code is completely platform independent, only the interpreter and a few native libraries need to be ported to get Java to run on a new computer or operating system. The rest of the runtime environment including the compiler and most of the class libraries are written in Java.

All these pieces, the javac compiler, the java interpreter, the Java programming language, and more are collectively referred to as Java. However this book restricts its usage of *Java* to mean only the Java programming language. It will be more specific and spell out the java interpreter or the Java environment when discussing those things.

What Java Does

Web page authors are excited about Java because of all the cool things it lets them do. Here are just a few things you can do on a Web page with Java that you couldn't do before:

- Play a sound whenever a user visits a page
- Play music in the background while the user reads a page
- Use vector graphics instead of bitmaps and GIFs
- Run animation sequences in realtime
- Create forms that verify the user's input
- Create realtime, multiplayer, interactive games

Java changes the Web from a static, fixed medium to a realtime interactive, dynamic, expandable multimedia environment.

Java Makes Web Pages Dynamic

Until Java, Web pages were static. They had text and they had pictures but they had very little else, and they didn't change much. For the most part text and pictures just sat there. If you wanted to see something new, you clicked on a link and loaded an entirely new page. Then that page sat there, doing nothing.

Java makes Web pages dynamic. By using Java you can make a page change while the user watches it. You can animate pictures. You can change the text that's displayed without reloading the entire page. For instance, there were stock price pages before Java, but it wasn't until Java that there were stock ticker pages, that is, pages that updated as stock prices changed like the one in Figure 1.1.

Hype Alert Since this is an introductory book, I am occasionally going to gloss over some fine points and make sweeping statements like, "it wasn't until Java that there were stock ticker pages, that is, pages that updated as stock prices changed." If you want the clearest path through this book, please allow me to get away with the occasional misstatement. However, since this is not *Java for Dummies*, I will expand on the point in blocks like these for those people who want the unexpurgated story.

In this case, those of you who have been around the Web for a while will have noticed that there were in fact dynamically updated stock ticker applications using server push. However Java is better than server push for several reasons:

1. Server push gives you the choice of reloading an entire page or an image on the page. There is no way to change just a few pieces of text on the page, for instance the price of one stock.

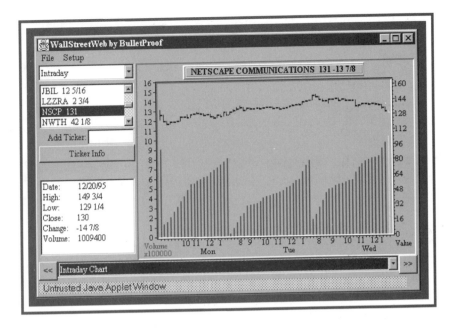

Figure 1.1: *The WallStreetWeb Online Investor Application from Bulletproof, http://www.bulletproof.com/*

2. Server push requires special support from the client and the server. For instance, MacHTTP 2.2 and earlier and WebStar 1.0 and 1.1 did not support server push. (WebStar 1.2 does support server push.) Java only needs to be supported by the client. Any Web server can serve Java pages.

Java Adds New Content Types to the Web

Before Java, users were limited to seeing the kinds of content their Web browsers supported; and Web developers were limited to the most basic content supported by their readers' Web browsers, generally HTML 2.0 and GIFs. Java lets developers expand the range of content types indefinitely.

For instance, HotJava was the first Web browser to include **inline** sound in a Web page. Inline means that the sound plays inside the browser automatically. The reader doesn't need to launch a separate helper application to view it. The sound can play when the reader first visits a page, it can play when the reader clicks a button on a page, or it can play continuously in the background.

However, Java is more than just a Web browser with special features. Although HotJava was the first browser to include inline sound and animation, Microsoft's Internet Explorer and Netscape Navigator 2.0 also have inline sound.

What makes Java special is not that it adds new types of content to pages as Netscape and Internet Explorer do. Rather it lets you add both the content and the code necessary to display that content. You no longer need to wait for a browser to be released that supports your preferred image format or special game protocol. With Java you send browsers both the content and the program necessary to view this content at the same time!

Think about what this means for a minute. Previously you had to wait for all the companies that make the Web browsers your readers use to update their browsers before you could use a new content type. Then you had to hope that all your readers actually did update their browsers. Java compatibility is a feature that any browser can implement and, by so doing, implement every feature!

For instance, suppose you want to use Encapsulated PostScript (EPS) files on your Web site. Previously you had to wait until at least one Web browser implemented EPS support. Now you don't wait. Instead you write your own code to view EPS files and send it to any client that requests your page at the same time they request the EPS file.

Or suppose you want people to be able to search your electronic card catalog. However, the card catalog database exists on a mainframe system that doesn't speak HTTP. Before Java you could hope that some browser would implement your proprietary card catalog protocol (fat chance); or you could try to program some intermediate cgi-bin on a UNIX box that could speak HTTP and talk to the card catalog (not an easy task). With Java, when a client wants to talk to your card catalog, you send them the code they need to do so. You don't have to try to force everything through an httpd server on port 80.

Java Lets Users Interact with a Web Page

Before Java, people browsed the Web. They moved from site to site passively reading the text and viewing the pictures there, but they rarely interacted with the page or changed it in any meaningful way.

Occasionally, someone might fill out a form which would be submitted back to the server, but even that was slow and limited to typing text and making menu choices. This was hot stuff in 1975 but isn't so exciting in an era where users are accustomed to the interactivity of Doom.

After Java, users can use the keyboard for more than typing text and the mouse for more than choosing from menus. Instead of just reading a page and perhaps filling out a form, users can now play games, calculate spreadsheets, draw pictures, and in general do anything they might do within a window displayed by a traditional computer program. Most importantly, users get immediate feedback. When you press the enter key in a spreadsheet cell, you don't want to wait for the entire spreadsheet to be sent back to the server and then the entire revised spreadsheet to be sent back to you. You want the update to happen instantaneously. With Java, the calculations are performed on the client system and the results updated locally rather than remotely as would have to be done using a CGI program.

Why Java's a Better Programming Language

If that were all Java was, it would still be more interesting than a <marquee> or <frame> tag in some new browser beta, but there's a lot more. Java isn't just for Web sites. Java is a programming language that can do almost anything a traditional programming language such as Fortran, Basic, or C++ can do. However, Java has learned from the mistakes of its predecessors. It is considerably easier to program and learn than those languages without giving up any of their power.

The Java language shares many superficial similarities with C, C++, and Objective C. For instance, loops have identical syntax in all four languages, but Java is not based on any of those languages nor have efforts been made to make it compatible with them.

Java is sometimes referred to as C++++--. James Gosling invented Java because C++ proved inadequate for programs he wanted to write. Since Java's designers were not burdened with compatibility with existing languages, they were able to learn from the experience and mistakes of previous object-oriented languages. They added a few things C++ doesn't have, such as garbage collection and multithreading (the ++), and they threw away C++ features that had proven to be better in theory than in practice, such as multiple inheritance and operator overloading (the --). A few advanced features such as closures and parameterized types that the Java team liked were nonetheless left out of the language due to time constraints. There's still argument over whether the right choices were made. For now, let's just say that none of these choices are likely to be reviewed soon.

Java has learned a lot from previous languages. Let's look at some of the advantages Java offers programmers.

Java Is Simple

Java was designed to make it much easier to write bug-free code. According to Sun's Bill Joy, shipping C code has, on average, one bug per 55 lines of code. The most important part of helping programmers write bug-free code is keeping the language simple.

Java has the bare-bones functionality needed to implement its rich feature set. It does not add lots of syntactic sugar or unnecessary features. The original language specification for Java was only about 80 pages long compared to a couple of hundred pages for C and even more for C++. Despite its simplicity Java has considerably more functionality than C.

Because Java is simple, it is easy to read and write. Obfuscated Java isn't nearly as common as obfuscated C. There aren't a lot of special cases or tricks that will confuse beginners.

About half of the bugs in C and C++ programs are related to memory allocation and deallocation. Therefore the second important addition Java makes to encouraging bug-free code is automatic memory allocation and deallocation. The C library memory allocation functions `malloc()` and `free()` are gone as are C++'s destructors.

Java is an excellent teaching language, and an excellent choice with which to learn programming. The language is small so it's easy to become fluent. The language is interpreted so the compile-run-link cycle is much shorter. The runtime environment provides automatic memory allocation and garbage collection so there's less for the programmer to think about. Java is object-oriented unlike Basic so the beginning programmer doesn't have to unlearn bad programming habits when moving into real-world projects. Finally, it's very difficult (if not quite impossible) to write a Java program that will crash your system, something that you can't say about any other language.

Java Is Object-Oriented

Object-oriented programming is the catch phrase of computer programming in the 1990s. Although object-oriented programming has been around in one form or another since the Simula language was invented in the 1960s, it's really begun to take hold in modern graphical user interface (GUI) environments like Windows, Motif, and the Mac.

In object-oriented programs data is represented by objects. Objects have two sections: fields and methods. Fields tell you what an object is. Methods tell you what an object does. These fields and methods are closely tied to the object's real-world characteristics and behavior. When a program is run, messages are passed back and forth between objects. When an object receives a message, it responds accordingly as defined by its methods.

Object-oriented programming is alleged to have a number of advantages including

- Simpler, easier to read programs
- More efficient reuse of code
- Faster time to market
- More robust, error-free code

In practice, object-oriented programs have been just as slow, expensive, and buggy as traditional nonobject-oriented programs. In large part this is because the most popular object-oriented language is C++. C++ is a complex, difficult language that shares all the obfuscation of C while sharing none of C's efficiencies. It is possible in practice to write clean, easy-to-read Java code. In C++ this is almost unheard of outside of programming textbooks.

 For C Programmers: How Java Differs from C and C++

Java, unlike C++, is object-oriented at its core. Almost everything in Java is either a class, a method, or an object. Only the most basic primitive operations and data types (`int`, `+`, `for`, `while`, etc.) are at a subobject level.

There are no redundant features like structs, typedefs, and unions in Java. Since Java has classes, it doesn't need them. C++ doesn't need them either, but they were kept in the language for compatibility with C (which does need them since it doesn't have classes). Bill Joy is fond of showing off a copy of Bjarne Stroustrup's *The C++ Programming Language* in which he's been highlighting all the sections that Java programmers don't need to concern themselves with. The last time I saw it almost half the book was highlighted and he wasn't finished yet.

There are no header files in Java. The Java compiler reads the actual code to find out what's going on rather than relying on what the programmer thinks is going on. Methods only need to be declared where they're defined.

There is no operator overloading in Java. Experience has shown that as good as it sounds in theory, operator overloading is almost impossible to use in practice, especially in multiperson programming projects.

Methods in Java always occur inside the class they belong to. They may not be defined outside it as in C++. This is sensible for any object-oriented language, but C++ was forced to do otherwise to maintain compatibility with legacy C code. In fact everything in Java happens inside a class. Unlike C++, there are no functions sitting off in global space that do everything you forgot to do when you wrote the classes. Java almost forces clean, object-oriented design on you.

There are no explicit pointers or pointer arithmetic in Java. Like global functions, pointers let you sneak through an object's access control. Since there are no pointers, there are no virtual functions. (Or, more precisely, every Java method is virtual.) Similarly there are no friend functions in Java.

Java Is Platform Independent

Java was designed not only to be cross-platform in source form like C, but also in compiled binary form. Since this is impossible across processor architectures, Java is compiled to an intermediate form called byte code.

A Java program never really executes natively on the host machine. Rather a special native program called the Java interpreter reads the byte code and executes the corresponding native machine instructions. Thus, to port Java programs to a new platform all that is needed is to port the interpreter and some of the library routines. Even the compiler is written in Java. The byte codes are precisely defined and remain the same on all platforms.

The second important part of making Java cross-platform is the elimination of undefined or architecture-dependent constructs. Integers are always four bytes long, and floating-point variables follow the IEEE 754 standard for computer arithmetic exactly. You don't have to worry that the meaning of an integer is going to change if you move from a Pentium to a PowerPC. In Java everything is guaranteed.

Java Is Safe

Java was designed from the ground up to allow for secure execution of code across a network, even when the source of that code was untrusted and possibly malicious.

This required the elimination of many features of C and C++. Most notably there are no pointers in Java. Java programs cannot access arbitrary addresses in memory. All memory access is handled behind the scenes by the (presumably) trusted runtime environment. Furthermore Java has strong typing. Variables must be declared, and variables do not change types when you aren't looking. Casts are strictly limited to casts between types that make sense. Thus you can cast an `int` to a `long` or a `byte` to a `short` but not a `long` to a `boolean` or an `int` to a `String`.

Java implements a robust exception handling mechanism to deal with both expected and unexpected errors. The worst that an applet can do to a host system is bring down the runtime environment. It cannot bring down the entire system.

Most importantly, Java applets can be executed in an environment that prohibits them from introducing viruses, deleting or modifying files, or otherwise destroying data and crashing the host computer. A Java-enabled Web browser checks the byte codes of an applet to verify that it doesn't do anything nasty before it will run the applet.

However, the biggest security problem is not hackers. It's not viruses. It's not even insiders erasing their hard drives and quitting your company to go to work for your competitors. The biggest security problem in computing today is bugs. Regular, ordinary, nonmalicious unintended bugs are responsible for more data loss and lost productivity than all other factors combined. Java, by making it easier to write bug-free code, substantially improves the security of all kinds of programs.

Java Is High Performance

Java byte codes can be compiled on the fly to code that rivals C++ in speed using a "just-in-time compiler." Several companies are also working on native-machine-architecture compilers for Java. These will produce executable code that does not require a separate interpreter and that is indistinguishable in speed from C++. While you'll never get that last ounce of speed out of a Java program that you might be able to wring from C or Fortran, the results will be suitable for all but the most demanding applications.

It is certainly possible to write large programs in Java. The HotJava browser, the Java Workshop integrated development environment, and the javac compiler are large programs that are written entirely in Java.

Java Is Multithreaded

Java is inherently multithreaded. A single Java program can have many different processes executing independently and continuously. Three Java applets on the same page can run together with each getting equal time from the CPU with very little extra effort on the part of the programmer.

This makes Java incredibly responsive to user input. It also helps contribute to Java's robustness and provides a mechanism whereby the Java environment can ensure that a malicious applet doesn't steal all of the host's CPU cycles.

Unfortunately, multithreading is so tightly integrated with Java that it makes Java rather difficult to port to architectures like Windows 3.1 that don't natively support multithreading.

In short Java is a safe, robust, garbage-collected, object-oriented, high-performance, multithreaded, interpreted, architecture-neutral, cross-platform, buzzword-compliant programming language.

In the late 1970s Bill Joy thought about doing a language that would merge the best features of MESA, an experimental language from Xerox, and C. However other projects (like cofounding Sun) intervened. In the late 1980s he got Sun's engineers started on a complete revision of the UNIX operating system that involved merging SunOS 4.x with AT&T's SYSVR4.

In 1989 Joy sold his Sun stock, invested heavily in Microsoft, and moved out of mainstream Sun to Aspen, Colorado. By the early 1990s Bill was getting tired of huge programs. He decided that he wanted to be able to write a 10,000-line program that made a difference. In late 1990 Bill wrote a paper called "Further" which pitched Sun engineers on the idea that they should produce an object environment based on C++. Today, however, Joy freely admits that C++ was too complicated and not up to the job.

Around this time Sun Distinguished Scientist James Gosling (of emacs fame) had been working for several months on an SGML editor called Imagination using C++. The Oak language (now Java) grew out of Gosling's frustration with C++ on his Imagination project. Gosling claims that he named Oak when he looked out his window and saw a tree. However, early Sun papers refer to Oak as the "Object Architecture Kernel." It is unknown whether the name or the acronym came first. In either case the Oak name did not survive a trademark search and was changed to Java in 1995.

Patrick Naughton, then of Sun and now vice-president of technology at StarWave, started the Green Project on December 5, 1990. Naughton defined the project as an effort to "do fewer things better." That December he recruited Gosling and Mike Sheridan to help start the project. Joy showed them his "Further" paper, and work began on graphics and user interface issues for several months in C.

In April 1991 the Green Project (Naughton, Gosling, and Sheridan) settled on smart consumer electronics as the delivery platform, and Gosling started working in earnest on Oak. Gosling wrote the original compiler in C, and Naughton, Gosling, and Sheridan wrote the runtime interpreter, also in C. (The Green project never wrote a single line of C++.) Oak was running its first programs in August 1991. Joy got his first demos of the system that winter, when Gosling and Naughton went skiing at Joy's place in Aspen.

By the fall of 1992 "*7," a cross between a PDA and a remote control, was ready. In October 1992 this was demoed to Scott McNealy, Sun's president, who was blown away. Following that demo the Green Project was set up as First Person Inc., a wholly owned Sun subsidiary.

In early 1993 the Green team heard about a Time Warner request for proposal for a set-top box operating system. First Person quickly shifted focus from smart consumer electronics (which was proving to be more hype than reality) to the set-top box OS market and placed a bid with Time Warner.

Fortuitously, Sun lost the bid. The Time Warner project went nowhere, the same place it probably would have gone if Sun had won the bid. First Person continued work on set-top boxes until early 1994, when it concluded that, like smart consumer electronics, set-top boxes were more hype than reality.

Without a market to be seen, First Person was rolled back into Sun in 1994. However, around this time it was realized that the requirements for smart consumer electronics and set-top box software (small, platform-independent secure reliable code) were the same requirements for the nascent Web.

For a third time the project was redirected, this time at the Web. A prototype browser called WebRunner was written by Patrick Naughton in one weekend of inspired hacking. After additional work by Naughton and Jonathan Payne, this became HotJava. The rest, as they say, is history.

Getting and Installing Java

In early 1996 when this book is being written, the development tools for Java are fairly primitive, and this book does not assume access to an integrated development environment. However, Natural Intelligence has released Roaster, a Java applet development environment for the PowerMac. Metrowerks has integrated Java support into Code Warrior 9. Borland has also promised a Java development environment for Windows to be released in the fall of 1996. Symantec has integrated Java support into its C++ environments for Windows and the Mac. If you have access to any of these tools, you may find that they make Java development much smoother. However they are not necessary by any means.

Sun has made a **Java Developer's Kit** (JDK for short) available for all the platforms it supports. The Java Developer's Kit does not include a Web browser. Instead it includes Applet Viewer, which lets you view and test your applets. The JDK also includes the javac compiler, the java interpreter, the javaprof profiler, the javah header file generator (for integrating C into your Java code), the Java debugger, and limited documentation. However, most of the documentation for the JDK is on Sun's web site.

The basic Java environment consists of a Web browser that can play Java applets, a Java compiler to turn Java source code into byte code, and a Java interpreter to run Java programs. These are the three key components of a Java environment. You'll also need a text editor such as Textpad or BBEdit. Other tools such as a debugger, a visual development environment, and a class browser are nice but aren't absolutely necessary.

Note that it isn't necessary to get all pieces from the same source. For instance, Netscape currently provides a Java-enabled Web browser. However, it only provides a Java compiler with version 2.0 and later of its server products.

Versions of the Java Developer's Kit at varying stages of completion are available from Sun for Windows 95 and Windows NT for X86, MacOS 7.5 on 68030, 68040, and PowerMacs, and Solaris. Natural Intelligence has independently produced a Java environment for the Mac called Roaster which has some advantages and some disadvantages relative to Sun's product. The Open Software Foundation has ported Java to UnixWare 2.0 and HP/UX. The BlackDown Organization has ported Java to Linux. Silicon Graphics has ported Java to Irix. IBM has ported Java to OS/2 and AIX and has announced plans to port Java to Windows 3.1, OS/400, and MVS. As of this writing there are no versions of Java available for MIPS, Alpha, or PowerPC-based NT, Windows 3.1, or SunOS 4.1 though several of these are in development.

You can ftp the programs from the following sites:

United States

ftp://ftp.javasoft.com/pub/

ftp://www.blackdown.org/pub/Java/pub/

ftp://sunsite.unc.edu/pub/languages/java/

ftp://java.dnx.com/pub/

Germany:

ftp://sunsite.informatik.rwth-aachen.de/pub/mirror/java.sun.com/

Korea:

ftp://ftp.kaist.ac.kr/pub/java/

China:

ftp://math01.math.ac.cn/pub/sunsite/

Japan:

ftp://ftp.glocom.ac.jp/mirror/java.sun.com/

Sweden:

ftp://ftp.luth.se/pub/infosystems/www/hotjava/pub/

Singapore:

ftp://ftp.iss.nus.sg/pub/java/

United Kingdom:

ftp://sunsite.doc.ic.ac.uk/packages/java/

Windows 95 and NT Installation Instructions

The Win32 X86 releases are self-extracting archives. You will need about six megabytes of free disk space to install the JDK. Execute the file by double-clicking on its icon in the File Manager or by selecting Run... from the Program Manager's File menu and typing the path to the file. This will unpack the archive including all necessary directories and subdirectories. The full path is unimportant, but for simplicity's sake this book assumes you installed it from the root of your C: drive. If this is the case, the files will live in C:\java. If you unpacked it somewhere else, just replace C:\ by the full path to the java directory in what follows.

You will need to add C:\java\bin directory to your PATH environment variable.

In addition to the java files, the archive includes two common DLLs:

- `MSVCRT20.DLL`
- `MFC30.DLL`

These two files will be installed in your java directory. If you do not already have copies of these two files on your system (there's a very good chance you do, probably in your system directory), copy them into the C:\java\bin directory. If you do already possess these two files, just delete these extra copies.

Unix Installation Instructions

If you're on a shared system at a university or an Internet service provider, there's a good chance Java is already installed. Ask your local support staff how to access it. Otherwise follow these instructions.

The Unix release is a compressed tar file. You will need about nine megabytes of disk space to uncompress and untar the JDK. Double that would be very helpful. You do this with the commands

```
% uncompress JDK-1_0_2-solaris2-sparc.tar.Z
% tar xvf JDK-1_0_2-solaris2-sparc.tar
```

The exact file name may be a little different if you're retrieving the release for a different platform such as Irix or if the version is different.

You can untar it in your home directory, or, if you have root privileges, in some convenient place like /usr/local where all users can have access to the files. However root privileges are not necessary to install or run Java.

Untarring the file creates all necessary directories and subdirectories. The exact path is unimportant, but for simplicity's sake this book assumes it's installed in /usr/local. If a sysop already installed it, this is probably where it lives. (Under Solaris it's also possible the sysop put it into /opt.) If this is the case, the files live in /usr/local/java. If you unpacked it somewhere else, just replace /usr/local by the full path to the java directory in what follows. If you installed it in your home directory, you can use ~/java instead of a full path.

You now need to add /usr/local/java/bin directory to your PATH environment variable. Depending on your shell, you use one of the following commands:

```
csh, tcsh:
    % set path=($PATH /usr/local/java/bin)
sh:
    % PATH=($PATH /usr/local/java/bin); export $PATH
```

You should also add these lines to the end of your .profile and .cshrc files so you won't have to do this every time you log in. Now you're ready to run some applets.

Macintosh Installation Instructions

The file you get will be a self-extracting archive called something like JDK-1_0_2-MacOS.sea.bin. If you use Fetch or Anarchie to download it will be automatically converted into the self-extracting JDK-1_0_2-MacOS.sea. Double-click it to extract it and the double-click the resulting installer JDK-1_0_2-MacOS. It will prompt you for a location to put it on your hard disk. Put it wherever is convenient.

It will probably be helpful to make aliases of the Applet Viewer, the Java Compiler, and the Java Runner and put them on your desktop for ease of dragging and dropping later, especially if you have a large monitor.

Running Your First Applet

Unix/Windows Instructions

Start the Applet Viewer by doing the following:

1. Go to a command line prompt and cd to one of the directories in /usr/local/java/demo, for example,

   ```
   % cd /usr/local/java/demo/TicTacToe
   ```

2. Run the applet viewer on the HTML file:

   ```
   % appletviewer example1.html
   ```

3. You should see something like the applet in Figure 1.2a (UNIX), or 1.2c (Windows). Play Tic-Tac-Toe! It is allegedly possible to win.

a   b   c

Figure 1.2: *Sun's Tic-Tac-Toe applet by Arthur van Hoff*

Macintosh Instructions

1. Start the Applet Viewer by double-clicking it.
2. Select **Open...** from the **File** menu and navigate into the java folder, then the Sample Applets folder, then the TicTacToe folder.
3. Select the file example1.html and click on the **Open** button. Alternately you can drag and drop this file onto the Applet Viewer.
4. Play Tic-Tac-Toe! The algorithm was deliberately broken so it is possible to win.

Applets in Netscape

Netscape 2.0 and later will run Java applets. Java support is included in the Solaris, SunOS, IRIX, and Windows 95 and NT versions. It is available in beta form on the Mac. It is not included in other releases, notably Windows 3.1.

Q & A

 Q : *What can't I do with Java?*

 A : If you believed everything you read in the last chapter unconditionally, please contact the author about a certain bridge he has for sale, cheap. On the other hand if you're understandably a bit skeptical about whether Java really is the greatest tool since Mosaic, let me point out a few weaknesses

- Programs written in Java aren't very fast, at least not yet. While Java is adequate for basic applets, you wouldn't want to use it to do heavy scientific programming, so don't throw away your Fortran compiler.
- Java can't call native Application Program Interfaces (APIs) like the Mac toolbox without using extra code written in C, so don't throw away your C compiler yet either.

 Q : *Leaving implementation issues aside, is Java the perfect language?*

 A : Once again there are a few weaknesses to be pointed out:

- Java doesn't have any support for "versionning" classes and only limited ability to avoid name space collision.
- There is no support for either parameterized types (templates to C++ programmers) or for passing methods as arguments to other methods. This makes fully abstract data types excessively hard to implement.
- Applications that require extremely high performance, such as databases like Oracle or Informix, need an intimate understanding of the native hardware and OS. Java doesn't provide this.
- Java follows IEEE 754 standards for floating-point arithmetic precisely. Unfortunately, IEEE 754 is designed for traditional languages like C and Fortran. It is less suit-

able to languages with strong runtime exception models that would be better off tossing DivideByZero Exceptions and ArithmeticExceptions rather than returning Infs and NaNs.

- The switch-case statement is insufficiently expressive to handle even a majority of the "Choose one of several options" blocks you're likely to encounter.

- String literals can't contain embedded newlines, tabs, control characters, and the like. You have to use escape sequences like \n and \t to insert them.

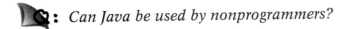

Q: *Can Java be used by nonprogrammers?*

A: Java isn't just for programmers. Just as you can write text with Microsoft Word without knowing how to write in C++, you can add animations, sounds, and other cool Java stuff to your web pages without writing a line of code, just by using other people's applets. However, this book is written for people who want to program in Java, and from here on in it will concentrate on developing the skills you need to write your own unique programs.

Q: *What's JavaScript? Where does it fit in?*

A: Java and JavaScript are about as closely related as the Trump Taj Mahal in Atlantic City is to the Taj Mahal in India. In other words, Java and JavaScript both have the word Java in their names. JavaScript is a programming language from Netscape which is incorporated in their browsers. It is superficially similar to Java in the same way C is similar to Java but differs in all important respects.

Q: *What's HotJava? Where does it fit in?*

A: HotJava is a particular Web browser from Sun Microsystems that can play Java applets. It is not the only one. Netscape 2.0 and Microsoft Internet Explorer 3.0 can also run Java applets.

Q: *Couldn't a Netscape plug-in be used to to do all the cool stuff an applet can do?*

A: In theory plug-ins can do a lot. However, they cannot be downloaded and installed into a user's system on the fly when they visit a Web page. Imagine if every web site you visited required a new plug-in. Furthermore, plug-ins are platform-specific. You need to write a plug-in for every platform that may be used by someone visiting your pages. Plug-ins are generally faster than Java applets though and don't have as many security restrictions. Therefore plug-ins are good if you're writing something that will be used by many unrelated Web sites and you have the resources to support a dozen or more platforms equally. However, if what you're creating is unique to your site or you don't want to port your software to a dozen platforms, then you should write it as a Java applet.

Exercises

1. Think of four ways you can use Java to improve your existing Web pages.

Summary

This chapter has given you a basic overview of why Java is so exciting. The things you learned in this chapter included

- What Java is
- What Java can do for your Web pages
- Why Java is superior to other programming languages
- The history of Java
- Where to get Java
- How to install Java
- How to run Java applets

Before you continue, you should have Sun's Java Development Kit 1.0 or later installed and you should have run the TicTacToe applet in the Applet Viewer.

Coming Up

In the next chapter you will write your first Java program, Hello World.

In later chapters you'll learn all the practical details of Java's advanced language features like objects and multi-threading that were discussed theoretically in this chapter. You'll learn how to write your own applets like TicTacToe or WallStreetWeb. Get ready. Your journey into Java is about to begin.

Further Reading

Sun's Web site has several white papers about the philosophy of Java. The most comprehensive one is often referred to simply as "The White Paper" and is available at

http://www.javasoft.com/whitePaper/java-whitepaper-1.html

Though doubtless one day tomes will be written about the genesis of Java and the Green project will be mentioned in the same hushed tones now reserved for the Home Brew Computer Club, not much has yet been written about the history of Java. Most of the details are being passed around by word of mouth. However, there have been a couple of decent articles about the genesis of Java. See

BANK, DAVID, "The Java Saga," *Wired*, December 1995, pp. 166–169, http://www.hotwired.com/wired/3.12/features/java.saga.html

O'CONNELL, MICHAEL, "Java: The Inside Story," *SunWorld Online*, July 1995, http://www.sun.com/sunworldonline/swol-07-1995/swol-07-java.html

So far only one of the original members of the Green Project has written about it publicly. For a rather surprising look at how the Green Project operated and how Java almost didn't happen see

NAUGHTON, PATRICK, "The Long Strange Trip to Java," *The Java Handbook*, pp. 391–409, Berkeley, CA: Osborne McGraw-Hill, 1996.

Not everyone agrees that C++ is as horrible as is argued here. For an interesting alternative viewpoint, you should read The Design and Evolution of C++ by Bjarne Stroustrup, the inventor of C++. It's a fascinating look at why C++ is what it is, for good or bad.

STROUSTRUP, BJARNE, *The Design and Evolution of C++*, New York: Addison-Wesley, 1995.

CHAPTER 2

HELLO WORLD: THE APPLICATION

How to type and save Java source code

How to compile a Java application

How to run a Java application

How to make your code easy to read

How to print text on the screen

This chapter begins your introduction to programming in Java. In this chapter you will write a simple Java application. The goal of this chapter is to be able to write, compile, and run a simple Java program. Once you can do that you're ready to move on.

The Hello World Program

Since the first edition of Kernighan and Ritchie's *The C Programming Language* it's been customary to begin programming tutorials and classes with the Hello World program, a program that prints the words "Hello World!" on the display. Being heavily influenced by Kernighan and Ritchie and not one to defy tradition, this book begins similarly. Here's the HelloWorld program in its entirety.

Program 2.1: HelloWorld

```
class HelloWorld {
  public static void main (String args[]) {
    System.out.println("Hello World!");
  }
}
```

HelloWorld is very close to the simplest program imaginable. When you successfully compile and run it, it prints the words "Hello World!" on your display. Although it doesn't teach very much programming, it gives you a chance to learn the mechanics of typing and compiling code. The goal of this program is not to learn how to print words to the terminal. It's to learn how to type, save and compile a program. This is often a nontrivial procedure, and there are a lot of things that can go wrong even if your source code is correct.

If you completed the last chapter, you should already have downloaded and installed the Java compiler and interpreter. You should also have looked at some applets written by other people. Also, if you're using Unix or Windows, you should have configured your PATH variable so that the command line can find the Java compiler and other utilities. To make sure you're set up correctly, bring up a command-line prompt and type

```
javac nofile.java
```

If your computer responds with

```
error: Can't read: nofile.java
```

you're ready to begin. If, on the other hand, it responds

```
javac: Command not found
```

or something similar, then you need to go back to the previous chapter and make sure you have the Java environment properly installed and your PATH configured.

Assuming that Java is properly installed on your system, there are three steps to creating a Java program: writing the code, compiling the code, and running the code.

STEP 1: WRITING THE CODE

To write the code you need a text editor. You can use any text editor like Notepad, Brief, emacs or vi. Personally I use BBEdit on the Mac and TextPad on Windows.

You should not use a word processor like Microsoft Word or WordPerfect since these save their files in a proprietary format and not in pure ASCII text. If you absolutely must use one of these, be sure to tell it to save your files as pure text. Generally this will require using **Save As...** rather than **Save**.

If you have an integrated development environment like Symantec's Cafe or Natural Intelligence's Roaster, that will include a text editor you can use to edit Java source code. It will probably change your words various colors and styles for no apparent reason. Don't worry about this yet. As long as the text is correct, you'll be fine.

When you've chosen your text editor, type Program 2.1 into a new file. For now type it exactly as it appears here. Like C and unlike Fortran, Java is case sensitive so System.out.println is not the same as system.out.println. CLASS is not the same as class, and so on.

Save this code in a file called HelloWorld.java. Use that name, including case, exactly. Congratulations! You've written your first Java program.

STEP 2: COMPILING THE CODE

Writing code is easy. Writing correct code is much harder. In the compilation step you find out whether the code you wrote is in fact

Tip Extraneous Extensions in Windows

Some Windows text editors including Notepad add a three letter ".txt" extension to all the files they save without telling you. Thus you can unexpectedly end up with a file called "HelloWorld.java.txt." This is wrong and will not compile. If your editor has this problem, you should get a better editor. However in the meantime enclose the filename in double quotes in the Save dialog box to make editor save the file with exactly the name you want.

legal Java code. Select the section which most closely matches your environment and follow the following instructions to compile and run your program.

UNIX AND WINDOWS: To compile the code from the command line, make sure you're in the same directory where you saved HelloWorld.java and type

```
javac HelloWorld.java
```

at the command prompt. If everything is well, then the compiler will silently return you to the command line prompt with no indication that anything has happened. However if you list the files in that directory, you'll see a new file there called HelloWorld.class. This file contains the Java byte codes for your program.

MACINTOSH JDK: Open the Java Compiler application, select **Compile File** from the **File** menu, and select HelloWorld.java in the resulting dialog box. Or you can drag and drop the HelloWorld.java file onto the Java Compiler icon. (If necessary, make an alias to the Java Compiler on your desktop and drop HelloWorld.java onto that.) You'll see a dialog box like the one in Figure 2.1 and a spinning beach ball cursor as the file is compiled.

If everything is well, then the compiler will finish, the cursor will revert back to an arrow, and you'll see the dialog shown in Figure 2.2.

Figure 2.1: Compile in progress

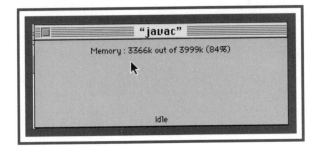

Figure 2.2: Compile successful

If you look in the folder where HelloWorld.java resides, you'll see a new file there called HelloWorld.class. This is the output of your program.

MACINTOSH WITH ROASTER: From Roaster's **Project** menu select **New Project** to create a new project. Call it HelloWorld. Then select **New** from the **File** menu to create a new untitled window. Type Program 2.1 into this window and then save it as HelloWorld.java. Then select **Add Window** from the **Project** menu to add HelloWorld.java to the project. Finally select **Make** from the **Project** menu to compile the file. If you look in the folder where HelloWorld.java resides, you'll see a new file there called HelloWorld.class. This is the output of your program.

IF AT FIRST YOU DON'T SUCCEED... Your first effort to compile the code may not succeed. In fact, it's probably more likely that it will fail than that it will work. In that case you may see one or more of the following error messages:

```
HelloWorld.java:7: ';' expected.
    System.out.println("Hello World!")
                                      ^

HelloWorld.java:2: Class or interface declaration
expected.
Class HelloWorld {
^

HelloWorld.java:9: '}' expected.
  }
```

These messages may or may not be helpful. For now, if you had a problem you should make sure that you did in fact type in the code exactly as written in Program 2.1. Here are a few common mistakes you can check for:

1. Did you put a semicolon after `System.out.println("Hello World!")`?

2. Did you include the closing brace? There should be two open braces and two closing braces.

3. Did you type everything exactly as it appears here? In particular, did you use the same capitalization? Remember, Java is case sensitive. `class` is not the same as `Class`. Also make sure your text editor used dumb quotes like " " and not smart quotes like " ".

Step 2 is by far the hardest part of this entire book. Do not get discouraged if you're having trouble getting code to compile. If after following the above suggestions you still can't compile HelloWorld.java, try the following:

1. Read the documentation, scant though it may be, for your development environment. This is particularly important if you're using an IDE like Borland's Latte that isn't covered here.

2. Get a knowledgeable friend to help you out. This is often the quickest road to success at this stage.

3. Get an unknowledgeable friend to help out. Sometimes it just takes a second pair of eyes to see what you can't.

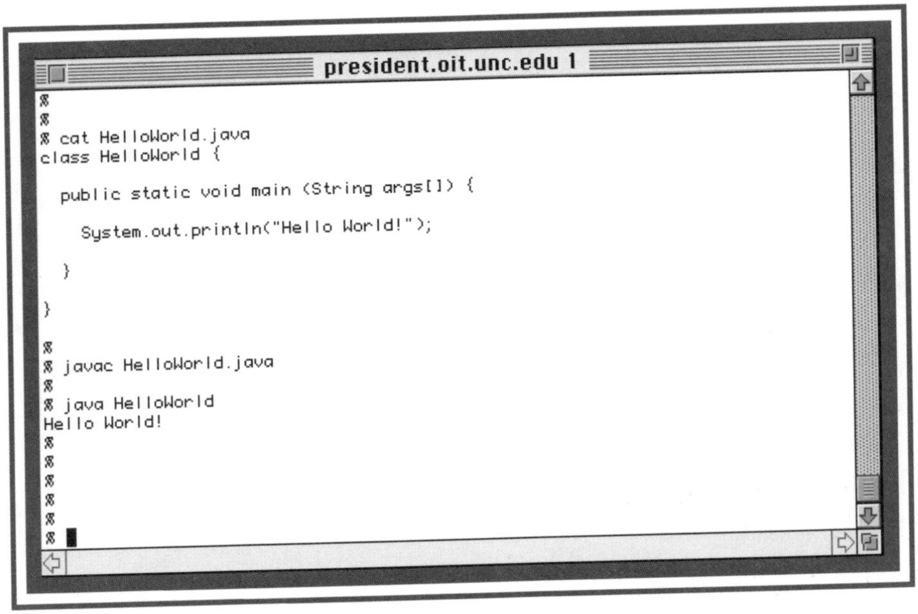

```
                    president.oit.unc.edu 1
%
%
% cat HelloWorld.java
class HelloWorld {

  public static void main (String args[]) {

    System.out.println("Hello World!");

  }

}

%
% javac HelloWorld.java
%
% java HelloWorld
Hello World!
%
%
%
%
%
%
```

Figure 2.3: Successful Unix compile

4. Post a message on comp.lang.java. Be sure to include your complete source code, the complete text of any error messages you get, and details of the development environment and platform you're using, for example, Sun's JDK 1.1, Solaris 2.5 for Sparc.

Step 3: Run the Program

After you have successfully compiled the program, you run the program to find out whether it in fact does what you expect it to do.

UNIX AND WINDOWS: When javac compiled HelloWorld.java, it wrote byte code in a file called HelloWorld.class in the same directory as HelloWorld.java. You run this program by typing

```
java HelloWorld
```

at the command prompt. As you probably guessed the program responds by printing "Hello World!" on your screen as shown in Figure 2.3.

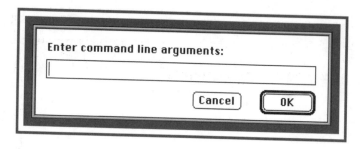

Figure 2.4: *The command-line argument dialog box.*

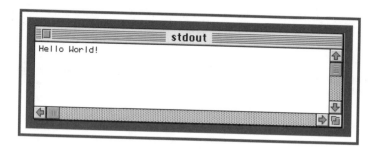

Figure 2.5: *HelloWorld on the Macintosh*

Congratulations! You've just finished your first Java program!

MACINTOSH JDK: Drag the HelloWorld.class file onto the Java runner icon. First you'll be asked for the command line arguments in a dialog box as shown in Figure 2.4. This program doesn't need any command-line arguments so click OK or press the return key.

Then the program prints "Hello World!" in a standard output window as shown in Figure 2.5.

At this point you may find yourself wondering how to quit since there doesn't appear to be a standard **File** menu with a **Quit** menu item. The **Quit** menu item is hiding in the **Java Runtime** menu in the Apple menu (🍎) as shown in Figure 2.6. This enables you to create your own menu bars in stand-alone applications that replace the standard Macintosh menu bars. You'll learn how to do this in Chapter 17.

MACINTOSH WITH ROASTER: Go to the HelloWorld project window and select HelloWorld.java by clicking on it. Then choose **Set**

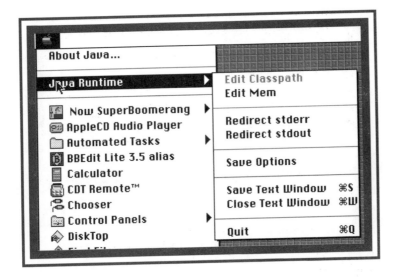

Figure 2.6: *The Java Runtime Menu*

Startup File from the **Project** menu as shown in Figure 2.7. A little blue arrow should appear to the left of HelloWorld.java in the project window indicating that this is the startup file. Then choose **Run** from the **Project** menu. As you may have expected, the program responds by printing "Hello World!" in a standard output window as shown in Figure 2.8.

Examining Hello World

Hello World is a Java application. A Java application is normally started from the command line prompt and contains a main method.

When you typed `java HelloWorld`, here's what happened. First the Java interpreter looked for a file called HelloWorld.class. When it found that file, it looked inside it for a method called `main()`. Once it found the main method, it executed, in order, the statements found there. In this case there was only one statement,

```
System.out.println("Hello World!")
```

which, as you probably guessed, prints "Hello World!" on the screen. Then, since there were no further statements in the main method, the program exited.

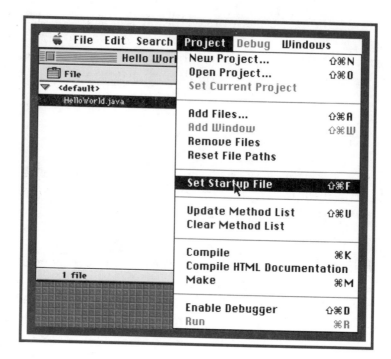

Figure 2.7: *Setting the Startup file Roaster*

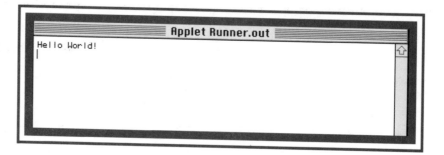

Figure 2.8: *Hello World on the Macintosh with Roaster*

The Microstructure of a Java Program

Java source code is composed of a number of different pieces. The lowest level is made up of **tokens**. Tokens are like atoms. A token cannot be split into smaller pieces without fundamentally altering its meaning. There are seven kinds of tokens: keywords, operators, comments, identifiers, separators, white space, and literals. These tokens are combined to make the molecules of Java programs, statements, and expressions; and these molecules are combined into still larger compounds of blocks, methods, and classes.

Keywords

Keywords are identifiers like `public`, `static`, and `class` that have a special meaning inside Java source code and outside of comments and Strings. Four keywords are used in HelloWorld: `public`, `static`, `void`, and `class`.

Keywords are reserved for their intended use and cannot be used by the programmer for variable or method names. There are 50 reserved keywords in Java 1.0. The 48 that are actually used are listed in Table 2.1. Don't worry if the purposes of the keywords seem a little opaque at this point. They will all be explained in much greater detail later.

Table 2.1: *Java Keywords Used in Java 1.0*

Keyword	Purpose
abstract	declares that a class or method is abstract
boolean	declares a boolean variable or return type
break	prematurely exits a loop
byte	declares a byte variable or return type
case	one case in a `switch` statement
catch	handles an exception
char	declares a character variable or return type
class	signals the beginning of a class definition
continue	prematurely returns to the beginning of a loop
default	default action for a `switch` statement
do	begins a `do-while` loop

Table 2.1 *Continued*

double	declares a double variable or return type
else	signals the code to be executed if an `if` statement is not true
extends	specifies the class of which this class is a subclass
final	declares that a class may not be subclassed or that a field or method may not be over-ridden
finally	declares a block of code guaranteed to be executed
float	declares a floating-point variable or return type
for	begins a `for` loop
if	execute statements if the condition is true
implements	declares that this class implements the given interface
import	permit access to a class or group of classes in a package
instanceof	tests whether an object is an instance of a class
int	declares an integer variable or return type
interface	signals the beginning of an interface definition
long	declares a long integer variable or return type
native	declares that a method is implemented in native code
new	allocates a new object
package	defines the package in which this source code file belongs
private	declares a method or field to be private

Table 2.1 Continued

47

Hello World: The Application

protected	declares a class, method, or field to be protected
public	declares a class, method, or field to be public
return	returns a value from a method
short	declares a short integer variable or return type
static	declares that a field or a method belongs to a class rather than an object
super	a reference to the parent of the current object
switch	tests for the truth of various possible cases
synchronized	indicates that a section of code is not thread-safe
this	a reference to the current object
throw	throw an exception
throws	declares the exceptions thrown by a method
transient	declares that a field should not be serialized
try	attempt an operation that may throw an exception
void	declare that a method does not return a value
volatile	warns the compiler that a variable changes asynchronously
while	begins a while loop

Two other keywords, const and goto, are reserved by Java but are not actually implemented. This allows compilers to produce better error messages if these common C++ keywords are improperly used in a Java program.

Literals

Literals are pieces of Java source code that mean exactly what they say. For instance `"Hello World!"` is a String literal and its meaning is the words "Hello World!"

The string `"Hello World!"` looks like it's several things, but to the compiler it's just one thing, a String. This is similar to how an expression such as 1,987,234 may be seven digits and two commas but is really just one number.

The double quote marks tell you this is a String. A String is an ordered collection of characters (letters, digits, punctuation marks, etc.). Although the String may have meaning to a human being reading the code, the computer sees it as no more than a particular set of letters in a particular order. It has no concept of the meaning of the characters. For instance it does not know that `"two"` + `"two"` is `"four."` In fact the computer thinks that `"two"` + `"two"` is `"twotwo."`

The quote marks show where the String begins and ends. However the quote marks themselves are not a part of the String. The value of this string is Hello World!, not "Hello World!" You can change the output of the program by changing Hello World to any other words you want.

A String in a Java program has no concept of italics, bold face, font family or other formatting. It cares only about the characters that compose it. Even if you're using an editor like NisusWriter that lets you format text files, **`"Hello World!"`** is identical to *`"Hello World!"`* as far as Java is concerned.

Character literals are similar to String literals except they're enclosed in single quotes and must have exactly one character. For example `'c'` is a character literal that means the letter c.

`true` and `false` are boolean literals that mean true and false.

Numbers can also be literals. `34` is an integer literal and it means the number thirty-four. `1.5` is a floating-point literal. `45.6`, `76.4E8` (76.4×10^8) and `-32.0` are also floating-point literals.

Grammar Alert: Why Is the Word String Capitalized?

The word string with a lowercase s is a generic term in programming that refers to an ordered sequence of characters. However, in Java all strings are members of the java.lang.String class. Since Java is case-sensitive, string is not the same as String. The case sensitivity of Java is responsible for a lot of apparently funky grammar in this book.

Identifiers

Identifiers are the names of variables, methods, classes, packages, and interfaces. Unlike literals they are not the objects themselves, just ways of referring to them. In the HelloWorld program, `HelloWorld`, `String`, `args`, `main`, and `System.out.println` are identifiers.

Identifiers must be composed of letters, numbers, the underscore _ and the dollar sign $. Identifiers may only begin with a letter, the underscore, or a dollar sign, not with a number.

White Space

White space consists mostly of the space character that you produce by hitting the space bar on your keyboard; it is commonly used to separate words in sentences. There are four other white space characters in Java: the horizontal tab, the form feed, the carriage return, and the linefeed. Depending on your platform, when you hit the return or enter key, you get either a carriage return (the Mac), a linefeed (Unix), or both (DOS, Windows, VMS). This produces a hard line break in the source code text.

Outside of String literals, Java treats all white space and runs of white space (more than one white space character in immediate succession) the same. It's used to separate tokens, and one space is as good as seven spaces, a tab, and two carriage returns. Exactly which white space characters you use is primarily a result of what's convenient for human beings reading the code. The compiler doesn't care.

Inside String and character literals the only white space permitted is the space character. Carriage returns, tabs, line feeds and form feeds must be inserted with special escape sequences like '\r', '\t' and '\n'.

Separators

Separators help define the structure of your program. The separators used in HelloWorld are parentheses, ( ), braces, { }, the period, ., and the semicolon, ;. Table 2.2 lists the five Java separators (eight if you count opening and closing separators as two).

Table 2.2: Separators in Java 1.0

Separator	Purpose
( )	Encloses arguments in method definitions and calling; adjusts precedence in arithmetic expressions; surrounds cast types and delimits test expressions in flow control statements
{ }	defines blocks of code and automatically initializes arrays
[ ]	declares array types and dereferences array values
;	terminates statements
,	separates successive identifiers in variable declarations; chains statements in the test expression of a for loop
.	selects a field or method from an object; separates package names from subpackage and class names

Comments

You might think it would be useful to be able to store information about what is going on in a program within the source code itself. In fact you can. This is done with **comments**.

Comments in Java are identical to those in C++. Everything between /* and */ is ignored by the compiler, and everything on a single line after // is also thrown away. Therefore, Program 2.2 is, as far as the compiler is concerned, identical to Program 2.1.

Program 2.2: HelloWorld with comments

```
// This is the Hello World program in Java
class HelloWorld {

  public static void main (String args[]) {

    /* Now let's print the line Hello World */
    System.out.println("Hello World!");

  } // main ends here

} // HelloWorld ends here
```

The /* */ style comments can comment out multiple lines so they're useful when you want to remove large blocks of code, perhaps for debugging purposes. // style comments are better for short notes of no more than a line. /* */ can also be used in the middle of a line whereas // can only be used at the end. However, putting a comment in the middle of a line makes code harder to read and is generally considered to be bad form.

Syntax Coloring

Comments are by far the most useful way to document source code. However, modern source code editors have the ability to change the text style and color of individual words to represent what those words stand for. For instance, language keywords can be made bold or blue or both, comments can be rendered in italics, and everything else can appear in the usual monospaced font. Aside from the blue keywords (color printing is still a little expensive), this book uses those conventions for Java programs. Thus Program 2.2 becomes Program 2.3.

Program 2.3: A syntax-colored HelloWorld program

```
// This is the HelloWorld program in Java
class HelloWorld {

  public static void main (String args[]) {

    /* Now let's print the line Hello World */
    System.out.println("Hello World!");

  } // main ends here

} // HelloWorld ends here
```

The bold words, **class**, **public**, **static** and **void** are Java keywords. The italicized words are comments. Everything else is part of the Java code but is not a keyword defined by the Java language specification.

Java cares not a whit about the style of the text, only about the characters used. Thus Program 2.3 is identical to Program 2.2 in all respects except legibility.

It will occasionally be necessary to add line numbers for ease of reference as in Program 2.4.

Program 2.4: A syntax-colored HelloWorld program with line numbers

```
1.  // This is the Hello World program in Java
2.  class HelloWorld {
3.
4.    public static void main (String args[]) {
5.
6.      /* Now let's print the line Hello World */
```

```
7.      System.out.println("Hello World!");
8.
9.    } // main ends here
10.
11. } // HelloWorld ends here
```

The line numbers exist solely to make it easier to refer to a particular line of code in the explanation of a program and are not part of the program itself. If you're typing in these programs, do not type in the line numbers.

Operators

An **operator** is a symbol that operates on one or more arguments to produce a result. The Hello World program is so simple it doesn't use any operators, but almost all other programs you write will.

Table 2.3 lists Java's operators. Don't worry if the purposes of the operators seem a little opaque at this point. They will all be explained in much greater detail later.

Table 2.3: Operators in Java 1.0

Operator	Purpose
+	add numbers, concatenate Strings
+=	add and assign numbers, concatenate and assign Strings
−	subtract
−=	subtract and assign
*	multiply
*=	multiply and assign
/	divide
/=	divide and assign
|	bitwise OR
=	bitwise OR and assign

Table 2.3: *Continued*

^	bitwise XOR
^=	bitwise XOR and assign
&	bitwise AND
&=	bitwise AND and assign
%	take remainder
%=	take remainder and assign
>	greater than
>=	greater than or equal to
<	less than
<=	less than or equal to
!	boolean NOT
!=	not equal to
++	increment by one
—	decrement by one
>>	shift bits right with sign extension
>>=	shift bits right with sign extension and assign
<<	shift bits left
<<=	shift bits left and assign
>>>	unsigned bit shift right
>>>=	unsigned bit shift right and assign
&&	boolean AND
||	boolean OR
==	boolean equals
=	assignment
~	bitwise NOT
?:	conditional

Language Law:
Are "true" and "false" Java Keywords?

According to the *New Hacker's Dictionary*, a language lawyer is "a person who will show you the five sentences scattered through a 200-plus-page manual that together imply the answer to your question 'if only you had thought to look there.'" Language law sections are included in this book to satisfy language lawyers and other pedants who enjoy sending authors flaming email to correct minor misstatements.

According to the Java language specification `true` and `false` are not Java keywords. Rather they are boolean literals, just as 1.2 is a floating-point literal and 42 is an integer literal. Therefore, technically, they should not be boldfaced. However the syntax coloring editor used to format these listings, Roaster from Natural Intelligence, does make true and false bold. I have elected to follow this convention rather than correcting it manually in every program.

Tokenizing HelloWorld

Now that you know what the tokens are, it's possible to break HelloWorld into tokens. Program 2.4 has the following tokens, one to a line.

```
// This is the Hello World program in Java
class
HelloWorld
{
public
static
void
```

```
main
(
String
args
[
]
)
{
/* Now let's print the line Hello World */
System.out.println
(
"Hello World!"
)
;
}
// main ends here
}
// HelloWorld ends here
```

There are 25 tokens in HelloWorld, four keywords, five identifiers, four comments, one literal, and eleven separators. That, in short, is the microstructure of HelloWorld.

The Macrostructure of Hello World

Hello World is very close to the simplest program imaginable. All it does is print two words and an exclamation point on the display. Nonetheless there's quite a lot going on inside it. All Java applications have a certain structure and since HelloWorld is a Java application, albeit a simple one, it shares that structure.

You might think that the only line in the code that mattered was `System.out.println("Hello World!");` since that was the only line that appeared to do anything. In some sense it was the only line that did anything. In fact it's the only statement in the program. However the rest of the code is not irrelevant. It sets up a structure that all Java applications must follow. Since there is so little going on in this program, the structure is rather exposed and easy to see. Therefore let's take this opportunity to investigate the structure of a simple Java application, line by line (comment lines are omitted).

Line 2: **class HelloWorld** {

The initial class statement may be thought of as defining the program name, in this case HelloWorld. The compiler actually got the name for the class file from the class HelloWorld statement in the source code, not from the name of the source code file. If there is more than one class in a file, then the Java compiler will store each one in a separate .class file. For reasons you'll see later it's advisable to give the source code file the same name as the primary class in the file followed by the .java extension.

Line 2: class HelloWorld **{**

After class HelloWorld, you open the class with a brace. The brace is used to separate blocks of code and must be matched by a closing brace. Thus somewhere (in this case all the way at the end of the file) is another brace which closes the class. Everything between those two braces is a part of this class.

Line 3:

The second line is blank. Blank lines are meaningless in Java and are used purely to make the code easier to read. You could take all the blank lines out of this program, and it would still produce identical results.

Line 4: public static void **main** (String args[]) {

The HelloWorld class contains one method, the main method. As in C the main method is where an application begins executing. The words before the braces declare what the main method is, what type of value it returns and what data it receives. Everything after the brace actually is the main method.

Line 4: **public static void** main (String args[]) {

The main method is declared public, meaning that the method can be called from anywhere. It is declared static, meaning that all instances of this class share this one method. It is declared void, which means, as in C, that this method does not return a value. Finally, you pass any command line arguments to the method in an array of Strings called args. In this simple program, there aren't any command-line arguments.

Line 4 is the most complicated line in the program. You'll investigate each piece of this line in much greater detail in later chapters so don't worry too much about it now. The primary thing you need to know is that every Java application (but not every applet) needs to have a main method and that method must be written exactly as this one is.

Finally, note that line 4 is indented by two spaces. This is because line 4 is inside the HelloWorld class and indentation helps keep track of how deep inside it is. Every time you open a new block with a brace, subsequent lines will be indented by two more spaces. When you leave the block with a closing brace. Subsequent lines are de-indented by two spaces.

To keep track of just how deep into braces you are at any particular point in the code, it's customary to indent by a space or a tab after every opening brace and to de-indent after every closing brace. This makes the code much easier to read since you can see at a glance which statements belong to which classes, methods, and blocks. However, this is purely a convention and not in any way part of the Java language. The code would produce identical output if it had no indentation. In fact you'll probably find a few examples in this book where the convention hasn't been followed precisely. Indentation makes code easier to read and understand, but it does not change its meaning.

White space in Java is significant as a separator between different things, but the amount of white space is not. The Java compiler treats three consecutive spaces the same as three consecutive tabs or just one space. Whether you use tabs or spaces to indent your code is mainly a matter of which is more convenient in your text editor.

Line 5 is another blank line. Line 6 is a comment.

```
Line 7: System.out.println("Hello World!");
```

Line 7 is indented by two more spaces since it is now two braces deep in the program (in the main method of the HelloWorld class).

When the main method is called, it does exactly one thing: print `Hello World!` to the standard output, generally a terminal monitor or console window of some sort. This is accomplished by the `System.out.println()` method. To be more precise, this is accomplished by calling the println method of the out object belonging to the System class, but for now just treat this as one method.

The `System.out.println()` method takes various arguments inside the parentheses. In this case it has the argument `"Hello World!"`

Next note that this line ends with a semicolon. Every **statement** in Java must end with a semicolon, and it's a very common mistake of even the most experienced programmers to omit semicolons. If you do, the compiler will generate an error message which, depending on how smart the compiler is, may or may not have anything to do with missing semicolons. For instance, if the semicolon is left out of this line, here's what javac says:

```
HelloWorld.java:7: ';' expected.
    System.out.println("Hello World!")
                                      ^
```

You may be wondering why the other lines of this program didn't end with a semicolon. They didn't because they're not statements. Rather they're definitions. When you open a block with a brace, you're signaling that you can't do everything you want to do with one statement. Instead, you're going to use a whole series of statements and execute them as a group. You're not finished so you'll continue with more statements. On the other hand, `System.out.println("Hello World!")` is complete unto itself so it is terminated with a semicolon.

Sometimes you'll have lines of code that continue for some distance. It is permissible to use a newline or carriage return instead of typing a space (except inside a String). The Java compiler treats all white space equally. This book makes frequent use of this feature to make long lines of code fit within the margins of the page. Remember, the line isn't finished until you see the semicolon.

Unlike the `printf` function in C, the `System.out.println` method does append a newline at the end of its output. There's no need to include a `\n` at the end of each string to break a line. There is also a `System.out.print()` method which doesn't add a new line at the end of each line.

Line 9 has a closing brace. This finishes the main method since the previous opening brace opened the main method. A closing brace closes the nearest preceding opening brace that has not already been closed.

Line 11 has the final closing brace which signals the end of the HelloWorld class.

Q&A

Q: *Does the compiler turn comments into white space or does it throw them away completely?*

A: As in ANSI C, the compiler turns comments into white space. In general, when you're uncertain how something may work, the way it works in ANSI C is a good first guess.

Q: *I thought Java was supposed to be cross-platform, how come there are all these different instructions for Unix, the Mac, and Windows?*

A: Programs you create with Java are cross-platform. The Java development environment regrettably isn't.

Q: *Can comments be included in the middle of a String?*

A: No. Inside a String / and * are just characters. They have no special meaning. For instance the following program prints `/* This is a test */`

```
class StringTest {

    public static void main (String args[]) {

        System.out.println(" /* This is a test */");

    }

}
```

Q: *Why isn't* `System.out.println` *boldfaced in the code samples?*

A: Many things that look like part of the Java language, at least at first glance, are instead part of the Java runtime library. The runtime library is made up of several different packages. `System` and `System.out` are part of the java.lang package. `println` is from the java.io package. They are not keywords of the Java language itself.

Quiz

1. What happens if you change the name of the source code file, for example, HelloEarth.java instead of HelloWorld.java?

2. What happens if you keep the name of the source code file the same (HelloWorld.java) but change the class's name, for example, class HelloEarth?

3. How would you write the HelloWorld program in French? Spanish? Latin? Arabic?

4. What's the difference between an operator and a separator?

5. What's the difference between a keyword and an identifier?

6. What's the difference between an identifier and a literal?

7. What would happen if you added the following line to the Hello World program?

```
/* THIS PROGRAM CANNOT BE EXECUTED WITHOUT SYSADMIN PRIVILEGES */
```

Exercises

1. Personalize the HelloWorld program with your name so that it tells you hello rather than the somewhat generic "World."

2. Write a program that produces the following output:

   ```
   Hello World!
   It's been nice knowing you.
   Goodbye world!
   ```

3. Write a program that draws the following figures one above the other.

   ```
   *  *  *  *  *                     *
   *  *  *  *  *                   *  *
   *  *  *  *  *                 *  *  *
   *  *  *  *  *               *  *  *  *  *
   ```

   Now modify it to draw them next to each other as they are above.

Summary

In this chapter you learned to write a simple Java application. The things you learned included:

- How to type and save Java source code
- How to compile a Java application
- How to run a Java application
- How Java programs are structured
- What operators, separators, keywords, identifiers, comments, and literals are and the difference between them.
- How to comment your source code
- How to print text on the screen.
- How to indent code to make it more legible.

The goal of this chapter is to be able to write, compile and run a simple Java program. If you can do that, you're ready to move on.

Coming Up

In the next chapter you'll expand the HelloWorld program to include multiple statements, different data, and user input. You'll learn a variation on `System.out.println`, how to use String variables and how to do simple arithmetic.

There isn't much more to learn about comments than you learned in this chapter. However in Chapter 22, you will learn how to use comments with javadoc to combine source code with its own documentation.

There is a lot more to learn about `println` than this chapter covered, though. You'll see more of it in Chapter 20.

Further Reading

The original HelloWorld program in C comes from

KERNIGHAN, BRIAN W. and DENNIS M. RITCHIE, *The C Programming Language*, Englewood Cliffs, NJ: Prentice-Hall, Inc., 1988, pp. 5–8.

Operators, literals, separators, white space, comments, and identifiers are covered fully if not always clearly in sections 3.6 through 3.10 of *The Java Language Specification.*

GOSLING, JAMES, BILL JOY and GUY STEELE, *The Java Language Specification*, Reading, MA: Addison-Wesley, Inc., 1996, pp. 15–25.

CHAPTER 3

EXTENDING HELLO WORLD

- ☑ Variables

- ☑ Strings

- ☑ Command-line arguments

- ☑ if statements and while loops

- ☑ Simple arithmetic

This chapter extends the HelloWorld program to call you by name, for example, Hello Rusty! or Hello Beth! Toward this end, the HelloWorld program of the previous chapter will be expanded in steps with something new added at each step of the way. Each HelloWorld program will be a little more capable than the previous one. Nonetheless, each one will indicate a direction for further improvement.

The constructs you encounter in this chapter form the basic building blocks of most programming languages. You'll revisit all these items later and explore them in much greater detail, but this chapter will give you the basic knowledge you need for your first programs.

Extending Hello World

Gauss, the most prolific mathematician of the nineteenth century and possibly the greatest mathematician of all time, was fond of saying that mathematical proofs should stand elegantly alone with no hint of the structure that was used to build them, much as when viewing the Cathedral of Notre Dame, you don't see all the wires and scaffolding that were in place for years during the cathedral's construction.

Sometimes programs are presented in the same way, as if they sprung from the programmer's mind like Athena from the head of Zeus. In reality, architecture, mathematics, and programming are not so orderly. There is quite a lot of scaffolding that must be erected before software is completed. Many times you don't even know what the cathedral will look like when you're building it. Other times you think you know what it will look like, but the archbishop changes the plans in the middle of construction. Other times it's only during actual construction that a better path becomes apparent, or you realize that your current goal is infeasible. In most instances programs start their life small, incomplete, and buggy and only slowly build themselves up to useful things. Working code is littered with debug statements, test conditions, false starts, obsolete algorithms and more. One of the tasks a programming team must complete before shipping a product is to remove all this scaffolding from the final build of the code.

In this chapter you'll see the construction of a simple program from start to finish including all the intermediate steps, ungainly and awkward though they may be. You begin building the expanded HelloWorld program by using variables to store a name. This program still won't be as general as you'd like so you'll use command-line arguments and arrays to allow the user to choose a name when the program is run. In the process some bugs will have been introduced, so in the next section you'll use `if` statements to fix the bugs. This will fix the serious bugs but also reveal some shortcomings in the program at the same time. Therefore in the final section of this chapter you'll use loops and simple arithmetic to dramatically expand the power of HelloWorld.

Data and Variables

The HelloWorld program of last chapter only used a method,

```
System.out.println("Hello World!");
```

This printed "Hello World!" on the screen. "Hello World!" is a String literal. `System.out.println` is a method call.

Now you're going to extend this program by adding a variable and some operators. The name of the person you want to say hello to will be stored inside a variable called `name`. Then, instead of saying hello to a rather generic world, the program will say hello to the person whose name it is. Program 3.1 is the generalization of the HelloWorld program.

Program 3.1 Hello Name

```java
// This is the Hello Name program in Java
class HelloName {

  public static void main (String args[]) {

    //Declare the variable name to be a String
    String name;

    // Replace "Rusty" with your own name
    name = "Rusty";

    // Say hello
    System.out.println("Hello " + name);

  }

}
```

Here's what happens when you compile and run the program:

```
% javac HelloName.java
% java HelloName Rusty
Hello Rusty
%
```

Success! Java has now said hello to you personally rather than to the entire world. You did this by creating a **String variable** called name, storing the value "Rusty" in it using the assignment operator =, and then printing out the concatenation of the constant String `"Hello "` with the variable name using the now-familiar `System.out.println()` method and the concatenation operator +. Let's look at each of these steps in detail.

A variable is a small area of computer memory with a name where you can store a value. You use the name to refer to the variable in your program. The value of the variable may change but the name stays the same. The value can be an integer like "2" or a word like "Rusty." Word variables are called Strings in most programming languages including Java. (Java is a little unusual in that it capitalizes the word String.) This value can be changed while the program is running. Hence the name "variable."

Java is **strongly typed** language. This means that you must declare what kind of value a variable will hold before you use it. In this case the line

```
String name;
```

declares that you will put Strings into name, not integers, not boolean values like true and false, not arrays, not anything else that isn't a String.

Once you've declared the variable name, you should put a value in it. The first time you do this is called "initializing the variable." If you put a different value in it later, that's called assigning a value to the variable. In this case you initialize name with the constant String "Rusty." (You may, of course, replace Rusty with your own name.)

```
name = "Rusty";
```

The equals sign is called the **assignment operator**. It's used to store values in variables. After the assignment has taken place, the variable name has the value "Rusty."[1]

---

[1]Before the assignment takes place, name has the value " ", that is, the empty String.

You print out `"Hello Rusty"` with the line

```
System.out.println("Hello " + name);
```

The plus sign is an operator that "adds" the string `"Hello "` to the value of name, that is, `"Rusty"`. The result is the longer String, `"Hello Rusty"`. Adding two or more Strings together is called **concatenating** the Strings.

You can change the name you say hello to by changing the value of the name variable. Program 3.2 says hello to Beth.

Program 3.2 Hello Beth

```java
class HelloName {

  public static void main (String args[]) {

    //Declare the variable name to be a String
    String name;

    // Replace "Beth" with your own name
    name = "Beth";

    // Say hello
    System.out.println("Hello " + name);

  }

}
```

The only thing that you had to change to say hello to Beth instead of to Rusty was the value of the variable name.

You may be asking yourself, Why bother with a variable at all? Why not just change the name in the String literal? The main reason is that you can change the value of the variable on the fly. For instance consider the following program:

Program 3.3 Hello Beth & Rusty

```java
class HelloTwoNames {

    public static void main (String args[]) {

        //Declare the variable name to be a String
        String name;
        // Say hello to Beth
        name = "Beth";
        System.out.println("Hello " + name);

        // Say hello to Rusty
        name = "Rusty";
        System.out.println("Hello " + name);

    }

}
```

Here's what you get when you compile and run this program:

```
% javac HelloTwoNames.java
% java HelloTwoNames
Hello Beth
Hello Rusty
%
```

Naming Your Variables

Each variable has a name by which it is identified in the program. It's a good idea to give your variables mnemonic names that are closely related to the values they hold. Variable names can include any alphabetic character or digit, the underscore _, and the dollar sign $. The main restriction on the names you can give your variables is that they cannot contain any white space. Also, you cannot begin a variable name with a number. It is important to note that as in C, but not as in Fortran or Basic, variable names are case-sensitive. MyVariable is not the same as myVariable. There is no limit to the length of a Java variable name.

The following are legal variable names:

- `MyVariable`
- `myvariable`
- `MYVARIABLE`
- `x`
- `i`
- `_myvariable`
- `$myvariable`
- `_9pins`
- `This_is_an_insanely_long_variable_name_that_just_keeps_going_and_going_and_going_and_well_you_get_the_idea_The_line_breaks_arent_really_part_of_the_variable_name_Its_just_that_this_variable_name_is_so_ridiculously_long_that_it_won't_fit_on_the_page_I_cant_imagine_why_you_would_need_such_a_long_variable_name_but_if_you_do_you_can_have_it`

The following are not legal variable names.

- `My Variable`   `// Contains a space`
- `9pins`   `// Begins with a digit`
- `a+c`   `// The plus sign is not an`
                    `// alphanumeric character`
- `testing1-2-3`   `// The hyphen is not an`
                    `// alphanumeric character`

Tip If you want to begin a variable name with a digit, prefix the name you'd like to have (e.g. 8ball) with an underscore, e.g. _8ball. You can also use the underscore like a space in long variable names.

Simultaneous Declaration and Initialization

Java is descended from C, and one thing C is notorious for is shortcuts. In many ways this makes C the obfuscated language it is. Java has wisely thrown out a lot of the more obfuscated shortcuts of C like pointer arithmetic and #defines.

However many of C's shortcuts are genuinely useful and quite legible. Java has kept these and even added a few of its own. One such shortcut in Java is the simultaneous declaration and initialization of variables. The previous program could have been written as in Program 3.4.

Program 3.4 Hello Rusty with a shortcut

```java
// This is the Hello Name program in Java

class HelloName {

  public static void main (String args[]) {

    String name ="Rusty";

    /* Say hello */
    System.out.println("Hello " + name);

  }

}
```

One line of code is saved by merging the declaration of the variable name and its initialization into the same line. The rest of this book will often do this where appropriate.

Command-Line Arguments

The Hello program still isn't very general. You can't change the name you say hello to without editing and recompiling the source code. This may be fine for the programmers, but what if the secretaries want their computers to say hello to them? (I know, this is a little far-fetched, but bear with me. I'm making a point.)

What you need is a way to change the name at runtime rather than at compile time. Runtime is when you type `java HelloName`. Compile time is when you type `javac HelloName.java`.

Language Law: Runtime

To be precise, runtime is everything that happens after the source code is translated into byte code including not only the actual running of the program but also linking different classes, loading files with the class loader, and even machine code generation and dynamic optimization by a just-in-time compiler.

To add this, the next version will make use of command-line arguments. To run a Java application, you normally type

```
% java program_name
```

where *program_name* is the name of the program you want to run. Any word you type after the program name is a **command-line argument**. For instance, if you typed

```
% java Hello Beth and Rusty
```

then there are three command line arguments, the words `Beth`, `and`, and `Rusty`. Java stores the command-line arguments in an array called `args`. The words `java` and `Hello` are not command-line arguments to the Hello program.

An array is a variable with many pieces stored in a particular order. To get a specific piece, you ask for it by number. `args[0]` is the first value in the array, `args[1]` is the second value, and so on. For instance, in the previous example, `args[0]` is `"Beth"`, `args[1]` is `"and"`, and `args[2]` is `"Rusty"`.

 **Tip Zero-Based Arrays**

At this point, almost everyone reading this is probably saying "Whoa, that can't be right." However, what you're saying depends on your background.

If you've never programmed before or if you've programmed only in Pascal or Fortran, you're probably wondering why the first element of the array is at position 0, the second at position 1, the third at position 2 instead of the clearly more sensible element 1 being the first element in the array, element 2 being the second, and so on. All I can tell you is that this is a holdover from C where this convention almost made sense.

On the other hand, if you've used to C, you're probably upset because args[0] is the first command line argument instead of the command name. The problem is that in Java it's not always clear what the command name is. For instance, in the above example, is it java or Hello?

Since there is no command line on the Macintosh, the Java Runner program brings up a dialog box in which you can enter command-line arguments. Figure 3.1 shows how you'd enter the command line arguments for Program 3.4 on a Macintosh.

If you're using Roaster, you can set the command-line arguments in the **Roaster Preferences:** Dialog under **Project** in the **Parameters for main()** input box as shown in Figure 3.2.

The next program reads the first command-line argument (which should be a name) and says hello to that person.

Program 3.5 Hello with command-line input

```java
// This is the Hello program in Java
class Hello {

    public static void main (String args[]) {

        /* Now let's say hello */
        System.out.println("Hello " + args[0]);

    }

}
```

Compile this program as usual and then type java Hello Gloria. You should see something like the following:

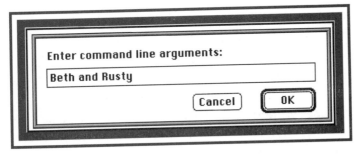

Figure 3.1: *Command-line arguments on a Macintosh*

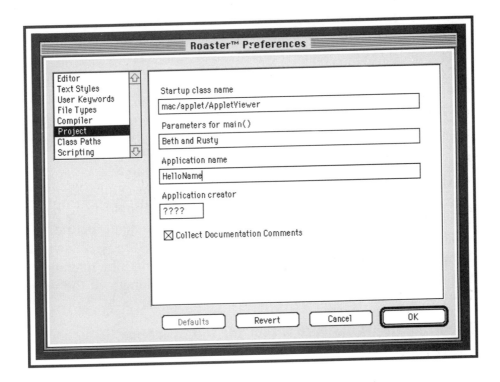

Figure 3.2: *Command-line arguments on Roaster*

```
% javac Hello.java
% java Hello Gloria
Hello Gloria
%
```

This isn't very hard, is it? In fact, the program has even been simplified by removing the name variable. args[0] is used instead.

Now try typing java Hello without any command-line arguments.

That was interesting wasn't it? You should have seen something very close to

```
Exception in thread "main"
java.lang.ArrayIndexOutOfBoundsException at
Hello.main(C:\javahtml\Hello.java:7)
```

Here's what happened. Since `Hello` didn't have any command-line arguments, there wasn't any value in `args[0]`. Therefore, Java kicked back this not very friendly error message about an `ArrayIndexOutOfBoundsException`. That's a mouthful. You'll see one way to fix it in the next section.

If

All but the most trivial computer programs need to make decisions. They test a condition and operate differently based on the outcome of the test. This is quite common in real life. For instance you stick your hand out the window to test if it's raining. If it is raining, then you take an umbrella with you. If it isn't raining then you don't.

All programming languages have some form of an `if` statement that tests conditions. In the previous program, you should have tested whether there actually were command-line arguments before you tried to use them.

Arrays have lengths and you can access that length by referencing the variable *arrayname*.`length`.[2] You test the length of the `args` array as follows.

Program 3.6 Hello with a test for the presence of command-line input

```java
// This is the Hello program in Java

class Hello {
    public static void main (String args[]) {

        if (args.length > 0) {
            System.out.println("Hello " + args[0]);
        }
    }
}
```

---

[2] Experienced Java programmers will note that this means that the array is an object that contains a public field called length.

Compile and run this program and toss different inputs at it. You should note that there's no longer an `ArrayIndexOut OfBoundsException` if you don't give it any command-line arguments at all.

`System.out.println(args[0])` was wrapped in a conditional test, if `(args.length > 0) {   }`. The code inside the braces, `System.out.println(args[0])`, now gets executed if and only if the length of the `args` array is greater than zero.

In Java, numerical greater-than and lesser-than tests are done with the > and < operators, respectively. You can test whether a number is less than or equal to or greater than or equal to another number with the <= and >= operators.

Testing for equality is a little trickier. You would expect to test if two numbers are equal by using the = sign. However, the = sign has already been used as an assignment operator that sets the value of a variable. Therefore a new symbol is needed to test for equality. Java borrows C's double equal sign, ==, for this purpose.

It's not uncommon for even experienced programmers to write == when they mean = or vice versa. In fact, this is a very common cause of errors in C programs. Fortunately in Java, you are not allowed to use == and = in the same places. Therefore, the compiler can catch your mistake and make you fix it before you run the program.

Else

It's often said that a good answer raises more questions than it answers. Often a solution to one bug causes more bugs to pop up in other places.

You may have noticed a minor **cosmetic bug** in Program 3.6. A cosmetic bug is one that doesn't crash the program or system, or produce incorrect results, but just looks different than it should. Cosmetic bugs are acceptable in quick hacks you'll only use once, but not in finished code.

The cosmetic bug in Program 3.6 occurred if you didn't provide any command-line arguments. Although the program didn't crash, it didn't say hello either. You can fix this by adding an additional `if` statement as in Program 3.7.

Program 3.7 Hello with two ifs

```java
// This is the Hello program in Java
class Hello {

    public static void main (String args[]) {

        if (args.length > 0) {
            System.out.println("Hello " + args[0]);
        }
        if (args.length <= 0) {
            System.out.println(
                "Hello whoever you are");
        }
    }

}
```

This corrects the bug, but the code is hard to read and maintain. It's very easy to miss a possible case. For instance, you might well have tested to see if args.length were less than zero and left out the more important case that args.length equals zero. What's needed is an else statement that will catch any result other than the one you hope for, and luckily Java provides exactly that. Here's the right solution:

Program 3.8 Hello with else

```java
// This is the Hello program in Java
class Hello {

    public static void main (String args[]) {
        if (args.length > 0) {
            System.out.println("Hello " + args[0]);
        }
        else {
            System.out.println(
                "Hello whoever you are.");
        }
    }

}
```

You're still not quite done. `java Hello` works and `Java Hello Rusty` works, but if you type `java Hello Elliotte Rusty Harold`, Java still only prints `Hello Elliotte`. Let's fix that.

Else If

`If` statements are not limited to two cases. You can combine an `else` and an `if` to make an `else if` and test a whole range of mutually exclusive possibilities. For instance, here's a version of the Hello program that handles up to four names on the command line:

Program 3.9 Hello with else if

```java
// This is the Hello program in Java

class Hello {

    public static void main (String args[]) {

        if (args.length == 0) {
          System.out.println(
            "Hello whoever you are");
        }
        else if (args.length == 1) {
          System.out.println("Hello " + args[0]);
        }
        else if (args.length == 2) {
          System.out.println("Hello " + args[0] +
            " " + args[1]);
        }
        else if (args.length == 3) {
          System.out.println("Hello " + args[0] +
            " " + args[1] + " " args[2]);
        }
        else if (args.length == 4) {
          System.out.println("Hello " + args[0] +
            " " + args[1] + " " args[2] +
            " " + args[3]);
        }
        else {
          System.out.println("Hello " + args[0] +
```

```
                      "   " + args[1] + "  "  args[2] + "  " +
               args[3] + "  and all the rest!");
         }

     }

 }
```

You can see that this gets mighty complicated mighty quickly. No experienced Java programmer would write code like this. There is a better solution and you'll explore it in the next section.

While Loops

When your only tool is a hammer, most problems look like nails. You may even be able to hammer them into submission. Still there's often more than one solution to a problem, and if your problem is a screw, you'll likely have an easier time if you go down to the local hardware store and buy a screwdriver.

In the last section, a problem that really needed a loop was attacked with `if` and `else`. It wasn't pretty but it worked. However, it will be a lot simpler when you add the `while` loop to your toolbox.

A loop is a section of code that is executed repeatedly until a test condition fails. A typical loop might look like

```
while (there's more data) {
   Read a Line of Data
   Write the Data In a File
}
```

This isn't working code but it does give you an idea of a very typical loop. There is a test condition (Is there more data?) and something to do if the condition is met (Read a Line of Data and Write the Data in a File). Once you've finished processing the data, you go back to the beginning of the loop and try again. Is there still more data? If so, execute the code between the braces again. This process continues until there's no more data.

A loop has three main parts: the **keyword**, the **body**, and the **test condition**. In the above pseudo-code, `while` is the keyword, (there's more data) is the test condition, and reading the data and doing something with it is the body. The keyword just tells you that a loop is starting and what kind of loop it is. In Java the test condition of the loop comes in parentheses after the keyword and the body comes in braces. Test conditions are normally short and simple. The body of the loop can be quite complex, however.

You need a loop that prints each of the command-line arguments in succession, starting with the first one. You don't know in advance how many arguments there will be, but you can easily find this out before the loop starts using `args.length`. Program 3.10 has the code.

Program 3.10 Hello with a while loop

```
1.  // This is the Hello program in Java
2.
3.  class Hello {
4.
5.    public static void main (String args[]) {
6.
7.      int i;
8.
9.      System.out.print("Hello ");    // Say Hello
10.     i = 0;                // Initialize loop counter
11.     while (i < args.length) {// Test and Loop
12.       System.out.print(args[i]);
13.       System.out.print(" ");
14.       i = i + 1;     // Increment Loop Counter
15.     }
16.     System.out.println();  // Finish the line
17.   }
18.
19.}
```

Line 1 of this program is just a comment. The program really begins in line 3 where the Hello class opens. Line 5 is the usual declaration of a main method.

The main method of the Hello class begins with variable declarations in line 7. In this case, there is one variable, the `int i`. `int` is the basic integer data type in Java. You'll use this variable to count how many times you've gone through the body of the loop. This is called a **loop index**.

> ## Tip Loop Index Names
>
> Programming tradition that dates back to Fortran in the 1950s insists that loop indices be named i, j, k, l, m, and n in that order. This is purely a convention and not a feature of Java. However, anyone who reads your code will expect you to follow this convention. If you choose to violate this convention, try to give your loop variables mnemonic names like counter or loop_index.

Line 9 says "Hello." However, here `System.out.print` is used instead of `System.out.println`. The difference between these methods is that `System.out.print` does not move the cursor to the next line when it's done. More text can still be printed on the same line.

Line 10 initializes the loop counter. This means its value is set for the first time. The loop counter is used to count through the values of the array so set it to the first position in the array, index 0.

Line 11 starts the `while` loop. At the beginning of every loop there is a test. In this case the test is (`i < args.length`), that is, whether or not `i` is less than the number of elements in the array. If `i` is less than the number of elements in the array, then the statements in the body of the loop are performed.

The body of the loop is everything between the opening brace and the closing brace four lines later. It consists of the three statements:

```
System.out.print(args[i]);
System.out.print(" ");
i = i + 1;
```

When `i` becomes equal to the number of arguments, `args.length`, the test fails, you exit the loop, and go to the first statement after the loop's closing brace. You might think you should test for `i` being less than or equal to the number of arguments, but remember that you began counting at zero, not one.

Why Algebra Teachers Hate Basic and Aren't That Fond of Java

The statement $i=i+1$ drives algebra teachers up the wall. It's an invalid assertion. There isn't a number in the world for which the statement $i=i+1$ is true. In fact, if you subtract i from both sides of that equation, you get the patently false statement that $0 = 1$. The trick here is that the symbol = does not imply equality. That is reserved for the double equals sign, ==. In almost all programming languages, including Java, a single equals sign is the assignment operator.

The one notable exception is Pascal (and the Pascal derivatives Modula-2, Modula-3, and Oberon) where = does in fact mean equality and where : = is the assignment operator. Math teachers are very fond of their equal sign and don't like to see it abused. This is one reason why Pascal is still a popular language for teaching programming, especially in schools where the Computer Science department is composed mainly of math professors.

Needless to say, math professors hate languages like Basic where, depending on context, = can mean either assignment or equality.

The first line inside the body of the loop, line 12, should be familiar. You simply print the `ith` command line argument. Line 13 prints a space. These two lines could just as easily have been combined as

```
System.out.print(args[i] + " ");
```

Finally, line 14 has the increment step, `i = i + 1`. This adds one to the value of `i` and therefore moves on to the next element of the array. This is executed at the end of each iteration of the loop.

Without this you'd loop forever since i would always be less than args.length (unless, of course, args.length were less than or equal to zero. When would this happen?).

Line 15 is the closing brace for the body of the while loop.

Line 16, System.out.println() without any arguments, prints the newline character that's needed to finish the line.

Line 17 closes the main method and line 19 closes the class.

 Q & A

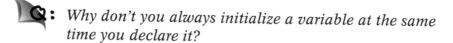

Q: *Why don't you always initialize a variable at the same time you declare it?*

A: Many times you don't have the information you need to initialize a variable when you're writing the code. For instance, a variable may need to be filled in by command-line arguments. Although you could fill a variable with dummy values, there's no need to do so and requiring it would defeat the goal of simplicity. You should set a variable's value when appropriate. Sometimes that's as soon as you define it. Other times it may be later in the code or even at runtime.

Q: *Why does the + operator sometimes mean addition and sometimes mean concatenation?*

A: There are only a finite number of keys on most people's keyboards, and something had to be chosen. Most of the time it should be completely obvious whether String concatenation or addition is meant. Nonetheless there are some questionable examples. For instance what do you think this code fragment prints?

```
System.out.println("2 + 2 is " + 2 + 2);
```

Quiz

1. What does the following program print?

```java
// This is the Hello Rusty program in Java

class HelloRusty {

    public static void main (String args[]) {

        String name = "Rusty";

        /* Now let's say hello */
        System.out.println("Hello + name");

    }

}
```

2. What's wrong with this program?

```java
// This is the Hello program in Java
class Hello {

    public static void main (String args[]) {

        int i;

        System.out.print("Hello ");   // Say Hello
        i = 0;               // Initialize loop counter
        while (i <= args.length) { // Test and Loop
            System.out.print(args[i] + " ");
            i = i + 1;       // Increment Loop Counter
        }
        System.out.println();     // Finish the line
    }

}
```

3. What happens if you don't give Program 3.10 any command-line arguments? You aren't testing the number of command line arguments anymore, so why isn't an ArrayIndexOutOfBounds Exception thrown?

4. For math whizzes only: I lied. In certain interpretations of certain number systems, the statement i = i + 1 does have a valid solution for i. What is it?

5. What does `System.out.println("2 + 2 is " + 2 + 2)` print?

Exercises

1. Write a program that prints all the integers between 0 and 36.

2. Imagine you need to open a standard combination dial lock but don't know the combination and don't have a pair of bolt cutters. Write a program that that prints all possible combinations you will need to try so you can print them on a piece of paper and check off each one as you try it. Assume the numbers on the dial range from 1 to 36 and three numbers in sequence are needed to open the lock.

3. Suppose the lock isn't a very good one and any number that's no more than one away from the correct number will also work. In other words, if the combination is 17-6-32 then 18-5-31 will also open the lock. Write a program that prints the minimum number of combinations you need to try.

4. The Fibonacci numbers are defined as follows. The zeroth Fibonacci number is 1. The first Fibonacci number is also 1. The second Fibonacci number is 1 + 1 = 2. The third Fibonacci number is 1 + 2 = 3. In other words, except for the first two numbers, each Fibonacci number is the sum of the two previous numbers. Write a program that prints the first 20 Fibonacci numbers.

 Summary

This chapter covered a lot of ground quite quickly. Before you go on, you should make sure you've got a firm grasp on this material, especially if you're new to programming. The main things you should have learned from this chapter are

- What a variable is
- How to declare a variable
- How to assign a value to a variable
- How to perform String concatenation with +
- How to use command line arguments in the `args` array
- How to test simple conditions with `if`
- How to use a `while` loop to repeatedly perform the same action
- How to do basic addition with +

Coming Up

In the next several chapters, you'll explore many more kinds of variables and data types as you move beyond Strings. Chapter 4 introduces number variables and the arithmetic you can do with them. Chapter 5 explores boolean values and sheds more light on the `if` and `while` statements. It also introduces several new kinds of loops to complement the `while` loop introduced here. Finally, Chapter 6 shows you how to create your own data types that go beyond the primitive ones built into Java.

CHAPTER 4

NUMBERS AND ARITHMETIC

- The different kinds of integers: bytes, shorts, ints, and longs.

- The different kinds of floating-point numbers: float and double.

- Basic arithmetic: addition, subtraction, multiplication and division.

- The char data type

So far most of your attention has been concentrated on Strings. However, although you can do a lot with Strings, and although there are in fact some programming languages where all variables are strings, there are many other data types that are equally useful.

Most notably missing are numbers. The first computers were invented to crunch numbers. Even today's modern computers that process text, keep track of huge databases, produce beautiful artwork, and perform other seemingly nonmathematical tasks do so by reducing everything to numbers and doing arithmetic on those numbers.

Java isn't as efficient a cruncher of numbers as C or Fortran, but it's still got enough raw number crunching power to make the eyes of the original atomic scientists of Los Alamos water.

This chapter is about numbers: big numbers, small numbers, whole numbers, real numbers, and more. You'll learn about the different kinds of numbers and why they're different. Then you'll learn what you can do with numbers including addition, subtraction, multiplication, division, and remainders. When this chapter is finished, you'll be able to do grammar school math in Java (but very quickly).

Numbers

There are two kinds of numbers in computer arithmetic: integers and floating-point numbers. Each of these comes in several sizes.

Integers

In classical arithmetic, an integer is a number like 1, 0, -72, or 10,342,853,036,854,775,979. Integers represent whole quantities of things and can be positive, negative, or zero. There is no limit to the size of an integer.

In computer arithmetic, there are no integers. The problem is that representing a number that's infinitely large requires an infinite amount of memory.[1] Therefore, Java restricts integer data types to one of four finite sizes. The default kind of integer in Java is an `int` which takes up four bytes of memory and can hold numbers between –2,147,483,648 and +2,147,483,647. That's a little over two billion, which should be sufficient to count most quantities you're liable to encounter in day-to-day life.

On the other hand, if you're Bill Gates and you want to count your wealth, an `int` isn't big enough. You can use a `long` instead. Longs occupy eight bytes of memory and range in size from

---

[1] More precisely, to represent any number that's arbitrarily large you need an infinite amount of memory. Java represents infinity quite compactly.

–9,223,372,036,854,775,808 to +9,223,372,036,854,775,807. That's almost ten thousand trillion. That's big enough to count Bill Gate's wealth and have room left over for the national debt. If you're counting anything more than that, perhaps the total number of neutrinos in the universe, you need to use a floating-point number instead.

Most people don't even need the full range of an int to count their wealth. On rare occasions when space is at a premium or when you're working on 16-bit architectures that deal more efficiently with two-byte integers, you can use a short which is only two bytes long and covers -32,768 to +32,767.

Finally, if you're very poor, either in money or memory, a byte is the shortest integer of all. It's one byte long and ranges in value from -128 to 127. Bytes aren't often used for counting in Java, but they are often used for input and output.

Although it's customary to write very large numbers like 9,223,372,036,854,775,808 with embedded commas to make reading them easier, Java doesn't allow this. In Java source code that number would be 9223372036854775808.

Floating-Point Numbers

A floating-point number has a decimal point and a fractional part. Examples include 0.0, 1.75, –83.4567, and 2.998×10^8. The last number can also be written as 2.998E8. The $\times 10$ is replaced by the E (for "Exponent").

A floating-point number can represent a whole quantity of things, but it can also represent parts of things. While you think of integers as exact, floating-point numbers are approximate. When you say there are two grapefruit in the refrigerator, you mean that there are exactly two grapefruit in the refrigerator, not one and not three. On the other hand, when you say that a grapefruit weighs 0.2 kilograms, you mean that it weighs somewhere between 0.15 and 0.25 kilograms, but you've chosen not to be more precise than one decimal place.

There are only two kinds of floating point numbers in Java: floats and doubles. A float is a four-byte number that can contain values as small as 1.40129846e-45 and as large as 3.40282347e+38. These numbers can be either positive or negative. It has nine places of

Scientific Notation

When a floating-point number is very large or very small, normal decimal notation becomes awkward. The speed of light is 299,792,456 meters per second. Avogadro's number is about 602,300,000,000,000,000,000,000. The mass of an electron is 0.00000000000000000000000091096 kilograms.

Scientific notation expresses a number as a value between 1.0 and 10.0 multiplied by a power of 10. Thus the speed of light becomes 2.99792456×10^8 meters per second. The two pieces of this number are called the mantissa (2.99792456) and the exponent (8). You always multiply by 10 so that number doesn't have a name. Avogadro's number is 6.023×10^{23}, and the mass of an electron is 9.1096×10^{-25} kg. This is much easier to write, read, and understand. In one glance you get a solid idea of both the precision (roughly, the number of decimal places) and the magnitude (size of the exponent) of the number.

Even 2.99792456×10^8 is awkward to type on computer keyboards that don't have multiplication signs or superscripts, so the accepted shorthand is 2.998E8. The E (for exponent) stands for times 10 to the power....

Although in pure scientific notation the mantissa must be greater than or equal to one and less than ten, Java allows a broader range of mantissas. For instance, 2.998E8 is the same as 0.2998E9, 29.98E7 or even 0.02998E10.

precision. A `double` takes up eight bytes and can signify numbers with magnitude between 4.94065645841246544e-324 to 1.79769313486231570e+308. It has 18 places of precision. Doubles are the default type so when you type a number with a decimal point, Java treats it as a double.

Most significantly, both floats and doubles comply with the IEEE 754 standards for floating-point arithmetic including proper handling of NaN and Inf values. Rounding is precisely defined and will be identical across all CPUs. Unlike Fortran or C, the same Java program should never produce different output on different computers.

Literals

1, 0, -72, 0.0, 1.75, 2.998E8, -83.4567, and 897.32 are all examples of "literals." A **literal** is a value that is written directly in the code without being stored in a variable first. 1 is an `int` literal. 1.75 is a `double` literal. 1.0 is also a `double` literal. `"Hello World"` in the first program in this book was a String literal.

With no further specification, a number like 75 in Java code is treated as an `int`. If you want it to be a `long`, suffix it with the letter L, i.e. 75L. Bytes and shorts are used only for storage in Java, never in an arithmetic operation, so there are no `byte` or `short` literals.

Similarly, a number like 75.07 is assumed to be a `double`. If you want it to be a `float`, then suffix it with an F, i.e. 75.07F.

Basic Arithmetic

You use `ints` and `doubles` in code pretty much as you expect. For instance, consider Program 4.1.

Program 4.1 Addition examples

```
1.   class AddInts {
2.
3.     public static void main (String args[]) {
4.
5.       int i = 1;
6.       int j = 2;
7.       int k;
8.
```

```
9.        System.out.println("i is " + i);
10.       System.out.println("j is " + j);
11.
12.       k = i + j;
13.       System.out.println("i + j is " + k);
14.
15.       k = i - j;
16.       System.out.println("i - j is " + k);
17.
18.    }
19.
20. }
```

Here's what happens when you compile and run AddInts:

```
% javac AddInts.java
% java AddInts
i is 1
j is 2
i + j is 3
i - j is -1
%
```

AddInts is straightforward.

Line 5 declares that i is an int and initializes it to 1.

Similarly Line 6 declares that j is an int and initializes it to 2.

Line 7 declares that k is an int but doesn't specify any value for it.

Lines 9 and 10 print the values of i and j. Note that Java is smart enough to handle the necessary conversion of an integer variable to a String before using the + operator to concatenate it to the String "i is ".

Line 12 sets k to be equal to i + j, in other words 3. Here the + operator means integer addition.

Line 13 prints k. Here the + operator means String concatenation. The Java compiler is able to figure out from context whether the + sign means addition or String concatenation. However the compiler isn't a mind reader. You'll see in the exercises that Java may not always behave as you expect (though it does always behave in a completely predictable manner).

Line 15 changes k's value to i - j, that is, –1, and Line 16 prints it. The minus sign is exactly what you expect. It signifies the subtraction of two numbers.

Line 18 closes the main method and line 20 closes the class.

doubles are treated much the same way, but now you get to use decimal points in the numbers. Program 4.2 is a similar program that does addition and subtraction on doubles.

Program 4.2: Addition and subtraction with doubles

```
class AddDoubles {

  public static void main (String args[]) {

    double x = 7.5;
    double y = 5.4;
    double z;

    System.out.println("x is " + x);
    System.out.println("y is " + y);

    z = x + y;
    System.out.println("x + y is " + z);

    z = x - y;
    System.out.println("x - y is " + z);

  }

}
```

Here's the result:
```
% javac AddDoubles.java
% java AddDoubles
x is 7.5
y is 5.4
x + y is 12.9
x - y is 2.1
%
```

Of course Java can also do multiplication and division. Since most keyboards don't have the × and ÷ symbols you learned in grammar school, Java uses * to mean multiplication and / to mean division. The syntax is straightforward as you see in Program 4.3.

Program 4.3: Multiplication and Division of Integers

```java
class MultiplyDivide {

  public static void main (String args[]) {

    int i = 10;
    int j = 2;
    int k;

    System.out.println("i is " + i);
    System.out.println("j is " + j);

    k = i/j;
    System.out.println("i/j is " + k);
    k = i * j;
    System.out.println("i * j is " + k);

  }

}
```

Here's the result:

```
% javac MultiplyDivide.java
% java MultiplyDivide
i is 10
j is 2
i/j is 5
i * j is 20
%
```

Floats and doubles are multiplied and divided in exactly the same way.

When faced with an inexact integer division, Java rounds the result down. For instance, dividing 10 by 3 produces 3.

Why i Is an int

Computers have evolved a lot since the first electronic computers were invented in the 1940s. Computer languages have evolved along with them but not always as fast.

The first high-level language invented was Fortran. Fortran did not share Java's strong data typing. In fact it was rare to see an early Fortran program that declared any variables at all. In Fortran, the type of a variable was determined by the first letter of a variable's name. If the variable began with the letter i, j, k, l, m, or n, then it was an integer. If it began with any other letter, it was a floating-point number.

Although more explicit data typing has long since been added to Fortran, the tradition of using the letters i, j, k, l, m, and n for integer variables has stuck with us, even among programmers who never learned Fortran.

Remainder

Java has one important arithmetical operator you may not be familiar with, %, also known as the modulus or remainder operator. The % operator returns the remainder of two numbers. For instance 10 % 3 is 1 because 10 divided by 3 leaves a remainder of 1. You can use % just as you might use any other more common operator like + or –. Program 4.4 demonstrates.

Program 4.4: The remainder operator

```
class Remainder {

    public static void main (String args[]) {
```

```
      int i = 10;
      int j = 3;
      int k;

      System.out.println("i is " + i);
      System.out.println("j is " + j);

      k = i%j;
      System.out.println("i%j is " + k);
    }

  }
```

Here's the output:

```
% java Remainder
i is 10
j is 3
i%j is 1
%
```

Perhaps surprisingly, the remainder operator can be used with floating-point values as well. It's surprising because you don't normally think of real number division as producing remainders. However, there are rare times when it's useful to ask exactly how many times does 1.5 go into 5.5 and what's left over? The answer is that 1.5 goes into 5.5 three times with one left over, and it's that one which is the result of `5.5 % 1.5` in Java.

Precedence and Order of Evaluation

It's possible to combine multiple arithmetic expressions in one statement. For instance, the following line adds the numbers one through five:

```
int m = 1 + 2 + 3 + 4 + 5;
```

A slightly more interesting example, Program 4.5 calculates the energy equivalent of an electron using Einstein's famous formula $E = mc^2$.

Program 4.5: The energy equivalent of the mass of an electron

```
class mc2 {

  public static void main (String args[]) {

    double mass = 9.1096E-25;
    double c = 2.998E8;
    double E = mass * c * c;
    System.out.println(E);
  }
}
```

Here's the output:

```
% javac mc2.java
% java mc2
8.18771e-08
%
```

This is all very obvious. However, if you use different operators on the same line, it's not always clear what the result will be. For instance, consider the following code fragment:

```
int n = 1 - 2 * 3 - 4 + 5;
```

Is n equal to –2? You might think so if you just calculate from left to right. However, if you compile this in a program and print out the result, you'll find that Java thinks n is equal to –4. Java got that number because it performs all multiplications before it performs any additions or subtractions. If you like you can think of the calculation Java did as being

```
int n = 1 - (2 * 3) - 4 + 5;
```

This is an issue of order of evaluation. Within the limited number of operators you've learned so far, here is the order in which Java calculates:

1. `*`, `/`, `%`   Do all multiplications, divisions, and remainders from left to right.
2. `+`, `-`   Do additions and subtractions from left to right.
3. `=`   Assign the right-hand side to the left-hand side.

Parentheses

Sometimes the default order of evaluation isn't what you want. For instance, the formula to change a Fahrenheit temperature to a Celsius temperature is °C = (5/9) (°F – 32). You must subtract 32 from the Fahrenheit temperature before you multiply by 5/9, not after. You can use parentheses to adjust the order much as they are used in the above formula. Program 4.6 prints a table showing the conversions from Fahrenheit and Celsius between 0 and 200 degrees Fahrenheit every ten degrees.[2]

Program 4.6: Parentheses used to change the order of evaluation

```java
// Print a Fahrenheit to Celsius table

class FahrToCelsius  {

  public static void main (String args[]) {

    double fahr, celsius;
    double lower, upper, step;

    // lower limit of temperature table
    lower = 0.0;

    // upper limit of temperature table
    upper = 300.0;

    // step size
    step  = 20.0;
```

---

[2] C programmers will recognize this as a Javaized version of the second program from Kernighan and Ritchie.

```
    fahr = lower;
    while (fahr <= upper) {
        celsius = (5.0 / 9.0) * (fahr-32.0);
        System.out.println(fahr + " " + celsius);
        fahr = fahr + step;
    }
  }
}
```

As usual here's the output:

```
% java FahrToCelsius
0 -17.7778
20 -6.66667
40 4.44444
60 15.5556
80 26.6667
100 37.7778
120 48.8889
140 60
160 71.1111
180 82.2222
200 93.3333
220 104.444
240 115.556
260 126.667
280 137.778
300 148.889
%
```

This program is a little more involved than the previous examples. Mostly it's stuff you've seen before though, so a line-by-line analysis isn't necessary. The line to be concerned with is

```
    celsius = (5.0 / 9.0) * (fahr-32.0);
```

This is a virtual translation of the formula C = (5/9) (°F - 32) with the single change that a * was added because Java does not implicitly multiply items in parentheses. The parentheses are used just as they are in regular algebra, to adjust the precedence of terms in a formula. In fact, the precedence of operations that use the basic arithmetic operators (+, −, *, /) is exactly the same as you learned in high school algebra.

Remember, you can always use parentheses to change the order of evaluation. Everything inside the parentheses will be calculated before anything outside of the parentheses is calculated. If you're in doubt it never hurts to put in extra parentheses to clear up the order in which terms will be evaluated.

Mixing Data Types

As well as combining different operations, you can mix and match different numeric data types on the same line. Program 4.7 uses both ints and doubles, for example.

Program 4.7: Different data types in one expression

```java
class IntAndDouble {

  public static void main (String args[]) {

    int i = 10;
    double x = 2.5;
    double k;


    System.out.println("i is " + i);
    System.out.println("x is " + x);

    k = i + x;
    System.out.println("i + x is " + k);
    k = i * x;
    System.out.println("i * x is " + k);
    k = i - x;
    System.out.println("i - x is " + k);
    k = x - i;
    System.out.println("x - i is " + k);
    k = i / x;
    System.out.println("i / x is " + k);
    k = x / i;
    System.out.println("x / i is " + k);

  }

}
```

Program 4.7 produces the following output:

```
% javac IntAndDouble.java
% java IntAndDouble
i is 10
x is 2.5
i + x is 12.5
i * x is 25
i - x is 7.5
x - i is -7.5
i / x is 4
x / i is 0.25
%
```

When Is an int Not an int?
Arithmetic Promotion and Casting

An int divided by an int is still an int, and a double divided by a double is still a double, but what about an int divided by a double or a double divided by an int? When doing arithmetic on unlike types, Java tends to **widen** the types involved so as to avoid losing information. After all, 3 * 54.2E18 will be a perfectly valid double but much too big for any int.

The basic rule is that if any of the variables on the right-hand side of an equals sign are doubles, then Java treats all the values on the right-hand side as doubles. If none of those values are doubles but some are floats, then Java treats all the values as floats. If there are no floats or doubles but there are longs, then Java treats all the values as longs. Finally if there are no doubles, floats or longs, then Java treats everything as an int, even if there aren't any ints in the equation. Therefore, when the right-hand side is finished calculating, the result will be a double, float, long or int depending on what was on the right-hand side to begin with.

If this is an assignment statement, that is, if there's an equals sign, then Java compares the type of the left-hand side to the final type of the right-hand side. It won't change the type of the left-hand side, but it will check to make sure that the value it has (double, float, int or long) can fit in the type on the left-hand side. Anything can fit in a double. Anything except a double can fit in a float. Any integral type can fit in a long, but a float or a double can't, and ints can fit inside `ints`. If the left-hand side can fit inside the right-hand side, the assignment takes place with no further ado.

However, if the left-hand side may not be able to fit into the right-hand side, then a series of operations takes place to chop the right-hand side down to size. For a conversion between a floating-point number and an `int` or a `long`, the fractional part of the floating-point number is truncated (rounded toward zero). This produces an integer. If the integer is small enough to fit in the right-hand side, the assignment is completed. On the other hand, if the number is too large, then the integer is set to the largest possible value of its type. If the floating-point number is too small, the integer is set to the smallest possible value of its type.

This can produce nasty bugs in your code. It can also be hard to find since everything may work perfectly 99 times out of 100 and only on rare occasions will the rounding become a problem. However, when it does, there will be no warning or error message. You need to be very careful when assigning floating-point values to integer types.

Assigning integer types to integer types or `doubles` to `floats` can be equally troublesome when the right-hand side is a larger number than the left-hand side can hold. In fact it's so troublesome the compiler won't let you do it unless you tell it you really mean it with a **cast**. A cast forces a value into a particular type. To cast a variable or a literal or an expression to a different data type, just precede it with the type in parentheses. For instance:

```
int i = (int) 9.0/4.0;
```

A cast lets the compiler know that you're serious about the conversion you plan to make.

Converting Strings to Numbers

When processing user input, it is often necessary to convert a String that the user enters into an `int`. The syntax is straightforward. It requires using the static `valueOf(String s)` and `intValue()` methods from the java.lang.Integer class. To convert the String `"22"` into the `int` 22, you would write

```
int i = Integer.valueOf("22").intValue();
```

Doubles, floats and longs are converted similarly. To convert a String like "22" into the long value 22, you would write

```
long l = Long.valueOf("22").longValue();
```

To convert "22.5" into a float or a double, you would write:

```
double x = Double.valueOf("22.5").doubleValue();
float y = Float.valueOf("22.5").floatValue();
```

If you want to read a byte or a short, read it as an int first and then cast it to the desired type.

The various valueOf methods are relatively intelligent and can handle plus and minus signs, exponents, and most other common number formats. However if you pass one something completely non-numeric like "pretty in pink," it will throw a NumberFormat-Exception. You haven't learned how to handle exceptions yet, so try to avoid passing non-numeric data to these methods.

You can now rewrite the $E = mc^2$ program to accept the mass in kilograms as user input from the command line. Many of the exercises will be similar.

Program 4.8: $E = mc^2$ with user input

```
class mc2 {
  public static void main (String args[]) {

    double mass;
    double c = 2.998E8;  // meters/second
    double E;

    mass = Double.valueOf(args[0]).doubleValue();
    E = mass * c * c;
    System.out.println(E + " Joules");
  }
}
```

Here's the output:

```
% javac mc2.java
% java mc2 0.0456
4.09853e+15 Joules
%
```

Char Variables and Literals

There are eight primitive data types in Java. In this chapter so far you've seen the numeric types, `byte`, `short`, `int`, `long`, `float`, and `double`. There is one remaining numeric data type in Java, the character type, `char`.

A `char` is a single character, that is, a letter, a digit, a punctuation mark, a tab, a space, or something similar. A `char` literal is a single character enclosed in single quote marks like this:

```
char myCharacter = 'g';
```

Some characters are hard to type. For these, Java provides **escape sequences**. This is a backslash followed by an alphanumeric code. For instance, `'\n'` is the newline character. `'\t'` is the tab character. `'\\'` is the backslash itself. The following escape sequences are defined:

\b	backspace
\t	tab
\n	linefeed
\f	formfeed
\r	carriage return
\"	double quote, "
\'	single quote, '
\\	backslash, \

The double quote escape sequence is used mainly inside Strings where it would otherwise terminate the String. For instance,

```
System.out.println("And then Jim said, \"Who's at
the door?\"");
```

It isn't necessary to escape the double quote inside single quotes. The following line is legal in Java

```
char doublequote = '"';
```

Unicode

Java uses the Unicode character set. Unicode is a two-byte character code set that has characters representing almost all characters in almost all human alphabets and writing systems around the world including English, Arabic, Chinese, and more.

Unfortunately, many operating systems and Web browsers do not handle Unicode. For the most part, Java will properly handle the input of non-Unicode characters. The first 128 characters in the Unicode character set are identical to the common ASCII character set. The second 128 characters are identical to the uppercase 128 characters of the ISO-Latin-1 extended ASCII character set. It's the next 65,280 characters that present problems.[3]

You can refer to a particular Unicode character by using the escape sequence \u followed by a four-digit hexadecimal number. For example,

\u00AE	©	The copyright symbol
\u0022	"	The double quote
\u00BD	1/2	The fraction 1/2
\u0394	Δ	The capital Greek letter delta
\u00F8	ø	A little o with a slash through it

You can even use the full Unicode character sequence to name your variables. For instance,

```
String Mjølner = "Hammer of Thor";
```

However, chances are your text editor doesn't handle more than basic ASCII very well.[4] You can use Unicode escape sequences instead like this:

```
String Mj\u00F8lner = "Hammer of Thor";
```

but frankly this is way more trouble than it's worth.

---

[3] Actually only about 34,000 of those characters are defined, even within Unicode. The rest are reserved for future extensions.

[4] Do not assume that just because you can use a particular font to produce these symbols in your word processor that the file you save is a valid Unicode file. Almost certainly it is not. Some text editors may handle ISO-Latin-1 properly, but even this is rare.

Q&A

Q: *Why not have a single integer type and a single floating-point type?*

A: Primarily for efficiency. There are many times when you don't need the extra size and precision of a `double` or a `long`, and a lot of memory and CPU time can be saved by using a smaller type. Most modern computers deal very efficiently with four-byte (32-bit) `ints` and `floats` and have to do extra work to handle the longer data types. On the other hand, there are times when you need the extra precision or length of a `long` or a `double`.

Quiz

1. In one line, how would you find the minimum of three values? of four? of five?

2. Write the Java equivalent of the following formulas:

Area of a square:	$A = s^2$
Area of a circle:	$A = \pi r^2$
Circumference of a circle:	$C = 2\pi r$
Slope of the line between two points:	$\text{slope} = \dfrac{Y2 - Y1}{X2 - X1}$

Exercises

1. Sales tax in New York City is 8.25%. Write a program that accepts a price on the command line and prints out the appropriate tax and total purchase price.

2. Modify the sales tax program to accept an arbitrary number of prices, total them, calculate the sales tax, and print the total amount.

3. Write a program that reads two numbers from the command line, the number of hours worked by an employee, and their base pay rate. Then output the total pay due.

4. Modify the previous program to meet the U.S. Dept. of Labor's requirement for time-and-a-half pay for hours over 40 worked in a given week.

5. Add warning messages to the payroll program if the pay rate is less than the minimum wage ($4.35 an hour as of mid-1996) or if the employee worked more than the number of hours in a week.

6. There are exactly 2.54 centimeters to an inch. Write a program that takes a number of inches from the command line and converts it to centimeters.

7. Write the inverse program that reads a number of centimeters from the command line and converts it to inches.

8. There are 454 grams in a pound and 1000 grams in a kilogram. Write programs that convert pounds to kilograms and kilograms to pounds. Read the number to be converted from the command line. Can you make this one program instead of two?

9. The equivalent resistance of resistors connected in series is calculated by adding the resistances of the individual resistors. Write a program that accepts a series of resistances from the command line and outputs the equivalent resistance.

10. The formula for resistors connected in parallel is a little more complex. Given two resistors with resistances $R1$ and $R2$ connected in parallel the equivalent resistance is given by the inverse of the sum of the inverses, that is,

$$R_{eqv} = \frac{1}{\dfrac{1}{R1} + \dfrac{1}{R2}}$$

If there are more than two resistors you continue to invert the sum of their inverses; for example, for four resistors you have

$$R_{eqv} = \frac{1}{\dfrac{1}{R1} + \dfrac{1}{R2} + \dfrac{1}{R3} + \dfrac{1}{R4}}$$

Write a program that calculates the resistance of a a group of resistors arranged in parallel.

Summary

In this chapter, you learned how to do basic arithmetic in Java. The things you learned included

- The difference between integers and floating-point numbers
- The different kinds of integers: `byte`, `short`, `int`, and `long`.
- The different kinds of floating point numbers: `float` and `double`.
- How to do basic addition, subtraction, multiplication, and division.
- What the remainder operator does
- How to use parentheses to change the order of evaluation
- How to convert between data types
- How to use character literals and variables

When the `while` loop and `if` statements of the last chapter are combined with the math of this chapter, you've got the tools to do some real work in Java. You should definitely try some of the programming exercises before moving on. Your input and output capabilities are still somewhat limited though. All the input will be from the command line and all output will be pure text.

Coming Up

In the next chapter, you'll meet boolean variables (two-state variables that can be either true or false and nothing else) and learn how they relate to various kinds of flow control, including `for`, `while`, and `do-while` loops.

In Chapter 8, you'll learn about the java.lang.Math package that lets you take square roots, exponentiate numbers, and do trigonometry, logarithms, and more. In short, you'll learn how to do high school math in Java (though once again, very quickly).

Further Reading

Most of the details of floating point, integer, and character data types in Java are found in the Java Language Specification, Chapters 3 and 4. The remainder can be found in

"IEEE Standard for Binary Floating-Point Arithmetic," ANSI/IEEE Std. 754-1985, New York: IEEE, 1985

Java's arithmetic operators, +, -, *, /, and %, including the details of what happens in the event of overflow or underflow, are covered in Chapter's 5 and 15 of the Java Language Specification.

For the complete story on Unicode, check out

http://www.unicode.org/

and

The Unicode Standard: Worldwide Character Encoding, Version 1.0, Volume 1 (ISBN 0-201-56788-1) and Volume 2 (ISBN 0-201-60845-6).

Numbers and Arithmetic

CHAPTER 5

BOOLEANS AND FLOW CONTROL

- What boolean data is

- How to use the relational operators
  <, >, <=, >=, ==, !=

- How to write for, while, and do while loops

This chapter covers two different but complementary topics: booleans and flow control. Flow control statements let your program do different things depending on the result of a test. The results of those tests are returned as booleans. Given two possible paths, which do you take? Booleans let you make that choice.

Boolean Variables

So far you've seen seven primitive data types: bytes, shorts, ints, longs, chars, floats, and doubles. The eighth and last is the boolean. Booleans are named after George Boole, a nineteenthcentury logician. Each boolean variable has one of two values: `true` or `false`. These are not the same as the Strings `"true"` and `"false"`. They are not the same as any numeric value like 1 or 0. They are simply `true` and `false`. Booleans are not numbers; they are not Strings. They are simply booleans.

Boolean variables are declared just like any other variable.

```
boolean test1 = true;
boolean test2 = false;
```

Note that `true` and `false` are reserved words in Java. These are called the Boolean literals. They are case-sensitive. `True` with a capital T is not the same as `true` with a little t. The same is true of `False` and `false`.

Relational Operators

Java has six relational operators that compare two numbers and return a boolean value. The relational operators are `<`, `>`, `<=`, `>=`, `==`, and `!=`.

`x < y`	Less than	True if x is less than y; otherwise false.
`x > y`	Greater than	True if x is greater than y; otherwise false.
`x <= y`	Less than	True if x is less than or equal to y; otherwise false.
`x >= y`	Less than	True if x is greater than or equal to y; otherwise false.
`x == y`	Less than	True if x equals y; otherwise false.
`x != y`	Less than	True if x is not equal to y; otherwise false.

Here are some code snippets showing the relational operators:

```java
boolean test1 = 1 < 2;   /* True. One is less than
two.*/

boolean test2 = 1 > 2;   /* False. One is not
greater than two.*/

boolean test3 = 3.5 != 1;   /* True. One does not
equal 3.5 */

boolean test4 = 17*3.5 >= 67.0 - 42; /* True.
59.5 is greater than 5 */

boolean test5 = 9.8*54 <= 654; /* True. 529.2 is
less than 654 */

boolean test6 = 6*4 == 3*8; // True. 24 equals 24

boolean test7 = 6*4 <= 3*8; /* True. 24 is less
than or equal to 24 */

boolean test8 = 6*4 < 3*8; /* False. 24 is not
less than 24 */
```

This, however, is an unusual use of booleans. Almost all use of booleans in practice comes in conditional statements and loop tests. You've already seen several examples of this. In Program 3.6 you saw this:

```java
if (args.length > 0) {
   System.out.println("Hello " + args[0]);
}
```

args.length > 0 is a boolean value. In other words, it is either true or it is false. You could write

```java
boolean test = args.length > 0;
if (test) {
   System.out.println("Hello " + args[0]);
}
```

instead. However, in simple situations like this the original approach is customary.

Similarly, the condition test in a while loop is a boolean. When you write

```java
while (i < args.length) {
```

i < args.length is a boolean.

For C programmers, I want to emphasize once again that condition tests must return booleans and that booleans are not numbers. This means that some of the more confusing tests in C like

```
if ( a = b)
```

will generate compiler errors in Java.

Relational Operator Precedence

Whenever a new operator is introduced, you have to ask yourself where it fits in the precedence hierarchy. If you look back at the example in the last section, you'll notice that it was implicitly assumed that the arithmetic was done before the comparison. Otherwise, for instance

```
boolean test8 = 6*4 < 3*8; /* False. 24 is not
less than 24 */
```

$4 < 3$ returns false which would then be multiplied by 6 and 8, which would generate a compile-time error because you can't multiply booleans. Relational operators are evaluated after arithmetic operators and before the assignment operator. `==` and `!=` have slightly lower precedences than `<`, `>`, `<=`, and `>=`. Here's the revised order:

1. `*`, `/`, `%`   Do all multiplications, divisions, and remainders from left to right.

2. `+`, `–`   Next, do additions and subtractions from left to right.

3. `<`, `>`, `>=`, `<=`   Then any comparisons for relative size.

4. `==`, `!=`   Then do any comparisons for equality and inequality.

5. `=`   Finally, assign the right-hand side to the left-hand side.

Testing for Equality

`<`, `>`, `<=`, and `>=` can only be used with numbers and characters. They cannot be used with Strings, booleans, arrays, or other compound types since there's no well-defined notion of order for these objects. Is true greater than false? Is "My only regret is that I have but one life to give for my country" greater than "I have a dream"?

Equality is a little easier to test, however. `true` is equal to `true` and `true` is not equal to `false`. Similarly, "My only regret is that I have but one life to give for my country" is not equal to "I have a dream." However you might be surprised if you ran Program 5.1.

Program 5.1: A test for String equality

```
class JackandJill {

  public static void main(String args[]) {

    String s1 = "Jack went up the hill.";
    String s2 = "Jack went up the hill.";

    if (s1 == s2) {
      System.out.println(
        "The strings are the same.");
    }
    else if (s1 != s2) {
      System.out.println(
        "The strings are different.");
    }
  }
}
```

The result is

```
The strings are different.
```

That's not what you expected. To compare Strings you need to use the `equals(String s)` method from java.lang.String. Program 5.2 is a corrected version that works as expected. The reasons for this odd behavior go fairly deep into Java and the nature of compound data types like Strings. You'll learn more about this in the next four chapters.

Program 5.2: A correct test for String equality

```
class JackAndJill {

  public static void main(String args[]) {
```

```
String s1 = "Jack went up the hill.";
String s2 = "Jack went up the hill.";

if (s1.equals(s2)) {
  System.out.println(
    "The strings are the same.");
}
else {
  System.out.println(
    "The strings are different.");
}

}

}
```

Loops

There are three different kinds of loops in Java. These are the `while`, `for`, and `do while` loops. They differ primarily in the stopping conditions used.

You've already seen `while` loops. They iterate continuously until a particular condition is met. If the condition is false when the loop is first entered, the body of the loop won't execute at all. You usually do not know in advance how many times a `while` loop will loop. The following code fragment is a `while` loop that counts to ten.

```
int i=1;
while (i <= 10) {
  System.out.println(i);
  i = i + 1;
}
```

`for` loops normally iterate a fixed number of times and then exit. The following code fragment is a `for` loop that counts to ten.

```
for (int i=1; i <= 10; i++) {
  System.out.println(i);
}
```

do `while` loops iterate until a condition is met, but the condition is tested at the end of the loop rather than at the beginning. Therefore, the body of a `do while` loop is guaranteed to execute at least once. The following code fragment is a `do while` loop that counts to ten.

```
int i=1;
do {
   System.out.println(i);
   i = i + 1;
} while (i <= 10)
```

Although each of these loops has slight advantages in terms of simplified code for a given problem, they are often more or less interchangeable.

For Loops

The final version of the Hello program in Chapter 3 needed a loop that would print each of the command-line arguments in succession, starting with the first one. You knew in advance how many arguments there were from the `args.length` variable.

This problem was solved with a `while` loop, and indeed that was a valid and useful solution. However, `while` loops are more commonly used for problems where there isn't a known number of iterations when the loop starts. Although `while` loops are well suited to that type of problem, that particular variation of a loop, where there's a counter that counts up to a certain variable, is so common that there's a somewhat redundant but nonetheless useful shorthand for this operation. That shorthand is a `for` loop, and you will now see how to solve this problem with a `for` loop. Here's the code.

Program 5.3: One Last Hello World

```
// This is the Hello program in Java

class Hello {

   public static void main (String args[]) {
```

```
      System.out.print("Hello ");
      for (int i=0; i < args.length; i++) {
        System.out.print(args[i]);
        System.out.print(" ");
      }
      System.out.println();
    }

}
```

This code is almost identical to Program 3.10. However the `for` loop compresses four lines of code into one. The lines that have been compressed are signified below in bold

```
int i;

System.out.print("Hello ");   // Say Hello
i = 0;                // Initialize loop counter
while (i < args.length) {  // Test and Loop
  System.out.print(args[i]);
  System.out.print(" ");
 i = i + 1;           // Increment Loop Counter
}
```

They have become the one line:

```
for (int i=0; i < args.length; i++) {
```

Let's investigate this very compact line. The `for` loop begins by declaring that the counter variable `i` is an `int` and then by initializing it to zero. This happens exactly once at the beginning of the loop. It is not repeated every time you pass through the loop. This takes the place of the two lines `int i;` and `i = 0;` in the original version.

`i < args.length` is still the test condition. This is the same test condition used before, and it has the same meaning: every pass through the loop, `i` is checked to see whether or not it is less than the value of `args.length`. If it is, then another pass is made through the loop. If it's not, then the program jumps to the first statement after the loop's closing brace.

Finally, there is the increment step, `i++`. `i++` is shorthand for `i=i+1`. Incrementing a variable by one is such a common operation that it's been given its own operator, `++`. This counter increment step is executed at the end of each iteration of the loop. Without the increment, the loop would continue forever since i would always be less than args.length (unless, of course, args.length were less than or equal to zero).

Language Law: Wraparound

I'm not being completely truthful. If you have a very fast machine or you wait long enough during an infinite loop, somewhere below negative two billion i will suddenly become a very large positive number and the program will halt. This happens because of vagaries in computer arithmetic discussed in the last chapter. Nonetheless, this is still a bug. If you don't want to wait for that to happen, just type Control-C to abort the program. This sort of behavior is referred to as an infinite loop and is a more common programming error than you might think.

If that's unclear look at a simpler example.

Program 5.4: A simple for loop

```java
//Count to ten

class CountToTen  {

  public static void main (String args[]) {

    for (int i = 1; i <= 10; i = i + 1) {
      System.out.println(i);
    }
    System.out.println("All done!");

  }
}
```

This program prints the numbers put:

```
% java CountToTen
1
2
3
4
5
6
7
8
9
10
All done!
```

Program 5.4 began by setting the see if 1 is in fact less than or equal program prints it. Finally it adds 1

i is now 2. The program checks the program prints "2" and adds 1 to i again.

i is now 3. Once again the code checks to see that 3 is less than or equal to 10. Most human beings get bored about here so let's skip ahead. Fortunately, computers don't get bored, and very soon the computer has counted to the point where i is 10. The computer prints "10" and adds 1 to i.

Now i is 11. Eleven is not less than or equal to 10, so the computer does not print it. Rather it moves to the next statement after the end of the for loop:

```
System.out.println("All done!");
```

The computer prints "All Done!" and the program ends.

for loops do not always work this smoothly. For instance, consider the following program:

Program 5.5: A for loop that counts backward

```
//Count to ten??

class BuggyCountToTen  {

  public static void main (String args[]) {
```

```
for (int i=1; i <= 10; i = i - 1) {
    System.out.println(i);
}
System.out.println("All done!");
    }
}
```

This program counts backward. There's nothing fundamentally wrong with a program counting backwards, but the exit condition is that i is bigger than 10. Since i is never going to be bigger than 10 in this program, the program never stops.[1]

Multiple Initializers and Incrementers

Sometimes it's necessary to initialize several variables before beginning a for loop. Similarly, you may want to increment more than one variable. Java lets you do this by placing a comma between the different initializers and incrementers like this:

```
for (int i = 1, j = 100; i < 100; i = i-1, j = j-1) {
    System.out.println(i + j);
}
```

You can't, however, include multiple test conditions, at least not with commas. The following line is illegal and will generate a compiler error:

```
for (int i = 1, j = 100; i <= 100, j > 0; i = i-1, j = j-1) {
```

To include multiple tests, you need to use the boolean logic operators && and ||, which will be discussed toward the end of this chapter.

Do While

while and for loops handle 99.9 percent of loops with ease. However, on rare occasions you are faced with a problem where you must execute the body of the loop at least once, even if the test

---

[1] Once again, if you wait long enough the value of i will wrap around to the largest positive value from the smallest negative value.

condition is false at the beginning of the loop. For this purpose, Java provides the do while loop. The syntax is as follows:

```
do {
   what you want to do
} while (condition)
```

The condition is tested at the end of the loop rather than at the beginning. This guarantees that the code in the body will be executed at least once. Program 5.6 is an example of do while in action. This example is a little forced. In practice, you almost never see do while. The entire source code for the Java 1.0.1 API doesn't use do while even a single time.

Program 5.6 Count to ten with a do-while loop

```
class CountToTen {

  public static void main (String args[]) {

    int i=1;
    do {
      System.out.println(i);
      i = i + 1;
    } while (i <= 10)


  }


}
```

Increment and Decrement Operators

++ is called the "increment operator." There is a corresponding decrement operator, −−. It works like this:

```
//Count to ten??

class BuggyCountToTen  {

  public static void main (String args[]) {

    for (int i=1; i <= 10; i = i--) {
      System.out.println(i);
    }
    System.out.println("All done!");
  }
}
```

i++ is shorthand for i = i + 1. Similarly i-- is shorthand for i = i - 1. Adding and subtracting 1 from a number are such common operations that these special increment and decrement operators have been added to the language. Increment and decrement operators also allow the compiler to be smarter about certain optimizations on some CPU architectures, but mainly they make code easier to write and read.

However, what do you do when you want to increment not by 1 but by 2? or 3? or 15? You could of course write i = i + 15, but this also happens frequently enough that there's another shorthand for the general add and assign operation, +=. You would normally write this as i += 15. Program 5.8 uses += to count from 0 to 20 by twos.

Program 5.8: += in a for loop

```
class CountToTwentyByTwos  {

  public static void main (String args[]) {
    int i;
    for (i=0; i <=20; i += 2) {
      System.out.println(i);
    }
    System.out.println("All done!");
  }
}
```

Here's the output:

```
% javac CountToTwentyByTwos.java
% java CountToTwentyByTwos
0
2
4
6
8
10
12
14
16
18
20
All done!
%
```

As you might guess, there is a corresponding –= operator. If you wanted to count down from 20 to 0 by twos you could write:

Program 5.9 Use –= to count down by twos

```java
class CountToZeroByTwos  {

  public static void main (String args[]) {
    int i;
    for (i=20; i >= 0; i -= 2) {
      System.out.println(i);
    }
    System.out.println("All done!");

  }

}
```

Here's the output:

```
% javac CountToZeroByTwos.java
% java CountToZeroByTwos
20
18
16
14
```

```
12
10
8
6
4
2
0
All done!
%
```

You should note that the initialization and test components of the `for` loop also had to be changed to count down instead of up.

There are also `*=` and `/=` operators that multiply and divide by their right-hand sides before assigning. In practice, you almost never see these because of the speed at which variables making use of them go to either zero or infinity. If you don't believe me, consider the following cautionary tale.

Many centuries ago in India, a very smart man is said to have invented the game of chess. This game greatly amused the king, and he became so enthralled with it that he offered to reward the inventor with anything he wished, up to half his kingdom and his daughter's hand in marriage.

Now the inventor of the game of chess was quite intelligent and not a little greedy. Not being satisfied with merely half the kingdom and the princess's hand in marriage, he asked the king for the following gift:

"Mighty King," he said, "I am but a humble man and would not know what to do with half of your kingdom. Let us merely calculate my prize as follows. Put onto the first square of the chessboard a single grain of wheat. Then onto the second square of the chessboard two grains, and onto the third square of the chessboard twice two grains, and so on until we have covered the board with wheat."

Upon hearing this the king was greatly pleased for he felt he had gotten off rather cheaply. He rapidly agreed to the inventor's prize. He called for a bag of wheat to be brought to him, and when it arrived he began counting out wheat. However he soon used up the first bag and was not yet halfway across the board. He called for a second, and a third, and more and more, until finally he was forced to admit defeat and hand over his entire kingdom for lack of sufficient wheat with which to pay the inventor.

How much wheat did the king need? Program 5.10 tries to calculate it. Although it doesn't use physical wheat, it soon finds itself in the same dire straits as the king. Remember that a chessboard has 64 squares.

Program 5.10: How much does the king owe?

```
class CountWheat   {

  public static void main (String args[]) {

    int i, j, k;

    j = 1;
    k = 0;

    for (i=1; i <= 64; i++) {
      j *= 2;
      k += j;
      System.out.print(k + "\t   ");
      if (i%4 == 0) System.out.println();
    }
    System.out.println("All done!");

  }

}
```

Here's the output:

```
% javac CountWheat.java
% java CountWheat
javac CountWheat.java
java CountWheat
% 2            6              14            30
62            126            254           510
1022          2046           4094          8190
16382         32766          65534         131070
262142        524286         1048574       2097150
4194302       8388606        16777214      33554430
67108862      134217726      268435454     536870910
1073741822    2147483646     -2            -2
```

```
-2          -2          -2          -2
-2          -2          -2          -2
-2          -2          -2          -2
-2          -2          -2          -2
-2          -2          -2          -2
-2          -2          -2          -2
-2          -2          -2          -2
-2          -2          -2          -2
All done!
%
```

What happened? After 2,147,483,646 grains of wheat were count-ed, the next number should have been 6,442,450,938. However an int can't be larger than 2,147,483,647. The number instead wrapped around into the negative numbers and stayed there.

You can improve your results slightly (but only slightly) by chang-ing the ints to longs. A long is an integer type variable that can hold up to 9,223,372,036,854,775,807. However, even that isn't enough to count how much wheat the king owed. To truly calculate the king's debt use a double, the largest type of all, as shown in Program 5.11.

Program 5.11 Count the wheat with doubles

```java
class CountWheat {

  public static void main (String args[]) {

    int i;
    double j, k;

    j = 1.0;
    k = 0.0;

    for (i=1; i <= 64; i++) {
       j *= 2.0;
       k += j;
       System.out.print(k + "\t  ");
       if (i%4 == 0) System.out.println();
    }
    System.out.println("All done!");
  }
}
```

A double can hold a number as large as 1.79769313486231570e+308. That turns out to be large enough to count the king's debt which comes to 1.84467e+019 grains of wheat, give or take a few trillion grains. That's a lot of wheat.

Making a Speedy Exit: Break and Continue

It is sometimes necessary to exit from the middle of a loop. Sometimes you'll want to start over at the top of the loop. Sometimes you'll want to leave the loop completely. For these purposes, Java provides the break and continue statements.

A continue statement returns to the beginning of the innermost enclosing loop without completing the rest of the statements in the body of the loop. If you're in a for loop, the counter is incremented. For example, this code fragment skips even elements of an array

```
for (int i = 0; i < m.length; i++) {

  if (m[i] % 2 == 0) continue;
  // process odd elements…

}
```

The continue statement is rarely used in practice, perhaps because most of the instances where it's useful have simpler implementations. For instance, the above fragment could equally well have been written as

```
for (int i = 0; i < m.length; i++) {

  if (m[i] % 2 != 0) {;
    // process odd elements…

  }

}
```

There are only seven uses of continue in the entire Java 1.0.1 source code for the java packages.

The break statement, however, is used more frequently. It is used over 80 times in the Java 1.0.1 source code. A break leaves a loop before an entry condition fails. For example, in this variation on the CountWheat program, an error message is printed, and you break out of the `for` loop if `j` becomes negative.

Program 5.12: Count the wheat but test for overflow

```java
class CountWheat {

  public static void main (String args[]) {

    int i, j, k;

    j = 1;
    k = 0;

    for (i=1; i <= 64; i++) {
      j *= 2;
      if (j <= 0) {
        System.out.println("Error: Overflow");
        break;
      }
      k += j;
      System.out.print(k + "\t  ");
      if (i%4 == 0) System.out.println();
    }
    System.out.println("All done!");

  }

}
```

Here's the output:

```
% javac CountWheat.java
% java CountWheat
2            6            14           30
62           126          254          510
1022         2046         4094         8190
16382        32766        65534        131070
262142       524286       1048574      2097150
4194302      8388606      16777214     33554430
67108862     134217726    268435454    536870910
1073741822   2147483646     Error: Overflow
```

```
All done!
%
```

The most common use of `break` is in `switch` statements, which you'll learn about in the next section.

Labeled Loops

Normally inside nested loops, `break` and `continue` exit the innermost enclosing loop. For example, consider the following loops:

```java
for (int i=1; i < 10; i++) {
  for (int j=1; j < 4; j++) {
    if (j == 2) break;
    System.out.println(i + ", " + j);
  }
}
```

This code fragment prints

```
1, 1
2, 1
3, 1
4, 1
5, 1
6, 1
7, 1
8, 1
9, 1
```

because you break out of the innermost loop when `j` is 2. However, the outermost loop continues.

To break out of both loops, label the outermost loop and indicate that label in the `break` statement like this:

```java
iloop: for (int i=1; i < 3; i++) {
  for (int j=1; j < 4; j++) {
    if (j == 2) break iloop;
    System.out.println(i + ", " + j);
  }
}
```

This code fragment prints

```
1, 1
```

and then stops because j is 2 and the outermost loop is exited.

Switch

Earlier you saw that a for loop is really just a shorthand for a certain kind of while loop. switch statements are shorthands for a certain kind of if statement. It is not uncommon to see a stack of if statements all relate to the same quantity like this:

```
if (x == 0) do something;
else if (x == 1) do something else;
else if (x == 2) do something else;
else if (x == 3) do something else;
else if (x == 4) do something else;
else do something else;
```

Java has a shorthand for these types of multiple if statements, the switch-case statement. Here's how you'd write the above using a switch statement:

```
switch (x) {
  case 0:
    do something;
    break;
  case 1:
    do something;
    break;
  case 2:
    do something;
    break;
  case 3:
    do something;
    break;
  default: do something else;
}
```

In this fragment, x must be a variable or expression that can be cast to an `int` without loss of precision.[2] This means the variable must be or the expression must return an `int`, `byte`, `short`, or `char`. x is compared with the value of each the case statements in succession. This fragment compares x to literals, but these too could be variables or expressions as long as the variable or result of the expression is an `int`, `byte`, `short`, or `char`.

Multiple cases can be matched if multiple `case` statements have the same value. This can trigger decidedly unexpected behavior. Therefore it is common to include the `break` statement at the end of each `case` block. It's good programming practice to put a `break` after each one unless you explicitly want multiple cases to be matched.

Finally, if no cases are matched, the default action is triggered. If the `break` statement is not present in the individual cases, all values of x will trigger the default action.

It's important to remember that the `switch` statement doesn't end when one `case` is matched and its action performed. The program continues to look for additional matches unless specifically told to `break`.

Logical Operators

The relational operators you've learned so far (`<`, `<=`, `>`, `>=`, `!=`) are sufficient when you only need to check one condition. However what if a particular action is to be taken only if several conditions are true? You can use a sequence of if statements to test the conditions, as follows:

```
if (x == 2) {
   if (y != 2) {
      System.out.println(
        "Both conditions are true.");
    }
}
```

---

[2] It can be a literal like 2 as well, but then why would you test multiple cases when you already know what it is? The only use I can imagine for this would be when you're debugging and you want to make sure you test every possible branch.

This, however, is hard to write and harder to read. It only gets worse as more conditions are added. Fortunately, Java provides an easy way to handle multiple conditions: the logic operators. There are three logic operators: `&&`, `||` and `!`.

`&&` is logical *and*. `&&` combines two `boolean` values and returns a `boolean` which is `true` if and only if both of its operands are `true`. For instance,

```
boolean b;
b = 3 > 2 && 5 < 7; // b is true
b = 2 > 3 && 5 < 7; // b is now false
```

`||` is logical *or*. `||` combines two boolean variables or expressions and returns a result that is `true` if either or both of its operands are `true`. For instance,

```
boolean b;
b = 3 > 2 || 5 < 7; // b is true
b = 2 > 3 || 5 < 7; // b is still true
b = 2 > 3 || 5 > 7; // now b is false
```

The last logic operator is `!` which means *not*. It reverses the value of a `boolean` expression. Thus if b is true, !b is false. If b is false, !b is true.

```
boolean b;
b = !(3 > 2); // b is false
b = !(2 > 3); // b is true
```

These operators allow you to test multiple conditions more easily. For instance, the previous example can now be written as

```
if (x == 2 && y != 2) {
   System.out.println("Both conditions are true.");
}
```

That's a lot clearer.

The ?: Operator

The value of a variable often depends on whether a particular boolean expression is or is not `true` and on nothing else. For instance, one common operation is setting the value of a variable to the maximum of two quantities. In Java you might write

```
if (a > b) {
    max = a;
}
else {
    max = b;
}
```

Setting a single variable to one of two states based on a single condition is such a common use of if-else that a shortcut has been devised for it: the conditional operator, ?:. Using the conditional operator, you can rewrite the above example in a single line like this:

```
max = (a > b) ? a : b;
```

(a > b) ? a : b; is an expression which returns one of two values, a or b. The condition, (a > b), is tested. If it is true, the first value, a, is returned. If it is false, the second value, b, is returned. Whichever value is returned is dependent on the conditional test, a > b. The condition can be any expression which returns a boolean value.

The expressions do not have to return a value, however; nor does this construct have to be used in an assignment statement. For instance, the following is a valid statement:

```
name.equals("Rumpelstiltskin") ? give_back_child()
: laugh();
```

This fragment tests whether the string name has the value "Rumpelstiltskin." If it does, the give_back_child() method is called. If it doesn't, the laugh() method is called. Regardless of whether an assignment is performed or not, exactly one of the two expressions following the question mark is executed. You never laugh and give back the child.

The Order of Evaluation of Logic Operators

When Java sees a && operator or a ||, the expression on the left side of the operator is evaluated first. For example, consider the following:

```
boolean b, c, d;
b = !(3 > 2); // b is false
c = !(2 > 3); // b is true
d = b && c;
```

When Java evaluates the expression `d = b && c;`, it first checks whether `b` is true. Here `b` is false, so `b && c` must be false regardless of whether `c` is or is not true, so Java doesn't bother checking the value of `c`.

On the other hand, when faced with an `||`, Java short-circuits the evaluation as soon as it encounters a true value since the resulting expression must be true.

This short-circuit evaluation is less important in Java than in C because in Java the operands of `&&` and `||` must be booleans which are unlikely to have side effects that depend on whether or not they are evaluated. Still it's possible to force them. For instance, consider this code:

```
boolean b = (n == 0) || (m/n > 2);
```

Even if `n` is 0, this line will never cause a division by 0, because the left-hand side is always evaluated first. If `n` is 0, then the left-hand side is true and there's no need to evaluate the right-hand side. Mathematically this makes sense because `m/0` is in some sense infinite, which is greater than 2.

This isn't a perfect solution though because `m` may be 0 or it may be negative. If `m` is negative and `n` is 0, then `m/n` is negative infinity, which is less than 2. And if `m` is also zero, then `m/n` is very undefined.

The proper solution at this point depends on your problem. Since real-world quantities aren't infinite, when infinities start popping up in your programs, nine times out of ten it's a sign that you've lost too much precision. The remaining times are generally signals that you've left out some small factor in your physical model that would remove the infinity.

Therefore, if there's a real chance your program will have a divide by zero error think carefully about what it means and how you should respond to it. If, upon reflection, you decide that what you really want to know is whether `m/n` is finite and greater than 0, you should use a line like this:

```
boolean b = (n != 0) && (m/n > 0);
```

Avoiding Short Circuits

If you want all of your boolean expressions evaluated regardless of the truth value of each, then you can use `&` and `|` instead of `&&` and

||. However, make sure you use these only on boolean expressions. Unlike && and ||, & and | also have a meaning for numeric types, which is completely different from their meaning for booleans.

Precedence

Finally, let's add the &&, ||, &, |, and ? operators to the precedence table:

1.	*, /, %	Multiplicative operators
2.	+, –	Additive operators
3.	<, >, >=, <=	Relational operators
4.	==, !=	Then do any comparisons for equality and inequality
5.	&	Bitwise &
6.	|	Bitwise *or*
7.	&&	Logical *and*
8.	||	Logical *or*
9.	? :	Conditional operator
10.	=	Assignment operator

Q&A

Q: *How much space does a boolean take up?*

A: This is implementation defined. In current implementations a boolean takes one byte.

Q: *Is there a way to change booleans to ints and ints to booleans?*

A: Although you can't cast ints to booleans and vice versa, if you must deal with data that assumes true is non-zero and false is zero, use the following assignments:

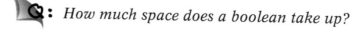

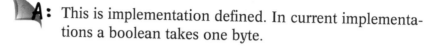

```
boolean b = (i != 0);
int i = b ? 1 : 0;
```

Quiz

1. Is a float large enough to count the king's wheat?

2. Why isn't there a `**` or a `//` operator?

3. Given that `b` is a boolean variable, what's the value of `(b || !b)`?

4. Here's one that stumped the author until he got some help from comp.lang.java. What's wrong with this program?

```java
public class BytePrint {

    public void main(String[] args) {
        for (byte b = -128; b <= 127; b++) {
            System.out.println(b);
        }
    }
}
```

Exercises

1. Write the FahrToCelsius program of the last chapter using a `for` loop instead of a `while` loop.
2. Write the combination lock programs of Chapter 3 using `for` loops.

Summary

In this chapter, you learned how to make choices based on boolean conditions. The tools used to make these choices include:

- boolean data
- The relational operators <, >, <=, >=, ==, and !=
- `for` loops
- The increment and decrement operators: ++ and --
- `do while` loops
- `break` and `continue`
- `switch-case` statements
- logic operators
- the conditional operator ?

Coming Up

In many ways you now have all the elements you really need to solve any problem. However that's like saying you can build a car out of steel, plastic, glass, rubber and a blow torch or two. You might be able to do it, but more powerful tools would certainly help. The next three chapters will concentrate on building those more powerful tools, starting with classes and objects.

Further Reading

Boolean data is covered in Section 4.2.5 of the *Java Language Specification*. `switch` statements and loops are covered in Chapter 13. The increment, decrement, logical, relational, equality operators, and ?: are in Chapter 14.

CHAPTER
INTRO TO OOP

▶ What a class is, what an object is, and the difference between them

▶ How to pass arguments to and return values from methods

▶ How to use Constructors and toString methods

▶ How to control access to your methods and fields

This chapter begins your introduction to classes and objects in Java. Here you'll learn the about abstract data typing through classes, objects, and methods. Abstract data typing produces code that is much easier to read, understand, and maintain.

What is Object-Oriented Programming?

Object-Oriented Programming (OOP for short) is the programming buzzword of the 90s. Everyone advertises their products as object-oriented. But what does object-oriented mean? To understand why object-oriented programming is so revolutionary, you need to take a brief glance back at the history of computing.

A Brief History of Programming

Different styles of programming are supported by different kinds of programming languages. These languages are loosely classified into first through fifth generation. The difference between the generations is the level of abstraction from the computer hardware the language provides. In a first-generation language, the programmer must understand the computer's hardware and think in terms of bits and bytes in the computer's memory. In fourth-generation languages, the programmer doesn't worry about the innards of the computer at all and merely asks it for the result he or she wants. "Select employees from accounting where salary > 25000" is a typical fourth-generation computer program. Fifth-generation languages (which are still a subject of intense research) take the abstraction even further to allow full natural language queries like, "Computer, give me the names of all the employees in accounting who make more than $25,000 a year."

Java is a third-generation language. In third-generation languages (3GLs for short), you don't worry about the internal state of memory or the CPU, but you do specify the algorithms and data structures to be used in fulfilling your requests.

In the early days of computers, computer memories were quite small, a few hundred bytes at most. Programs were loaded into a computer by toggling switches on a panel. In those days it was possible for a programmer to keep track of every memory location and every machine instruction in his or her head. Since computer memories were so small and the machines so slow, program efficiency was the primary concern. Any program was acceptable as long as it worked. Algorithms were very closely tied to the capabilities of the specific machine they ran on. The toggling of individual memory locations (by switch or other means) is called a **first-generation language**, and this requires a very liberal definition of *language*. In a first-generation language, there is almost no abstraction. This is also known as machine-language programming.

As computers grew in power and memory, it was no longer possible for a programmer to keep track of what was happening at every location in the machine's physical memory. Card readers and assembly language were invented to make programming more feasible. Assembly language uses mnemonic codes like MOV to represent particular CPU instructions. These codes map directly to individual instructions on the CPU, and memory is still addressed directly. One code means exactly one CPU instruction.[1] Algorithmically, the philosophy of "use whatever works" continued.

Assembly language was still a bear to program in, especially when it came to arrays and storage in memory. Therefore, the first high-level programming language, Fortran, was invented to spare programmers from the pains of keeping track of the location of their variables in memory.[2] Fortran was the first example of a third-generation language. In a third-generation language, the programmer tells the computer the algorithms and data structures it should use to calculate the results, but the programmer uses more abstract logical and mathematical operators rather than directly manipulating addresses in memory and CPU instructions. Fortran is named for "*For*mula *trans*lation." Fortran statements were meant to be English that a human being could read and understand. The Fortran code would be compiled into the machine language the computer would understand. In a third-generation language, a single statement often represents several machine instructions. Which instructions they represent may even depend on their context. This level of abstraction made considerably more powerful algorithms and data structures possible.

Java is a very advanced third-generation language. Most of the other computer languages you're probably familiar with—Fortran,

---

[1] More modern assembly languages don't always map as directly to the CPU as the older ones did.

[2] It's interesting to note that this lesson has had to be learned again and again and again. The buggiest parts of C and C++ programs result from programmers being allowed to access arbitrary bytes of memory. Java has wisely removed this capability. Ninety-nine times out of 100 you don't need it. A large part of training C or C++ programmers to use Java consists of convincing them of this fact.

Basic, C, C++, Cobol, Pascal, Perl—as well as most of the ones you're not familiar with—AppleScript, Frontier, Eiffel, Modula-3, ADA, PL/I, etc.—are also third-generation languages (or 3GLs for short).

When third-generation languages were invented, they were supposed to make computers so easy to use even the CEO could write programs. This turned out not to be true. Fourth-generation languages (or 4GLs for short) moved the abstraction level a step higher. In these languages the programmer tells the computer the results desired rather telling it how to calculate those results. For instance, you would ask for the total sales for the year, without specifying the loops necessary to sum all the sales of all the salespeople. SQL (Structured Query Language) is the most popular fourth-generation language.

Of all these languages, there's no question that 3GLs have been the most successful by almost any measure. A number of different styles of 3GL programming and programming languages have sprung up, most learning from the experience and mistakes of their predecessors. Fortran was the first. It shared with assembly language an attitude of "whatever works, no matter how ugly." It had limited flow control (essentially for loops and if statements as well as goto) and one data structure, the array. All variables were global, and it was impossible to hide one part of the program from any other. Although it was possible to write maintainable, legible code in Fortran, few people did. Basic was invented in the 1960s as an even simpler language that could be used for teaching programming and could be implemented on very small computers.

Pascal and C were the next widely successful languages. They made possible a style of programming known as **structured programming**. Structured programming languages have many different flow control constructs (switch statements, while loops, and more) as well as tools for more complicated data structures (structs, records and pointers). Goto is deprecated in structured programming though not eliminated entirely. (It is still necessary for some error handling.) Finally structured programming languages have subroutines with local variables that are capable of splitting the code into more manageable and understandable chunks. These languages allowed programmers to write larger, more maintainable programs. However, they too began to bog down when faced with the need to share code among programmers and to write very large (greater than 50,000 line) programs.

Some of the above history may sound a little funny to those readers with experience in the languages being discussed. The fact is, successful computer languages have continued to evolve. Fortran now has pointers so it can create more complicated data structures. Basic has while loops. Cobol has objects. And on some architectures like Alpha/VMS, the assembly language bears little to no resemblance to the underlying machine architecture. These features were not parts of the first versions of the language, however. And despite these improvements, the modern versions of these languages are their parents' children. Basic and Fortran programmers still often produce spaghetti code. Assembly language is quick to run but long to program. C is obfuscated beyond the comprehension of mere mortals.

The third generation of 3GLs (3.3 GLs) began to take hold in the late 1980s. These were the object-oriented languages. Although object-oriented languages had been around since Simula in the late 1960s, it wasn't until the late 80s that computer hardware became fast enough and memory cheap enough to support them.[3]

Object-oriented programming included all the features of structured programming and added still more powerful ways to organize algorithms and data structures. There are three key features of OOP languages: encapsulation, polymorphism, and inheritance. All of them are tied to the notion of a class.

Classes and Objects

Classes and objects are the primary distinguishing feature of OOP languages. A class is a user-defined data type that can associate the methods which act on an object with the object itself. The earliest 3GLs (Fortran, Basic) provided a few basic data types like real and double, and that is all you had to work with. In the second generation of 3GLs (C and Pascal) programmers could create their own data types using structs or records. However these types were separate from the functions that acted on them. In OOP languages, data and methods are both part of programmer-defined classes.

Java provides a number of simple data types like `int`, `float`, and `String`. However, very often the data you want to work with is not an `int`, a `float`, or a `String`. Classes let programmers define their own more complicated data types.

---

[3] Object-oriented programming is not a panacea. It exacts a speed penalty over plain vanilla C or Fortran code and often requires much more memory.

For instance, suppose your program needs to keep a database of web sites. Each site has a name, a URL, and a description. In traditional programming languages, you'd have three different String variables for each web site. With a class, you combine these into one thing like this:

Program 6.1: A web site class

```
public class website {

    public String name;
    public String url;
    public String description;

}
```

These variables (name, url, and description) are called the **member variables** or **fields** of the class. The fields tell you what a class is and what its properties are. Each of the variables in this example has been declared to be public. That means that any other object can use these variables.

The web site database will have many thousands of websites. Each specific web site is an object. The definition of a web site though, which is given above, is a class. This is a very important distinction. A class defines what an object is, but it is not itself an object. An object is a specific **instance** of a class. Thus when you create a new object, you are **instantiating** the class. Each class exists only once in a program, but there can be many thousands of objects that are instances of that class. On the other hand, some classes may never be instantiated at all.

Another way of thinking of it: The class is a cookie cutter while an object is a cookie. The cookie cutter defines what the cookie will look like, but it is not itself a cookie. You can use a particular cookie cutter to make as many or as few cookies as you want.

To instantiate an object in Java use the keyword **new**. Here's how you'd create a new web site variable called w:

```
website w = new website();
```

The first word, `website`, declares the type of the variable `w`. Classes are types, and variables of a class type need to be declared just like variables that are `int`s or `double`s. The equal sign is the assignment operator and `new` is the construction operator. Finally, notice the `website()` method. The parentheses tell you this is a method and not a data type like the `website` on the left-hand side of the assignment. This is a constructor, a method that creates a new instance of a class. You'll learn more about constructors soon. For now, Java provides a default constructor, which takes no arguments.

Once you've created a website, you want to know something about it. To access the members of the website you use the `.` separator. The website class has three fields: `name`, `url`, and `description`, so `w` has three fields as well: `w.name`, `w.url`, and `w.description`. You use these just like you'd use any other String variables. For instance,

```
website w = new website();

w.name = "Cafe Au Lait";
w.url = "http://sunsite.unc.edu/javafaq/";
w.description = "Really cool!";

System.out.println(w.name + " at " + w.url +
    " is " + w.description);
```

The `.` separator selects a specific member of a website object by name.

Program 6.2 creates a new website, sets its fields, and prints the result:

Program 6.2: Create and print a website

```
class OOPTest {

  public static void main(String args[]) {

    website w = new website();

    w.name = "Cafe Au Lait";
    w.url = "http://sunsite.unc.edu/javafaq/";
    w.description = "Really cool!";
```

```
        System.out.println(w.name + " at " + w.url +
            " is " + w.description);

    }
```

Program 6.2 requires not just the OOPTest class but also the web-site class. To make them work together, put Program 6.1 in a file called website.java. Put Program 6.2 in a file called OOPTest.java. Put both these files in the same directory. Then compile both files in the usual way. Finally, run OOPTest. Note that website does not have a main method so you cannot run it. It can exist only when called by other programs that do have main methods. Here's the output:

```
% javac website.java
% javac OOPTest.java
% java OOPTest
Cafe Au Lait at http://sunsite.unc.edu/javafaq/ is
Really cool!
%
```

Many of the applications you write from now on will use multiple classes. It is customary in Java to put every class in its own file. In Chapter 8, you'll learn how to use packages to organize your com-monly used classes in different directories. For now, keep all your .java source code and .class byte code files in one directory.

Member Variables versus Local Variables

Until this chapter, all the programs were quite simple in structure. Each had exactly one class. This class had a single method, main, which contained all the program logic and variables. The variables in those classes were all local to the main method. They could not be accessed by anything outside the main method. These are called **local variables**.

This sort of program is the amoeba of Java. Everything the program needs to live is contained inside a single cell. It's quite an efficient arrangement for small organisms, but it breaks down when you want to design something bigger or more complex.

The `name`, `url`, and `description` variables of the website class, however, belong to a website object, not to any individual method. They are defined outside of any methods but inside the class and are used in different methods. They are called **member variables** or **fields**.

The rest of this book will concentrate on larger programs. Each class will be more complex and will contain multiple methods and member variables (as well as whatever local variables are necessary). Most programs are composed of multiple classes, each of which can have several member variables and methods and can be instantiated many times.

Methods

Data types aren't much use unless you can do things with them. For this purpose, classes have methods. Fields say what a class is. Methods say what a class does. The fields and methods of a class are collectively referred to as the **members** of the class.

The classes you've seen in previous chapters have all had a single method, main. However, many classes will have many different methods to do many different things. For instance, the website class might have a method to print its data. Such a class might look like Program 6.3.

Program 6.3: A website class with a print method

```java
public class website {

    public String name;
    public String url;
    public String description;

    public void print() {
        System.out.println(name + " at " + url + " is " +
            description);
    }
}
```

The fields are the same as in Program 6.2 but now there's also a method called `print`. It begins with the Java keyword `public`, which means that other classes can call this method.

That is followed by the keyword `void`, which is the **return type** of the method. Every method must have a return type, which will be some data type like `int`, `byte`, `float`, or `String`. The return type says what kind of value will be sent back to the calling method when all calculations inside the method are finished. If the return type is `int`, for example, you can use the method anywhere you use an `int` constant. If the return type is `void`, then no value will be returned.

`print` is the name of this method. The name is followed by two empty parentheses. Any arguments passed to the method would be passed here. This method has no arguments. Finally, a { begins the body of the method.

There is one line of code inside the method. This is the call to `System.out.println`, a system-supplied method, which prints this information. Notice that within the website class you don't need to prefix the field names with `w.` like `w.name` or `w.url`. Just `name` and `url` are sufficient. That's because the print method must be called by a specific instance of the website class, and this instance knows what its data is. Or, another way of looking at it: every object has its own print method.

Finally, the print method is closed with a } and the class is closed with another }.

Outside the website method, you call the print method just like you reference member variables, using the name of the object you want to print and the `.` separator as demonstrated in Program 6.4.

Program 6.4: An OOP test that uses the print method

```java
class OOPTest {

  public static void main(String args[]) {

    website w = new website();

    w.name = "Cafe Au Lait";
    w.url = "http://sunsite.unc.edu/javafaq/";
    w.description = "Really cool!";
```

```
        w.print();

    }

}
```

The print method is completely enclosed within the website class. Every method in a Java program must belong to a class. Unlike C++ programs, Java programs cannot have a method hanging around in global space that does everything you forgot to do inside your classes.

Passing Arguments to Methods

It's generally considered bad form to make your fields public. Instead, it is considered good object-oriented practice to make all your fields nonpublic and only allow access to them through public methods.

Of course, before the fields of the website class can be made private, a means must be provided to set their values. To do this you need to be able to send information into the website class. This is done by passing arguments. For example, to allow other classes to change the value of the name field in a website object, the website class would need this method:

```
public void setName(String s) {
    name = s;
}
```

The first line of the method is called its **signature**. The signature

```
public void setName(String s)
```

indicates that setName is a public method that returns no value and takes a single argument, a String, which will be referred to as s inside the method.

The line

```
    name = s;
```

sets the name field to s.

More than one argument can be passed to a method. If so, successive arguments are separated by commas. For example,

```
public void setNameURLDescription(String s1,
String s2, String s3) {
  name = s1;
  url = s2;
  description = s3;
}
```

though this is an artificial example no one would actually use in practice. The section on constructors explains why.

Program 6.5 is a website class that makes the fields nonpublic. They can then be set with the three set methods as demonstrated in Program 6.6.

Program 6.5: A website class with no public fields

```
public class website {

  String name;
  String url;
  String description;

  public void setName(String s) {
    name = s;
  }

  public void setURL(String s) {
    url = s;
  }

  public void setDescription(String s) {
    description = s;
  }
  public void print() {
    System.out.println(name + " at " + url + " is " +
      description);
  }

}
```

```
class OOPTest {

  public static void main(String args[]) {

    website w = new website();

    w.setName("Cafe Au Lait");
    w.setURL("http://sunsite.unc.edu/javafaq/");
    w.setDescription("Really cool!");

    w.print();

  }

}
```

Returning Values from Methods

It's often useful to have a method return a value to the object that called it. This is accomplished by the **return** keyword at the end of a method and by declaring the data type that is returned by the method at the beginning of the method.

For example, the following getName method returns the current value of the name field in the website class:

```
public String getName() {
  return name;
}
```

The signature **public String** getName() indicates that getName is a public method that returns a value of type String and takes no arguments. Inside the method, the line

```
return name;
```

returns the String contained in the name field to whoever called this method. It is important that the type of value returned by the return statement match the type declared in the method signature. If it does not, the compiler will complain.

It is not possible to return more than one value from a method. You cannot, for example, return the name, url, and description fields with a single method. You could combine them into an object of some kind and return the object. However, this would be poor object-oriented design.

The right way to solve this problem is to define three separate methods: getName, getURL, and getDescription, each of which returns its respective value. Program 6.7 demonstrates this.

Program 6.7: A website class with get methods

```java
public class website {

  String name;
  String url;
  String description;

  public String getName() {
    return name;
  }

  public String getURL() {
    return url;
  }

  public String getDescription() {
    return description;
  }

  public void setName(String s) {
    name = s;
  }

  public void setURL(String s) {
    url = s;
  }

  public void setDescription(String s) {
    description = s;
  }
```

```
public void print() {
    System.out.println(name + " at " + url + " is " +
        description);
}

}
```

The programs you've seen in the first five chapters have been quite simple, under 100 lines of code each. As programs grow in size, it begins to make sense to break them into methods. Each method can perform a particular calculation or perform some action and possibly produce a result. This is especially useful when the calculation or action needs to be repeated at several different places in the program because the same block of code can be called from each of several different places. Breaking your program into methods can also help define a clearer picture of the flow of the program, much like an outline shows the flow of a book.

A method can be thought of as a black box which receives a specified input and produces some output. Some methods don't produce any output. These are called void methods. Some methods change the input they're given, but in Java this is rare. Methods are similar to C's functions, Pascal's procedures and functions, and Fortran's functions and subroutines.

Constructors

The first method most classes need is a **constructor**. A constructor creates a new instance of the class. It initializes all the fields and does any work necessary to prepare the class to be used. In the line

```
website w = new website();
```

`website()` is the constructor. A constructor method has the same name as the class.

If no constructor exists, Java provides a generic one, but it's better to write your own. You make a constructor by writing a method that has the same name as the class. Thus the website constructor is called `website()`.

Most of the time you will want to make this method public as well, though this is not required.

Constructors do not have return types. They are the only method for which this is true. They do return an instance of their own class; but this is implicit, not explicit.

The following method is a constructor that initializes all the fields of a website to empty `Strings`.

```
public website() {
  name = "";
  url  = "";
  description = "";
}
```

Better yet, you can create a constructor that accepts three Strings as arguments and use those to initialize the member variables as in Program 6.8.

Program 6.8: A website class with a constructor

```
public class website {

  String name;
  String url;
  String description;

  public website(String n, String u, String d) {
    name = n;
    url  = u;
    description = d;
  }

  public String getName() {
    return name;
  }

  public String getURL() {
    return url;
  }

  public String getDescription() {
    return description;
  }
```

```
public void setName(String s) {
  name = s;
}

public void setURL(String s) {
  url = s;
}

public void setDescription(String s) {
  description = s;
}

public void print() {
  System.out.println(name + " at " + url + " is " +
    description);
}

}
```

Program 6.9 uses the constructor instead of the set methods to prepare the website to be printed.

Program 6.9: An OOP test that uses the constructor

```
class OOPTest {

  public static void main(String args[]) {

    website w = new website("Cafe Au Lait",
      "http://sunsite.unc.edu/javafaq/",
      "Really cool!");
    w.print();

  }

}
```

If all you want to do is create new web sites and print them, you no
longer need to know about the fields name, url, and description.

All you need to know is how to construct a new website and how to print it.

You may ask whether the `setURL`, `setDescription`, and `setName` methods are still needed since all three of these are now set in a constructor. The general answer to this question depends on the use to which the website class is to be put. The specific question is whether a website may need to be changed after it is created. If you're using this class to create a database of web sites like that at Yahoo, for example, then it is entirely possible that the URL may change while the name and description remain the same or that the site may update its description so set methods are necessary for this class. However, some other classes may not change after they're created; or , if they do change, they'll represent a different object. The most common such class is `String`. You cannot change a `String`'s data without creating a new `String`.

toString Methods

Print methods are common in some languages, but most Java programs operate differently. You can use `System.out.println` to print any object. However, for good results your class should have a toString method that formats the object's data in a sensible way and returns a `String`. Otherwise all that's printed is the name of the class, which is normally not what you want. For example, a good toString method for the website class might be

```java
public String toString() {
  return (name + " at " + url + " is " + description);
}
```

Program 6.10 is a variant of the website class that replaces `print` with a `toString` method.

Program 6.10: A website class with a toString method

```java
public class website {

  String name;
  String url;
  String description;
```

```
public website(String n, String u, String d) {
  name = n;
  url  = u;
  description = d;
}

public String getName() {
  return name;
}

public String getURL() {
  return url;
}

public String getDescription() {
  return description;
}

public void setName(String s) {
  name = s;
}

public void setURL(String s) {
  url = s;
}

public void setDescription(String s) {
  description = s;
}

public String toString() {
  return (name + " at " + url + " is " +
    description);

}
}
```

Since the print method has been removed from website, the OOPTest program won't work any longer. This is a bad thing to do to shipping software, but is not uncommon in the development stage. Program 6.11 is an OOPTest that uses toString and System.out.println instead of print and thus works with the new website class.

Program 6.11: OOPTest with toString

```java
public class OOPTest {

    public static void main(String args[]) {

        website w = new website("Cafe Au Lait",
            "http://sunsite.unc.edu/javafaq/",
            "Really cool!");
        System.out.println(w);

    }

}
```

Public, Private, and Protected Access

Global variables are classic causes of bugs in most programming languages. Some unknown function can change the value of a variable when the programmer isn't expecting it to change. This plays all sorts of havoc.

Most OOP languages, including Java, allow you to protect variables from external modification. This allows you to guarantee that your class remains consistent with what you expect it to be as long as the methods of the class themselves are bug-free. For example, suppose you have a car class with a field for current speed and a field for fuel consumption. If the speed increases, the fuel consumption should also increase. By protecting fields from external modification, you can ensure that whenever the speed goes up the fuel consumption goes up too, and whenever the speed goes down, the fuel consumption goes down.

A class presents a picture of itself to the world. This picture says that the class has certain methods and certain fields. Everything else about the class including the detailed workings of the class's methods is hidden. As long as the picture the class shows to the world doesn't change, the programmer can change how the class implements that picture. Among other advantages, this allows the programmer to change and improve the algorithms a class uses without worrying that some piece of code depends in unforeseen ways on the details of the algorithm used. This is called **encapsulation**.

A common way to think about encapsulation is that a class signs a contract with all the other classes in the program. This contract says that a class has methods with unambiguous names that take particular types of arguments and return a particular type of value. The contract may also say that a class has fields with given names and of a given type. However, the contract does not specify how the methods are implemented. Furthermore it does not say that there aren't other private fields and methods which the class may use. A contract guarantees the presence of certain methods and fields. It does not exclude all other methods and fields. This contract is implemented through access protection. Every class, field, and method in a Java program is defined as either `public`, `private`, `protected`, or unspecified.

The public variables and methods of an object can be accessed from anywhere the object itself can be seen. Anyone can touch an object's public members. They should be kept to a minimum. Public fields should relate very closely to the core functionality of the class. They should not show intimate details of the inner workings of the class. Except in very simple instances fields should probably not be public.

The private fields and methods of an object can only be accessed by the object itself and by other objects of the same class (**siblings**). An object may touch its sibling's private parts. A sibling is an object in the same class which is not the same object.

Protected fields and methods may be accessed by objects in the same package as the class and by objects in a subclass of the class. You'll learn about subclasses and inheritance in the next chapter, and you'll learn more about packages in Chapter 8. For now you may safely assume that all classes defined in the same source code file are in the same package. Siblings may touch each others' protected parts.

Finally, if a member variable or method is not specifically declared as either `public`, `private`, or `protected`, then it is **unspecified**. An unspecified method or field is accessible to anything in the same package but not to any subclasses that are in different packages. Note that unspecified is not a Java keyword. It is simply the default behavior when no access specifier is prefixed to a member or class.

Static Members

A method or a field in a Java program can be declared `static`. This means the member belongs to the class rather than to an individual object. If a variable is static, then when any object in the class changes the value of the variable, that value changes for all objects in the class.

One possible use of `static` is to add version information to a class. A static `String` field called `version` can be used to store the version information and a static method called `getVersion` can return it. Since the version is a property of the class rather than of an object, it is static.

Program 6.12 is a website class with such a `version` field and `getVersion` method.

Program 6.12: A website class with a static version

```java
public class website {

  String name;
  String url;
  String description;
  static String version = "1.0";

  public website(String n, String u, String d) {
    name = n;
    url  = u;
    description = d;
  }

  public static String getVersion() {
    return version;
  }

  public String getName() {
    return name;
  }

  public String getURL() {
    return url;
  }
```

```
public String getDescription() {
  return description;
}

public void setName(String s) {
  name = s;
}

public void setURL(String s) {
  url = s;
}

public void setDescription(String s) {
  description = s;
}

public String toString() {
  return (name + " at " + url + " is " +
    description);
}

}
```

If a method is declared `static`, you access it by using the name of the class rather the name of a particular instance of the class.

Therefore instead of writing

```
website w = new website("Cafe Au Lait",
  "http://sunsite.unc.edu/javafaq/",
  "Really cool!");
String s = w.getVersion();
```

you just write

```
String s = website.getVersion();
```

Static methods may not call nonstatic members of the same class directly. Rather they must specify which instance of the class they are referring to. Trying to call a nonstatic member is a very common compile-time error. The specific error message generated by the javac compiler will look something like this:

```
Error:   Can't make static reference to method
void print() in class test.
```

Of course the names and signature will be changed to match the specific method and class.

Classes as Atoms, a Metaphor

Classes are the atoms of Java programs. Methods are the electrons of a Java class, responsible for most of its behavior. The detailed structure of a class is hidden inside its nucleus, the fields. The public methods of a class are like the valence electrons that do most of the interacting with other atoms. Normally all interaction between different objects takes place through methods, not through the fields in the nucleus.

The exception to the rule that only a class's methods interact with unrelated classes is very simple classes. If there aren't many fields and only the most basic methods, then it may make sense to expose your fields to the world. For instance, java.awt.Point has two public member variables, x and y, each ints. There really isn't any other intelligent way to represent a point in the graphics coordinate system so there's no reasonable expectation that the implementation of a point will ever need to change. Therefore the fields are exposed and direct access to them is allowed rather than wrapping them in excessively inconvenient getX() and setX(int x) methods.

To continue with the chemistry analogy, in the simplest atom, hydrogen, it's easy for the single electron to be stripped away leaving only the nucleus. Then other atoms interact directly with the nucleus. However even in a two-proton atom (Helium) it's rare for the nucleus to be exposed.

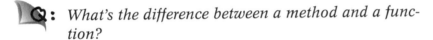

Q: *What's the difference between a method and a function?*

A: Partially this is just a difference in terminology. We could just as easily have written function everywhere we wrote method and this book would not have been substantially changed. However, there's a deeper difference. In traditional programming languages, functions are assumed to be global in scope. They exist independently of the data they work on. A method, however, is attached to a particular object (or, in the case of static methods, a class) and it can only operate in conjunction with the object that contains it.

Q: *Why do you switch between the words "member variable" and "field"?*

A: In traditional object-oriented languages, notably C++, the words "member variable" are used for what the *Java Language Specification* calls a "field." Since most people using Java started programming in other languages, they use the term "member variable" more commonly. Unlike methods and functions, there isn't even a theoretical difference between a member variable and a field though.

Q: *Can a class be declared private?*

A: No. If a class were private, it couldn't be instantiated or subclassed anywhere which would defeat the purpose of its existence. A class can be declared public or protected or left unspecified, but it may not be private.

Q: *Can a method be recursive?*

A: Yes. Java fully supports recursive methods (that is, methods that call themselves) to the limits of available memory.

Intro to OOP

Quiz

1. What's the difference between an object and a class?

2. What's the difference between an instance of a class and an object in that class?

3. What's the difference between a local variable and a member variable?

4. What's the difference between a static field and a nonstatic field?

Exercises

1. Convert the command line programs of exercises 1, 5, 7, 8, 9, 10, 11, and 12 from Chapter 4 into methods that do the calculations but don't handle any input. Then write a main method to handle the input and call the new methods. Do you notice anything similar about the new main methods?

2. Java lacks a complex data type. Write a Complex class that represents a single complex number and includes methods for all the usual operations, that is, addition, subtraction, multiplication, division, and so forth.

3. Hard: Create a VeryLong class that will store an integer of arbitrary length. The methods of this class should be similar to those of the Complex class.

4. Using the VeryLong class of the last exercise, create a Rational class that handles arbitrarily precise fractions.

5. Modify the `toString()` method of the Rational class so that it outputs results as mixed numbers in reduced form (i.e., 1 + 3/8 instead of 1 + 6/16 or 11/8). Hint: The greatest common denominator of two numbers u and v is the same as the greatest common denominator of u and u − v.

Summary

This chapter covered a lot of ground quite quickly. Before you go on, make sure you've got a firm grasp on this material, especially if you're new to OOP. The main things you should have learned from this chapter are

- What a class is, what an object is, and the difference between them

- How to instantiate an object with the new keyword

- What a member variable is, what a local variable is, and the difference between them

- How to use methods to break up the logic of a program

- How to write and use a constructor

- How and when to use a toString method

- The meaning and use of public and private

- The meaning and use of static methods and fields

Coming Up

In Chapter 7 you'll continue your exploration of OOP as polymorphism and inheritance are introduced.

The rest of this book will rely heavily on the concepts introduced in this chapter. From now on, you're going to see many different classes representing everything from games to rectangles to windows.

Further Reading

There are a number of good books about object-oriented programming. Regrettably, most of them assume the language you're using is C++. Nonetheless, two of the better ones are

ECKEL, BRUCE, *Thinking in C++*, Englewood Cliffs, NJ: Prentice-Hall, 1995.

ENTSMINGER, GARY, *The Tao of Objects*, 2nd Ed., New York: M&T Books, 1995.

CHAPTER

POLYMORPHISM AND INHERITANCE

- Polymorphism

- Inheritance

- The java.lang.Object class

- Abstract methods and classes

- Interfaces

The last chapter concentrated on abstract data typing through classes, objects, and methods. Abstract data typing produces code that is much easier to read, understand, and maintain. This chapter continues the exploration of OOP by investigating its other two primary features: polymorphism and inheritance. Polymorphism allows the programmer to choose an operation without worrying excessively about the data types involved. Inheritance promotes code reuse and increases programmer productivity.

Polymorphism

Polymorphism is when the same method or operator can be used on many different types of data. For instance the + sign is used to add `ints` as well as concatenate Strings. The plus sign behaves differently depending on the type of its arguments. Therefore, the plus sign is inherently polymorphic. `System.out.println` can print a String or a number. You don't have to call one method to print Strings and another to print `ints`. Polymorphism takes care of it.

Polymorphism can be implemented in programmer-defined classes as well. To do this, simply write two methods with the same name but different argument lists. For instance, the last chapter had two different versions of the website constructor: one that took three arguments and one that took no arguments. You can use both of these in a single class.

Program 7.1: Polymorphic website constructors

```java
public class website {

   String name;
   String url;
   String description;

   public website(String n, String u, String d) {
     name = n;
     url  = u;
     description = d;
   }

   public website() {
     name = "";
     url  = "";
     description = "";
   }

}
```

Operator Overloading

Some OOP languages, notably C++, allow you to not only overload methods but also operators like + or −. This is very useful when dealing with user-defined mathematical classes like complex numbers where + and − have well-defined meanings.

However, most non-mathematical classes do not have obvious meanings for operators like + and −. Experience has shown that operator overloading is a large contributor to making multi-person programming projects infeasible. Therefore, Java does not support operator overloading.

Normally a single identifier refers to exactly one method. When, as above, one identifier refers to more than one method, the method is said to be **overloaded**. You could argue that this should be called identifier overloading rather than method overloading since it's the identifier that refers to more than one method, not the method that refers to more than one identifier. However, common usage calls this method overloading.

Which method an identifier refers to depends on the **signature**. The signature is the number, type, and order of the arguments passed to a method. The signature of the first constructor in Program 7.1 is three Strings. The signature of the second method is no arguments of any type. Thus the first version of the website constructor is called when there are three String arguments and the second version is used when there aren't any arguments.

If there are one, two, four, or more String arguments to the constructor, or arguments that aren't Strings, then the compiler generates an error because it doesn't have a method whose signature matches the requested method call. For example,

```
Error:    Method website(double) not found in
    class website.
website.java   line 17
```

Many of the system-supplied methods are polymorphic. For instance, `println` can print a `String`, an `int`, or many other kinds of data types. The compiler is responsible for determining what is being passed to the `println` method and calling the right variant of the method accordingly.

Inheritance

Code reusability is claimed to be a key advantage of OOP languages over non-object-oriented languages. Inheritance is the mechanism by which this is achieved. An object can inherit the fields and methods of another object. It can keep those it wants and replace those it doesn't want.

For instance, suppose there is a class which represents a car. A car has a make, a model, a year, a maximum speed, a weight, a price, a number of passengers it can carry, four wheels, either two or four doors, and many other properties you can represent with fields. Here's how you might write a class definition for a car:

Program 7.2: The Car class

```java
class Car {

    String make;
    String model;
    int year;
    int max_speed;
    int weight
    float price;
    int num_passengers;
    int num_wheels = 4;
    int num_doors;

}
```

Obviously, this doesn't exhaust everything there is to say about a car. Which properties you choose to include in your class depends on your application.

Now suppose you also need a class for a motorcycle. A motorcycle also has a make, a model, a year, a maximum speed, a weight, a price, a number of passengers it can carry, two wheels, and many other properties you can represent with fields. A class that represents a motorcycle might look like this:

Program 7.3: A Motorcycle Class

```
class Motorcycle {

    String make;
    String model;
    int year;
    int max_speed;
    int weight
    float price;
    int num_passengers;
    int num_wheels = 2;
}
```

There's a lot of overlap between these two class definitions. OOP languages provide a mechanism for taking advantage of the overlap. This mechanism is inheritance. This example begins by defining a more general MotorVehicle class, as shown in Program 7.4.

Program 7.4: A Motor Vehicle Class

```
class MotorVehicle {

    String make;
    String model;
    int year;
    int max_speed;
    int weight
    float price;
    int num_passengers;
    int num_wheels;
}
```

The MotorVehicle has all the characteristics shared by motorcycles and cars, but it leaves the number of wheels unspecified, and it doesn't have a `num_doors` variable since not all motor vehicles have doors.[1] Next you define two subclasses of MotorVehicle: one for cars and one for motorcycles. To do this you use the keyword `extends`, as shown in Programs 7.5 and 7.6.

Program 7.5: A Motorcycle subclass

```
class Motorcycle extends MotorVehicle {

  int num_wheels = 2;

}
```

Program 7.6: A Car subclass

```
class Car extends MotorVehicle {

  int num_wheels = 4;
  int num_doors;

}
```

It may look as if these classes aren't as complete as the earlier ones, but that's incorrect. Car and Motorcycle each **inherit** the members of their **superclass**, MotorVehicle. Since a MotorVehicle has a make, model, year, max_speed, weight, price, and num_passengers, Cars and Motorcycles also have makes, models, years, max_speeds, weights, prices, and num_passengers.

Car and Motorcycle are subclasses of MotorVehicle. If you instantiate a Car or a Motorcycle with `new`, you can use that object anywhere you can use a MotorVehicle, because Cars are MotorVehicles. Similarly, you can use a Motorcycle anywhere you can use a MotorVehicle.

---

[1] Depending on your application, it might make sense to allow motorcycles to have a `num_doors` varible and just set `num_doors` to zero.

Language Law: Vectors and subclasses

Note that I said you shouldn't give a method that expects a Car a MotorVehicle. I didn't say you couldn't. Objects can be cast into their subclasses. This is useful when using data structures like Vectors that handle only generic objects. It's up to the programmer to keep track of what kind of object is stored in a Vector, and to use it accordingly.

The converse is not true. Although all Cars are MotorVehicles, not all MotorVehicles are Cars. Some are Motorcycles. Therefore, if a method expects a Car, you shouldn't give it a MotorVehicle instead.

The proper choice of classes and subclasses is a skill learned primarily through experience. There are often different ways to define classes.

Multilevel Inheritance

The example given above shows single-level inheritance. There's nothing to stop you from going further. You can define subclasses of cars for compacts, station wagons, sports coupes, and more. They might look like this:

Program 7.7: A compact subclass of Car

```
class compact extends Car {

    int num_doors = 2;
}
```

Multiple Inheritance

Some OOP languages, notably C++, allow a class to inherit from more than one unrelated class. This is called multiple inheritance and is different from the multilevel inheritance in this section. Most of the things that can be accomplished via multiple inheritance in C++ can be handled by interfaces in Java.

Program 7.8: A wagon subclass of Car

```java
class wagon extends MotorVehicle {

  int num_doors = 5;

}
```

Program 7.9: A coupe subclass of Car

```java
class coupe extends MotorVehicle {

  int num_doors = 2;

}
```

Each of these inherits from not only its immediate superclass, Car, but also from Car's superclass, MotorVehicle. Thus the coupe class also has a make, a model, a year, and so on. There's no limit to this chain of inheritance, though getting more than four or five classes deep makes code excessively complex.

Overriding Methods

Suppose that one day you've just finished your website class. It's been plugged into an object-oriented database, which is chugging along merrily serving out files and responding to requests from the world. Then the the webmaster rolls in the door, and tells you that he needs a toString method that formats the web site's data as three Strings on three lines like

```
Cafe Au Lait

http://sunsite.unc.edu/javafaq/

Really cool
```

rather than

```
Cafe Au Lait at http://sunsite.unc.edu/javafaq/ is
Really cool!
```

What are you going to do? Your first reaction may be to change the class that you already wrote so that it formats String output in the requested form. However, you're using that class elsewhere and things will break if you change it.

You could create a completely new class in a different file, either by starting from scratch or by copying and pasting. This would work, but it would mean that if you found a bug in the website class now, you'd have to fix it in two files. And if you wanted to add new methods to the website class (as you will in the next few sections), you'd have to add them in two files. Still this is the best you could do if you were writing in C or some other traditional language.

But you're not writing in C, are you? The OOP solution to this problem is to define a new class, call it returnDelimitedWebsite, which inherits from website and **overrides** website's toString method. You'll only need to write those parts of the class that have changed. Everything else can remain the same as in the website class and as bug free as that class is. If you do find and fix a bug in the website class, it will be fixed in the returnDelimitedWebsite class too.

Here's the returnDelimitedWebsite class:

Program 7.10: The returnDelimitedWebsite class

```java
public class returnDelimitedWebsite
  extends website {

  public returnDelimitedWebsite(String n,
    String u,
    String d) {

      super(n, u , d);

  }

    public String toString() {

    return getName() + '\r' + getURL() +
      '\r' + getDescription() + '\r';

  }

}

public class returnDelimitedWebsite
  extends website {

  public returnDelimitedWebsite(String n,
    String u,
    String d) {

      super(n, u , d);

  }

    public String toString() {

    return getName() + '\r' + getURL() +
      '\r' + getDescription() + '\r';

  }

    public boolean over256() {

    if (getDescription().length() > 256) {
      return true;
    }
```

```
        return false;

    }

}
```

The first thing to note about this class is what it doesn't have: getURL, getDescription, getName, setName, setURL, or setDescription methods or name, url, and description fields. All of these are provided by the superclass website. Nothing about them has changed so they don't need to be repeated here.

Next look at the toString method. This is different than the toString method in website. Its output formats as return-delimited lines of text rather than as a single line of text. Since the name, url, and description fields from website are not accessible to the subclass, they're retrieved using the getName, getURL, and getDescription methods. These methods are public so they are accessible to the returnDelimitedWebsite class.

The returnDelimitedWebsite constructor is a little more complicated. First note that if you're going to use a nondefault constructor, that is a constructor with arguments, you do need to write a constructor for the subclass, even if it's just going to do the exact same thing as the matching constructor in the superclass. You cannot simply inherit website's constructor because that constructor is named website and this one must be named returnDelimitedWebsite. When a new returnDelimitedWebsite is created, the constructor that's looked for is `returnDelimitedWebsite`, not `website`.

The constructor needs to set the value of `name`, `url`, and `description`. However they're not accessible from the subclass. Instead they are set by calling the superclass's constructor using the new keyword `super`. When `super` is used as a method in the first non-blank line of a constructor, it stands for the constructor of this class's superclass, in this case `website(String n, String u, String d)`.

The immediate superclass's constructor *will* be called in the first nonblank line of the subclass's constructor. If you don't call it explicitly, then Java will call it for you with no arguments. It's a compile-time error if the immediate superclass doesn't have a constructor with no arguments and you don't call a different constructor in the first line of the subclass's constructor.

Adding New Methods

A subclass isn't restricted to changing the behavior of its superclass. You can also add completely new methods and fields that are not shared with the superclass. For instance, if a class represents a user of a multiuser database, the user class might start off with no access. Secretaries could be given read-only access. Therefore, the secretary class would have additional methods to read data that aren't part of the user class.

Data entry clerks might be allowed to read the database and to create new records but not to modify old records. Therefore, the data entry class would inherit from the secretary class and have methods to allow adding new records. A supervisor class would inherit from the data entry class and also have methods that allow modification of existing records. Finally, a database manager would inherit from supervisor but have new methods that allowed database managers to change the structure of the database.

As a practical example, suppose the webmaster wants a quick way to test if the length of the description field in returnDelimitedWebsite is greater than 256 characters. You can add a boolean method called over256 to the returnDelimitedWebsite class like this:

Program 7.11: The returnDelimitedWebsite Class with an additional method

```
public class returnDelimitedWebsite
 extends website {

  public returnDelimitedWebsite(String n,
    String u, String d) {

      super(n, u , d);

  }

  public String toString() {

  return getName() + '\r' + getURL() +
     '\r' + getDescription() + '\r';

}
```

```
public boolean over256() {

if (getDescription().length() > 256) {
   return true;
}
else {
   return false;
}


}

}
```

The `over256` method is simple. It gets the description String using getDescription and then tests the length of that String with the `length` method from java.lang.String. If the length is greater than 256, the method returns `true`. Otherwise it returns `false`. Nothing at all like this is present in the website class and nothing needs to be.

The java.lang.Object Class

All objects in Java inherit from the java.lang.Object class. If you don't specify which class your class extends, then it is assumed to extend the Object class. java.lang.Object provides a number of methods that are common to all objects. `toString` is the most important such method. Since the default `toString` method produces only the name of the class, you should override it in all classes you define. Three others you should be aware of are

Object clone()

Clone creates a clone of a particular object in a particular state. When the object is cloned, the clone is identical in all respects to the original object, except that it has its own storage space and can be changed independently of the original object. For security reasons, Netscape won't run any applet that calls `Object.clone()` so you should be very sparing in its use. If you expect to use it at all, you should probably override `clone()` with a method of your devising.

For example, here is a clone method you can use for the website class:

```
public website clone() {

    return new website(name, url, description);

}
```

boolean equals(Object o)

The equals method tests whether two objects are equal to each other in all respects. This is not the same as using the == operator, which tests if two objects are the same object. An object created by a clone method will pass the equals test if neither object has changed since the clone was created. However, the clone will fail to be == to the original object.

For example, here is an equals method you could use for the website class. Two web sites are equal if and only if their URLs are equal, and that's what this method tests for.

```
public boolean equals(website w) {

    if (url.equals(w.url)) return true;
    else return false;

}
```

This example is particularly interesting because it demonstrates the impossibility of writing a useful generic equals method that tests equality for any object. It is not sufficient to simply test for equality of all the fields of two objects. It is entirely possible that some of the fields may not be relevant to the test for equality as in this example, where changing the description or name of a web site does not change the actual web site that's pointed to.

In fact, a still more sophisticated web site applet could actually use the URL and InetAddress classes in java.net to test whether apparently different URLs in fact pointed at the same file, but this is beyond the scope of this book.

Class getClass()

The getClass() method returns a class descriptor that you can use to test the type of a particular object at runtime. You should not need to override this.

Finality

You will notice that a number of the classes in Java library are declared final, e.g.

public final class String

This means this class will not be subclassed and informs the compiler that it can perform certain optimizations it otherwise could not. The compiler will not let you subclass any class that is declared final. You probably won't want or need to declare your own classes final though.

You can also declare that methods are final. A method that is declared final cannot be overridden in a subclass. The syntax is simple: just put the keyword final after the access specifier and before the return type like this:

public final String convertCurrency()

You may also declare variables to be final. This is not the same thing as declaring a method or class to be final. When a variable is declared final, it is a constant which will not and cannot change. Attempts to change it will generate either a compile-time error or an exception (depending on how sneaky the attempt is).

Variables that are both final and static are effectively constant. For instance, a physics program might define the speed of light as

public static final double c = 2.998E8;

Abstract Methods and Classes

Java allows methods and classes to be declared abstract. An abstract method is not actually implemented in the class. It is merely declared there. The body of the method is then implemented in subclasses of that class. An abstract method must be part of an abstract class. You create abstract classes by adding the keyword abstract after the access specifier, for example,

```
public abstract MotorVehicle
```

Abstract classes cannot be instantiated. It is a compile-time error to try something like

```
MotorVehicle m = new MotorVehicle;
```

when MotorVehicle has been declared to be abstract. MotorVehicle is actually a pretty good example of the sort of class that might be abstract. You're unlikely to be interested in a generic motor vehicle. Rather, you'll have trucks, motorcycles, cars, go-carts, and other subclasses of MotorVehicle, but nothing that is only a MotorVehicle.

Interfaces

Interfaces are the next level of abstraction. An interface is like a class with nothing but abstract methods and final, static fields. All methods and fields of an interface must be public.

However, unlike a class, an interface can be added to a class that is already a subclass of another class. Furthermore, an interface can apply to members of many different classes. For instance, you can define an Import interface with the single method called calculate_tariff().

Program 7.12

```
public interface Import {

  public abstract double calculate_tariff();

}
```

You might want to use this interface on many different classes, cars among them, and also for clothes, food, electronics, and more. It would be inconvenient to make all these objects derive from a single class. Furthermore, each different type of item is likely to have a different means of calculating the tariff. Therefore, you define an Import interface and declare that each class implements Import.

The syntax is simple. Import is declared public so that it can be accessed from any class. It is also possible to declare that an interface is protected so that it can only be implemented by classes in a particular package. However, this is very unusual. Almost all interfaces will be public. No interface may be private because the whole purpose of an interface is to be inherited by other classes.

The `interface` keyword takes the place of the `class` keyword.

The single method looks like a classic method definition. It's public (as it must be). It's abstract, also as it must be. And it returns a `double`. The method's name is `calculate_tariff` and it takes no arguments. The difference between this and a method in a class is that there is no method body. That remains to be created in each class that implements the interface.

To actually use this interface, you create a class that includes a `public double calculate_tariff()` method and declare that the class `implements Import`. For instance, here's one such class:

Program 7.13: A Car class that implements Import

```
class Car implements Import {

    String make;
    String model;
    int year;
    int max_speed;
    int weight
    float price;
    int num_passengers;
    int num_wheels = 4;
    int num_doors;

    public double calculate_tariff() {
        return price * 0.1;
    }
}
```

You can declare many different methods in an interface. These methods may be polymorphic. An interface can have member variables, but if so they must be final and static (in other words constants).

Q&A

Q: *Can two methods in a class have the same name but return different types?*

A: As long as the signatures are different two overloaded methods can return different types. For instance java.lang.Math.abs(float) returns a `float` while java.lang.Math.abs(int) returns an `int`. However, a class cannot have two methods with the same signature and the same name that return different types. That is, you can't have one abs method that takes an `int` and returns an `int`, and another that takes an `int` but returns a `float`. Polymorphic methods in Java are distinguished only by their signature, never by their return type.

Q: *What's the difference between overriding a method and overloading a method?*

A: A method is overloaded when the same class has several methods by the same name which are distinguished by their signatures. A method is overridden when a subclass implements a different version of the method with the same name and signature. Overloading provides different arguments. Overriding provides different behavior.

Q: *Final variables are constant. Are fields in a final class also constant?*

A: No. If a class is final, that only means it can't be sub-classed. You can still change its fields unless they have been independently declared final. In the following example, num_doors can be changed but num_wheels is constant.

```java
final class Car extends MotorVehicle {

    final int num_wheels = 4;
    int num_doors;

}
```

Quiz

1. Why can't a class be declared private?

2. If you can add methods and fields to a subclass, why can't you remove them?

3. What's the difference between an abstract class and an interface?

Summary

This chapter completes your very brief introduction to object-oriented programming. You learned

- What polymorphism is
- What inheritance is and why you'd want to use it.
- That all objects inherit from the Object class, including the `toString()`, `clone()`, `getClass()` and `equals()` methods.
- What final variables and classes are
- What an abstract method is
- What an interface is

Coming Up

In later chapters almost everything you learn about will be one sort of object or another. You will see many, many more examples of classes, objects, and methods. In the next chapter, you'll learn how to group classes into packages and how to use prewritten classes in the Java library.

Further Reading

Information about classes, objects, inheritance, and polymorphism is scattered throughout the *Java Language Specification*. However, you should now read Chapter 8, which has most of the detailed information. You can find more about interfaces in Chapter 9.

CHAPTER 8

PACKAGES

- What a package is

- What packages are included

- How to import a class or package

- How to do high school math in Java

Related classes can be combined into packages. Packages can be stored anywhere in the user's CLASSPATH and made available to different classes. Java provides a number of packages with several hundred classes that handle input and output, networking, mathematical functions, graphical user interfaces, and more. This chapter shows you how to unlock the power of Java's packages.

Importing Packages

A package is a group of functionally related classes that add capabilities to Java. You can reuse the code in a package in many different programs. In a more generic sense, it can be called a library. Some methods and classes you've already seen are part of the java.lang package. When you call `System.out.println`, `System` refers to the java.lang.System class and `out` is a static field in the System class, and an instance of the PrintStream class in the java.io package.

There are two ways to gain access to a method or class in a particular package. First, you can refer to it using its full package name. For instance,

```
java.util.Date now = new java.util.Date();
```

This is useful if you are only going to use a class once, but if you're using it multiple times, you'll find this notation gets tiresome very quickly. Therefore, you can import the class and refer to its public fields and methods as if they were part of your own file. Write

```
import java.util.Date;
.
.
.
   Date now = new Date();
```

Import statements must come at the top of a file, before any class or interface definitions.

It's often useful to import an entire package rather than just a single class. This book tries to be very specific about what classes are imported so you can see what classes come from where. However in real-world programming, it's more common to replace the specific class with an asterisk, `*`. Thus to import all the packages in java.util, you would write at the top of your program

```
import java.util.*;
```

This imports java.util.Date, java.util.Random, and several other public classes in the java.util package. You normally don't need each and every one of these classes, but it's often the case that you need enough of them that it's easier to ask for them all.

When you import an entire package you get access to all the public classes contained in the package. You do not get access to any of the private, protected, or unspecified classes in the package.

> **Tip** Whether you import an entire package or just the classes you need does not affect the final byte code .class file at all. However, importing just the classes you use makes compile times slightly faster. On the other hand, you'll often find yourself recompiling because you forgot to import a class you used. Although importing specific classes is cleaner and helps you keep closer tabs on what your program is doing, it's almost always faster to import entire packages.

Name Conflicts

It is possible that you will try to import a package that contains public classes which have the same name as a class in your own source code. The two classes may or may not mean the same thing. In general you should probably rename the class in your own source code rather than in the package. However, if the two classes with conflicting names are related functionally, it may make sense to implement your class as a subclass of the class in the package.

> **Warning** Although the compiler could theoretically warn you of this problem, it does not. The compiler will use the first definition of a class it finds. This is perhaps the best reason to import classes individually rather than in a package. If you import each needed class separately, there's very little chance you'll accidentally import a class that has the same name as one of your own classes.

java.lang

The java.lang package is special. It is automatically imported. Thus you neither have to import `java.lang.*` nor prefix all your calls to java.lang's methods and classes with java.lang, for example you don't have to write

```
java.lang.System.out.println("Hello World");
```

At the same time, this means that you can have a name conflict with one of the java.lang classes without even importing the class you conflict with. The classes in java.lang are

- Boolean
- Character
- Class
- ClassLoader
- Compiler
- Double
- Float
- Integer
- Long
- Math
- Number
- Object
- Process
- Runtime
- SecurityManager
- String
- StringBuffer
- System
- Thread
- ThreadGroup
- Throwable

Avoid creating a class with any of these names. There are also two interfaces and about two dozen assorted exceptions in java.lang.

Where Does Java Look for Classes?

When you import a package, Java looks at the complete name of the package and the CLASSPATH environment variable to determine where it can find the requested .class and .java files.

CLASSPATH should contain a list of directories, separated by the java.io.File.separatorChar. This is a platform-dependent separator between directories. It is a semicolon on Unix and Windows and a forward slash on the Mac. For example

```
~/classes;/usr/local/netscape/classes
```

These directories are the roots for the search for an imported class.

Java changes the periods in the full name of the class it's looking for into directory separators (/ on Unix, \ on Windows, : on the Mac). Thus if it wants the java.awt.GridBagLayout class, it looks for java/awt/GridBagLayout.class in each of the root directories listed in the CLASSPATH variable from left to right until it finds the file. With the CLASSPATH listed above Java first looks for

```
~/classes/java/awt/GridBagLayout.class
```

Then for

```
/usr/local/netscape/classes/java/awt/GridBagLayout
.class
```

The specification of the CLASSPATH is somewhat platform dependent. For instance, ~ means the home directory on Unix but has no meaning on the Mac.

The CLASSPATH variable is also important when you run Java applets, not just when you compile them. It tells the Web browser or applet viewer where it should look to find the referenced .class files. If the CLASSPATH is set improperly, you'll probably see messages about "Applet could not start."

Zip Classes

Since large packages can contain many, many .class files, Sun has built the capability to read zip archives into Java. Therefore, an entire directory structure can be zipped to save space. If you want to see what's inside the zip file, just unzip it. The compiler and runtime don't care whether or not a directory has been zipped. You just need to make sure that the .zip file is named the same as the directory it replaces plus the .zip extension and that it is in the same location.

Using the System Packages

Learning the language is only part of learning to program modern applications. A large part consists of learning the application programming interface (API) for a particular system. Although the Java language is quite small, the Java API is quite large. It includes methods for displaying text on the screen, drawing windows and graphics, sending data over the network, common mathematical functions like sine and cosine, and common data structures like vectors and hash tables.

The Java language is quite small. There are only 50 keywords and two of those aren't even implemented. In theory, these words plus Java's operators, literals and separators are sufficient to do just about anything you might want to do that doesn't require access to the operating system. In practice, most programmers don't want to bother themselves with the details of calculating sines, cosines, or square roots using just +, – and *, even though they could. A few programmers might want to implement their own data structures like linked lists, but most would prefer to be spared the details. And almost everyone wants access to the host API, but applets are specifically prohibited from doing this.

All these capabilities are provided through packages. A package is a prewritten group of related classes that contains many methods a programmer can use as if they were part of the language. This includes both methods that could be written in Java, like sine and cosine methods, and methods like `println` that could not because they require access to the underlying OS.

Before this chapter, you've used several methods provided by the java.lang package, most commonly `System.out.println`. The `System.out.println` method actually requires quite a lot of code, but it is all stored in the java.lang and java.io packages. Thus rather than including that code every time you need to print, you just call `System.out.println`.

There are eight packages of system routines in Java 1.0. They are

- java.applet
- java.awt

JAVA DEVELOPER'S RESOURCE

- java.awt.image
- java.awt.peer
- java.io
- java.lang
- java.net
- java.util

These packages include hundreds of methods and classes that you can use in your programs. Fortunately, you don't need to know all of them. The java.applet and java.awt packages are primarily useful when writing applets. Most of the middle third of this book will cover those two packages. java.io contains various kinds of input and output streams. For now, `System.out.println` is the only one of those you'll need. You'll see more routines from java.io in Chapter 20. java.net includes networking routines for opening, closing, and reading sockets. If your applications don't do any of that, you don't need it. java.util contains efficient implementations of some common data structures such as hash tables and stacks. You'll learn about these in Chapter 22.

java.lang is the package that concerns you now. It contains the most common classes and methods that are guaranteed to be available to your program. You've seen several pieces of this class already. Strings are defined in java.lang.String. The System that you used for `System.out.println` is java.lang.System. The Integer, Float, Double and Long classes and their valueOf methods you used to perform String to number conversion in Chapter 4 are also part of java.lang. You'll see more of java.lang along the way. Right now let's take a good look at one of the more useful java.lang classes, java.lang.Math.

java.lang.Math

Math is a large subject. There's a lot more than simple addition, multiplication, subtraction, and division. Numbers are raised to powers, square roots are taken, sines and cosines of angles are calculated and a lot more. Although Java doesn't have built-in operators for these operations, it has a math class that can handle all of them. This class is called java.lang.Math and includes static methods that perform just about every operation you learned about in high school algebra.

To use a static method from a package, prefix its name with the name of the class followed by a period. For instance,

```
x = java.lang.Math.sqrt(9);
```

If the package is part of java.lang, then you can skip the name of the package. Thus

```
x = Math.sqrt(9);
```

is equivalent to the above. However this only works if the package is part of java.lang. If you're going to be using one of the classes frequently, then you can import it at the very start of your file. Then you won't even need to use the class prefix. For example,

```
import java.lang.Math;
.
.
.

  x = sqrt(9);
.
.
.
```

Program 8.1 is an example program that exercises most of the routines in java.lang.Math. Almost all of these methods are straightforward. If you have any doubts about how they work, run the program and look at the output. If your high school math is a little rusty, don't worry if you don't remember the exact meaning of logarithms or cosines. Just know that they're here in Java if you need them.

Program 8.1 The math library

```
class MathLibraryExample {

  public static void main(String args[]) {

    int i = 7;
    int j = -9;
    double x = 72.3;
    double y = 0.34;
```

```
System.out.println("i is " + i);
System.out.println("j is " + j);
System.out.println("x is " + x);
System.out.println("y is " + y);

// The absolute value of a number is equal to
// the number if the number is positive or
// zero and equal to the negative of the number
// if the number is negative.

System.out.println("|" + i + "| is " +
   Math.abs(i));
System.out.println("|" + j + "| is " +
   Math.abs(j));
System.out.println("|" + x + "| is " +
   Math.abs(x));
System.out.println("|" + y + "| is " +
   Math.abs(y));

// Truncating and Rounding functions

// You can round off a floating point number
// to the nearest integer with round()
 System.out.println(x + " is approximately " +
   Math.round(x));
 System.out.println(y + " is approximately " +
   Math.round(y));

// The "ceiling" of a number is the
// smallest integer greater than or equal to
// the number. Every integer is its own
// ceiling.
 System.out.println("The ceiling of " + i +
   " is " + Math.ceil(i));
 System.out.println("The ceiling of " + j +
   " is " + Math.ceil(j));
 System.out.println("The ceiling of " + x +
   " is " + Math.ceil(x));
 System.out.println("The ceiling of " + y +
    " is " + Math.ceil(y));
```

```
// The "floor" of a number is the largest
// integer less than or equal to the number.
// Every integer is its own floor.
System.out.println("The floor of " + i +
  " is " + Math.floor(i));
System.out.println("The floor of " + j +
  " is " + Math.floor(j));
System.out.println("The floor of " + x +
  " is " + Math.floor(x));
System.out.println("The floor of " + y +
  " is " + Math.floor(y));

// Comparison operators

// min() returns the smaller of the two
// arguments you pass it
System.out.println("min(" + i + "," + j +
  ") is " + Math.min(i,j));
System.out.println("min(" + x + "," + y +
  ") is " + Math.min(x,y));
System.out.println("min(" + i + "," + x +
  ") is " + Math.min(i,x));
System.out.println("min(" + y + "," + j +
  ") is " + Math.min(y,j));

// There's a corresponding max() method
// that returns the larger of two numbers
System.out.println("max(" + i + "," + j +
  ") is " + Math.max(i,j));
System.out.println("max(" + x + "," + y +
  ") is " + Math.max(x,y));
System.out.println("max(" + i + "," + x +
  ") is " + Math.max(i,x));
System.out.println("max(" + y + "," + j +
  ") is " + Math.max(y,j));

// The Math library defines a couple
// of useful constants:
System.out.println("Pi is " + Math.PI);
System.out.println("e is " + Math.E);

// Trigonometric methods
// All arguments are given in radians
```

```java
// Convert a 45 degree angle to radians
double angle = 45.0 * 2.0 * Math.PI/360.0;
System.out.println("cos(" + angle +
  ") is " + Math.cos(angle));
System.out.println("sin(" + angle +
  ") is " + Math.sin(angle));

// Inverse Trigonometric methods
// All values are returned as radians

double value = 0.707;

System.out.println("acos(" + value +
  ") is " + Math.acos(value));
System.out.println("asin(" + value +
  ") is " + Math.asin(value));
System.out.println("atan(" + value +
  ") is " + Math.atan(value));

// Exponential and Logarithmic Methods

// exp(a) returns e (2.71828...) raised
// to the power of a.

System.out.println("exp(1.0) is " +
  Math.exp(1.0));
System.out.println("exp(10.0) is " +
  Math.exp(10.0));
System.out.println("exp(0.0) is " +
  Math.exp(0.0));

// log(a) returns  the natural
// logarithm (base e) of a.
System.out.println("log(1.0) is " +
  Math.log(1.0));
System.out.println("log(10.0) is " +
  Math.log(10.0));
System.out.println("log(Math.E) is " +
  Math.log(Math.E));
```

```
  // pow(x, y) returns the x raised
  // to the yth power.
  System.out.println("pow(2.0, 2.0) is " +
    Math.pow(2.0,2.0));
  System.out.println("pow(10.0, 3.5) is " +
    Math.pow(10.0,3.5));
  System.out.println("pow(8, -1) is " +
    Math.pow(8,-1));

  // sqrt(x) returns the square root of x.
  for (i=0; i < 10; i++) {
    System.out.println("The square root of " +
      i + " is " + Math.sqrt(i));
  }


  // Finally there's one Random method
  // that returns a pseudo-random number
  // between 0.0 and 1.0;

  System.out.println(
    "Here's one random number: " + Math.random());
  System.out.println(
    "Here's another random number: " +
    Math.random());

  }

}
```

Here's the output:

```
i is 7
j is -9
x is 72.3
y is 0.34
|7| is 7
|-9| is 9
|72.3| is 72.3
|0.34| is 0.34
72.3 is approximately 72
0.34 is approximately 0
The ceiling of 7 is 7
```

```
The ceiling of -9 is -9
The ceiling of 72.3 is 73
The ceiling of 0.34 is 1
The floor of 7 is 7
The floor of -9 is -9
The floor of 72.3 is 72
The floor of 0.34 is 0
min(7,-9) is -9
min(72.3,0.34) is 0.34
min(7,72.3) is 7
min(0.34,-9) is -9
max(7,-9) is 7
max(72.3,0.34) is 72.3
max(7,72.3) is 72.3
max(0.34,-9) is 0.34
Pi is 3.14159
e is 2.71828
cos(0.785398) is 0.707107
sin(0.785398) is 0.707107
acos(0.707) is 0.785549
asin(0.707) is 0.785247
atan(0.707) is 0.615409
exp(1.0) is 2.71828
exp(10.0) is 22026.5
exp(0.0) is 1
log(1.0) is 0
log(10.0) is 2.30259
log(Math.E) is 1
pow(2.0, 2.0) is 4
pow(10.0, 3.5) is 3162.28
pow(8, -1) is 0.125
The square root of 0 is 0
The square root of 1 is 1
The square root of 2 is 1.41421
The square root of 3 is 1.73205
The square root of 4 is 2
The square root of 5 is 2.23607
The square root of 6 is 2.44949
The square root of 7 is 2.64575
The square root of 8 is 2.82843
The square root of 9 is 3
Here's one random number: 0.820582
Here's another random number: 0.866157
```

Wrapping Your Own Packages

Java does not limit you to using only the system-supplied packages. You can write your own as well. You write packages just as you write any other Java program. Make sure you follow these rules:

1. There must be no more than one public class per file, even if you've figured out how to get the compiler to let you get around this restriction.

2. All files in the package must be named classname.java where classname is the name of the single public class in the file.

3. At the very top of each file in the package, before any import statements, put the statement

```
package myPackage;
```

To use the package in other programs, compile the .java files as usual and then move the resulting .class files into the appropriate subdirectory of one of the directories referenced in your CLASSPATH environment variable. For instance, if /home/elharo/classes is in your CLASSPATH and your package is called package1, you would make a directory called package1 in /home/elharo/classes and then put all the .class files in the package in /home/elharo/classes/package1.

Naming Your Packages

As you saw earlier, name space conflicts arise if two pieces of code declare the same name. Java keeps track of what belongs to each package internally. Thus if Sun decides to put a website class in java.lang in Java 2.0, it won't conflict with a website class defined in an http package. Since they're in different packages, Java can tell them apart. Just as you tell John Smith apart from John Jones by their last names, so too does Java tell two website classes apart by their package names.

However, this scheme breaks down if two different classes share the same package name as well as class name. In a world in which many different packages can be downloaded from many different sites, all landing in the user's CLASSPATH, it's not unthinkable that two differ-ent people might write packages called http with a class called Website.

To ensure that package names don't conflict with each other, Sun asks that you prefix all your packages with a reversed domain name. Thus if your domain name is sunsite.unc.edu, your package names should begin with edu.unc.sunsite. Within that domain, you are responsible for making sure that no one else writes a package that conflicts with yours.

If you don't have a personal domain name and only an account with an Internet service provider, then add your username to this as well. For instance under this scheme, the package prefix for foo@sunsite.unc.edu would be edu.unc.sunsite.foo.

This is primarily of interest to applet writers, not applet users. If you're surfing the net and you load one applet from MIT that has a http.Website class and another from NYU that has a different http.Website class, Java can still tell them apart because before it runs any package it downloads off the net, it prefixes everything with the site from which it got it. In other words, it sees edu.nyu.www.http.Website and edu.mit.www.http.Website. It's only when you download a package manually and install it in one directo-ry in your CLASSPATH and install another package elsewhere in your CLASSPATH that real name conflicts can arise if packages aren't carefully prefixed with a domain or email address.

Rant This scheme works but it's unbelievably kludgy. Does anyone really want to distribute a package called edu.njit.math.elharo.http? Wouldn't elharo.http be a lot simpler? Even Sun itself doesn't use com.sun for its own packages. What's needed is an organization which assigns reasonable, single-word package names to entities that have a legitimate need for them. Thus Borland's http package could be borland.http and Symantec's could be symantec.http, and so on. This entity would have to use reasonable checks on whether the package name made sense, that is, it shouldn't assign the kaplan package name to the Princeton Review as Internic did a while ago with the kaplan.com domain. It would also need to be careful not to give away generic package names like graphics or statis-tics. Otherwise there'd be a rush to grab up all the available names like you saw in early 1996 when Procter & Gamble grabbed several dozen domain names including hotdogs.com and badbreath.com simply because they could and it wouldn't cost them anything.

Q & A

 Q: *Can one class be part of two or more packages?*

 A: No. Since packages are closely tied to the location of a file on the disk, being part of more than one package would require the same file to be in two places at once.

 Q: *What's a pseudo-random number?*

 A: Java uses a known algorithm to create allegedly random numbers. This algorithm takes a seed, generally some measure of the current time, multiplies it by other numbers, truncates parts of it, and twiddles the bits in a predictable fashion. As long as the seed isn't guessable this may give the appearance of producing random numbers, but if you use the same seed you'll get the same "random" number back.

 Q: *Since* Math.Random() *only returns a number between 0.0 and 1.0, how would you get a random number in some other range? For instance, an integer between 1 and 6?*

 A: Multiply the random number by the difference between the high end and the low end of the range of the random numbers you want and add the low end. For instance, to get a floating point number between 1.0 and 6.0 you could use

```
double x = Math.random() * (6.0-1.0) + 1.0;
```
If you want an integer in this range then just use Math.round like so:

```
int die = Math.round(Math.random() * (6.0-1.0)
  + 1.0);
```

 Quiz

1. What happens if you try to take the square root of a negative number?

2. What happens if you use java.lang.Math.pow to raise zero to the zeroth power?

3. What, if anything, can come before a `package` statement in a Java source code file?

4. What, if anything, can come before an `import` statement in a Java source code file?

5. Can one source code file import from more than one package?

Exercises

1. Although mathematicians prefer to work in radians, most scientists and engineers find it easier to think in degrees. Write sine, cosine, and tangent methods that accept their arguments in degrees.

2. Write the corresponding set of inverse trigonometric methods that return their values in degrees instead of radians.

3. The math library is missing secant, cosecant, and cotangent methods. Write them.

4. The math library lacks a log10 method for taking the common logarithm. Write one.

5. Computer scientists often use log2 (log base 2). java.lang.Math doesn't have one of those either. Write it.

6. A simple model for the growth of bacteria with an unlimited supply of nutrients says that after t hours an initial population of p_0 will have grown to $p_0 e^{1.4t}$. Write a Java application that calculates the growth of a colony of bacteria. As usual get the value of p_0 and t from the command line.

7. Modify the bacteria growth program so that the time can be input in minutes. Note that the formula still requires a time in hours.

8. Carbon dating is used to estimate the age of once living objects according to the following formula:

$$age = \frac{-\ln \texttt{ fraction } C\texttt{-14 remaining}}{1.22 \times 10^{-4}}$$

Write a Java application that calculates the age of an object given the percentage of carbon 14 remaining.

9. Put the Complex, VeryLong, and Rational classes of the exercises in Chapter 6 into your own package.

Summary

In this chapter you learned how to take advantage of the large blocks of code that have already been written for you by Java's designers. Things you learned include

- What a package is
- What packages are available
- How to import a class or package
- How to use methods in the Java library
- How to use mathematical functions like square root, sine, and cosine.
- How to put your own classes in packages

Coming Up

The system packages have only been touched on here. From Chapter 10 on, almost every chapter is going to spend the bulk of its pages on one part of the Java packages or another.

CHAPTER
ARRAYS

9

- Arrays, their declaration, initialization, and use

- Multidimensional arrays

- Searching lists

- Sorting lists

Nontrivial computing problems often require lists of items. Often these items can be referred to by their position in the list. Sometimes this ordering is natural as in a list of the first ten people to arrive at a sale. The first person would be item one in the list, the second person to arrive would be item two, and so on. Other times the ordering doesn't really mean anything, but it's still convenient to be able to assign each item a unique number and enumerate all the items in a list by counting out the numbers.

There are many ways to store lists of items, including linked lists, sets, hash tables, binary trees, and arrays. Which one you choose depends on the requirements of your application and the nature of

I[0] 4
I[1] 2
I[2] 76
I[3] -90
I[4] 6

Figure 9.1: *A one-dimensional array of ints with five components*

your data. Java provides classes for many of these. In this chapter, you'll explore the simplest and most common, the array.

One-Dimensional Arrays

Arrays are the oldest and still the most generally effective means of storing groups of variables. An array is a group of variables that share the same name and are ordered sequentially from zero to one less than the number of variables in the array. The number of variables that can be stored in an array is called the array's **length**. Each variable in the array is called a **component** of the array.

An integer array called I can be visualized as a column of data, as shown in Figure 9.1. This is an integer array named I with five components, that is, the type of the array is int and the array has length 5. It is very important to note that the first component of the array is component zero, not component one. Array indexes begin counting with zero. This means that an array with length five does not have a component five, only components zero through four.

There are three steps to creating an array: declaring it, allocating it, and initializing it.

Declaring Arrays

Like all other variables in Java, an array must have a specific type like byte, int, String, or double. This type may be a user-defined class such as website from Chapter 6. Only variables of the appropriate type can be stored in an array. One array cannot store both `int`s and `String`s, for instance.

Like all other variables in Java, an array must be **declared**. When you declare an array variable, you suffix the type with `[]` to indicate that this variable is an array. Here are some examples:

```
int[] k;
float[] yt;
String[] names;
```

This says that `k` is an array of `int`s, `yt` is an array of `float`s and `names` is an array of `String`s. In other words, you declare an array the way you declare any other variable except that you append brackets to the end of the type.

You also have the option to append the brackets to the variable instead of the type.

```
int k[];
float yt[];
String names[];
```

The choice is primarily one of personal preference. You can even use both at the same time like this:

```
int[] k[];
float[] yt[];
String[] names[];
```

I can think of no reason why you might want to do this.

Creating Arrays

Declaring arrays merely says what kind of values the array will hold. It does not create them. Java arrays are objects, and as with any other object, you use the `new` keyword to create them.[1] When you create an array, you must tell the compiler how many components will be stored in it. Here's how you'd create the variables declared above:

```
k = new int[3];
```

---

[1] On the other hand, arrays are a very funny kind of object since, as you see by this syntax, they don't really have constructors as any other object would. Nonetheless, arrays are objects and you can use all the methods of java.lang.Object on an array.

```
yt = new float[7];
names = new String[50];
```

The numbers in the brackets specify the length of the array, that is, how many slots it has to hold values. `k` can hold three `int`s, `yt` can hold seven `float`s, and `names` can hold 50 `String`s. This step is sometimes called **allocating the array** since it allocates the memory the array requires.

Initializing Arrays

Individual components of an array are referenced by the array name and by an integer which represents a position in the array. The numbers you use to identify them are called **subscripts** or **indexes** into the array.

Subscripts are consecutive integers beginning with 0. Thus the array `k` above has components `k[0]`, `k[1]`, and `k[2]`. Since you start counting at zero, there is no `k[3]`, and trying to access it will throw an ArrayIndexOutOfBoundsException.

You can use array components wherever you'd use a similarly typed variable that wasn't part of an array. For example, this is how you'd store values in the arrays above:

```
k[0] = 2;
k[1] = 5;
k[2] = -2;
yt[17] = 7.5f;
names[4] = "Fred";
```

This step is called **initializing the array** or, more precisely, initializing the components of the array. Sometimes the phrase "initializing the array" is used to mean when you initialize all the components of the array.

For even medium-sized arrays, it's unwieldy to specify each component individually. It is often helpful to use `for` loops to initialize the array. Here is a loop that fills an array with the squares of the numbers from 0 to 100:

```
float[] squares;
squares = new float[101];
```

```
for (int i=0, i <= 100; i++) {
    squares[i] = i*i;
}
```

You should note two things about this code fragment:

1. Watch the end points! Since array subscripts begin at zero, you need 101 components if you want to include the square of 100.

2. Although i is an int, it is promoted to a float when it is stored in squares, since squares is declared to be an array of floats.

Shortcuts

It may seem like a lot of work to set up arrays, particularly if you're used to a more array-friendly language like Fortran. Fortunately, Java has several shorthands for declaring, allocating, and initializing arrays.

You can declare and allocate an array at the same time like this:

```
int[] k = new int[3];
float[] yt = new float[7];
String[] names = new String[50];
```

You can even declare, allocate, and initialize an array at the same time by providing a list of the initial values inside braces like this:

```
int[] k = {1, 2, 3};
float[] yt = {0.0f, 1.2f, 3.4f, -9.87f, 65.4f,
0.0f, 567.9f};
```

Counting Digits

You saw one example of an array in Chapter 3. Main methods store command-line arguments in an array of Strings called args.

As the second example, consider a class that counts the occurrences of the digits 0–9. For example, you might wish to test the randomness of a random number generator. If a random number generator is truly random, all digits should occur with equal frequency over a sufficiently long period of time.[2]

You will do this by creating an array of ten longs called `ndigit`. The zeroth component of `ndigit` tracks the number of zeros; the first component tracks the numbers of ones, and so forth. Program 9.1 tests Java's random number generator to see if it produces apparently random numbers.

Program 9.1: Test the randomness of a random number generator

```java
import java.util.Random;

class RandomTest {

  public static void main (String args[]) {

    int[] ndigits = new int[10];
    double x;
    int n;

    Random myRandom = new Random();

    // Initialize the array
    for (int i = 0; i < 10; i++) {
      ndigits[i] = 0;
    }

    // Test the random number generator
    // a whole lot
    for (long i=0; i < 100000; i++) {
      // generate a new random number
      // between 0 and 9
      x = myRandom.nextDouble() * 10.0;
```

---

[2] This is only part of a test for randomness. A more realistic test would try to make sure there are no patterns in the digit sequence. For instance, in the decimal expansion of the rational number 123,456,789/999,999,999 = 0.12345678901234567890..., all digits occur with equal frequency and yet this number would hardly be considered random in any sense of the word.

```
      n = (int) x;
      //count the digits in the random number
      ndigits[n]++;
   }


   // Print the results
   for (int i = 0; i < 10; i++) {
      System.out.println(i+": " + ndigits[i]);
   }

}

}
```

Below is one possible output from this program. If you run it, your results should be slightly different. After all, this is supposed to be random. These results are pretty much what you would expect from a reasonably random generator. If you have a fast CPU and some time to spare, try bringing the number of tests up to a billion or so and see if the counts for the different digits get any closer to each other.

```
% java RandomTest
0: 10171
1: 9724
2: 9966
3: 10065
4: 9989
5: 10132
6: 10001
7: 10158
8: 9887
9: 9907
%
```

There are three `for` loops in Program 9.1: one to initialize the array, one to perform the desired calculation, and a final one to print out the results. This is quite common in code that uses arrays.

System.arraycopy

Although copying an array isn't particularly difficult, it is an operation that benefits from a native implementation. Therefore, java.lang.System includes an arraycopy method you can use to copy one array to another.

The syntax is simple:

```
System.arraycopy(Array src, int src_position,
    Array dst, int dst_position, int n)
```

System.arraycopy copies n elements from the array src, beginning with the element at src_position, to the array dst starting at dst_position. The destination array must already exist when arraycopy is called. The method does not create it. The src and dst arrays must be of the same type.

Multidimensional Arrays

So far, all these arrays have been one dimensional. That is, a single number could locate any value in the array. However, sometimes data is naturally represented by more than one number. For instance, a position on the Earth requires a latitude and a longitude.

The most common kind of multidimensional array is the two-dimensional array. If you think of a one-dimensional array as a column of values, you can think of a two-dimensional array as a table of values, as shown in Figure 9.2.

This is an array with five rows and four columns. It has a total of 20 components. This array is not the same as a five-by-four array like the one shown in Figure 9.3.

Two numbers are required to identify a position in a two-dimensional array. These are the component's row and column positions. For instance, if the array in Figure 9.3 is called J, then J[0][0] is 0, J[0][1] is 1, J[0][2] is 2, J[0][3] is 3, J[1][0] is 1, and so on.

Figure 9.4 shows how the components in a four-by-five array called M are referred to.

	column 0	column 1	column 2	column 3
row 0	0	1	2	3
row 1	1	2	3	4
row 2	2	3	4	5
row 3	3	4	5	6
row 4	4	5	6	7

Figure 9.2: A two-dimensional array of ints with five rows and four columns where each component is given by a sum of the indexes

	column 0	column 1	column 2	column 3	column 4
row 0	0	1	2	3	4
row 1	1	2	3	4	5
row 2	2	3	4	5	6
row 3	3	4	5	6	7

Figure 9.3: A two-dimensional array of ints with four rows and five columns

Declaring, Allocating, and Initializing Two-Dimensional Arrays

Two-dimensional arrays are declared, allocated, and initialized much like one-dimensional arrays. However, you have to specify two dimensions rather than one and you typically use two nested for loops to fill the array.

M[0][0]	M[0][1]	M[0][2]	M[0][3]	M[0][4]
M[1][0]	M[1][1]	M[1][2]	M[1][3]	M[1][4]
M[2][0]	M[2][1]	M[2][2]	M[2][3]	M[2][4]
M[3][0]	M[3][1]	M[3][2]	M[3][3]	M[3][4]

Figure 9.4: *Indexes for a four by five array M*

The array examples above were filled with the sum of their row and column indices. Program 9.2 creates and fills such an array.

Program 9.2: Fill a two-dimensional array with the sum of the row and column indexes

```java
class FillArray {

  public static void main (String args[]) {

    int[][] M;
    M = new int[4][5];

    for (int row=0; row < 4; row++) {
      for (int col=0; col < 5; col++) {
        M[row][col] = row+col;
      }
    }

  }

}
```

Of course the algorithm you use to fill the array depends completely on the use to which the array is to be put. Program 9.3 calculates the identity matrix for a given dimension. The identity matrix of dimension *N* is a square matrix which contains ones along the diagonal and zeros in all other positions.

```java
class IDMatrix {

  public static void main (String args[]) {

    double[][] ID;
    ID = new double[4][4];

    for (int row=0; row < 4; row++) {
      for (int col=0; col < 4; col++) {
        if (row != col) {
          ID[row][col]=0.0;
        }
        else {
          ID[row][col] = 1.0;
        }
      }
    }

  }

}
```

In two-dimensional arrays, ArrayIndexOutOfBoundsExceptions occur whenever you exceed the maximum column index or row index.

You can also declare, allocate, and initialize a two-dimensional array at the same time by providing a list of the initial values inside nested brackets. For instance the three-by-three identity matrix could be set up like this:

```java
double[][] ID3 = {
  {1.0, 0.0 , 0.0},
  {0.0, 1.0, 0.0},
  {0.0, 0.0, 1.0}
};
```

The spacing and the line breaks used above are purely for the programmer. The compiler doesn't care. The following works equally well:

```java
double[][] ID3 = {{1.0, 0.0, 0.0},{0.0, 1.0, 0.0},
  {0.0, 0.0, 1.0}};
```

Even Higher Dimensions

You don't have to stop with two-dimensional arrays. Java permits arrays of three, four, or more dimensions. However, chances are pretty good that if you need more than three dimensions in an array, you're using the wrong data structure. Even three-dimensional arrays are exceptionally rare outside of scientific and engineering applications.

The syntax for three-dimensional arrays is a direct extension of that for two-dimensional arrays. Program 9.4 declares, allocates, and initializes a three-dimensional array. The array is filled with the sum of its indexes.

Program 9.4: Fill a three-dimensional array with the sum of the row and column indexes

```java
class Fill3DArray {

  public static void main (String args[]) {

    int[][][] M;
    M = new int[4][5][3];

    for (int row=0; row < 4; row++) {
      for (int col=0; col < 5; col++) {
        for (int ver=0; ver < 3; ver++) {
          M[row][col][ver] = row+col+ver;
        }
      }
    }

  }

}
```

You need the additional nested `for` loop to handle the extra dimension. The syntax for still higher dimensions is similar. Just add another pair of brackets and another dimension.

Unbalanced Arrays

Like C, Java does not have true multidimensional arrays. Java fakes multidimensional arrays using arrays of arrays. This means that it is possible to have unbalanced arrays. An unbalanced array is a multi-dimensional array where the dimension isn't the same for all rows. In most applications this is a horrible idea and should be avoided.

Searching

One common task is searching an array for a specified value. Sometimes the value is known in advance. Other times you want to know the largest or smallest component of the array.

Unless you have some special knowledge of the contents of the array, for instance, that it is sorted, the quickest algorithm for searching an array is a straightforward linear search. Use a `for` loop to look at every component of the array until you find the component you want. Here's a simple method that prints the largest and smallest components of an array:

```java
public static void
printLargestAndSmallestcomponents (int[] n) {

  int max = n[0];
  int min = n[0];

  for (int i=1; i < n.length; i++) {
    if (max < n[i]) {
      max = n[i];
```

```
    }
    if (min > n[i]) {
      min = n[i];
    }
  }

  System.out.println("Maximum: " + max);
  System.out.println("Minimum: " + min);

  return;

}
```

If you're going to search an array many times, you may want to sort the array before searching it. Then by knowing the largest and smallest elements you can interpolate a reasonable starting guess for the position of any value in the array. Sorting algorithms are the subject of the next section.

Sorting

All sorting algorithms rely on two fundamental operations: comparison and swapping. Comparison is straightforward. Swapping is a little more complex. Consider the following problem. You want to swap the value of a and b. Many novices propose something like Program 9.5 as the solution.

Program 9.5: An incorrect swapping algorithm

```
class Swap1 {

  public static void main(String args[]) {

    int a = 1;
    int b = 2;

    System.out.println("a = " + a);
    System.out.println("b = " + b);
```

```
// swap a and b

a = b;
b = a;

System.out.println("a = " + a);
System.out.println("b = " + b);


  }
}
```

This produces the following output:

```
a = 1
b = 2
a = 2
b = 2
```

That isn't what you expected! The problem is that you lost the original value of a when you put the value of b into a. To correct this, you need to introduce a third variable, temp, to hold the original value of a.

Program 9.6: A correct swapping algorithm

```
class Swap2 {

  public static void main(String args[]) {

    int a = 1;
    int b = 2;
    int temp;

    System.out.println("a = " + a);
    System.out.println("b = " + b);

    // swap a and b

    temp = a;
    a = b;
    b = temp;

    System.out.println("a = " + a);
```

```
      System.out.println("b = " + b);

   }

}
```

This program produces the output you expect:

a = 1

b = 2

a = 2

b = 1

Bubble Sort

Now that you know how to swap the values of two variables properly, let's proceed to sorting. There are many different sorting algorithms. One of the simplest and the most popular algorithms is called the **bubble sort**.

Start at the top of the array. Compare each component to the next component. If it is greater than the next component, then swap the two. Pass through the array as many times as necessary to sort it. The smallest value bubbles up to the top of the array while the largest value sinks to the bottom. (You could equally well call it a sink sort, but then nobody would know what you were talking about.) Program 9.7 demonstrates this by filling an array with ten random numbers and then sorting them.

Program 9.7: Bubble Sort

```java
import java.util.Random;

class BubbleSort {

  public static void main(String args[]) {
```

```
int[] n;
n = new int[10];
Random myRand = new Random();

// initialize the array
for (int i = 0; i < 10; i++) {
  n[i] = myRand.nextInt();
}

// print the array's initial order
System.out.println("Before sorting:");
for (int i = 0; i < 10; i++) {
  System.out.println("n["+i+"] = " + n[i]);
}

boolean sorted = false;
// sort the array
while (!sorted) {
  sorted = true;
  for (int i=0; i < 9; i++) {
    if (n[i] > n[i+1]) {
      int temp = n[i];
      n[i] = n[i+1];
      n[i+1] = temp;
      sorted = false;
    }
  }
}

// print the sorted array
System.out.println();
System.out.println("After sorting:");
  for (int i = 0; i < 10; i++) {
    System.out.println("n["+i+"] = " + n[i]);
  }

}
```

This program sorts the array in ascending order, smallest component first. It would be easy to change it to sort in descending order.

Q&A

 Q: *I've heard about elements of an array. What are those?*

A: Elements is just another word for components. Some languages, notably Fortran, prefer to speak about elements whereas in Java the preferred term is component.

 Q: *What's the maximum number of components an array can have?*

A: Array indexes are `int`s. Therefore an array index can range from 0 to 2,147,483,647 for a theoretical limit for a one-dimensional array of 2,147,483,648 total components. In practice, you'd almost certainly run out of memory before you were finished allocating such a large array.

 Quiz

1. What's the index of the first component of a 100-component array? of a 200-component array? of a 1024-component array?

2. What's the index of the last component of a 100-component array? of a 200-component array? of a 1024-component array?

3. What's the mininum number of components an array can have?

4. What's the difference between a brace and a bracket?

 Exercises

1. Write a program that randomly fills a three-by-four-by-six array and then prints the largest and smallest values in the array.

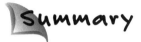 Summary

In this chapter you learned

- How to declare and initialize arrays of varying dimension
- How to search an array
- How to sort an array

You've completed the discussion of basic Java syntax. You now have the knowledge to do just about anything in Java you could do in a traditional language like C or Fortran.

Coming Up

The next part shows you how to write applets that exploit the Java Abstract Window Toolkit (AWT). This will occupy you for the next eight chapters. However after that, you'll return to Java's syntax to explore some more advanced features including exceptions, streams, and threads.

Arrays are the simplest data structure in Java. In Chapter 22, you'll see some more complicated ones including vectors, trees, hash tables, and queues.

Further Reading

Arrays are covered in Chapter 10 of the *Java Language Specification*. This is actually one of the more intelligible sections of that book and you should definitely read it.

Searching and sorting are discussed in great detail in many programming texts. One of the better treatments can be found in

SEDGEWICK, ROBERT, *Algorithms in C++*, New York: Addison Wesley, 1992.

PART TWO

Applets and the AWT

Applet Viewer: Bullseye.class

CHAPTER 10

WRITING YOUR FIRST APPLET

How to include an applet on a Web page

How to write an applet

How to read parameters into an applet from a Web page

How applets are and aren't secure

Until now, the programs in this book have been command-line applications. Command-line applications are useful for many problems, but you can write them in any language. Even though Java's syntax for writing command-line applications is much cleaner and more powerful than most languages', that's not why people are excited about Java.

What excites people about Java are **applets**, interactive secure programs that can be embedded in a Web page. Applets are not the only thing you can write with Java, but they are the only thing you can only write in Java. Therefore, we're going to spend much of this book discussing applets.

A large part of writing real-world programs consists of learning the application programming interface, or API, of the target platform. Knowing the C language backwards and forwards does not mean that you know how to write a Macintosh, Windows, or Motif program in C. There's a lot of information the programmer needs to understand that is almost completely separate from the particular language used to do the programming. Most of that is related to the API. A smaller part is related to understanding the quirks of the host system.

In the next several chapters, you're going to explore the API for Java applets. You'll see how an applet differs from a Java application, and you'll investigate many different methods provided by the Java class library. So far you've only seen a few methods from the class library, most notably println. There are many, many more.

Hello World: The Applet

The reason people are excited about Java as more than just another OOP language is because it allows them to write interactive applets on the Web. HelloWorld isn't a very interactive program, but let's look at a Webbed version.

Program 10.1: The Hello World Applet

```java
import java.applet.Applet;
import java.awt.Graphics;


public class HelloWorldApplet extends Applet {

  public void paint(Graphics g) {
    g.drawString("Hello world!", 50, 25);
  }

}
```

The applet version of HelloWorld is a little more complicated than the HelloWorld application of Chapter 2, and it will take a little more effort to run it as well.

First, type in the source code and save it into file called HelloWorldApplet.java. Compile this file in the usual way. If all is well, a file called HelloWorldApplet.class will be created. Now you need to create an HTML file that will include your applet. The following simple HTML file will do:

```
<HTML>
<HEAD>
<TITLE> Hello World </TITLE>
</HEAD>

<BODY>

This is the applet:<P>
<applet code="HelloWorldApplet.class" width="200"
height="200">
</applet>
</BODY>
</HTML>
```

Save this file as HelloWorldApplet.html in the same directory as the HelloWorldApplet.class file. When you've done that, load the HTML file into a Java-enabled browser like Netscape 2.0 or the Applet Viewer. You should see something like Figure 10.1, though of course the exact details depend on which browser you use.

If the applet compiled without error and produced a HelloWorldApplet.class file, and yet you don't see the string "Hello World" in your browser, chances are that the .class file is in the wrong place. Make sure HelloWorldApplet.class is in the same directory as HelloWorld.html. Also make sure that you're using a version of Netscape which supports Java. Not all versions do. In any case, Netscape's Java support is less than perfect so if you have trouble with an applet, the first thing to try is loading it into Sun's Applet Viewer instead. If the Applet Viewer has a problem, then chances are pretty good the problem is with the applet and not with the browser. Figure 10.2 shows the Hello World applet running in the Applet Viewer. In the interest of saving paper, the rest of the applets in this book will be shown running in Applet Viewer.

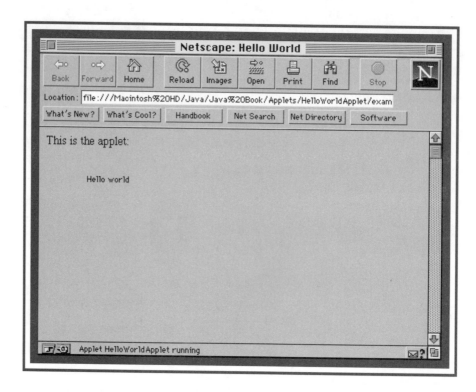

Figure 10.1: *The Hello World applet in Netscape 2.0*

Figure 10.2: *The Hello World applet in Sun's Applet Viewer*

Examining the Hello World Applet

The Hello World applet adds several things to what you saw in the Hello World application. Moving from top to bottom, the first thing you notice is the two lines

```
import java.applet.Applet;
import java.awt.Graphics;
```

These two lines import the public classes java.applet.Applet and java.awt.Graphics. Depending on the phase of the moon, awt stands for "advanced window toolkit," "applet window toolkit," "abstract window toolkit" or "another window toolkit." You'll see a lot more of it.

The next change from the application is the class definition:

```
public class HelloWorldApplet extends Applet
```

All applets must be public. HelloWorldApplet extends the java.applet.Applet class; or, to put it another way, HelloWorldApplet is a subclass of java.applet.Applet. The Applet class is defined in the java.applet.Applet class which is imported so it's not necessary to spell out java.applet.Applet in the code. Applet alone is sufficient. Since HelloWorldApplet is a subclass of the Applet class, the HelloWorldApplet automatically inherits all the functionality of the generic Applet class. Anything an applet can do, the HelloWorldApplet can do too.

The simplicity of this applet is an example of the advantages of OOP, particularly inheritance. Applets need to do a lot of things including handling mouse clicks, starting and stopping, processing keyboard input, updating the screen, and any of two dozen other things. However, you don't have to write the code to do any of this. As long as you're willing to accept the default behavior of an applet, you can reuse the code Java's designers kindly wrote and included in the class java.applet.Applet. If you do want your applet to have its own unique behavior in one or more of these areas, you can override the default methods.

The next difference between the Hello World applet and the HelloWorld application is far less obvious (except maybe to a long-time C programmer). There's no main method! Applets don't need them. The main method is actually in the browser or the Applet

Viewer, not in the applet itself. Applets are like plug-in code modules for Adobe Photoshop that provide extra functionality, but can't run without a main program to host them.

```
public void paint(Graphics g) {
```

HelloWorldApplet has one method, paint(Graphics g). Any applet that draws on the screen needs a paint method. This is where all drawing takes place. The applet host (either a Web browser or Applet Viewer) calls the applet's paint method whenever a part of the applet's visible area is uncovered and needs to be drawn again. You don't need to worry about the details of when the paint method is called. You just need to be ready to respond to it.

The paint method has one argument, a Graphics object, here called g. The Graphics class is defined in the java.awt.Graphics package, which was imported in the second line of the program. java.awt.Graphics contains a number of methods for drawing text, lines, circles, and other things on the screen. Within the paint method, g's drawString method is called to draw the string "Hello World!" at the coordinates (50, 25). That's 50 pixels across and 25 pixels down from the upper-left-hand corner of the applet. Coordinate systems will be covered in more detail in the next chapter.

The <APPLET> HTML Tag

Applets are embedded in Web pages using the <APPLET> and </APPLET> tags. The <APPLET> tag is similar to the <IMG> tag. Like <IMG>, <APPLET> references a source file that is not part of the HTML page on which it is embedded. IMGs do this with the SRC attribute. APPLET's do this with the CODE attribute. The CODE attribute tells the browser where to look for the compiled .class file. It is relative to the location of the source document. Thus if you're browsing http://sunsite.unc.edu/javafaq/index.html and that page references an applet with CODE="animation.class," then the file animation.class should be at the URL http://sunsite.unc.edu/javafaq/animation.class.

For reasons that remain a mystery to HTML authors everywhere, if the applet resides somewhere other than the same directory as the page it lives on, you don't just give a URL to its location. Rather you point at the CODEBASE. The CODEBASE attribute is a URL that points at the directory where the .class file is. The CODE attribute is the name of the .class file itself. For instance, if on the HTML page of the previous section you had written

```
<applet code="HelloWorldApplet.class"
CODEBASE="classes" width=200 height=200>
```

then the browser would have tried to find HelloWorldApplet.class in the classes directory in the same directory as the HTML page that included the applet. On the other hand, if you had written

```
<applet code="HelloWorldApplet.class"
CODEBASE="http://www.foo.bar.com/classes"
width=200 height=200>
```

then the browser would try to retrieve the applet from http://www.foo.bar.com/classes/HelloWorldApplet.class regardless of where the HTML page was.

In short, the applet viewer will try to retrieve the applet from the URL given by the formula (CODEBASE + "/" + code). Once this URL is formed, all the usual rules about relative and absolute URL's apply.

Also like IMG, APPLET has several attributes to define how the applet is positioned on the page. HEIGHT and WIDTH attributes work exactly as they do with IMG, specifying how big a rectangle the browser should set aside for the applet. These numbers are specified in pixels. ALIGN also works exactly as for images defining how the applet's rectangle is placed on the page relative to other elements. Possible values include LEFT, RIGHT, TOP, TEXTTOP, MIDDLE, ABSMIDDLE, BASELINE, BOTTOM, and ABSBOTTOM. As with IMG, you can specify an HSPACE and a VSPACE in pixels to set the amount of blank space between an applet and the surrounding text.

Finally, also like IMG, APPLET has an ALT attribute. As of this writing ALT has not yet been implemented in any browsers. An ALT attribute is used by a browser that understands the APPLET tag but for some reason cannot play the applet. For instance, if an applet needs to write a file on your hard drive, but your preferences are set not to allow that, then the browser should display the ALT text.

> **Tip Choosing the Right Size for an Applet**
>
> Unlike images, applets don't often have a preset size. However, you will find that they look better at one size than another. To avoid lots of editing of the HTML file as you go back and forth trying to find the perfect size for an applet, just run it in Sun's Applet Viewer, size the applet until it looks best., and then select Tag from the Applet menu. A window will pop up that shows an <APPLET> HTML tag for this applet, including the current size, as shown in Figure 10.3.

ALT is not used by browsers that do not understand APPLET at all. For that purpose, APPLET has been defined to require a closing tag, </APPLET>. All raw text between the opening and closing APPLET tags is ignored by a Java-capable browser. However, a non-Java-capable browser will ignore the APPLET tags instead and read the text between them. For example, the following HTML fragment says Hello to people both with and without Java-capable browsers:

```
<applet code="HelloWorldApplet.class" width=200
height=200>
Hello World<P>
</applet>
```

Finding the Applet's Size

When running inside a Web browser, the size of an applet is set by the Height and Width attributes and cannot be changed by the applet. Many applets need to know their own size. After all, you don't want to draw outside the lines. Retrieving the applet size is straightforward with the size() method. size() returns a Dimension object. A Dimension object has two public int fields: height and width. Program 10.2 is a simple applet that prints its own dimensions.

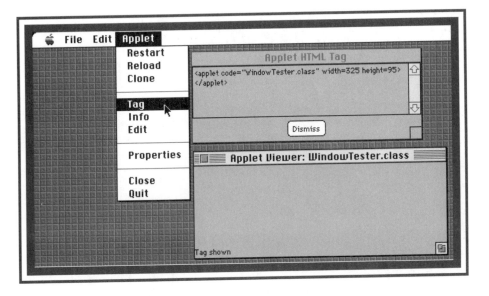

Figure 10.3 *Picking a size for an applet*

Program 10.2: An applet that knows how big it is

```
//Print out the applet's size

import java.applet.Applet;
import java.awt.Graphics;
import java.awt.Dimension;


public class getSizeApplet extends Applet {

  public void paint(Graphics g) {

    Dimension d = size();
    int AppletHeight = d.height;
    int AppletWidth = d.width;

    g.drawString("This applet is " +
      AppletHeight + " pixels high by " +
      AppletWidth + " pixels wide.",
      15, AppletHeight/2);

  }

}
```

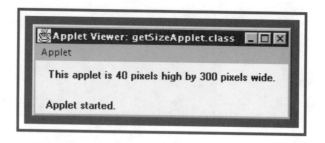

Figure 10.4: *An applet that knows its size*

Figure 10.4 shows the result.

Note how the applet's height is used to decide where to draw the text in Program 10.2. You'll often want to use the applet's dimensions to determine how to place objects on the page. The AppletWidth wasn't used because it made more sense to left-justify the text rather than center it. In other programs, you'll have occasion to use the AppletWidth too.

Passing Parameters to Applets

As well as providing alternate text for non-Java-capable browsers, the area between the opening and closing APPLET tags is used to pass parameters to applets. This is done with the PARAM HTML tag and the getParameter method of the java.applet.Applet class. Program 10.3 demonstrates this with a generic string-drawing applet. The applet parameter "Message" is the string to be drawn.

Program 10.3: An applet that is configurable through a parameter

```
import java.applet.Applet;
import java.awt.Graphics;

public class DrawStringApplet extends Applet {

  String input_from_page;
```

```
public void init() {
    input_from_page = getParameter("Message");
}

public void paint(Graphics g) {
    g.drawString(input_from_page, 50, 25);
}

}
```

You also need an HTML file that references your applet. The following simple HTML file will do:

```
<HTML>
<HEAD>
<TITLE> Draw String </TITLE>
</HEAD>

<BODY>

This is the applet:<P>

<APPLET code="DrawStringApplet.class" width="350"
height="100">
<PARAM name="Message" value="Howdy, there!">
This page will be very boring if your
browser doesn't understand Java.
</APPLET>
</BODY>
</HTML>
```

Figure 10.5 shows the result.

Of course you are free to change "Howdy, there!" to a "message" of your choice. You only need to change the HTML, not the Java source code. PARAMs let you customize applets without changing or recompiling the code.

This applet is very similar to the Hello World applet. However, rather than hard-coding the message to be printed, it's read into the field input_from_page from a PARAM in the HTML. This happens in a new applet method, init(). init() is the first method run by an applet when a Web browser starts it up. This is where execution of your program begins. It's a good place to do any setup necessary for the rest of the program such as initializing fields.

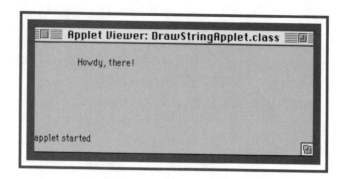

Figure 10.5: *The DrawStringApplet*

In this applet, there is one field to initialize: `input_from_page`. You do this with the `getParameter` method. Pass `getParameter` a String that names the parameter you want. This String should match the name of a PARAM tag in the HTML page. `getParameter` returns the value of the parameter. All values are passed as Strings. If you want to get another type, such as an integer, then you'll need to pass it as a String and convert it to the type you really want using the methods of Chapter 4.

The PARAM HTML tag is also straightforward. It occurs between <APPLET> and </APPLET>. It has two attributes of its own: NAME and VALUE. NAME identifies which PARAM this is. VALUE is the value of the PARAM as a String. Both should be enclosed in double-quote marks if they contain white space.

An applet is not limited to one PARAM. You can pass as many named PARAMs to an applet as you want. An applet does not necessarily need to use all the PARAMs that are in the HTML. Additional PARAMs can be safely ignored.

Processing an Unknown Number Of Parameters

Most of the time you have a fairly good idea of what parameters will and won't be passed to your applet. However, some of the time there will be an undetermined number of parameters. For instance, Sun's imagemap applet passes each "hot button" as a parameter. Different imagemaps have different numbers of hot buttons. Another applet might want to pass a series of URLs to different sounds to be played in sequence. Each URL could be passed as a separate parameter.

Or perhaps you want to write an applet that displays several lines of text. While it would be possible to cram all this information into one long string, that's not too friendly to authors who want to use your applet on their pages. It's much more sensible to give each line its own PARAM tag. If this is the case, you should name the tags via some predictable and numeric scheme. For instance, in the text example, the following set of PARAM tags would be sensible:

```
<PARAM name="Line1" value="There once was a man
from Japan">

<PARAM name="Line2" value="Whose poetry never
would scan">

<PARAM name="Line3" value="When asked reasons
why,">

<PARAM name="Line4" value="He replied, with a
sigh:">

<PARAM name="Line5" value="I always try to get as
many syllables into the last line as I can.">
```

Program 10.4 prints this limerick. Lines are accumulated into an array of Strings called poem. A for loop fills the array with the different lines of poetry. There are 101 spaces in the array, but since you won't normally need that many, an if clause tests to see whether the attempt to get a parameter was successful by checking to see if the line is null. As soon as one fails, the loop is broken. Once the loop is finished, num_lines is set to i − 1, the number of lines that have been successfully read.

The paint method loops through the poem array and prints each String on the screen, incrementing the y position by 15 pixels each step so you don't draw one line on top of the other.

Program 10.4: A Poetry applet that processes an unknown number of parameters

```java
import java.applet.Applet;
import java.awt.Graphics;

public class PoetryApplet extends Applet {

    String[] poem;
    int numlines = 101;
```

```
public void init() {

    int i;
    String nextline;
    poem = new String[numlines];

    for (i = 1; i < numlines; i++) {
        nextline = getParameter("Line" + i);
        if (nextline == null) break;
        poem[i] = nextline;
    }
    numlines = i-1;

}

public void paint(Graphics g) {

    int y = 15;

    for (int i=1; i <= numlines; i++) {
        g.drawString(poem[i], 5, y);
        y += 15;
    }

}
}
```

Figure 10.6 shows the result.

Applet Security

The possibility of surfing the Net, wandering across a random page, playing an applet, and catching a virus is a fear that has scared many uninformed people away from Java. This fear has also driven a lot of the development of Java in the direction it's gone. Chapter 1 discussed various security features of Java, including automatic garbage collection, the elimination of pointer arithmetic, and the Java interpreter. These serve the dual purpose of making the language simple for programmers and secure for users. You can surf the Web without

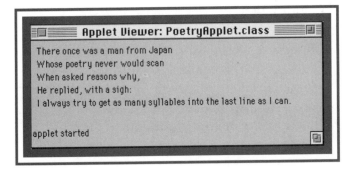

Figure 10.6: *The Poetry Applet*

What You Can't Do

You might think it would be useful to be able to process an arbitrary list of parameters without knowing their names in advance, if nothing else so you could return an error message to the page designer. Unfortunately, there's no way to do it in Java 1.0. It may be possible in future versions.

worrying that a Java applet will format your hard disk or introduce a virus into your system.

In fact, both Java applets and applications are much safer in practice than code written in traditional languages. This is because even code from trusted sources is likely to have bugs. However, Java programs are much less susceptible to common bugs involving memory access than are programs written in traditional languages like C. Furthermore, the Java runtime environment provides a fairly robust means of trapping bugs before they bring down your system. Most users have many more problems with bugs than they do with deliberately malicious code. Although users of Java applications aren't protected from out-and-out malicious code, they are largely protected from programmer errors.

Applets implement additional security restrictions that protect users from malicious code too. This is accomplished through the java.lang.SecurityManager class. This class is subclassed to provide different security environments in different virtual machines. Regrettably, implementing this additional level of protection does somewhat restrict the actions an applet can perform. Let's explore exactly what an applet can and cannot do.

What Can an Applet Do?

An applet can

- Draw pictures on a Web page
- Create a new window and draw in it
- Play sounds
- Receive input from the user through the keyboard or the mouse.
- Make a network connection to the server from which it came and send and receive arbitrary data from that server.

Anything you can do with these abilities you can do in an applet. An applet cannot

- Write data on any of the host's disks without the user's permission. In some environments, notably Netscape, an applet cannot write data on the user's hard drive even with permission.
- Read any data from the host's disks without the user's permission. In some environments, notably Netscape, an applet cannot read data from the user's disks even with permission.
- Delete files.
- Read from or write to arbitrary blocks of memory, even on a nonmemory-protected operating system like the MacOS. All memory access is strictly controlled.
- Call the native API directly (though Java API calls may eventually lead back to native API calls).
- Introduce a virus or trojan horse into the host system.
- Crash the host system. However, in practice, Java isn't quite stable enough to make this claim yet.

To Whom Can an Applet Talk?

By default, an applet can only open network connections to the system from whence the applet came. It cannot talk to an arbitrary system on the Internet. Any communication between different client systems must be mediated through the server.

The concern is that if connections to arbitrary hosts were allowed, then a malicious applet might be able to make connections to other systems and launch network-based attacks on other machines in an organization's internal network. This would be an especially large problem because the machines inside a firewall may be configured to trust each other more than they would trust any random machine from the Internet. If the internal network is properly protected by a firewall, this might be the only way an external machine could even talk to an internal machine. Furthermore, arbitrary network connections would allow crackers to more easily hide their true location by passing their attacks through several applet intermediaries.

HotJava and Sun's Applet Viewer (but not Netscape) let you grant applets permission to open connections to any system on the Internet, though this is not enabled by default. Several people have used this functionality to create white board applets and networked games that allow multiple people to talk to each other.

How Much CPU Time Does an Applet Get?

As of this writing, one of the few legitimate concerns about hostile applets is excessive use of CPU time. It is possible on a non-preemptively multitasking system (specifically the Mac) to write an applet that uses so much CPU time in a tight loop that it effectively locks up the host system. This is not a problem on preemptively multitasking systems like Solaris and Windows NT. Even on those platforms, though, it is possible for an applet to force the user to kill their web browser, possibly losing accumulated bookmarks, email, and other work.[1]

It's also possible for an applet to use CPU time for purposes other than the apparent intent of the applet. For instance, a popular applet

The Chinese Lottery

Suppose the Chinese government has an encrypted file they want to decrypt. Let's further assume this file has only a one-in-a-billion chance of being decrypted in an hour's time using a conventional computer that chooses keys at random. This is not an unreasonable estimate for certain kinds of encryption, especially DES (Data Encryption Standard). Now let's suppose the government sells everyone in China a television set that has a special processor designed to break the encryption of encrypted files. They can broadcast the encrypted file along with the nightly news. All one billion televisions go to work decrypting the file. Whichever one succeeds displays the key on the screen along with a message saying that the owners have won the lottery and should write the key down and bring it to their local police station to claim the prize. A problem that is effectively unsolvable by normal computers becomes easily solvable by one billion computers.

When I first read about the proposed Chinese television super-parallel computer, it seemed a little far-fetched, even for an authoritarian society like China. However, as I write this, the U.S. Congress is debating a bill which would require every new television in America to contain a special V-chip that lets parents block out violent programs. Consumers would be forced to pay extra for this chip whether they wanted it or not. Television stations would be required to broadcast V-chip info whether they wanted to or not. The Chinese lottery suddenly seems a little less far-fetched.

could launch a Chinese lottery attack on a Unix password file. A popular game applet could launch a thread in the background that tried a random assortment of keys to break an encrypted file. If the key were found, then a network connection could be opened to the applet server to send the decryption key back. The more popular the applet was, the faster the key would be found. The ease with which Java applets are decompiled would probably mean that any such applet would be discovered, but there really isn't a way to prevent it from running in the first place.

There's an upside too. Some advances in data encryption and many other fields have been made in recent years by splitting tasks across multiple computers. Before Java, this required a network of computers, all running the same operating system, and all more or less had to trust each other. Now these same programs can be written in Java, and anyone who wants to participate in a particular project (for example predicting hurricane formation in the Gulf of Mexico in 1998) can just point their web browser at a web page that contains the hurricane applet. Each of these cooperating computers will get its own small piece of the problem. This way the power of the millions of computers that don't normally do anything most of the day and at night can be leveraged to solve immensely difficult problems.

User Security Issues and Social Engineering

Contrary to popular belief, most computer break-ins by external hackers don't happen because of great knowledge of operating system internals and network protocols. They happen because a hacker dug through a company's garbage and found a piece of paper with a password written on it, or perhaps because they talked to a low-level bureaucrat on the phone, convinced this person they were from the local data processing department, and that they needed him or her to change their password to "DEBUG."

This sort of attack is called **social engineering**. Java applets introduce a new path for social engineering. For instance, imagine an applet that pops up a dialog box that says, "You have lost your

---

[1] In practice this may not be an issue since Netscape, at least, writes this data to disk as it changes, rather than at quit time.

Figure 10.7: *An applet window with a warning message from Netscape 3.0b3*

connection to the network. Please enter your username and password to reconnect." How many people would blindly enter their username and password without thinking? Now what if the box didn't really come from a lost network connection but from a hacker's applet? And instead of reconnecting to the network (a connection that was never lost in the first place), the username and password were sent over the Internet to the cracker? See the problem?

To help prevent this, Java applet windows are specifically labeled as such with an ugly bar that says: "Warning: Applet Window" or "Unsigned Java Applet Window," as shown in Figure 10.7. The exact warning message varies from browser to browser but in any case should be enough to prevent the more obvious attacks on clueless users. It still assumes the user understands what "Unsigned Java Applet Window" means and that they shouldn't type their password or any sensitive information in such a window. User education is the first part of any real security policy.

Content Issues

Some people claim that Java is insecure because it can show the user erotic pictures and play flatulent noises. By this standard, the entire Web is insecure. Java makes no determination of the content of an applet. Any such determination would require artificial intelligence and computers far more powerful than those we have today.

Q&A

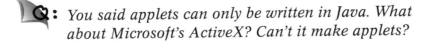

Q: *You said applets can only be written in Java. What about Microsoft's ActiveX? Can't it make applets?*

A: To answer this question, you first have to define what you mean by "applet." While most people think of an applet as either a small application or a program that plays on a Web page, the definition used here is intimately related to security. An applet is an interactive secure program that can be embedded in a Web page.

ActiveX is based around OLE and Visual Basic. Neither of these was designed for execution of potentially malicious code in a secure environment. Although some security can be grafted onto ActiveX, it's a little like attaching a big rig to the back of a Toyota Corolla. The Corolla was never meant to pull such a heavy load and will break down sooner rather than later. Security is similar. It needs to be planned for from the initial design of the language, not grafted on to meet the needs of a press release.

Quiz

1. What happens if you have two PARAMs with the same name but different values?

2. What would be the problems with writing a telnet program as an applet?

3. What would be the biggest problems with trying to write a word processor as an applet?

Exercises

1. Modify Program 10.2 so that it does not need AppletHeight or AppletWidth variables or their equivalents. Hint: you won't need to import java.awt.Dimension either.

2. Assume that each letter occupies a box 15 pixels wide by 15 pixels high. Write an applet which takes a single letter as a parameter and fills the available space with that letter.

3. The PoetryApplet handles at most 100 lines because that is all the space that's been allotted to the poem array. Adjust the PoetryApplet so that it includes a numlines parameter that will set the size of the poem array at runtime.

Summary

In this chapter you learned

- What an applet is
- What an applet's paint method does
- What an applet's init method does
- How to include an applet on an HTML page
- How to read parameters into an applet from the HTML page
- How to process an arbitrary number of parameters
- How applets are and aren't secure

Coming Up

You've just begun to scratch the surface of what's possible in an applet. In the next chapter you'll see how to draw vector-based graphics in an applet including lines, circles, rectangles and polygons. You'll also learn many more details about drawing text including fonts, sizes and styles.

In future chapters you'll learn how to write applets that respond to user input and create their own windows, menu bars and more.

Further Reading

If you need some brush-up work on HTML, check out the *Beginner's Guide to HTML* at

http://www.ncsa.uiuc.edu/General/Internet/WWW/HTMLPrimer.html

For more information about Java security, see the Java Secutiry FAQ at

http://www.javasoft.com/java.sun.com/sfaq/index.html

Also see the applet security FAQ at

http://www.javasoft.com/sfaq/

For the details of the byte code verifier, see

http://www.javasoft.com/sfaq/verifier.html

All the methods of java.applet.Applet are documented at

http://www.javasoft.com/JDK-1.0/api/java.applet.Applet.html

For more details about DES and the Chinese television attack on it, see

SCHNEIER, BRUCE, *Applied Data Encryption*, New York: John Wiley and Sons, 1994, pp. 156–157.

CHAPTER

DRAWING PICTURES

The Java coordinate system

Drawing text in different fonts and colors

Drawing straight and curved lines

Java has a full range of graphics objects and methods that draw rectangles, ovals, lines, polygons, and more. These are all part of the java.awt.Graphics class. Every applet has a graphics context which is an instance of java.awt.Graphics. This object is passed into the paint method where you call its individual methods.

The Java Coordinate System

Before you can begin drawing pretty pictures in Java applets, you need to understand Java's coordinate system. The first thing to note is that the fundamental unit of computer displays is the pixel. A pixel is a dot of phosphor on the screen. Each pixel is a certain color. The choice of colors may range from two (black or white) to as many as 16,000,000 different hues. All computer graphics need to be translated to pixels before they're drawn on the screen.

A typical computer monitor has 640 pixels across and 480 pixels down. Other common resolutions include 832 by 624, 800 by 600 and 1024 by 768. The actual size of a pixel can vary from monitor to monitor depending on the viewable area and the resolution. On a small monitor at a high resolution, everything will look smaller than on a larger monitor at the same resolution.

Because of the variation in monitors, it is hard to specify an exact size of an object in inches or meters. Most of the time you make a rough estimate that an inch equals 72 pixels. However, depending on the monitor, an inch can be as few as 68 pixels or as many as 100.

In a typical windowing system, you generally don't have access to the entire display, but only to some rectangular subset of the display called a window. Within the window you have complete control and a separate coordinate system that allows you to draw where you like. The parent window system handles the mapping between your window and the computer display. It also handles window movement so if the user drags your window around the screen none of your variables change. You can even draw outside the window, but nothing you draw there will be displayed.

Figure 11.1 shows the coordinate system for a small window with 100 pixels (ten down and ten across). There are two coordinates, x and y. (0,0) is the top left pixel. x increases to the right and y increases downwards. Since both start at 0, x and y range from 0 to 9. A particular pixel is identified by giving its x coordinate and its y coordinate.

The choice of the letters x and y is arbitrary. They could be swapped or replaced with two completely different variables, and it wouldn't change the final results at all. However x and y are what most computer graphics programmers use, including Java programmers; and all the Java documentation uses x and y as they're used

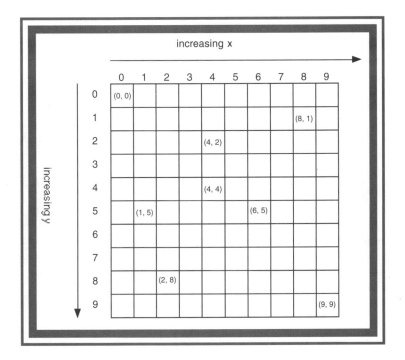

Figure 11.1: *The Java coordinate system*

here. This convention will be followed in the rest of this book without further comment.

Drawing pictures by turning individual pixels off and on is not an easy task. In fact, there isn't even a command in Java to address an individual pixel.[1] Fortunately, Java (and most other graphics-oriented window systems) provides a series of more abstract commands for drawing lines, circles, text, rectangles, and more. You tell Java what you want to draw and where you want to put it, and the library translates that into pixels.

Graphics Objects

In Java, all drawing takes place via a Graphics object. Graphics is an abstract base class that is a part of many different Java classes including applets. Initially, the Graphics object you use will be the one

---

[1] It is possible to fake it with one-pixel-long lines.

passed as an argument to an applet's paint method. In later chapters you'll see other Graphics objects too. Everything you learn in this chapter about drawing in an applet transfers directly to drawing in other objects like Panels, Frames, Buttons, Canvases, and more.

Each Graphics object has its own coordinate system, and all the methods of Graphics including those for drawing Strings, lines, rectangles, circles, polygons, and more. Drawing in Java starts with a particular Graphics object. You get access to the Graphics object through the `paint(Graphics g)` method of your applet. Each draw method call will look like `g.drawString("Hello World", 0, 50)` where g is the particular Graphics object with which you're drawing.

For convenience's sake in this chapter and the next, g will always refer to a preexisting object of the Graphics class. As with any other method, you are free to use some other name for the particular Graphics context—`myGraphics` or `appletGraphics` perhaps.

Drawing Text

You've already seen one example of drawing text in the Hello World Applet of the last chapter. You call the drawString method of the Graphics object. This method is passed the String you want to draw as well as an x and y coordinate. If g is a Graphics object, then the syntax is

```
g.drawString(String s, int x, int y)
```

The String is simply the text you want to draw. The two integers are the x and y coordinates of the lower-left-hand corner of the String. The String will be drawn above and to the right of this point. However, letters with descenders like y and p may have their descenders drawn below the line.

Working with Fonts

Until now, all the applets have used the default font, probably some variation of Helvetica, though this is platform-dependent. However, Java does allow you to choose your fonts. Java implementations are guaranteed to have the fonts Helvetica, Courier, Times Roman, and Symbol available or some reasonable facsimile thereof. Program 11.1 lists the fonts available on the system it's running on. It does this by using the getFontList method from java.awt.Toolkit. This method returns an array of Strings containing the names of the available fonts. These may or may not be the same as the fonts installed on your system. It is implementation-dependent whether or not all the fonts a system has are available to the applet.

Program 11.1: An applet that shows the available fonts

```java
import java.applet.Applet;
import java.awt.Toolkit;
import java.awt.Graphics;

public class FontList extends Applet {

  String availableFonts[];

  public void init () {

    Toolkit t = Toolkit.getDefaultToolkit();
    availableFonts = t.getFontList();

  }

  public void paint(Graphics g) {

    for (int i=0; i<availableFonts.length; i++) {
      g.drawString(availableFonts[i], 5,
        15*(i+1));
    }
  }
}
```

Figure 11.2a shows this applet running on a Mac. The Mac lists five fonts, Dialog, Helvetica, Courier, Times Roman, and Symbol. The font Times will be substituted for Times Roman on most Macs. Dialog is the font used for Dialogs on the host system, Chicago on Macs. Figure

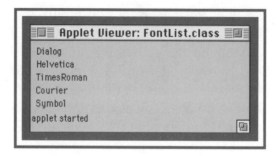

Figure 11.2a: *The available fonts on a Mac*

Figure 11.2b: *The available fonts on Windows 95*

Figure 11.2c: *The available fonts on Solaris*

11.2b shows the same applet on Windows 95. Figure 11.2c shows the same applet on Solaris. Both of these platforms have the fonts Dialog, Helvetica, TimesRoman, Courier, DialogInput and Zapf Dingbats. Dialog and DialogInput are the same font in Windows 95 but different fonts in Solaris.

Choosing a font face is easy. First you create a new Font object; then you call `g.setFont(Font f)`. To instantiate a Font object, use the

```
Font(String name, int style, int size)
```

constructor. name is the name of the font family, e.g. "Helvetica" or "Times Roman." Size is the size of the font in points. In computer graphics, a point is considered to be equal to one pixel. Twelve points is a normal-size font. Fourteen points is probably better on most computer displays. Smaller point sizes look good on paper printed with a high-resolution printer, but not in the lower resolutions of a computer monitor. style is a mnemonic constant from java.awt.Font that tells whether the text will be bold, italic, or plain. The three constants are java.awt.Font.PLAIN, java.awt.Font.BOLD, and java.awt.Font.ITALIC. Program 11.2 is a modification of Program 11.1 that prints each font in its own face and 14-point bold.

Program 11.2: An applet that shows the available fonts in their own faces

```java
import java.applet.Applet;
import java.awt.Toolkit;
import java.awt.Graphics;
import java.awt.Font;


public class FontList extends Applet {

  String availableFonts[];

  public void init () {

    Toolkit t = Toolkit.getDefaultToolkit();
    availableFonts = t.getFontList();

  }

  public void paint(Graphics g) {

    for (int i=0; i<availableFonts.length; i++) {
      Font f = new Font(availableFonts[i],
        Font.BOLD, 14);
      g.setFont(f);
      g.drawString(availableFonts[i], 5,
        15*i + 15);
    }
  }

}
```

Figure 11.3: *The available fonts in 14-point bold*

Figure 11.3 shows the output on the Mac, Windows 95, and Solaris. Since ZapfDingbats wasn't installed on the system where the Solaris screenshot was taken, Helvetica was substituted.

Font Metrics

No word wrapping is done when you draw a String in an applet, even if you embed newlines in the String with \n. If you expect that your String may not fit in the applet, you should probably use a TextArea Component instead. You'll learn about TextAreas and other AWT Components in Chapter 14. However, there are times when you will need to concern yourself with how much space a particular String will occupy. You find this out with a **FontMetrics** object. FontMetrics allow you to determine the height, width, and other useful characteristics of a particular String, character, or array of characters in a particular font. As an example, Program 11.3 expands on the DrawString applet of the previous chapter. Previously, text would run off the side of the page if the String was too long to fit in the applet. Now the String will wrap around if necessary.

In order to tell where and whether to wrap the String, you need to measure the String—not its length in characters but rather its width and height in pixels. Measurements of this sort clearly depend on the font that's used to draw the String. All other things being equal, a 14-point String will be wider than the same String in 12- or 10-point type.

To measure character and String sizes, get a FontMetrics object for the current Graphics object using the `java.awt.Graphics.getFontMetrics()` method. From java.awt.FontMetrics, you'll need `fm.stringWidth(String s)` to return the width of a String in a particular font, and `fm.getLeading()` to get the appropriate line spacing for the font. There are many more methods in java.awt.FontMetrics that let you measure the heights and widths of specific characters as well as ascenders, descenders, and more, but these three methods will be sufficient for this program.

Finally, you'll need the StringTokenizer class from java.util to split up the String into individual words. However, you do need to be careful lest some annoying beta tester (or, worse yet, end user) tries to see what happens when they feed the word antidisestablishmentarianism or supercalifragilisticexpialidocious into an applet that's 50 pixels across.

Program 11.3: An applet that wraps text

```java
import java.applet.Applet;
import java.awt.Graphics;
import java.awt.FontMetrics;
import java.util.StringTokenizer;

public class WrapTextApplet extends Applet {

  String input_from_page;

  public void init() {
    input_from_page = getParameter("Text");
  }
```

```java
public void paint(Graphics g) {
    int i = 0;
    int linewidth = 0;
    int margin = 5;
    StringBuffer sb = new StringBuffer();
    FontMetrics fm = g.getFontMetrics();
    StringTokenizer st = new
        StringTokenizer(input_from_page);

    while (st.hasMoreTokens()) {
        String nextword = st.nextToken();
        if (fm.stringWidth(sb.toString() +
            nextword) < size().width) {
            sb.append(nextword);
            sb.append(' ');
        }
        else if (sb.length() == 0) {
            g.drawString(nextword, margin,
                ++i*fm.getHeight());
        }
        else {
            g.drawString(sb.toString(), margin,
                ++i*fm.getHeight());
            sb = new StringBuffer(nextword + " ");
        }

    }
    if (sb.length() > 0) {
        g.drawString(sb.toString(), margin,
            ++i*fm.getHeight());
    }
}
}
```

Changing Color

Color is a class in the AWT. Individual colors like red or mauve are instances of this class, java.awt.Color. Be sure to import it if you want to use other than the default colors. You create new colors using the same RGB (red-green-blue) triples that you use to set background colors on Web pages. However, you use decimal numbers instead of the hex values used by the <bgcolor> tag. For example, medium gray is Color(127, 127, 127). Pure white is Color(255, 255, 255). Pure red is (255, 0, 0) and so on. As with any variable, you should give your colors descriptive names. For instance,

```
Color medGray = new Color(127, 127, 127);

Color cream = new Color(255, 231, 187);

Color lightGreen = new Color(0, 55, 0);
```

A few of the most common colors are available by name. These are

- `Color.black`
- `Color.blue`
- `Color.cyan`
- `Color.darkGray`
- `Color.gray`
- `Color.green`
- `Color.lightGray`
- `Color.magenta`
- `Color.orange`
- `Color.pink`
- `Color.red`
- `Color.white`
- `Color.yellow`

Color is not a property of a particular rectangle, String, or other thing you may draw. Rather color is a part of the Graphics object that does the drawing. To change colors, you change the color of your Graphics object. Then everything you draw from that point forward will be in the new color, at least until you change it again.

When an applet starts running, the color is set to black by default. You can change this to red by calling `g.setColor(Color.red)`. Then you can change it back to black again by calling `g.setColor(Color.black)`. The following code fragment shows how you'd draw a pink String followed by a green one:

```
g.setColor(Color.pink);

g.drawString("This String is pink!", 50, 25);

g.setColor(Color.green);

g.drawString("This String is green!", 50, 50);
```

Remember, everything you draw after the last line will be drawn in green. Therefore, before you start messing with the color, its a good idea to make sure you can go back to the color you started with. For this purpose, Java provides the getColor() method. You use it as follows:

```
Color oldcolor = g.getColor();
g.setColor(Color.pink);
g.drawString("This String is pink!", 50, 25);
g.setColor(Color.green);
g.drawString("This String is green!", 50, 50);
g.setColor(oldcolor);
```

Drawing Lines

Drawing straight lines with Java is easy. Just call

```
g.drawLine(int x1, int y1, int x2, int y2)
```

where (x1, y1) and (x2, y2) are the endpoints of your lines and g is the Graphics object you're drawing with.

Program 11.4 draws a line diagonally across the applet.

Program 11.4: Draw a diagonal line

```
import java.applet.Applet;
import java.awt.Graphics;

public class SimpleLine extends Applet {

 public void paint(Graphics g) {

    g.drawLine(0, 0, size().width, size().height);

 }

}
```

Figure 11.4 shows the result.

Figure 11.4: *A line.*

Drawing Curved Lines

You can also use the drawLine method to draw non-straight figures. It is shown in advanced calculus that any reasonably well behaved function can be approximated arbitrarily well by straight lines where quantities like "well behaved" and "arbitrarily" are precisely defined. I'll spare you the details of the mathematical proof, but I will demonstrate its probability by showing how you can graph almost any function using only straight lines.

The key to the trick is to break the image up into many small straight lines. For instance, Figure 11.5 shows a semicircle approximated by varying numbers of lines.

As you can see, by the time you use eight line segments, you've got a pretty good approximation to the semicircle. With Java, it's easy to use not just eight but hundreds of line segments. In fact, you can draw one line segment between every two consecutive pixels.

As an example, Program 11.5 draws a sine wave from the left-hand side of the applet to the right-hand side.

Program 11.5: A sine wave

```
import java.applet.Applet;
import java.awt.Graphics;
import java.awt.Dimension;
```

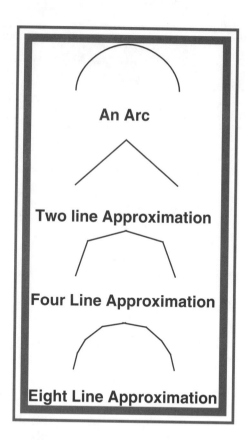

Figure 11.5: *Different straight line approximations to a semicircle*

```java
public class SineApplet extends Applet {

  public void paint(Graphics g) {

    int x0 = 0;
    int xN = size().width-1;
    int y0=0;
    int yN=size().height-1;

    for (int x = x0; x < xN; x++) {
      g.drawLine(x,(int)(yN*Math.sin(x)), x+1,
      (int) (yN*Math.sin(x+1)));
    }

  }

}
```

Figure 11.6: *A sine wave*

The meat of this applet is in the `for` loop of the paint method.

```
for (int x = x0; x < xN; x++) {
    g.drawLine(x,(int) (yN*Math.sin(x)),x+1,
    (int) (yN*Math.sin(x+1)));
}
```

This loops across every x coordinate in the applet. The sine of each point is calculated. At the same time, the sine of the next pixel is calculated. This gives two 2-D points and a line is drawn between them. Since the sine of a real number is always between one and negative one, the y value is scaled by the height of the applet. Finally the y values are cast to `ints` since Math.sine returns a floating-point number but drawLine requires an `int`. Figure 11.6 shows the results.

This applet runs, but it's got a lot of problems. All of them can be related to two factors:

1. Sines are floating-point operations. To create a really useful graphing applet, you need to use floating-point numbers.

2. The coordinate system of an applet counts from (0,0) at the upper-left-hand corner to the right and down. The standard Cartesian coordinate system you expect graphs to use counts from (0,0) in the lower-left-hand corner to the right and up. The origin can be moved in both systems, for instance to the center of the applet, but you still need to transform between the y down and the y up coordinates.

There are several ways to resolve this. The key to all of them, however, is to separate the data from the display. Since you are graphing a well-behaved mathematical function, you may assume that the data is completely described by a rectangle in Cartesian space within which you wish to plot a function. The display, on the other hand, is described by a rectangle of discrete points of fixed size and width. You need to calculate in the general Cartesian plane and display in the particular applet window.

To do this you need a program that converts a point in the applet window into a point in the Cartesian plane, and one that converts it back. Program 11.6 is it.

Program 11.6: A nicer sine wave

```java
import java.applet.Applet;
import java.awt.Graphics;

public class SineApplet extends Applet {

  public void paint(Graphics g) {

    int i, j1, j2;

    j1 = yvalue(0);
    for (i = 0; i < size().width; i++) {
      j2 = yvalue(i+1);
      g.drawLine(i, j1 ,i+1, j2);
      j1 = j2;
    }

  }

  // Given an xpoint calculate
  // the Cartesian equivalent
  private int yvalue(int ivalue)  {

    double xmin = -10.0;
    double xmax =  10.0;
    double ymin = -1.0;
    double ymax =  1.0;
    double x, y;
    int jvalue;
```

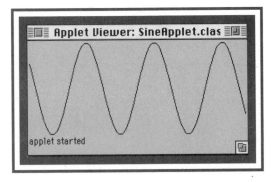

Figure 11.7: *A sine wave*

```
x = (ivalue * (xmax - xmin)/
    (size().width - 1)) + xmin;

// Take the sine of that x
y = Math.sin(x);

// Scale y into window coordinates
jvalue = (int) ((y - ymin) *
    (size().height - 1)/(ymax - ymin));

/* Switch jvalue from Cartesian coordinates
   to computer graphics coordinates */
jvalue = size().height - jvalue;

return jvalue;

    }

}
```

Figure 11.7 shows the output from this applet. Isn't that a much nicer looking sine wave?

This program separates the actual drawing from the logic that decides what lines to draw. This makes it very easy to modify this applet to draw other functions or to change the Cartesian rectangle in which you draw. For instance, to make this applet graph a cosine function just replace `Math.sin(x)` with `Math.cos(x)`.

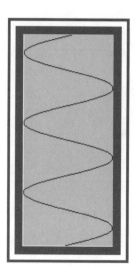

Figure 11.8: *A non-function*

The only real restriction on this applet is that the curved line you draw must be a valid function, that is, each x coordinate must map to exactly one y coordinate. If you wanted to draw a relation that crosses back on itself like Figure 11.8, you would have to change the paint method to loop on y instead of x.

 Q: *How can you draw from outside the paint method?*

A: To draw in an applet, you must have access to that applet's Graphics object. This object is passed into the paint method as an argument and may be passed from there to other methods. You can also use the applet's getGraphics method to get the applet's Graphics object at any point, but this is a rather dangerous thing to do. You should try to keep all drawing inside the paint method if at all possible.

Quiz

1. What happens if you try to draw objects at negative coordinates? For example, `g.drawLine(-5, -4, 64, 50)`?

2. What's the difference between `g.drawLine(0, 1, 5, 6)` and `g.drawLine(5, 6, 0, 1)`?

3. What's the difference between `g.drawLine(0, 1, 5, 6)` and `g.drawLine(1, 0, 6, 5)`?

Exercises

1. Modify the WrapText applet so that it optionally accepts FONT, SIZE, and STYLE PARAMs that set the font face, point size, and style in which the String is drawn. Be sure to gracefully handle the case when the APPLET tag does not include any or all of these PARAMs or includes invalid values (e.g., STYLE="UNDERLINE").

2. The default StringTokenizer used by the WrapText applet breaks words on white space, i.e. spaces, tabs, newlines, and carriage returns. Make it more intelligent about choosing line breaks. In particular, let it break a line on a hyphen and have it jump to the next line (i.e., end a paragraph) on a newline or a carriage return. To do this, you'll need to use a different StringTokenizer constructor, specifically `StringTokenizer(String s, String delimiters)`, where s is the String to tokenize and `delimiters` is a String that contains all the characters you want to break on.

3. If the String won't fit in the applet, even after breaking into pieces, shrink the font size so that it does fit. What's the smallest font size you can use?

4. Add labeled coordinate axes to the SineApplet graph. Make sure they adjust if the applet is resized.

5. Modify the SineApplet so that it looks for xmin, xmax, ymin, and ymax to be specified via parameters. However, for robustness if the author of the HTML forgets to specify them, supply some reasonable default values. You will probably need to make these fields rather than local variables.

Summary

In this chapter you learned

- How the Java coordinate system is structured
- How to draw Strings
- How to draw straight lines
- How to draw curved lines
- How to change the color of the pen
- How to map between Cartesian coordinates and graphic system coordinates

Coming Up

The next chapter continues the explication of graphics as rectangles, ovals, and polygons are added to your toolbox. In Chapter 15, you'll learn a better way to wrap text than drawing text directly.

Further Reading

For a complete listing of the methods of the java.awt.Graphics class, see

http://www.javasoft.com/JDK-1.0/api/java.awt.Graphics.html

For a deeper understanding of general computer graphics including how vector oriented quantities like lines are translated into bitmapped screen displays, the classic text is

FOLEY, JAMES, ANDRIES VAN DAM, STEVEN FEINER, and JOHN HUGHES, *Computer Graphics*, 2nd Ed., New York: Addison-Wesley, 1990.

A somewhat less intimidating text is

HEARN, DONALD and M. PAULINE BAKER, *Computer Graphics*, Englewood Cliffs, NJ: Prentice-Hall, 1994.

Drawing Pictures

CHAPTER 12

RECTANGLES, OVALS, POLYGONS, AND IMAGES

Rectangles and squares

Ovals and circles

Polygons

Bitmapped images

In this chapter, you'll learn about Java's methods to draw two-dimensional shapes including rectangles, squares, ovals, circles, and polygons. These are all part of the java.awt.Graphics class. You'll also learn how to use bitmapped GIF and JPEG images in your applet.

Drawing Rectangles

Drawing rectangles is simple. Start with a Graphics object `g` and call its `drawRect(int left, int top, int width, int height)` method. As the variable names suggest, the first `int` is the left-hand side of the rectangle, the second is the top of the rectangle, the third is the width, and the fourth is the height. This is in contrast to some APIs where the four sides of the rectangle are given.

Program 12.1 uses drawRect to draw a rectangle around the sides of an applet.

Program 12.1: Frame an applet by drawing a rectangle around it

```java
import java.applet.Applet;
import java.awt.Graphics;

public class RectangleApplet extends Applet {

  public void paint(Graphics g) {

    g.drawRect(1, 1, size().width - 1,
      size().height - 1);

  }

}
```

Figure 12.1 shows the result.

Remember that `size().width` is the width of the applet and `size().height` is its height. Why was the rectangle drawn only to `size().height-1` and `size().width-1`? Remember that the upper-left-hand corner of the applet starts at (0, 0), not at (1, 1). This means that a 100-by-200 pixel applet includes the points with x coordinates between 0 and 99, not between 0 and 100. Similarly the y coordinates are between 0 and 199 inclusive, not 0 and 200.

There is no separate drawSquare method. Squares are rectangles with equal length sides, so to draw a square, call drawRect and pass the same number for both the height and width arguments.

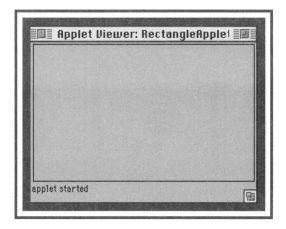

Figure 12.1: *A rectangle*

The drawRect method draws an open rectangle, a box if you prefer. If you want to draw a filled rectangle, use the fillRect method. Otherwise the syntax is identical. Program 12.2 draws a filled square in the center of the applet. This requires you to separate the applet width and height from the rectangle width and height.

Program 12.2: Draw a filled rectangle

```
import java.applet.Applet;
import java.awt.Graphics;

public class FillAndCenter extends Applet {

  public void paint(Graphics g) {

    int AppletHeight = size().height;
    int AppletWidth = size().width;
    int RectHeight = AppletHeight/3;
    int RectWidth = AppletWidth/3;
    int RectTop = (AppletHeight - RectHeight)/2;
    int RectLeft= (AppletWidth - RectWidth)/2;

    g.fillRect(RectTop, RectLeft, RectWidth-1,
      RectHeight-1);

  }
}
```

Figure 12.2: *A filled rectangle*

Figure 12.2 shows the result.

The rectangle is drawn in the current color, black by default. You can change the color of the rectangle by calling `g.setColor` before drawing the rectangle as you did in the last chapter.

It is also possible to clear a rectangle that you've drawn. The syntax is exactly what you'd expect, `g.clearRect(int left, int top, int width, int height)`.

Mondrian

Now that you've learned how to draw rectangles, both filled and unfilled, let's make life a little more exciting. The next example is a small graphics applet that adds a little class to Web pages. This applet is called Mondrian after the painter Piet Mondrian whose style it imitates. Mondrian randomly selects a series of rectangles to be painted on the screen. Each will have a random position, width, height, and color.[1]

To randomly select the position and size of the rectangle, use the random method from java.lang.Math. This method returns a `double`

---

[1] Macintosh programmers will recognize this as a Javaized version of the Mondrian program from Dave Mark and Cartwright Reed's *Macintosh C Programming Primer* (Addison-Wesley, 1989). Macintosh programmers may also note how much smaller and simpler this program is than the Mac version. This is a result of the relative simplicity of writing applets in Java versus Macintosh programs in C.

between 0.0 and 1.0, so multiply the results by the applet's height or width to get a reasonably sized rectangle that fits into the applet space. This will use the following Randomize method:

```java
private int Randomize( int range ) {
  double  rawResult;

  rawResult = Math.random();
  return (int) (rawResult * range);

}
```

Randomize forces the result of Math.random into an `int` in the range you require.

Program 12.3 Mondrian

```java
//Draw many random rectangles

import java.applet.Applet;
import java.awt.Graphics;
import java.awt.Color;

public class Mondrian extends Applet {

  public void paint(Graphics g) {

    int numberRectangles = 20;
    int RectHeight, RectWidth, RectTop, RectLeft;
    int AppletHeight = size().height;
    int AppletWidth = size().width;
    Color RectColor;

    for (int i=0; i < numberRectangles; i++) {
      RectColor = new Color(Randomize(255),
        Randomize(255), Randomize(255));
      g.setColor(RectColor);
      RectTop = Randomize(AppletHeight);
      RectLeft= Randomize(AppletWidth);
      RectHeight = Randomize(AppletHeight -
        RectTop);
      RectWidth = Randomize(AppletWidth -
        RectLeft);
      g.fillRect(RectTop, RectLeft,
```

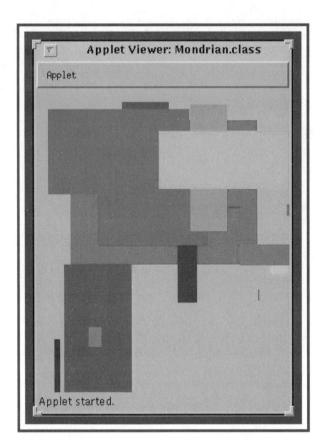

Figure 12.3: *Mondrian*

```
                  RectWidth-1, RectHeight-1);
    }

}

private int Randomize(int range) {
  double  rawResult;

  rawResult = Math.random();
  return (int) (rawResult * range);

}

}
```

Figure 12.3 shows one possible result.

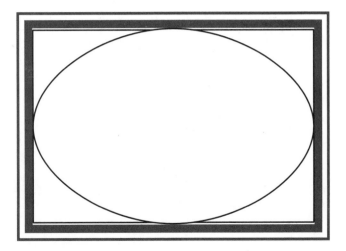

Figure 12.4: *An oval defined by a rectangle*

Drawing Circles and Ovals

Java has methods to draw outlined and filled ovals. As you'd probably guess, these methods are called drawOval and fillOval respectively. As you'd probably also guess, they draw in the current color just like drawRect and fillRect. As you might not guess, they take identical arguments to drawRect and fillRect, that is,

```
drawOval(int left, int top, int width, int height)
```

and

```
fillOval(int left, int top, int width, int height)
```

Instead of the dimensions of the oval itself, the dimensions of the smallest rectangle that can enclose the oval are specified. The oval is drawn as large as it can be to touch the rectangle's edges at their centers. Figure 12.4 may help.

The arguments to drawOval are the same as the arguments to drawRect. The first int is the left-hand side of the enclosing rectangle, the second is the top of the enclosing rectangle, the third is the width, and the fourth is the height.

There is no special method to draw a circle. Just draw an oval inside a square.

Java also has methods to draw outlined and filled arcs. They're similar to drawOval and fillOval, but you must also specify a starting and ending angle for the arc. Angles are given in degrees. The syntax is

```
drawArc(int left, int top, int width, int height,
int startangle, int stopangle)
```

```
fillArc(int left, int top, int width, int height,
int startangle, int stopangle)
```

The rectangle is filled with an arc of the largest circle that could be enclosed within it. The location of 0 degrees and whether the arc is drawn clockwise or counterclockwise are currently platform dependent.

Bullseye

Program 12.4 is a simple applet that draws a series of filled, concentric circles alternating red and white, in other words a bullseye.

Program 12.4: Bullseye

```java
import java.applet.Applet;
import java.awt.Graphics;
import java.awt.Color;


public class Bullseye extends Applet {

  public void paint(Graphics g) {

    int RectLeft, RectTop, RectHeight, RectWidth;
    int AppletHeight = size().height;
    int AppletWidth = size().width;

    for (int i=8; i >= 0; i--) {
       if ((i % 2) == 0) g.setColor(Color.red);
       else g.setColor(Color.white);
       RectHeight=AppletHeight*i/8;
       RectWidth=AppletWidth*i/8;
       RectLeft=AppletWidth/2 - i*AppletWidth/16;
```

Figure 12.5: *Bullseye. The .class file that draws this image is only 684 bytes. The equivalent GIF image is 4,608 bytes, almost seven times larger.*

```
        RectTop=AppletHeight/2 - i*AppletHeight/16;
        g.fillOval(RectLeft, RectTop, RectWidth,
           RectHeight);
    }
  }
}
```

Figure 12.5 shows the result.

Almost all the work in this applet consists of centering the enclosing rectangles inside the applet. The following lines do that:

```
RectHeight = AppletHeight*i/8;
RectWidth = AppletWidth*i/8;
RectLeft = AppletWidth/2 - i*AppletWidth/16;
RectTop = AppletHeight/2 - i*AppletHeight/16;
```

The first two lines just set the height and the width of the rectangle to the appropriate fraction of the applet's height and width. The next two lines set the position of the upper-left-hand corner. Once the rectangle is positioned, drawing the oval is easy.

Drawing Polygons

In Java, rectangles are defined by the position of their upper-left-hand corner, their height, and their width. However, it is implicitly assumed that there is in fact an upper-left-hand corner. Not all rectangles have an upper-left-hand corner. For instance, consider the rectangle in Figure 12.6. Where is its upper left hand corner? What's been assumed so far is that the sides of the rectangle are parallel to the coordinate axes.[2] You can't yet handle a rectangle that's been rotated at an arbitrary angle.

There are some other things you can't handle either—triangles, stars, rhombuses, kites, octagons, and more. To take care of this broad class of shapes, Java has a Polygon class. Polygons are defined by their corners. No assumptions are made about them except that they lie in a 2-D plane.

The basic constructor for the Polygon class is

```
Polygon(int xpoints[], int ypoints[], int npoints)
```

xpoints is an array that contains the x coordinates of the polygon. ypoints is an array that contains the y coordinates. Both should have the length npoints. Thus to construct a 3-4-5 right triangle with the right angle on the origin you would type

```
int[] xpoints = {0, 3, 0};
int[] ypoints = {0, 0, 4};
Polygon myTriangle = new Polygon(xpoints, ypoints,
3);
```

To actually draw the polygon, you use java.awt.Graphics's drawPolygon(Polygon p) method within your paint method like this:

```
g.drawPolygon(myTriangle);
```

---

[2] It's also been assumed that you're only working in two dimensions. For most of the things you're likely to do in Java, this is a safe assumption.

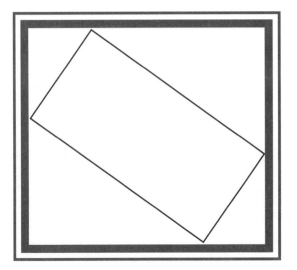

Figure 12.6: *A slanted rectangle*

You can pass the arrays and number of points directly to the drawPolygon method if you prefer:

```
g.drawPolygon(xpoints, ypoints, xpoints.length());
```

There's also a polymorphic fillPolygon method. The syntax is exactly what you'd expect:

```
g.fillPolygon(myTriangle);

g.fillPolygon(xpoints, ypoints, xpoints.length());
```

Java does not automatically close polygons it draws. That is, it draws polygons that look like the one on the left in Figure 12.7 rather than the one on the right.

If you want your polygons to be closed, repeat the first point as the last point. This means that a closed triangle will need four points, a closed rectangle 5, and so on. The extra point isn't necessary for filled polygons, but it doesn't hurt.

Drawing Images

Polygons, ovals, lines and text cover a lot of ground. The remaining graphic object you need is an image. Images in Java are bitmapped GIF or JPEG files that can contain pictures of just about anything. You

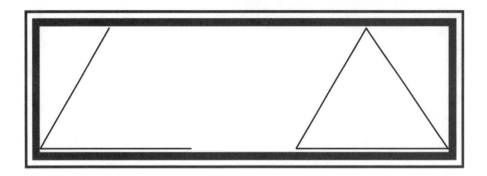

Figure 12.7: *An unclosed and a closed polygon*

can use any program at all to create them as long as that program can save in GIF or JPEG format.

Images displayed by Java applets are retrieved from the Web via a URL that points to the image file. An applet that displays a picture must have a URL to the image its going to display. Images can be stored on a Web server, a local hard drive, or anywhere else the applet can point to via a URL. Make sure you put your images somewhere the person viewing the applet can access them. A file URL that points to your local hard drive may work while you're developing an applet, but it won't be of much use to someone who comes in over the Web. Typically, you'll put images in the same directory as either the applet or the HTML file. Though it doesn't absolutely have to be in one of these two locations, storing it there will probably be more convenient. Put the image with the applet .class file if the image will be used for all instances of the applet. Put the applet with the HTML file if different instances of the applet will use different images. A third alternative is to put all the images in a common location and use PARAMs in the HTML file to tell Java where the images are.

If you know the exact URL for the image you wish to load, you can load it with the following command:

```
URL imageURL = new java.net.URL(
"http://www.prenhall.com/logo.gif");
java.awt.Image img = getImage(imageURL);
```

You can compress this as follows:

```
Image img = getImage(new java.net.URL(
"http://www.prenhall.com/logo.gif"));
```

The getImage method is provided by java.applet.Applet. The URL class is provided by a class you haven't seen before, java.net.URL. Be sure to import it.

If you don't know the exact URL of the Image but you do know its name and that it's in the same directory as the applet, you can use an alternate form of getImage that takes a URL and a filename. Use the applet's getCodeBase method to return the URL to the applet directory like this:

```
Image img = getImage(getCodeBase(), "test.gif");
```

The getCodeBase method returns a URL that points to the directory where the applet came from.

Finally, if the image file is stored in the same directory as the HTML file, use the same getImage method but pass it getDocumentBase instead. This returns a URL that points at the directory which contains the HTML page in which the applet is embedded.

```
Image img = getImage(getDocumentBase(),
"test.gif");
```

If an image is loaded from the Internet, it may take some time for it to be fully downloaded. Most of the time you don't need to worry about this. You can draw the Image as soon as you've connected it to a URL using one of the above methods. Java will update it as more data becomes available without any further intervention on your part.

Load all the images your applet needs in the init method. In particular, do not load them in the paint method. If you do, they will be reloaded every time your applet repaints itself, and applet performance will be abysmal.

Once the image is loaded, draw it in the paint method using the drawImage method like this

```
g.drawImage(Image img, int x, int y, ImageObserver io)
```

img is a member of the Image class, which you should have already loaded in your init method. x is the x coordinate of the upper-left-hand corner of the Image. y is the y coordinate of the upper-left-hand corner of the Image. The `ImageObserver io` is a member of a class that implements the ImageObserver interface. The ImageObserver interface is how Java handles the asynchronous updating of an Image when an Image is loaded from a remote Web site rather than directly from the hard drive. java.applet.Applet implements ImageObserver, so for now just pass the keyword **this** to drawImage to indicate that the current applet is the ImageObserver that should be used.

A paint method that does nothing more than draw an Image starting at the upper-left-hand corner of the applet may look like this:

```
public void paint(Graphics g) {
   g.drawImage(img, 0, 0, this);
}
```

This draws the Image as actual size. You can scale it into a particular rectangle using

```
g.drawImage(Image img, int width, int height,
ImageObserver io)
```

Width and height specify the size of the rectangle to scale the Image into. All other arguments are the same as before. If the scale is not in proportion to the size of the Image, it can end up looking quite squashed.

To avoid disproportionate scaling, use the Image's `getHeight(ImageObserver observer)` and `getWidth(Image-Observer observer)` methods to determine the actual size. Then scale appropriately. For instance, this is how you would draw an Image scaled by one quarter in each dimension:

```
g.drawImage(img, 0, 0, img.getWidth(this)/4,
img.getHeight(this)/4, this);
```

Program 12.5 reads a GIF file in the same directory as the HTML file and displays it at a specified magnification. The name of the GIF file and the magnification factor are specified via PARAMs.

Program 12.5 Magnify Image

```
import java.awt.Graphics;
import java.applet.Applet;
import java.awt.Image;

public class MagnifyImage extends Applet {
```

```
Image theImage;
int scalefactor;
int scaleWidth, scaleHeight;

public void init() {

  String filename=getParameter("imagefile");
  theImage = getImage(getDocumentBase(),
    filename);
  scalefactor = Integer.valueOf(getParameter
    ("scalefactor" )).intValue();

}

public void paint (Graphics g) {
  int x = theImage.getWidth(this);
  int y = theImage.getHeight(this);
  scaleWidth =  x * scalefactor;
  scaleHeight =  y * scalefactor;
  g.drawImage(theImage, 0, 0, scaleWidth,
    scaleHeight, this);
}

}
```

This applet is straightforward. The init method reads two PARAMs: one the name of the image file, the other the magnification factor. The paint method calculates the scale and then draws the image.

You may ask why the scale factor is calculated in the paint method rather than in the init method. Some time could be saved by not recalculating the Image's height and width every time the Image is painted. After all, the Image size should be constant.

In this application the size of the Image doesn't change, and indeed it will be a rare Image that changes size in the middle of an applet. However, in the init method the Image probably hasn't fully loaded. If instead you were to try Program 12.6, which does exactly that, you'd see that the Image wasn't scaled at all. The reason is that in this version the Image hasn't loaded when you make the calls to getWidth and getHeight so they both return -1.

Program 12.6 Broken Magnify Image

```java
public class MagnifyImage extends Applet {

    Image theImage;
    int scaleWidth, scaleHeight;

    public void init() {

        String filename=getParameter("imagefile");
        theImage = getImage(getDocumentBase(),
            filename);
        int scalefactor = Integer.valueOf(
            getParameter("scalefactor")).intValue();
        int x = theImage.getWidth(this);
        int y = theImage.getHeight(this);
        scaleWidth =  x * scalefactor;
        scaleHeight =  y * scalefactor;
    }

    public void paint (Graphics g) {

        g.drawImage(theImage, 0, 0, scaleWidth,
            scaleHeight, this);

    }

}
```

Q&A

Q: *What's missing?*

A: Although the last two chapters may seem like a lot to digest, Java's graphics support is still lacking a few crucial areas, most notably

- More common image formats like TIFF and PNG.
- Arbitrary rotation of figures. You can rotate a rectangle using a polygon, but this doesn't work for an oval.

- Bezier curves for smoother line drawing.
- Many of the draw methods such as drawRect and drawOval are insufficiently polymorphic. For instance, it's impossible to pass a java.awt.Rectangle into Graphics.drawRect.
- There's no way to specify a width for a line.

Quiz

1. What happens if you try to draw objects at negative coordinates? e.g. g.drawRect(–5, –4, 64, 50)?

2. What happens if you specify a negative height or width for a rectangle? e.g. g.drawRect(10, 10, -20, -20)?

Exercises

1. You may have noticed that the clearRect method allows a simplistic sort of animation. While a more effective animation will require external timing and thus needs to wait for the discussion of threads in Chapter 19, you can begin simple animations now. The key is to write an animation loop completely within the paint method and call `g.clearRect(0, 0, size().width-1, size().height-1)` between each successive frame. Use this technique to write an applet that moves a rectangle from the lower-left-hand corner to the upper-right-hand corner. What happens if you comment out the call to `clearRect`?

2. For the artistically inclined: Write a version of Mondrian that draws pictures that are more believably in the style of Piet Mondrian. You should probably restrict your color choices and not allow rectangles to overlap.

3. The Bullseye applet was so convoluted because it is relatively hard to center concentric rectangles inside another rectangle. On the other hand, if you think of circles as being defined by

their center point and a radius, it's not particularly difficult to draw concentric circles. Just keep the center point the same and draw circles with progressively larger radii. Write a CircleToRect method with the following signature:

public Rectangle CircleToRect(Point p, **int** radius)

which takes as its arguments a java.awt.Point and a radius and returns a java.awt.Rectangle that encloses the given circle. Before beginning you should review the documentation for points and rectangles at

http://www.javasoft.com/JDK-1.0/api/java.awt.Rectangle.html

and

http://www.javasoft.com/JDK-1.0/api/java.awt.Point.html

4. Modify the Bullseye applet so that it always draws a circular bullseye even if the applet isn't square.

Summary

In this chapter you learned

- How to draw ovals and circles
- How to draw rectangles
- How to draw polygons
- How to load and display bitmapped images

Coming Up

The last two chapters have concentrated on applet output. Chapter 13 introduces applet input through event processing. You'll learn how to make your applets respond to user input like mouse clicks, key presses, and more.

In later chapters, you'll see how to develop full-blown graphical user interfaces with stand-alone windows, menus, dialog boxes, radio buttons, and more. You'll discover that the drawing methods of the last two chapters can be used to draw on these objects too, vastly expanding their power.

Further Reading

This chapter's only scratched the surface of Java's image support. It's also possible to create images from scratch. For complete details about java.awt.Image, see

http://www.javasoft.com/JDK-1.0/api/java.awt.Image.html

For a more realistic look at the style of Piet Mondrian, see

JAFFE, HANS L. C., *Mondrian*, New York: Harry N. Abrams, Inc., 1985.

CHAPTER 13
EVENTS

- The life cycle of a Java applet including the init, start, stop, and destroy methods

- The paint, repaint, and update methods and the difference between them

- Processing input from the keyboard

- The structure of Event Objects

- The handleEvent method

This chapter introduces event-driven programming. This style of programming should be very familiar to Macintosh and Windows programmers. In those environments, program logic doesn't flow from the top to the bottom of the program as it does in most procedural code. Rather the operating system collects events and the program responds to them. These events may be mouse clicks, key presses, network data arriving on the Ethernet port, or any of about two dozen other possibilities. The operating system looks at each event, determines what program it was intended for, and places the event in the appropriate program's event queue.

Every application in one of these environments has an event loop. This is just a while loop which loops continuously. On every pass through the loop, the application retrieves the next event from its event queue and responds accordingly. For example, a double-click on a word may select the word.

Java applets behave similarly. However the runtime environment (i.e., the browser) provides the event loop for the applet so there's no need to write one explicitly. Rather, methods in your applet respond to each kind of event you want to process. Events that occur in a Java applet are mated with the methods that handle them. You override these methods when you want to do something special when an event happens. You ignore those events you aren't interested in.

The Life, Death, and Rebirth of A Java Applet

First you're born. Then you start going to preschool. Then you graduate from preschool, and you stop going to preschool. Then you start going to school again, but this time it's called kindergarten, and you still remember some of what you learned in preschool. Then you graduate again and stop going to school. After a summer of being stopped, you go to school again. Then next summer you stop going to school again. Eventually you stop going to school completely and get a job. Then you stop that job and start another. Hopefully, you still remember most of what came before. Finally, you retire and stop completely. Then you die. Sometimes you get hit by a bus when you're 32 and die unexpectedly. If you believe in reincarnation, you get to come back and start all over again, though this time you don't remember anything about your previous lives. If you're smart you can write what you learned down and hope that in your next life you're smart enough to read what you wrote in the last life so you don't have to learn everything again.

Applets are a lot like life. They're born. They start running. They stop running. They start again. They stop again. Maybe they do something interesting or important while they're running and maybe they don't. Eventually they stop for the final time, and then they die. Then later they're loaded into someone else's Web browser or even into the same Web browser, but they don't remember anything that happened before and they have to start all over.

When a Java applet is born, it is inited; that is, its init method is called. When it starts running, its start method is called. When it stops running, its stop method is called. An applet's start and stop methods may be called many times, but eventually it stops for good and then it is destroyed, that is, its destroy method is called. At this point the applet may be loaded again, but if it is it remembers nothing about what happened before.

Program 13.1 is an applet that does nothing more than trace the life cycle of a typical Java applet. It uses an array called events to hold the events that are tracked. The array has finite length so if you run it long enough it will crash with an ArrayIndexOutOfBounds Exception. However, that will take quite some time. There are several alternatives to this approach for storing an indefinite number of Strings which you'll see in this and upcoming chapters.

Program 13.1 The life cycle of an applet

```java
import java.applet.Applet;
import java.awt.Graphics;

public class LifeCycle extends Applet {

  String[] events = new String[2048];
  int i = 0;

  public void init() {
    events[i++] = "initializing... ";
    repaint();
  }

  public void start() {
    events[i++] = "starting... ";
    repaint();
  }

  public void stop() {
    events[i++] = "stopping...";
```

```
        repaint();
    }

    public void destroy() {
        events[i++] = "destroying...";
        repaint();
    }

    public void paint(Graphics g) {
        for (int j=0; j <= i; j++) {
            g.drawString(events[j], 5, 15*j + 15);
        }
    }

}
```

Run this applet in the Applet Viewer, Netscape, and HotJava. Be sure to try the following things:

- Restart the applet
- Reload the applet
- Minimize the applet's window
- Switch out of the applet into another application

You should see a list of the events that occur. However, this list will likely be different in Netscape and in the Applet Viewer or HotJava. Figure 13.1 shows what the applet looks like after several restarts in Sun's Applet Viewer. Figure 13.2 shows the same applet after several reloads in Netscape 2.0.

There are four key milestones in an applet's life: init, start, stop, and destroy.

The init method is called at the birth of an applet. Generally, you use this method to set up any data structures or perform any tasks you need to get ready to run the applet. For instance, past programs in this book have used the init method to read the parameters passed to the applet.

The start method is called when a user brings their attention back to an applet, for instance after maximizing a window or returning to the applet's page. It is called at least once in the life of any applet

Figure 13.1: The LifeCycle applet after two restarts.

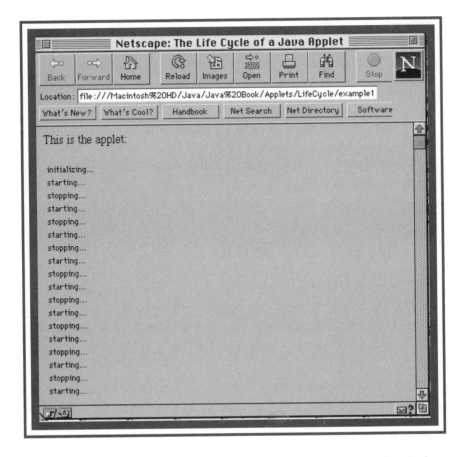

Figure 13.2: The LifeCycle Applet after being reloaded several times in Netscape 2.0.

immediately after the init method.[1] Code that needs to be performed every time an applet is restarted should be put here. Most of the time you probably won't do anything except restart processing the stop method stopped.

A stop event says the user is no longer looking at the page that contains the applet. This is usually because the user left the page or minimized the window. At this time you should stop any CPU eating activities that don't matter when the user isn't looking at your page. For instance, your Doom applet should stop tracking monster movement if the user isn't actually playing. On the other hand, a spreadsheet applet in the middle of a long calculation should continue calculating because the user is likely to want the result later. When the user returns to the page, the start method will be called. Stop may be called multiple times in your applet's life.

The destroy method is called just before the applet is unloaded completely. It is called after the stop method. Users may reload the applet later, but if they do, it will be as if they've never seen it before. All variables—static, member, local, or otherwise—will have been initialized to their initial state. If you have any final cleanup to do, do it here. If you're trying to implement some form of persistence by storing state information on the server, this is a good place to do it.

As of this writing, all of this is questionable. Sun's documentation does not always agree with the behavior of an applet. Don't be surprised if the browser you use to test this applet acts differently than those above.

Paint, Repaint, and Update

If life were nothing more than being born, starting school, stopping school, starting work, stopping work, starting work, stopping work, retiring, and dying, then it would be pretty boring. It's what happens in the spaces in between starting and stopping that makes life worth living.

So too in a Java applet most of the action happens between starts and stops. Unlike life, almost nothing happens in an applet when it's

---

[1] This assumes the init method doesn't do anything too evil. It is possible for an applet to get stuck in an infinite loop inside init or even to exit the Applet Viewer. However, this would be a truly pathological case.

stopped, only when it's started. In life, summer vacation or even unemployment can be a lot of fun.

There are three things that happen in between starts and stops, input, output (I/O in geek-speak), and calculations. The proper handling of long calculations requires Threads and will be taken up in Chapter 19. The remainder of this chapter discusses input and output methods.

In a well-designed Java applet, almost all output takes place via painting, the drawing of pixels on the display. You learned how to paint in the last chapter. Now you'll learn how the paint method is called.

There are three key methods involved in painting the screen: `paint (Graphics g)`, `repaint()`, and `update(Graphics g)`. All drawing, that is, all conversions of lines, text, rectangles, and other objects to the actual pixels that will be placed on the screen, happens in the paint method. In a simple applet, paint is all you need to worry about. Your paint method should draw the entire applet as it should look at a particular moment in time. It should not assume that anything will be left from a previous call to paint.

You rarely need to call paint directly. If you want the screen redrawn, call repaint instead. The screen may not be redrawn immediately. The repaint method does not guarantee an immediate redraw. It just signals the applet that the screen should be redrawn as soon as it gets a chance.

The actual painting of the screen, that is, the copying of the appropriate pixel values from the computer's RAM into the display's video RAM, happens at the end of the update method. In a basic applet you don't need to override update or worry much about what happens inside the update method. In more advanced applets, though, you can take advantage of the dichotomy between the drawing (in paint) and the painting (in update) to do some neat tricks with clipping and flicker-free animation.

Alternative Outputs: ShowStatus and println()

People who view your applet will expect the output to be communicated to them primarily through painting in the applet panel. However, you do have some quick and dirty alternatives. These are primarily useful for debugging.

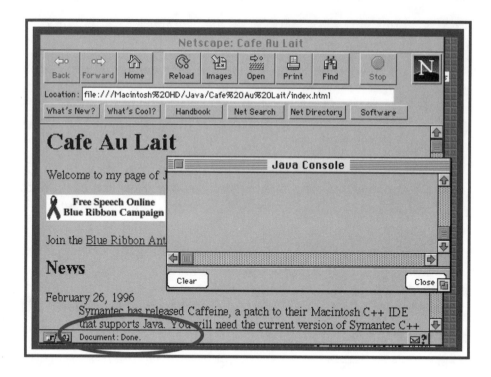

Figure 13.3: Netscape's status bar is circled. The Java console is showing.

First of all, you can call System.out.println from inside an applet. If the applet is running in the Applet Viewer on Windows or Unix, then this output will be printed on the command line from whence the applet viewer was launched. If the applet is running in Netscape or on the Mac, then this output will be printed in the Java console as shown in Figure 13.3. Well-behaved applets won't do this, but it can be immensely useful when you're debugging since it allows you to print debugging information right when you need it rather than waiting until the next time paint is called.

The second output alternative is the status line of the browser or the Applet Viewer. You can use `java.applet.Applet.showStatus(String s)` to print a short String in the status bar of the browser or applet viewer. You can use showStatus much like you'd use System.out.println in an application except that each message you print overwrites the previous one, and you don't have much space to work with. Many Net surfers do not pay attention to things happening in the status bar, so it's unwise to depend on anything you put there being seen by anybody but yourself.

Output is only half the user interface equation. Input's the other half. Java applets may assume that they are running on a system with a keyboard and a mouse. They may assume that they will get events from the keyboard and the mouse. They should not assume that the mouse will have more than one button. They should not assume that the keyboard will have a QWERTY layout in U.S. English. Fortunately, Java provides a sufficiently high level of abstraction for user input events that you do not need to assume any of these things. There is one method that handles keyboard input and six methods for mouse input.

Keyboard Methods

The single keyboard method is quite simple so let's look at it first. A keyDown event is generated whenever the user presses a key while your applet is active. An `int` keycode is returned indicating which key was pressed. If the key pressed is an alphanumeric or punctuation key, then the `int` can be cast to a `char` to find out what key was pressed. The syntax of the method is as follows:

```java
public boolean keyDown(Event e, int key) {
    char c = (char) key;
    showStatus("The " + key + " was pressed.");
    return true;
}
```

The `keyDown` method is called whenever the user presses a non-modifier key on their keyboard. (A modifier key is a key like Shift, Command, Control, Option, Escape, Alt, or Meta.) `keyDown` returns a `boolean`. If it returns `true`, that signals the applet's parent (normally the Web browser or Applet Viewer) that the keypress has been dealt with. On the other hand, if it returns `false`, then the parent must deal with the keypress so the parent's keyDown method will also be called. Parents will be discussed in the next two chapters. For now, you'll probably just want to return `true` from any event-handling method.

The keyDown method is called as soon as the user presses the key. It does not wait for the user to release the key. You will see that this in sharp contrast to the mouse methods. The key is not presented to the applet raw. Some processing is done by the operating system first. For instance, if the user presses and holds down the s key, it is up to the operating system whether to send the applet a single s or a stream of sssssssss. If the OS does send a stream of s's, then each one appears as a separate keypress to the applet. Thus in some sense this is a virtual keypress.

Program 13.2 is an applet that acts like a typewriter. It reads keypresses and then prints them on the screen. When the return key is pressed, it moves to the next line. It also does limited word wrapping.

Program 13.2: The TypeWriter applet

```java
import java.applet.Applet;
import java.awt.Event;
import java.awt.Graphics;

public class tw extends Applet {

  int numcols = 80;
  int numrows = 25;
  int row = 0;
  int col = 0;
  char page[][] = new char[numrows][];

  public void init() {

    for (int i = 0; i < numrows; i++) {
      page[i] = new char[numcols];
    }
    for (int i = 0; i < numrows; i++) {
      for (int j = 0; j < numcols; j++) {
        page[i][j] = '\0';
      }
    }

  }


  public boolean keyDown(Event e, int key) {
    char c = (char) key;

    if (c == '\n' || c == '\r') {
```

```
      row++;
      col = 0;
    }
    else if (row < numrows) {
      if (col >= numcols) {
      col = 0;
      row++;
      }
  page[row][col] = c;
  col++;
}
    else { // row >= numrows
      col++;
    }
    repaint();
    return true;
  }


public void paint(Graphics g) {

  for (int i=0; i < numrows; i++) {
    String tempString = new String(page[i]);
      g.drawString(tempString, 5, 15²i + 15));
  }

  }

}
```

Figure 13.4 is an example of the applet running.

If you're having trouble getting this applet to run, make sure you click once in the applet window to give it the focus before typing.

Special Keys

Not all keys on the keyboard map to ASCII or even Unicode characters. For instance, most keyboards have a plethora of function keys, possibly a numeric keypad, four arrow keys, and more. Although exact keyboard layouts are very platform-dependent, Java does provide ways to access these keys.

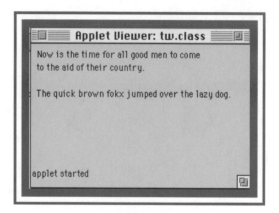

Figure 13.4: The Typewriter applet. You can see from the typos that this applet doesn't yet support any sort of editing.

The java.awt.Event class defines 20 mnemonic constants[2] you can use to test for these keys in your methods. They are separated into three groups.

<u>Page Position Keys</u>

- Event.HOME   the home key
- Event.END   the end key
- Event.PGUP   page up
- Event.PGDN   page down

<u>Arrow Keys</u>

- Event.UP   the up arrow
- Event.DOWN the down arrow
- Event.LEFT   the left arrow
- Event.RIGHT the right arrow

<u>Function Keys</u>

- Event.F1
- Event.F2
- Event.F3
- Event.F4
- Event.F5

---

[2] Final static `int` fields, to be precise.

- Event.F6
- Event.F7
- Event.F8
- Event.F9
- Event.F10
- Event.F11
- Event.F12

This still doesn't handle every key on many keyboards. An Apple Extended keyboard has three more function keys, command and option keys, a power key, and help, delete, and escape keys too. On the other hand, you can't assume all these keys are available either. PowerBook keyboards are missing page up, page down, home, and end keys. Sun workstations have L1 through L10 keys in addition to F1 to F12 keys. Nonetheless, these constants are often useful.

Since they're `ints`, you can use them in a `switch` statement in the keydown method to see what was pressed, as in this slightly more useful keyDown method for the TypeWriter applet.

```java
public boolean keyDown(Event e, int key) {

  char c = (char) key;

  switch (key) {
    case Event.HOME:
      row = 0;
      col = 0;
      break;
    case Event.END:
      row = numrows-1;
      col = numcols-1;
      break;
    case Event.UP:
      if (row > 0) row--;
      break;
    case Event.DOWN:
      if (row < numrows-1) row++;
      break;
    case Event.LEFT:
      if (col > 0) col-;
      else if (col == 0 && row > 0) {
        row--;
```

```
          col=numcols-1;
     }
     break;
  case Event.RIGHT:
     if (col < numcols-1) col++;
     else if (col == numcols-1 &&
        row < numrows-1) {
        row++;
        col=0;
     }
     break;
  default:
     if (c == '\n' || c == '\r') {
        row++;
        col = 0;
     }
     else if (row < numrows) {
        if (col >= numcols) {
       col = 0;
       row++;
        }
        page[row][col] = c;
        col++;
     }
  else { // row >= numrows
     col++;
     }
  }
  repaint();
  return true;
}
```

Mouse Methods

There is one keypress event. There are six mouse events. This reflects the relative complexity of mice and keyboards. At first glance it may seem that keyboards are more complex. After all, the typical keyboard has over 100 keys that can form an infinite number of words. The mouse has at most three buttons and sometimes only one. However, simplicity can be deceiving.

Keyboards are scalar input devices. There are 100+ keys, but each of them only has one value. Even multiplying the number of keys by four to account for modifier keys, the keyDown event still only produces an `int`. A mouse click, by contrast, has two coordinates. It's a vector. Mouse clicks aren't just "what" keyboard events. They're also a "where."

There are six mouse events your applet should be aware of:

- `mouseUp(Event e, int x, int y)`
- `mouseDown(Event e, int x, int y)`
- `mouseMove(Event e, int x, int y)`
- `mouseDrag(Event e, int x, int y)`
- `mouseExit(Event e, int x, int y)`
- `mouseEnter(Event e, int x, int y)`

Each of these methods has the same argument list, (`Event e, int x, int y`). Thus each mouse method has access to the event itself, which you mostly won't make use of, and the x and y coordinates of the position where the mouse button was pressed.

mouseDown

The mouseDown method is called whenever a mouse button is pressed in your applet. In most cases, you should wait for a mouseUp before taking any action though. A user interface object like a button or a menu item is highlighted when the mouse button is pressed while the cursor is over it, but it is not activated until the user releases the mouse button. This gives the user a chance to change their mind by moving the cursor off the object without releasing it.

The exception would be when you want an action to continue as long as the mouse button is held down—a fast forward button on a movie-playing applet, for instance.

mouseUp

The mouseUp method is called when the mouse button is released inside your applet. In most cases, this is the event you watch out for, not mouseDown. This is the event that triggers the action (if any).

mouseMove

mouseMove events occur when a user moves the mouse without holding down the mouse button. mouseMove methods receive the coordinates of the point where the mouse is when the event occurs.

You'll almost always get a steady stream of mouseMove events. Only rarely will you see a single mouseMove event in isolation. As with mouseDown, you normally won't take any action on a mouseMove event since when the user is moving the mouse, they're just moving it from one object to another object. Mouse action should only occur when the mouse button is held down.

mouseDrag

mouseDrag methods occur when a user moves the mouse while holding down the mouse button. mouseDrag methods are virtually identical to mouseMove methods except that now you should be taking some action that depends on your applet, for instance, drawing a line or moving an object.

mouseExit

Your applet receives a mouseExit event whenever the cursor leaves the applet. You'll also receive the coordinates of the point at which the cursor exited your applet but that's only rarely relevant. Depending on the details of your program, it may be wise to stop processing when `mouseExit()` is called.

mouseEnter

Your applet receives a mouseEnter event whenever the cursor enters your applet from somewhere else. You'll also receive the coordinates of the point at which the cursor entered your applet. The mouseEnter event is typically followed by a stream of mouseMove events as the cursor continues through the applet. If your applet stops doing anything while the cursor is outside the applet, it should restart in this method, perhaps by calling the applet's start method.

Event Tutor Applet

Program 13.3 is designed to give you a feel for what event-driven programming is like and the various events you're likely to encounter. Whenever an event occurs, the applet responds by printing the name of the event in the status bar.

Even if you've just been reading along until now, it's important to type in the following listing, compile it, write an HTML file that includes it, and load it into your Web browser.

Once you've compiled and loaded this applet, play with it. Click the mouse in the applet window. Double-click the mouse. Click and drag. Type some text. Resize the browser window. Cover it and then uncover it. Keep your eye on the standard output (Java console in Netscape) while doing this.

Here are some questions to answer:

1. Is a mouseDown event always followed by a mouseUp event?

2. Can there be a mouseDown event that is not followed by a mouseDrag event?

3. Can you have a mouseUp Event that is not preceded by a mouseDown event?

4. What has to happen for a paint event to occur?

5. What's the most common event? Why?

6. Are there any events you don't see?

7. How many times can the start event be called? the stop event?

8. Of those events you can make occur, exactly how do you do it? How many different ways can you do it?

Program 13.3: The Event Tutor Applet

```
import java.applet.Applet;
import java.awt.Event;
import java.awt.Graphics;
import java.util.StringTokenizer;

public class EventTutor extends Applet {

  private String events;
```

```java
private int num_events = 0;

public void init() {
  listEvent("initializing the applet");
}

public void start() {
  listEvent("starting the applet");
  repaint();
}

public void stop() {
  listEvent("stopping the applet");
  repaint();
}

public void destroy() {
  listEvent("destroying the applet");
}

public boolean mouseUp(Event e, int x, int y)
{
  listEvent("mouseUp at (" + x + "," + y +
    ")");
  return false;
}

public boolean mouseDown(Event e, int x, int y)
{
  listEvent("mouseDown at (" + x + "," + y +
    ")");
  return false;
}

public boolean mouseDrag(Event e, int x, int y)
{
  listEvent("mouseDrag at (" + x + "," + y +
    ")");
  return false;
}

public boolean mouseMove(Event e, int x, int y)
{
  listEvent("mouseMove event at (" + x + "," +
    y + ")");
  return false;
}
```

```java
public boolean mouseEnter(Event e, int x, int y)
{
    listEvent("mouseEnter at (" + x + "," + y +
    ")");
    return false;
}

public boolean mouseExit(Event e, int x, int y)
{
    listEvent("mouseExit at (" + x + "," +
    y + ")");
    return false;
}

public boolean keyDown(Event e, int x) {
    listEvent("keyDown: " + (char) x);
    return false;
}

public void paint(Graphics g) {

    int i = 0;
    int j = 1;
    int lineheight = 15;
    int numlines = 20;

    StringTokenizer st;
    st = new StringTokenizer(events.toString(),
    "\t");
    while (st.hasMoreTokens()) {
        if (num_events - i++ < numlines) {
            g.drawString(st.nextToken(), 5,
                lineheight * j++);
        }
    }

}

private void listEvent(String st) {
    events += st + "\t";
    showStatus(st);
    System.out.println(st);
    num_events++;
    repaint();
}
}
```

> **Tip** Some events are very easy to miss. You may catch the start event, but only if you're looking closely when the applet loads. Try using System.out.println to write the events to the standard output so you can keep a record of what has gone before.

The Structure of an Event

One of the arguments passed to each event-handling method is the Event itself. Event is a class defined by java.awt.Event that contains six public methods, three constructors, and nine public fields. In basic Java programming, you don't need to know about the constructors. The public methods and fields, however, provide potentially crucial information.

The three methods you'll use most frequently are `controlDown()`, `shiftDown()`, and `metaDown()`. These methods tell you whether the Control, Shift and Meta keys are pressed.[3] You may use this information to change the meaning of a particular event. For instance, if the shift key is held down in a drawing program, this generally means the action should be constrained in some sense. For example, all ovals are circles, all rectangles are squares, and all lines are vertical or horizontal.

java.awt.Event also provides access to nine different fields and a host of predefined constants.

id

`id` is an `int` that identifies the type of event. There are about 27 different possible events, each represented by a final static variable that's available as a mnemonic constant in java.awt.Event. For instance, java.awt.Event.MOUSE_DOWN is the `id` of the event posted when the mouse button is pressed. By the time control passes to the event methods like mouseDown, you already know the type of

---

[3] Meta is a special key from emacs (and other UNIX programs) that is often mapped to the escape key or the backquote (') key on normal keyboards, since non-emacs users don't have meta keys on their keyboards and won't know what you mean if you ask them to press the meta key, it's a good idea to avoid it entirely.

the event. However `id` will be more important in the next section where you write a custom event handler. The available event constants are

- KEY_PRESS
- KEY_RELEASE
- KEY_ACTION
- KEY_ACTION_RELEASE
- MOUSE_DOWN
- MOUSE_UP
- MOUSE_MOVE
- MOUSE_ENTER
- MOUSE_EXIT
- MOUSE_DRAG
- SCROLL_LINE_UP
- SCROLL_LINE_DOWN
- SCROLL_PAGE_UP
- SCROLL_PAGE_DOWN
- SCROLL_ABSOLUTE
- LIST_SELECT
- LIST_DESELECT
- ACTION_EVENT
- LOAD_FILE
- SAVE_FILE
- GOT_FOCUS
- LOST_FOCUS
- WINDOW_DESTROY
- WINDOW_EXPOSE
- WINDOW_ICONIFY
- WINDOW_DEICONIFY
- WINDOW_MOVED

This chapter only covers the first ten that have default handlers.[4] You'll see the others in the next several chapters.

---

[4] Actually, GOT_FOCUS, LOST_FOCUS, and ACTION_EVENT have default handlers as well. However, they're only useful when an applet contains multiple components. Since everything you've seen so far only contains a single component, the applet itself, discussion of those handlers is left for later.

target

The target is the Component for which this event is intended. Right now there's only one target, the applet itself; but in the next few chapters you'll see that buttons, scrollbars, textfields, and other user interface items all have their own event handlers. This field defines which part of a multicomponent applet the event is destined for.

when

when is a long variable that tells you when the event occurred in seconds since a certain date and time. That date and time is platform dependent, however, so this is primarily useful for comparing it to the times of other events.

x and y

x and y tell you where the cursor was when the event occurred in the applet's coordinate space. x is the horizontal location and y is the vertical location. The mouse events pass x and y as separate arguments too, but these are useful for determining the mouse location in non-mouse events like key presses. For instance, in an arcade game, the key pressed might indicate which weapon to fire, but the cursor would indicate which target to shoot at.

key

key is an int that specifies which key was pressed or released. It is valid only in keyboard-related events. Since it is also passed as a separate argument to keyboard methods, its primary use is if you're writing a custom-event handler.

modifiers

modifiers is an int that specifies the state (pressed or unpressed) of the control, meta, and shift keys. Since this information is more easily available through the `getShift()`, `getMeta()`, and `getControl()` methods, there's no real reason to access this variable. Do not be surprised if this variable is made private in a future version of the AWT.

clickCount

This is an `int` that specifies the number of consecutive clicks. One is a single click, two is a double click, and so on. It applies only to MOUSE_DOWN events. In other events, it is guaranteed to be zero.

arg

`arg` is an Object of any type that you can use for your own data in a user-defined event. It allows events to handle arbitrarily complex data by encapsulating it in an object. In system-defined events, `arg` will be `null` (though this may change in the future).

evt

`evt` is an instance of java.awt.Event. This is not the event you're looking at now, but rather the next one in the queue. This exists primarily for the convenience of the system. You should have no reason to access it.

The handleEvent Method

The events described in this chapter are sufficient to implement basic interactivity. Sometimes, however, you need to get more control over the events you respond to, or you need to respond to events that aren't normally available to you. To do this, you need to override the `handleEvent(Event e)` method in your applet.

The handleEvent method is just a big `switch` statement that tests the id of the event and dispatches it to the appropriate method. It returns a boolean value which should be `true` if the event was handled and `false` if it wasn't.

Program 13.4 uses a custom handleEvent method to print out the name of each event it sees on the standard output. Since this just peeks at the events, but doesn't properly respond to them, at the end of the handleEvent method, `super.handleEvent` is called to pass the event back to the default eventHandler.

Program 13.4: Print All Events

```java
import java.applet.Applet;
import java.awt.Event;

public class AllEvents extends Applet {

  public boolean handleEvent(Event evt) {
    switch (evt.id) {
      case Event.KEY_PRESS:
        System.out.println("Key Press Event");
        return super.keyDown(evt, evt.key);

      case Event.KEY_ACTION:
        System.out.println("Key Action Event");
        return super.keyDown(evt, evt.key);

      case Event.KEY_RELEASE:
        System.out.println("Key Release Event");
        return super.keyUp(evt, evt.key);

      case Event.KEY_ACTION_RELEASE:
        System.out.println(
          "Key Action Release Event");
        return super.keyUp(evt, evt.key);

      case Event.MOUSE_ENTER:
        System.out.println("Mouse Enter Event");
        return super.mouseEnter(evt, evt.x, evt.y);

      case Event.MOUSE_EXIT:
        System.out.println("Mouse Exit Event");
        return super.mouseExit(evt, evt.x, evt.y);

      case Event.MOUSE_MOVE:
```

```
          System.out.println("Mouse Move Event");
          return super.mouseMove(evt, evt.x, evt.y);

    case Event.MOUSE_DOWN:
          System.out.println("Mouse Down Event");
          return super.mouseDown(evt, evt.x, evt.y);

    case Event.MOUSE_DRAG:
          System.out.println("Mouse Drag Event");
          return super.mouseDrag(evt, evt.x, evt.y);

    case Event.MOUSE_UP:
          System.out.println("Mouse Up Event");
          return super.mouseUp(evt, evt.x, evt.y);

    case Event.SCROLL_LINE_UP:
          System.out.println("Scroll Line Up Event");
          return true;

    case Event.SCROLL_LINE_DOWN :
          System.out.println("Scroll Line Event");
          return true;

    case Event.SCROLL_PAGE_UP:
          System.out.println("Mouse Exit Event");
          return true;

    case Event.SCROLL_PAGE_DOWN:
          System.out.println("Mouse Move Event");
          return true;

    case Event.SCROLL_ABSOLUTE:
          System.out.println("Scroll Absolute Event");
          return true;

    case Event.LIST_SELECT:
          System.out.println("List Select Event");
         return true;

    case Event.LIST_DESELECT:
          System.out.println("List Deselect Event");
          return true;

    case Event.ACTION_EVENT:
          System.out.println("Action Event");
          return super.action(evt, evt.arg);
```

```java
    case Event.LOAD_FILE:
      System.out.println("Load File Event");
      return true;

    case Event.SAVE_FILE:
      System.out.println("Save File Event");
      return true;

    case Event.GOT_FOCUS:
      System.out.println("Got Focus Event");
      return super.gotFocus(evt, evt.arg);

    case Event.LOST_FOCUS:
      System.out.println("Lost Focus Event");
      return super.lostFocus(evt, evt.arg);

    case Event.WINDOW_DESTROY:
      System.out.println("Window Destroy Event");
      return true;

    case Event.WINDOW_EXPOSE:
      System.out.println("Window Expose Event");
      return true;

    case Event.WINDOW_ICONIFY:
      System.out.println(
        "Window Iconify Event");
      return true;

    case Event.WINDOW_DEICONIFY:
      System.out.println(
        "Window Deiconify Event");
      return true;

    case Event.WINDOW_MOVED:
      System.out.println("Window Moved Event");
      return true;

    default:
      return false;
  }

  }

}
```

If you write your own handleEvent method, it will probably look something like Program 13.4. Subtract cases for events you do not want your applet to respond to. If you want to completely replace the default handleEvent method, then have your handleEvent return `true`. On the other hand, if you just want to supplement the default handleEvent, then have your handler return `super.handleEvent(evt)`. If you do return true, the mouseUp, keyDown, and similar methods will not be called unless you explicitly call them from handleEvent.

Q&A

Q: *Why are the key pressed and the location of the cursor passed both inside an Event and as separate arguments?*

A: There's no particular reason for this. It is slightly more convenient to be able to access just the key pressed or just the cursor location rather than dereferencing the Event to find its member variables. Mostly, however, this seems to be a holdover from the alpha API where the Event was not passed to the event handler methods.

Quiz

1. *What's the difference between reloading and restarting an applet?*

Exercises

1. The typewriter applet is really very basic. Try to spruce it up enough to pass as a simple word processor. This exercise is fairly open-ended. Possibilities include

- A data structure that can handle arbitrary amounts of text
- Breaking for word wrapping on spaces
- Inserting a blinking vertical bar at the position of the insertion point
- Dynamically adjusting the text flow based on the size of the window and the size of the font
- Handling the delete key
- Using the mouse to position the insertion point
- An insert mode as well as the current typeover mode
- Setting the font to Courier
- Cleaning up the (by now quite messy) keyDown method by breaking it up into smaller pieces. Try creating a cursor object that responds to moveLeft, moveRight, moveTo(), and other such messages.

Don't get too wrapped up in this though. You'll see in Chapter 15 that Java does provide a TextArea class that gives you all this functionality, essentially for free.

Summary

In this chapter you learned

- When the init, start, stop, and destroy methods are called, what they do, and what you should use them for.
- How to repaint
- How to get input from the keyboard
- How to get input from the mouse
- How an Event Object is structured
- What handleEvent is and when you should use it.

Coming Up

The next two chapters introduce user interface components for applets, that is buttons, scrollbars, checkboxes, and more. You'll discover that a lot of what has been said about applets in the last three chapters applies more broadly, in fact, to any instance of the class java.awt.Component or one of its subclasses. It will turn out that everything you've learned about Graphics including Images, lines, rectangles, colors, and more as well as everything you've learned in this chapter about events derives from the java.awt.Component class. You'll also learn the details of events like SCROLL_ABSOLUTE and LIST_SELECT that apply only to particular user interface components. Chapter 17 introduces windows. Among other things, you'll see six new events that windows produce. Finally, in Chapter 20 you'll see the two events that occur when a file is opened or closed.

Further Reading

More information about java.awt.Event is available from

http://www.javasoft.com/JDK-1.0/api/java.awt.Event.html

CHAPTER 14
WIDGET WIZARDRY

- What a Component is

- What a Container is

- What a Label is

- How to use Buttons

Twelve years ago, drawing lines, text, and pictures was pretty hot stuff. Today users expect more. Modern applications have dialog boxes, menus, radio buttons, scroll bars, checkboxes, tool palettes, hot tips and more. Java provides premade components to implement many of these more modern application features. These include buttons, checkboxes, scrollbars, list boxes, pop-up menus, and more.

Collectively these user interface items are called **widgets**. In Java, widgets are all subclasses of java.awt.Component and are also called **Components**. And although there aren't any premade widgets to implement some of the more modern user interface elements like hot tips or floating palettes, you'll see how to use the basic classes to roll your own.

325

Components and Containers

All user interface elements like buttons and scrollbars are Components. That is, they are subclasses of java.awt.Component. The applets you've seen before have contained only one Component, the applet itself. (java.awt.Applet is a subclass of java.awt.Panel, which is a subclass of java.awt.Container, which is a subclass of java.awt.Component.) This applet had an event loop that allowed you to respond to user input, a Graphics object you could draw with, and a coordinate system to help you decide where to draw. All of this, it turns out, is inherited from java.awt.Component.

The other Components—buttons, checkboxes and so on—also have event loops, Graphics objects, and coordinate systems. And, just as applets overrode methods of java.awt.Component to provide painting, event handling, and more, so too do these components override the generic behavior of java.awt.Component to act as appropriate for buttons, scrollbars, or their own type.

In general, components will be contained in a Container.[1] An applet is one Container. Other Containers include windows and dialogs, which you'll see in Chapter 17. You can nest Containers inside other Containers.

Every Container has a LayoutManager that determines how different Components are placed within the Container. The LayoutManager is not something you see. Rather it is a way of thinking about how to place Components. For instance, a BorderLayout let's you place components in the North, South, East, West, and Center areas of your Container. The GridLayout lets you place components in cells of an evenly spaced grid.

In short, Containers contain Components. Components are positioned inside the Container according to a LayoutManager. Since Containers are themselves Components, Containers may by placed inside other Containers. This is really a lot simpler than it sounds. Applets provide a ready-made Container and a default LayoutManager, so let's begin with some examples that just add user interface Components to an applet.

---

[1] I say "in general" because java.awt.Container is itself a subclass of java.awt.Component.

Figure 14.1: An applet with a Label

Labels

The simplest component is java.awt.Label. A Label is one line of read-only text, pretty much perfect for a Hello World variant. Program 14.1 prints the String "Hello Container" in a Label in the applet.

Program 14.1: Hello Container

```
1.  import java.applet.Applet;
2.  import java.awt.Label;
3.
4.  public class HelloContainer extends Applet {
5.
6.    public void init() {
7.      Label l;
8.      l = new Label("Hello Container");
9.      add(l);
10.   }
11. }
```

Figure 14.1 shows the applet.

As usual, you begin by importing the classes you need. In this case, you need only two—java.applet.Applet and java.awt.Label—and lines 1 and 2 import them.

Line 4 declares the class in the usual way as an extension of Applet. The class has a single method, init.

Line 6 starts the init method. The init method does three things. First, Line 7 declares that l is a Label. Then, l is instantiated with the `Label(String s)` constructor in Line 8. Finally, l is added to the layout in line 9. Components don't have to be added to the layout in the init method nor do they need to be instantiated there, but it's often convenient to do so.

The key thing to remember about adding components to the applet is the three steps:

1. Declare the component
2. Initialize the component
3. Add the component to the layout

The first two steps must be performed when creating an instance of any class so it's really only the third that's new.

You can often combine the three steps into one like this:

```
add(new Label("Hello Container"));
```

The disadvantage to this shortcut is that you no longer have a variable which references the Label. Thus, you can't easily access the Label later. However, Labels are fairly constant things, so you're unlikely to want to access them anyway. Other, more dynamic components have other means to get references to them when necessary so most of the time there isn't any significant disadvantage to this shortcut.

When the applet is drawn, the Label appears in the center of the top of the applet. It appears there because that's where the default LayoutManager chose to put it. The default LayoutManager for an applet is FlowLayout. In a FlowLayout, Components are added in order from left to right, starting in the center and spreading out across the applet as necessary.

The first component is added in the middle of the top row. The second component is added to the right of the first component, and both components are slid over to the left so they're still centered. Subsequent components are added to the right while previous components are pushed to the left so that the row of components remains centered. When enough components have been added to fill the first row, the next component is added in the center of the second row. This is the same as a word processor set to center alignment. You'll explore LayoutManagers in much more detail in Chapter 16. For now you can rely on the defaults to at least make your widgets accessible.

Where's the paint Method?

You may have noticed something funny about the above applet. There's no paint method! And yet the text gets drawn on the screen anyhow. How does this happen?

The key is that Components know how to paint themselves. When a container like an applet is repainted, it not only calls its own paint method, it also calls the paint method for all the Components it contains. java.awt.Label has its own paint method that knows how to paint itself. The short of it is that you don't need to worry about painting Components unless you create your own unique Components or modify the appearance of the system-supplied components.

Label Methods

Labels are simple objects which have only two constructors and four methods of their own, separate from the general methods of java.awt.Component (which java.awt.Label subclasses). You've already seen the basic constructor for a label. You can also create a label with no text at all using the `Label()` constructor with no arguments. There's little to no reason to do this.

The two methods of java.awt.Label which you may occasionally have reason to call are `getText()` and `setText(String s)`. These allow you to retrieve and change the text of a Label while the applet is running. Given a Label l, here is how they might be used:

```
String s = l.getText();

l.setText("Here's the new label");
```

Buttons and Actions

Buttons are instances of java.awt.Button. You create them with the `Button(String label)` constructor. This creates a new button with the label printed on it. Then you add the button to the layout. Here's one example:

```
Button b;
b = new Button("My First Button");
add(b);
```

If this looks familiar, it should. It's almost identical to the syntax for creating a new Label. You'll use this syntax over and over again for all the different user interface Components including TextFields, TextAreas, Scrollbars, Canvases, and more. The only thing thing that will change will be the constructor.

The shortcut is the same also. The three lines can often be combined into the single line:

```
add(new Button("My First Button"));
```

Unlike labels, Buttons do things when you press them. When the mouse is clicked on a Button, the Button puts an ACTION_EVENT in the event queue. You respond to this event by including an action method in the applet. An action method looks like this:

```
public boolean action(Event e, Object o) {
    // Here you should handle the event


    return true;
}
```

The action method returns `true` if the event was successfully handled and `false` if it was not handled.

Program 14.2 is a very small applet that displays a single button and prints a message on standard output when the button is pressed.

Program 14.2: Button Action

```
import java.applet.Applet;
import java.awt.Button;
import java.awt.Event;

public class ButtonTest extends Applet {
```

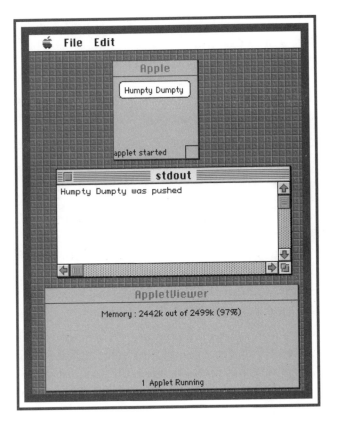

Figure 14.2: *After the button was pushed*

```
public void init () {

    add(new Button("Humpty Dumpty"));

}

public boolean action(Event e, Object o) {
    System.out.println("Humpty Dumpty was pushed");
    return true;
}

}
```

Figure 14.2 shows what the applet looks like after someone has pushed the button.

Program 14.2 works because there is only one Component. Therefore, there's only one thing that can send an ACTION_EVENT. Normally there will be several Components in the applet which may or may not be Buttons. Therefore, you'll use the arguments passed to the action method to determine which Component is responsible for the event and respond appropriately.

Since there will potentially be many Buttons and many other Components in a Java applet, it's possible for the action method to get quite crowded. Therefore, it's customary to have only an `if-else-if` block in the action method that determines what kind of Component was pressed. When you know what kind of Component was pressed, call a handleComponent method (where Component is replaced with the name of the class of Component hit, like Button or TextArea), which then determines which particular Component of that type was pressed. Based on that information, the program calls a third method to perform the appropriate action.

Recall that two arguments are passed to the action method. One is the Event itself which is here called `e`. The other is an Object `o`. `o` is an arbitrary object the Component uses for its own purposes. In the case of a Button, `o` is a String that is the label of the button. It's up to the method that handles a particular kind of action to know what, if anything, to do with the Object `o`.

The Event `e` is a full-featured event object from the last chapter. It has all the public methods and fields you learned there. The most important one is the target field. `e.target` is a reference to the Component that generated the action. You use this to distinguish between different Components in the applet.

Normally this is a two-step procedure. The action method tests what kind of Component `e.target` is with the `instanceof` operator. Then, when the class of the Component is determined, it's dispatched to a user-defined method that distinguishes between different Components of the same type and responds accordingly.

Here's an action method that tests for the one component which generates actions that you've learned about so far[2]

```
1.  public boolean action(Event e, Object o) {
2.     if (e.target instanceof Button) {
3.        return handleButton((Button) e.target,
           (String) o);
```

---

[2] Labels don't generate actions.

```
4.      }
5.      else { // We weren't able to handle the event
6.        return false;
7.      }
8.  }
```

Line 1 is the standard signature for an action method.

Line 2 tests to see whether the target of the Event was an instance of the Button class. If it is, then `e.target` and `o` are sent to a method that just handles Buttons. Since you now know that `e.target` is a Button and `o` is a String, you cast those variables to those types before passing them on. How did you know that `o` was a String? Simply because that is how the actions generated by Buttons behave. The handleButton method returns a boolean—`true` if it can handle the Button and `false` if it can't. Line 3 passes that boolean result back to whomever called action.

In Line 5, you see that the object that generated the Event was something this method did not test for. (As you learn more kinds of Components, `else if`'s will be added to this method that tests for the other Components.) Therefore, you cannot handle this event and should return `false`. This signals your Container to try and handle the event in its action method.

The handleButton method will be specific to the applet. For one example, here's a handleButton method that could have been used in Program 14.2:

```
public boolean handleButton(Button b, String s) {

    System.out.println(b.getLabel + " was pushed");

    return true;

}
```

Program 14.3 puts buttons and labels together to tell your fortune.

Program 14.3: The fortune teller applet

```
import java.applet.Applet;
import java.awt.Label;
import java.awt.Button;
import java.awt.Event;
```

```
public class Fortune extends Applet {

  String fortune1 ="You will be happy";
  String fortune2 ="You will be wealthy";
  String fortune3 = "You will have long life.";
  Label l;
  Button b;
  private int i = 1;

  public void init() {
    l = new Label();
    l.setText("Your Fortune for a nickel");
    add(l);
    Button b = new Button("A Nickel");
    add(b);
  }

  public boolean action(Event e, Object o) {
    if (e.target instanceof Button) {
      changeFortune();
    }
    return true;
  }

  public void changeFortune() {
    if (i == 1) {
      l.setText(fortune1);
      i++;
    }
    else if (i == 2) {
      l.setText(fortune2);
      i++;
    }

    else {
      l.setText(fortune3);
      i = 1;
    }
  }

}
```

Figure 14.3 shows the applet.

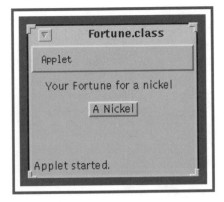

Figure 14.3: *The Fortune Teller Applet*

Handling Multiple Buttons

As implemented, the Fortune program only works for one button. What the action method says is that if a button has been pressed, then the fortune is changed. It does not check to see which button has been pressed. This works fine for an applet with only one button but it needs some modification to handle the more general case of an arbitrary number of buttons.

The following applet has two buttons: one for good news and one for bad. You pick which one you want first. In the `handleButton()` method, you find out which Button was pressed by looking at the button's label. Recall that the Button's label is passed to the action method as the Object o and that you pass that down to handleButton after casting it back to a String.

Program 14.4: Two buttons

```
import java.applet.Applet;
import java.awt.Label;
import java.awt.Button;
import java.awt.Event;


public class DoubleFortune extends Applet {

    String goodnews = "You will win the lottery";
```

```
String badnews =
  "The government will take half your " +
  "money for taxes.";
Label l;

public void init() {
  l = new Label();
  l.setText(
    "Do you want to hear the good news " +
    "or the bad news?");
  add(l);
  add (new Button("Good News"));
  add (new Button("Bad News"));

}

public boolean action(Event e, Object o) {

  if (e.target instanceof Button) {
    return handleButton((Button) e.target,
      (String) o);
  }
  else {
    return false;
  }

}

public boolean handleButton(Button b, String s)
{

  if (s.equals("Good News")) {
    l.setText(goodnews);
  }
  else if (s.equals("Bad News")) {
    l.setText(badnews);
  }
  else {
    l.setText(b.getLabel());
  }

  return true;
}
}
```

Figure 14.4 shows this applet running.

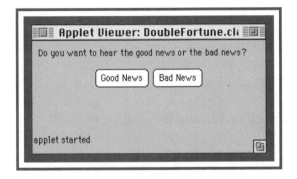

Figure 14.4: *Two Buttons and a Label*

Button Methods

Buttons are simple objects. Most of the time all you need to do is add them to the layout and respond to any ACTION_EVENTs that occur. The two methods of java.awt.Button that you may occasionally have reason to call are getLabel() and setLabel(String s). These allow you to retrieve and change the text of the button while the applet is running. Given a Button b, here is how they might be used:

```
String s = b.getLabel();

b.setLabel("Here's the new label");
```

Note that despite the suggestive name, getLabel returns a String, not a Label.

Q&A

Q: *Why not use a* switch *statement to test all the possible types of actions?*

A: switch statements can only switch based on char, byte, short, or int. They cannot switch based on whether the value of an expression is an instance of a class. Although you could write classes and methods to map between particular widget classes and ints, by the time you were finished, it would have been simpler just to use if and a lot of else if's.

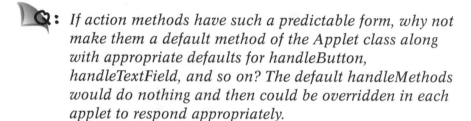 **Q:** *If action methods have such a predictable form, why not make them a default method of the Applet class along with appropriate defaults for handleButton, handleTextField, and so on? The default handleMethods would do nothing and then could be overridden in each applet to respond appropriately.*

A: There's no reason not to. In fact, feel free to go ahead and write your own subclass of java.applet.Applet that does exactly this and then extend this subclass rather than extending java.applet.Applet directly.

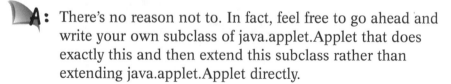 **Q:** *What's the difference between a widget and a Component?*

A: A widget is a generic term used across many platforms that refers to a graphical user interface object like a button or a scrollbar. In Java's AWT, widgets are all subclasses of java.awt.Component. However, some other things that are also subclasses of java.awt.Component would not be considered widgets. For instance, an applet is itself an instance of java.awt.Component. This is not a widget to most people's thinking.

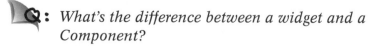 ## Quiz

1. What is the purpose of an action method?

2. When is the action method called?

Exercises

1. Modify the fortune teller applet so that it reads the fortunes out of an indefinite number of PARAM tags and randomly selects the fortune.

Summary

In this chapter you learned

- What a Component is
- How to add Components to an applet
- How to use Labels
- How to use Buttons

Coming Up

Now that you understand the basics of Components, the next chapter explores many new Components including TextAreas, TextFields, Canvases, Checkboxes, scroll bars, and more.

In Chapter 16, you'll learn how to gain more control over the placement of Components using LayoutManagers. Finally, in Chapter 17 you'll learn that the use of Components isn't restricted to applets, that you can also use the AWT to create GUI applications.

Further Reading

http://www.javasoft.com/JDK-1.0/api/java.awt.Component.html

http://www.javasoft.com/JDK-1.0/api/java.awt.Button.html

http://www.javasoft.com/JDK-1.0/api/java.awt.Label.html

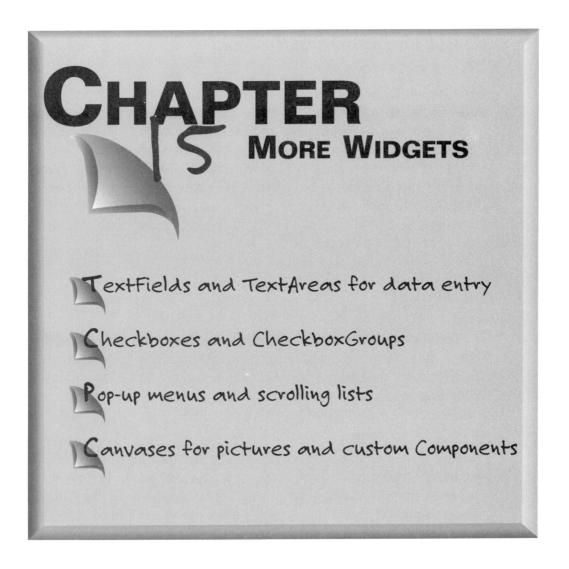

CHAPTER 15

MORE WIDGETS

- TextFields and TextAreas for data entry

- Checkboxes and CheckboxGroups

- Pop-up menus and scrolling lists

- Canvases for pictures and custom Components

In the last chapter, you learned the basic behavior of members of the class java.awt.Component. You also learned about the specific classes java.awt.Label and java.awt.Button. This chapter looks at the remaining Components, concentrating on the unique behavior of each.

TextComponents

The typewriter applet you saw in Chapter 13 is at the limits of what's possible in an applet using nothing more than the basic events and Graphics objects. Fortunately, Java provides a much more capable set of widgets for both freeform text input and output. These are based on the TextComponent class. A TextField is a TextComponent that allows the user to edit a single line of text. A TextArea is a TextComponent that lets the user edit several lines of text. Both handle selections, scrolling, copy and paste, and everything else you expect text to do in a modern GUI environment.

TextFields

TextFields are used for user input when the user is not expected to input more than a single line of text. For instance, you might use a TextField to get the user's name, zip code, or credit card number. However, you would not use a TextField to ask for the user's address since that would take more than a single line.

You can create empty TextFields with the `TextField()` constructor. However, you almost always want to specify the width of the field in characters using `TextField(int num_characters)`. This won't be an exact number unless you're using a monospaced font like Courier, but it should be good enough. Add a few extra spaces just in case.

TextFields don't have labels so you should add a Label next to each TextField to tell the user what to enter in that field. You also have the option of giving the TextField some default text. You can use this to tell the user what they should enter rather than using Labels if you like. Program 15.1 is an applet that asks the user for their name and phone number. Figure 15.1 shows this applet in action.

Program 15.1: TextField Example

```java
import java.applet.Applet;
import java.awt.Label;
import java.awt.TextField;
```

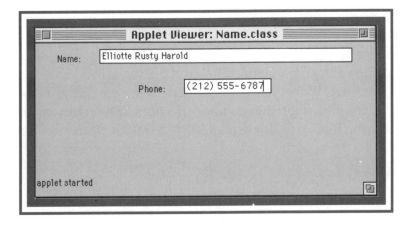

Figure 15.1: *Two TextFields and two Labels*

```
public class Name extends Applet {

  public void init() {
    add(new Label("Name: ", Label.LEFT));
    add(new TextField(40));
    add(new Label("Phone: ", Label.LEFT));
    add(new TextField(12));
  }

}
```

You can retrieve the value that's been stored in a TextField using the field's getText() method.

TextFields produce actions like most other Components. An action occurs in a TextField when the user hits the return key while the user is typing in the TextField. You trap this just like you trapped Button actions in the last chapter.

Most of the time TextFields are used for input. However, you can use them for output as well. Just call the TextField's setText(String s) method where s is the text you want to put in the TextField. If you only want to use the TextField for output and not allow the user to edit the text, then you should call the TextField's setEditable(false) method to turn off editing. If you later want to allow editing, you can call setEditable(true).

TextAreas

Sometimes one line of text isn't enough. If the user needs to enter several lines of text or you need to output several lines of text, you can use a TextArea. When you create a TextArea, you first give the number of lines and then the number of characters across a line. For instance, the following line adds a TextArea with three rows and forty columns to the applet:

```
add(new TextArea(3,40));
```

You can also pass a String to a TextArea to start it off with some text like this:

```
add(new TextArea("Thank you for visiting.", 3, 40));
```

TextAreas come complete with scrollbars so the user can enter as much text as they need to, regardless of the size of the TextArea.

For example, the address to which a pizza is to be delivered may require a street address, an apartment number, and a town. There may be some special instructions too, for instance, "Ring the bell twice, wait for the dog to stop barking, and then unlatch the gate and walk around to the back." You can use a TextArea to enter an unlimited amount of this sort of freeform text. Program 15.2 uses two TextAreas to ask where a pizza should be delivered. Figure 15.2 shows this applet in action.

Program 15.2: TextArea Example

```
import java.applet.Applet;
import java.awt.Label;
import java.awt.TextArea;


public class Delivery extends Applet {

  public void init() {
    add(new Label("Address: ", Label.LEFT));
    add(new TextArea(4, 30));
    add(new Label("Instructions: ", Label.LEFT));
    add(new TextArea(4, 30));
  }

}
```

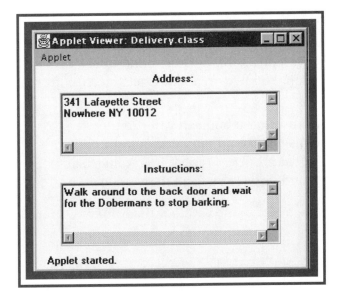

Figure 15.2: *Two TextAreas*

Checkboxes

Checkboxes are used to indicate a boolean value. Each Checkbox has a label that should be used to tell the user what the Checkbox represents. For instance, a Checkbox with the label "Anchovies" would be checked if the user wants anchovies on their pizza and unchecked if they don't.

Checkboxes are often used to select from a list of possible choices when as few selections as zero or as many as everything on the list may be made. Adding a Checkbox to an applet is simple. Just declare it, construct it, and add it.

```
Checkbox c;

c = new Checkbox("Pepperoni");

add(c);
```

As usual these steps may be combined into the single line

```
add(new Checkbox("Pepperoni"));
```

By default Checkboxes are unchecked when created. If you want a Checkbox to start life checked, use the following constructor instead:

```
add(new Checkbox("Pepperoni", null, true));
```

The **null** is a reference to a CheckboxGroup. Passing **null** for this argument says that this Checkbox does not belong to a CheckboxGroup. You'll learn about CheckboxGroups in the next section.

Every Checkbox has a boolean value, either `true` or `false`. When the Checkbox is checked, that value is `true`. When it is unchecked, that value is `false`. You access this value using the Checkbox's `getState()` and `setState(boolean b)` methods. For example,

```
private void handleCheckbox(Checkbox c) {


    if (c.getState()) price += 0.50f;
    else price -= 0.50f;


}
```

When the user checks or unchecks a Checkbox, an ACTION_EVENT is generated. Most of the time you ignore this event. Instead, you manually check the state of a Checkbox when you need to know it. However, if you want to know immediately when a Checkbox changes state, you watch out for action events generated by instances of java.awt.Checkbox in your action method.

For instance, Program 15.3 is an applet that asks the age-old question, "What do you want on your pizza?" When an ingredient is checked, the price of the pizza goes up by 50 cents. When an ingredient is unchecked, 50 cents is taken off. The price is shown in a TextField. Figure 15.3 shows this applet running.

Program 15.3: What do you want on your pizza?

```
import java.applet.Applet;
import java.awt.Checkbox;
import java.awt.Label;
import java.awt.TextField;
import java.awt.Event;

public class Ingredients extends Applet {
```

Figure 15.3: *Checkboxes*

```
/* You need access to t in the handleCheckbox
  method so make it a field. */
TextField t;
float price = 7.00f;

public void init() {
  add(new Label(
    "What do you want on your pizza?",
    Label.CENTER)
  );
  add(new Checkbox("Pepperoni"));
  add(new Checkbox("Olives"));
  add(new Checkbox("Onions"));
  add(new Checkbox("Sausage"));
  add(new Checkbox("Peppers"));
  add(new Checkbox("Extra Cheese"));
  add(new Checkbox("Ham"));
  add(new Checkbox("Pineapple"));
  add(new Checkbox("Anchovies"));
  t = new TextField(String.valueOf(price));

// so people can't change the price of the pizza
  t.setEditable(false);
  add(t);
}
```

```
public boolean action(Event e, Object o) {
    if (e.target instanceof Checkbox) {
        handleCheckbox((Checkbox) e.target);
    }

    return true;
}

private void handleCheckbox(Checkbox c) {

    if (c.getState()) price += 0.50f;
    else price -= 0.50f;
    // Change the price
    t.setText(String.valueOf(price));

    }

}
```

CheckboxGroups

CheckboxGroups are collections of Checkboxes with the special property that no more than one Checkbox in the same group can be selected at a time. The Checkboxes in a CheckboxGroup are often called **radio buttons**. Checkboxes that are members of the same CheckboxGroup cannot be checked simultaneously. When the user checks one, all others are unchecked automatically.

The constructor for a CheckboxGroup is trivial. No arguments are needed. You do not even need to add the CheckboxGroup to the applet since CheckboxGroups are themselves not user-interface widgets, just ways of arranging Checkboxes.

```
CheckboxGroup cbg = new CheckboxGroup();
```

To make Checkboxes act like radio buttons, use this Checkbox constructor

```
Checkbox(String label, CheckboxGroup cbg, boolean checked)
```

for each Checkbox in the group. The label is the label for this Checkbox, just as in Checkboxes of the last section. The

Figure 15.4: *Checkboxes*

CheckboxGroup is the group you want this Checkbox to belong to and must already exist. Program 15.4 asks the customer how they're going to pay for their pizza: Visa, Mastercard, American Express, Discover, cash, or check. Someone may want both anchovies and pineapple on their pizza, but they're unlikely to pay with both Visa and American Express. Figure 15.4 shows the applet in action.

Program 15.4: CheckboxGroup or Radio Buttons

```java
import java.applet.Applet;
import java.awt.Label;
import java.awt.Checkbox;
import java.awt.CheckboxGroup;

public class PaymentMethod extends Applet {

  public void init() {
    add(new Label("How will you pay for your pizza?"));
    CheckboxGroup cbg = new CheckboxGroup();
    add(new Checkbox("Visa", cbg, false));
    add(new Checkbox("Mastercard", cbg, false));
    add(new Checkbox("American Express", cbg, false));
    add(new Checkbox("Discover", cbg, false));
    add(new Checkbox("Cash", cbg, true));
  }

}
```

There isn't any action in this simple example applet. If you need to take action as radio buttons are checked and unchecked, you do it just the same as for any other Checkbox.

Program 15.4 brings up all the radio buttons unchecked. You could have chosen one to be checked by default (probably Cash in this example).

Choice Menus

Radio buttons are useful for a few items, but they take up a lot of space. More than six radio buttons in a group is probably too many. When you want the user to select one item from a medium-sized list of values, use a Choice menu, more commonly called a **pop-up menu**.

Creating a pop-up menu is a little more complex than creating the other user interface components you've seen. There's an extra step: adding the menu items to the menu. That is, the four steps are

1. Declare the Choice
2. Allocate the Choice
3. Add the menu items to the Choice
4. Add the Choice to the layout

Here's an example:

```
Choice ch;
ch = new Choice();
ch.addItem("Item 1");
ch.addItem("Item 2");
ch.addItem("Item 3");
add(ch);
```

Program 15.5 lets the customer choose the size of their pizza. It displays a price based on the size chosen. Figure 15.5 shows this applet running.

Program 15.5: A Choice Menu

```
import java.applet.Applet;
import java.awt.Choice;
```

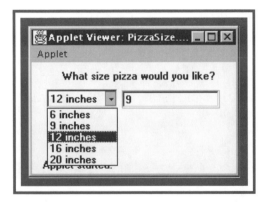

Figure 15.5: *A Choice menu*


```java
import java.awt.Label;
import java.awt.Event;
import java.awt.TextField;
import java.util.StringTokenizer;

public class PizzaSize extends Applet {

  /* You need access to t in the handleChoice
     method so make it a field. */
  TextField t;

  public void init() {
    add(new Label (
      "What size pizza would you like?",
      Label.CENTER)
    );
    Choice ch = new Choice();
    ch.addItem("6 inches");
    ch.addItem("9 inches");
    ch.addItem("12 inches");
    ch.addItem("16 inches");
    ch.addItem("20 inches");
    add(ch);
    t = new TextField(12);
    t.setEditable(false);
    add(t);
  }

  public boolean action(Event e, Object o) {
    if (e.target instanceof Choice) {
```

```java
        handleChoice((Choice) e.target);
      }
      return true;
    }

    private void handleChoice(Choice c) {

      String s = c.getSelectedItem();
      StringTokenizer st = new StringTokenizer(s);
      int size = Integer.parseInt(st.nextToken());
      float price = 2.0f;
      switch (size) {
        case 6:
          price = 2.0f;
          break;
        case 9:
          price = 6.0f;
          break;
        case 12:
          price = 9.0f;
          break;
        case 16:
          price = 12.0f;
          break;
        case 20:
          price = 16.0f;
          break;
      }
      t.setText(String.valueOf(price));

    }

  }
```

Lists

Scrolling lists are useful for storing long lists of things one to a line. You create a new List with the constructor List(**int** num_lines, **boolean** allow_multiple_selections) like this:

```java
List l = new List(8, true);
```

num_lines is the number of items you want to be visible in the scrolling list. It is not necessarily the same as the number of items in the list which is limited only by available memory.

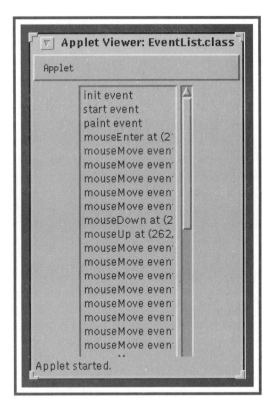

Figure 15.6: *The Event List applet*

`allow_multiple_selections` says whether the user is allowed to select more than one item at once (typically by Shift-clicking).

As an example of a List, Program 15.6 reworks the EventTutor applet from Chapter 13 so that it puts the output in a scrolling List rather than directly on the screen or in some inconvenient standard output stream. Figure 15.6 shows the applet in action.

Program 15.6: A Revised Event Tutor

```java
import java.applet.Applet;
import java.awt.List;
import java.awt.Event;
import java.awt.Graphics;

public class EventList extends Applet {

  List theList;
```

```java
public void init() {
  theList = new List(25, false);
  add(theList);
  theList.addItem("init event");
}

public void paint(Graphics g) {
  theList.addItem("paint event");
}

public void start() {
  theList.addItem("start event");
  repaint();
}

public void destroy() {
  theList.addItem("destroy event");
}

public void update(Graphics g) {
  theList.addItem("update event");
}

public boolean mouseUp(Event e, int x, int y) {
  theList.addItem("mouseUp at (" + x + "," +
    y + ")");
  return false;
}

public boolean mouseDown(Event e, int x, int y) {
  theList.addItem("mouseDown at (" + x + "," +
    y + ")");
  return false;
}

public boolean mouseDrag(Event e, int x, int y) {
  theList.addItem("mouseDrag at (" + x + "," +
    y + ")");
  return false;
}

public boolean mouseMove(Event e, int x, int y) {
  theList.addItem("mouseMove event at (" + x + "," +
    y + ")");
  return false;
```

```
    }

    public boolean mouseEnter(Event e, int x, int y) {
        theList.addItem("mouseEnter at (" + x + "," +
        y + ")");
        return false;
    }

    public boolean mouseExit(Event e, int x, int y) {
        theList.addItem("mouseExit at (" + x + "," +
        y + ")");
        return false;
    }

    public boolean keyDown(Event e, int x) {
        theList.addItem("keyDown: " + (char) x);
        return false;
    }

}
```

You should definitely run this applet. When you do, note that the only events that get listed are those that occur outside the List. The List handles and eats any events that occur inside its region before the broader applet gets a chance to look at them. This isn't just true of lists. It's standard behavior for any Component.

Scrolling lists can also be used for making multiple selections when there are too many choices for Checkboxes or pop-up menus to be feasible. You can retrieve the selected items at any time by using the List's `getSelectedItem()` and `getSelectedItems()` methods.

Canvases

You'll often want to have user interface Components like Buttons and TextArea's in the same applet where you do drawing with a Graphics object in the paint method. If you want to use Graphics primitives like drawLine and drawOval in an applet with Components, you normally put them inside a Canvas. A Canvas is just a rectangular area you can draw on.

Canvases must be subclassed to be useful. You override three methods in your subclass: `preferredSize()` to say how big a Canvas you want, `minimumSize()` to say what's the smallest size you can live with, and `paint(Graphics g)` to actually draw the picture in your Canvas. If your Canvas is interactive, for instance if it lets the user draw lines by clicking and dragging, you can override the various mouse and keypress methods as well, but most of the time this won't be necessary.

The Canvas in Program 15.7 draws a pizza, shown in Figure 15.7, but you can replace it with a mouth-watering bitmapped picture of a pizza and use g.drawImage instead if you like.

Program 15.7: A pizza on a Canvas

```java
import java.applet.Applet;
import java.awt.Canvas;
import java.awt.Label;
import java.awt.Dimension;
import java.awt.Graphics;

public class DrawPizza extends Applet {

  public void init() {
    add(new Label("This is a pizza", Label.CENTER));
    add(new PizzaCanvas());
  }

}

class PizzaCanvas extends Canvas {

  public void paint(Graphics g) {
    int CanvasWidth = size().width;
    int CanvasHeight = size().height;

    g.drawOval(0, 0, CanvasWidth-1,
      CanvasHeight-1);
    // Slice the pizza
    g.drawLine(0, CanvasHeight/2, CanvasWidth-1,
      CanvasHeight/2);
    g.drawLine(CanvasWidth/2, 0, CanvasWidth/2,
      CanvasHeight-1);
    int gap = (int) ((CanvasWidth/2) * (1.0 -
```

Figure 15.7: *A Pizza on a Canvas*

```
        1.0/Math.sqrt(2.0)));
      g.drawLine(gap, gap, CanvasWidth - 1 - gap,
         CanvasHeight - 1 - gap);
      g.drawLine(CanvasWidth - 1 - gap, gap, gap,
         CanvasHeight - 1 - gap);

   }

   public Dimension minimumSize() {
      return new Dimension(50, 50);
   }

   public Dimension preferredSize() {
      return minimumSize();
   }

}
```

Creating Custom Components

Try to use the default Components whenever possible. Consistency may be the "hobgoblin of little minds, teachers, poets, and divines" as Emerson wrote, but a lot of those people will be using your applet.

Nonetheless there are times when you'll find it necessary to create a custom Component that looks different from the standard

Components provided by the AWT. To do this, use a subclass of Canvas with its own paint, minimumSize, and preferredSize methods as in the last section.

You'll also want to add event handling to your new Component. There are three things your Component can do with each event:

1. Ignore it and pass it on to the component's Container by returning `false` (the default).
2. Ignore it, but eat the event by returning `true`.
3. Do something as a result of the event.

Let's say you want to make a PanicButton Component, that is, a big red button with yellow letters spelling out "Panic." Here's how you might do it:

Program 15.8: A Customized Panic Component

```java
import java.applet.Applet;
import java.awt.Graphics;
import java.awt.Canvas;
import java.awt.Label;
import java.awt.Color;
import java.awt.Dimension;
import java.awt.Event;
import java.awt.Font;

public class Panic extends Applet {

  public void init () {
    add(new Label("Don't Panic"));
    add(new PanicButton());

  }

}

class PanicButton extends Canvas {

  int radius = 101;

  public void paint(Graphics g) {

    g.setFont(new Font("Helvetica",Font.BOLD,24));
```

```
        g.setColor(Color.red);
        g.fillOval(0, 0, 2*radius, 2*radius);
        g.setColor(Color.yellow);
        g.drawString("Panic", 65, radius+12);


    }

    public boolean mouseUp(Event e, int x, int y) {

        // Was the click inside the circle??
        if (Math.sqrt( (x-radius)*(x-radius) +
            (y-radius)*(y-radius)) <= radius)   {
            System.exit(1);
            return true;
        }
        else {
            return false
        }


    }

    public Dimension minimumSize() {
        return new Dimension(2*radius,2*radius);
    }

    public Dimension preferredSize() {
        return minimumSize();
    }

}
```

Figure 15.8 shows the result.

The Panic class is simple. All it does is add a Label and a PanicButton to the applet. It doesn't even need to handle events, because the PanicButton knows what to do when it's pressed (kill everything).

The PanicButton class has one field and four methods. The member variable `radius` specifies the radius of the button. You use this inside `paint` to draw the button and inside `mouseUp` to determine whether the mouse was in fact clicked inside the button.

The paint method draws a big red circle with yellow letters. The coordinate system used is that of the Canvas, (0, 0, 100, 100), not the

Figure 15.9: *The PanicButton*

applet's. In the next chapter you'll see how to position the PanicButton in the center of the applet. Also remember that the coordinate system starts at the upper-left-hand corner of the Canvas, not at the more natural center of the circle. The center of the circle is at (50, 50).

The mouseUp method tests whether or not the mouse button was released inside the circle. Remember that although you get mouse clicks from inside the Canvas, the button doesn't cover the entire Canvas. If the mouse was pressed on the button, then you panic, that is, call System.exit. After panicking, you return `true` to indicate that this event has been handled. This return may seem superfluous because it will never be executed given that the applet is destroyed immediately before calling it. However, the compiler will complain if you don't include it. If the mouse was clicked outside the button, then you return `false` to say that the Container (the applet) still needs to process this event.

The last two methods of this class are `minimumSize()` and `preferredSize()`. They're the same as they were in the last chapter. They let the Container in which this Component is placed know how much size this Component wants and how much it will settle for.

Not all custom Components will be able to take all the action they need to take. You can test for events generated by your own Components in an applet's event loop too. For instance, if you wanted to panic from the applet rather than the button, you'd remove the call to System.exit from the mouseUp method in PanicButton and instead post an ACTION_EVENT telling the Container (i.e., the applet) that the PanicButton had been pressed. However, you still need to test the exact location of the hit inside the PanicButton class to determine whether the button was really hit. You can't just pass all mouse clicks up to the applet without any preprocessing. Program 15.9 is the revised Panic program:

Program 15.9: The revised PanicButton

```java
import java.applet.Applet;
import java.awt.Graphics;
import java.awt.Canvas;
import java.awt.Label;
import java.awt.Color;
import java.awt.Dimension;
import java.awt.Event;
import java.awt.Font;

public class Panic extends Applet {

  public void init () {

    add(new Label("Don't Panic"));
    add(new PanicButton());

  }

  public boolean action(Event e, Object arg) {

    if (e.target instanceof PanicButton) {
      System.exit(1);
      return true;
    }
    else {
      return false;
    }
  }
}
```

```
class PanicButton extends Canvas {

  int radius = 100;

  public void paint(Graphics g) {

    g.setFont(new Font("Helvetica",Font.BOLD,24));
    g.setColor(Color.red);
    g.fillOval(0, 0, 2*radius, 2*radius);
    g.setColor(Color.yellow);
    g.drawString("Panic", 65, radius+12);

  }

  public boolean mouseUp(Event e, int x, int y) {

    // Was the click inside the circle??
    if (Math.sqrt( (x-radius)*(x-radius) +
      (y-radius)*(y-radius)) <= radius)  {
      postEvent(new
        Event(this, Event.ACTION_EVENT, "Panic"));
      return true;
    }
    else {
      return false;
    }

  }

  public Dimension minimumSize() {
    return new Dimension(2*radius,2*radius);
  }

  public Dimension preferredSize() {
    return minimumSize();
  }
}
```

Program 15.9 adds an action method to the Panic class in order to test for and respond to the ACTION_EVENT generated by the PanicButton. The PanicButton itself is mostly unchanged except that System.exit(1) has been replaced by

```
postEvent(new Event(this, Event.ACTION_EVENT,
  "Panic"));
```

This is your first example of creating and posting your own events. The constructor used creates a new Event whose target is **this** (i.e., this instance of the PanicButton class) and whose ID is given by the mnemonic constant `Event.ACTION_EVENT`. Finally, you're allowed to pass one object of any type to the method that eventually responds to this event. In this applet you pass the String "Panic".

Having created the event, you then place it in the event queue by passing it to postEvent from java.awt.Component. This puts it in the event queue of this PanicButton, but since PanicButton doesn't respond to ACTION_EVENTs, it gets tossed up to the Container, that is, the Panic applet, where it is handled by Panic's action method.

This is actually the more common way to handle events generated by custom Components. It's quite rare that you can do everything you need to do within the Component itself.

Q&A

Q: *Why is PanicButton a subclass of Canvas and not a subclass of Button?*

A: Subclassing Button is the first thing most people try when faced with a problem like the PanicButton. The problem is that although you can change the behavior of a Button, you can't change its appearance on all platforms because it's implemented as a **peer**. A peer is an interface between the Java widget and the native windowing system's idea of a widget. Thus when your applet draws a Button, it doesn't say, "Draw a rounded rectangle 40 pixels across and 20 high." Rather it says, "Give me a native button 40 pixels across and 20 high." What that button looks like is up to the underlying windowing system.

Quiz

1. What would happen if you tried to set more than one Checkbox in a CheckboxGroup to true initially?

Exercises

1. Write a Headline Component that implements the same methods as java.awt.Label but draws all text in 24 point Helvetica bold.

2. Add two constructors to the PanicButton class: one that takes no arguments and produces a PanicButton with a 50 pixel radius, and one that takes an `int` and produces a PanicButton with that size radius.

3. Write a CircleButton class that creates a circular button as a subclass of Canvas. It should allow (but not require) the creator to specify the label and the radius of the button. Furthermore, it should post an action event if the mouse is pressed and released inside the circle.

4. Add getLabel and setLabel methods to the PanicButton class. If the size of the button was not specified at creation time, adjust the minimum size of the button to be large enough for the text in the current font.

5. Add setColor, setTextColor, and setFont methods to the CircleButton. You now have a fairly generic circular button.

Summary

In this chapter you learned

- How to use TextFields for single line data entry
- How to use TextArea for longer data entry
- How to set the text of TextComponents
- How to create and check the value of Checkboxes
- How to make Checkboxes mutually exclusive with CheckboxGroups
- How to make pop-up menus with java.awt.Choice
- How to make scrolling lists with java.awt.List

- How to handle Scrollbars
- How to use Canvases to draw pictures
- How to create custom Components with Canvases

Coming Up

Some of the applets presented in this chapter were functional but not nearly as attractive as they could be. In the next chapter, you'll learn how to use LayoutManagers and Panels to give yourself control over where Components are placed. Then in Chapter 17, you'll learn how to add these widgets to free-standing windows in applets and applications.

Further Reading

http://www.javasoft.com/JDK-1.0/api/java.awt.TextComponent.html

http://www.javasoft.com/JDK-1.0/api/java.awt.TextArea.html

http://www.javasoft.com/JDK-1.0/api/java.awt.TextField.html

http://www.javasoft.com/JDK-1.0/api/java.awt.Canvas.html

http://www.javasoft.com/JDK-1.0/api/java.awt.Choice.html

http://www.javasoft.com/JDK-1.0/api/java.awt.Checkbox.html

http://www.javasoft.com/JDK-1.0/api/java.awt.CheckboxGroup.html

http://www.javasoft.com/JDK-1.0/api/java.awt.Choice.html

http://www.javasoft.com/JDK-1.0/api/java.awt.List.html

CHAPTER 16

LayoutManagers

The five basic LayoutManagers

Nesting Panels for multiple layouts

Absolute positioning

You may have noticed that despite the GUI widgets, the last few applets didn't look so hot. Strings were sometimes cut off. Buttons lay on top of Labels, and other things weren't just the way you wanted them. LayoutManagers provide control over the locations of individual widgets in Java applets. Since you're never sure how big an area you'll have to work with or how it will be shaped, most of the controls are relative in nature. That is, you say this widget should be above that one or left-aligned with the other one; but you don't say that this widget's upper-left-hand corner is at pixel (42, 65).

In this chapter, you'll learn the five basic LayoutManagers included in the AWT and some additional tricks for handling complicated applets.

The Five LayoutManagers

A FlowLayout arranges widgets from left to right until there's no more space left. Then it begins a row lower and moves from left to right again. Each Component in a FlowLayout gets as much space as it needs and no more. A FlowLayout is useful for laying out buttons but not for much else. This is the default LayoutManager for applets and Panels (special Containers to aid with layouts about which you'll learn more very shortly).

A BorderLayout organizes an applet into North, South, East, West, and Center sections. North, South, East, and West are the rectangular edges of the applet. They're continually resized to fit the sizes of the widgets included in them. Center is whatever's left over in the middle.

A CardLayout breaks the applet into a deck of cards, each of which has its own LayoutManager. Only one card appears on the screen at a time. The user flips between cards, each of which shows a different set of Components. The common analogy is with HyperCard on the Mac and Toolbook on Windows. In Java, this might be used for a series of data input screens where more input is needed than can comfortably fit on one screen.

A GridLayout divides an applet into a specified number of rows and columns which form a grid of cells, each equally sized and spaced. As Components are added to the layout, they are placed in the cells, starting at the upper-left-hand corner and moving to the right and down the page. Each Component is sized to fit into its cell. This tends to squeeze and stretch Components unnecessarily. However the GridLayout is great for arranging Panels.

GridBagLayout is the most precise of the five AWT LayoutManagers. It's similar to the GridLayout, but Components do not need to be the same size. Each Component can occupy one or more cells of the layout. Furthermore, Components are not necessarily placed in the cells beginning at the upper-left-hand corner and moving to the right and down.

In simple applets with just a few Components, you often need only one of these LayoutManagers. In more complicated applets, however, you'll often split your applet into Panels, lay out the Panels according to a LayoutManager, and give each Panel its own LayoutManager.

A FlowLayout arranges components from left to right until there's no more space left. Then it begins a row lower and moves from left to right again. Each Component in a FlowLayout gets as much space as it needs and no more. FlowLayout is most commonly used for a series of buttons.

FlowLayout is the default LayoutManager for a Panel (of which Applet is a subclass), so you don't need to do anything special to create a FlowLayout in an applet. However, you do need to use the following constructors if you want to use a FlowLayout in a Window (which will be discussed in the next chapter).

LayoutManagers have constructors like any other class. The constructor for a FlowLayout is `FlowLayout()`. Thus, to create a new FlowLayout, write

```
FlowLayout fl;

fl = new FlowLayout();
```

As usual, this can be shortened to

```
FlowLayout fl = new FlowLayout();
```

You tell an applet to use a particular LayoutManager instance by passing the LayoutManager object to the applet's setLayout method like so:

```
setLayout(fl);
```

Most of the time setLayout is called in the init method. You normally just create the LayoutManager right inside the call to setLayout like this:

```
setLayout(new FlowLayout());
```

Program 16.1 uses a FlowLayout to position a series of buttons that mimic the buttons on a tape deck. The applet is shown in Figure 16.1.

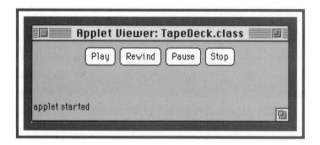

Figure 16.1: *Buttons arranged according to a FlowLayout*

Program 16.1: FlowLayout example

```java
import java.applet.Applet;
import java.awt.Button;
import java.awt.FlowLayout;

public class TapeDeck extends Applet {

  public void init() {
    setLayout(new FlowLayout());
    add( new Button("Play"));
    add( new Button("Rewind"));
    add( new Button("Pause"));
    add( new Button("Stop"));
  }

}
```

If you wish, you can exercise a little more control over a FlowLayout. First, you can change the alignment of the layout. The items are normally centered in the applet. You can make them left- or right-justified instead. To do this, just pass one of the mnemonic constants `FlowLayout.LEFT`, `FlowLayout.RIGHT`, or `FlowLayout.CENTER` to the constructor, that is,

```java
flL = new FlowLayout(FlowLayout.LEFT);
flR = new FlowLayout(FlowLayout.RIGHT);
flC = new FlowLayout(FlowLayout.CENTER);
```

Figure 16.2 shows how the TapeDeck applet looks if you replace

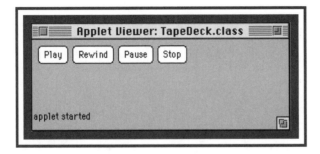

Figure 16.2: *Buttons arranged according to a left-aligned FlowLayout*

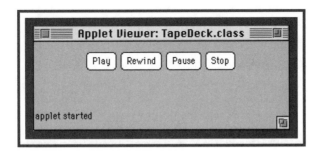

Figure 16.3: *Buttons arranged according to a center-aligned FlowLayout with a five-pixel horizontal spacing and ten-pixel vertical spacing*

```
setLayout(new FlowLayout());
```

with

```
setLayout(new FlowLayout(FlowLayout.LEFT));
```

You can also add some additional space between the Components so they don't squeeze each other quite so much. To do this, use the constructor

```
FlowLayout(int alignment, int hspace, int vspace);
```

Pass this constructor your chosen alignment variable, then the horizontal space between the Components, then the vertical space between the Components. For instance, to set up a FlowLayout with a five-pixel horizontal gap and a ten-pixel vertical gap, aligned with the left edge of the panel, you would type

```
FlowLayout fl = new FlowLayout(FlowLayout.CENTER,
    5, 10);
```

Figure 16.3 shows the result of adding this space to the FlowLayout.

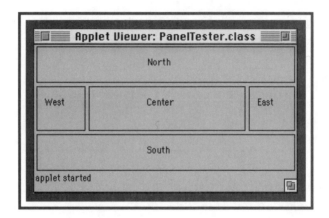

Figure 16.4: *A BorderLayout. The rectangles were drawn deliberately so you could see the boundaries between sections and are not a feature of a generic BorderLayout.*

BorderLayout

A BorderLayout places objects in the North, South, East, West, and center of an applet. You create a new BorderLayout much like a FlowLayout, in the init method inside a call to setLayout like this:

```
setLayout(new BorderLayout());
```

As with FlowLayout, you can add horizontal and vertical gaps between the areas. Here's how you'd add a five-pixel horizontal gap and a ten-pixel vertical gap to a BorderLayout:

```
setLayout(new BorderLayout(5, 10));
```

To add Components to a BorderLayout, include the name of the section you wish to add them to like this:

```
add("South", new Button("Start"));
```

Figure 16.4 shows a Border Layout. As you can see, the North and South sections extend across the applet from left to right. The East and West sections do not extend from the top of the applet to the bottom, but only from the bottom of the North section to the top of South section. The North, South, East and West sections will be made large enough for whatever Components they hold. The Center gets whatever is left over. The exact size is unpredictable.

Similarly the exact packing of Components inside a section is unpredictable as well.

CardLayout

The CardLayout is unusual. It breaks the applet into a deck of cards, each of which normally has a panel with its own LayoutManager. Only one card appears on the screen at a time. You then flip between cards, each of which shows a different set of Components. The common analogy is with HyperCard on the Mac and Toolbook on Windows. In Java, this might be used for a series of data input screens, where more input is needed than can comfortably be fit on one screen. Conversely, you can use a CardLayout for a slide show, where there's more data to be presented than will fit on one screen.

You create a CardLayout with the `CardLayout()` constructor:

```
setLayout(new CardLayout());
```

As before, you can create a CardLayout with a specified gap between Components like this:

```
setLayout(new CardLayout(3, 4));
```

In this example, there will be a three-pixel horizontal gap and a four-pixel vertical gap between each Component.

Each card has a name. A new card is created when you add a Component to the card. Add Components to cards by passing the name of the card and the Component to add to the add method like this:

```
setLayout(new CardLayout());
add("Pizza",
  new Label("How do you like your pizza?"));
add("Pizza", new Button("OK"));
add("Payment",
  new Label("How would you like to pay?"));
add("Payment", new Button("OK"));
add("Address", new Label("Delivery
Instructions"));
```

```
add("Address", new Button("Order"));
```

One common technique is to name each card after a number.

```
setLayout(new CardLayout());
add("1", new Label("First Card"));
add("2", new Label("Second Card"));
add("3", new Label("Third Card"));
add("4", new Label("Fourth Card"));
add("5", new Label("Fifth Card"));
add("6", new Label("Sixth Card"));
```

Technical Note Internally, the list of cards and their names is stored in a Hashtable. This means that there's no guaranteed or built-in order to the cards. You need to keep track of this yourself.

Normally, you add a Panel with its own LayoutManager to each card. Each Card should have some means for navigating between cards. The AWT does not provide one. Finally, note that you can add the same Component to more than one card. This is useful, for example, for creating a Choice Menu with the names of all the cards as a navigation aid.

GridLayout

For a GridLayout, you specify a number of rows and columns. The applet is broken up into a table of equal-sized cells.

GridLayout is useful when you want to place a number of similarly sized objects. It's great for putting together lists of Checkboxes and radio buttons as you did in the Ingredients applet of the last chapter.

Program 16.2 is a modified version that sets aside eight rows and one column. This gives one row for each Checkbox. Compare Figure 16.5 to Figure 15.3 to see how much nicer everything looks with proper use of a GridLayout.

```java
import java.applet.Applet;
import java.awt.Checkbox;
import java.awt.Label;
import java.awt.TextField;
import java.awt.Event;
import java.awt.GridLayout;

public class Ingredients2 extends Applet {

  /* You need access to t in the handleCheckbox
     method so make it a field. */
  TextField t;
  float price = 7.00f;

  public void init() {

    setLayout(new GridLayout(11,1));

    add(new Label(
      "What do you want on your pizza?",
      Label.CENTER)
    );
    add(new Checkbox("Pepperoni"));
    add(new Checkbox("Olives"));
    add(new Checkbox("Onions"));
    add(new Checkbox("Sausage"));
    add(new Checkbox("Peppers"));
    add(new Checkbox("Extra Cheese"));
    add(new Checkbox("Ham"));
    add(new Checkbox("Pineapple"));
    add(new Checkbox("Anchovies"));
    t = new TextField("$" + String.valueOf(price));
    // People can't change the price of the pizza
    t.setEditable(false);
    add(t);
  }

  public boolean action(Event e, Object o) {
    if (e.target instanceof Checkbox) {
      return handleCheckbox((Checkbox) e.target);
    }
    else {
      return false;
```

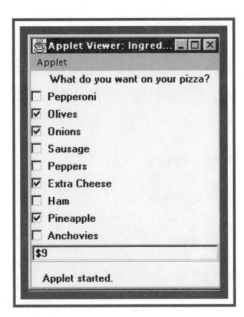

Figure 16.5: *A GridLayout that arranges
Components into one column and 11 rows*

```
        }

    }

    private boolean handleCheckbox(Checkbox c) {

        if (c.getState()) price += 0.50f;
        else price -= 0.50f;
        // Change the price
        t.setText("$" + String.valueOf(price));
        return true;


    }

}
```

GridLayouts are very easy to use. This applet is just three lines different from the previous version and one of those is a change in the
name of the class that wasn't really necessary.

A Panel is a fairly generic Container whose primary purpose in life is to subdivide your drawing area into separate rectangular pieces. Since each Panel can have its own LayoutManager, you can do many things with Panels that you couldn't do with a single LayoutManager.

For example, the Panic applet of the last chapter could use a BorderLayout to place the single Label in the North and the big red button in the center. However, you'd also like to center those Components within each of those areas. The BorderLayout doesn't let you center Components inside an area, but the FlowLayout does. Program 16.3 uses Panels to combine the two.

Program 16.3: Panel Example

```java
import java.applet.Applet;
import java.awt.Graphics;
import java.awt.Canvas;
import java.awt.Label;
import java.awt.Color;
import java.awt.Dimension;
import java.awt.Event;
import java.awt.Font;
import java.awt.BorderLayout;
import java.awt.FlowLayout;
import java.awt.Panel;


public class Panic extends Applet {

  public void init () {

    setLayout(new BorderLayout());
    Panel p1 = new Panel();
    p1.setLayout(new FlowLayout());
    p1.add(new Label("Don't Panic",
      Label.CENTER));
    add("North", p1);
    Panel p2 = new Panel();
```

```java
        p2.setLayout(new FlowLayout());
        p2.add(new PanicButton());
        add("Center", p2);

    }

    public boolean action(Event e, Object arg) {

        if (e.target instanceof PanicButton) {
            System.exit(1);
            return true;
        }
        else {
            return false;
        }
    }

}

class PanicButton extends Canvas {

    int radius = 100;

    public void paint(Graphics g) {

        g.setFont(new Font("Helvetica",
            Font.BOLD, 24));
        g.setColor(Color.red);
        g.fillOval(0, 0, 2*radius, 2*radius);
        g.setColor(Color.yellow);
        g.drawString("Panic", 65, radius+12);

    }

    public boolean mouseUp(Event e, int x, int y) {

        // Was the click inside the circle??
        if (Math.sqrt( (x-radius)*(x-radius) +
            (y-radius)*(y-radius)) <= radius) {
            postEvent(new Event(this, Event.ACTION_EVENT,
                "Panic"));
            return true;
        }
        else {
```

Figure 16.6: *Apple's Macintosh Calculator DA*

```
      return false;
    }


  }

public Dimension minimumSize() {
  return new Dimension(2*radius,2*radius);
}

public Dimension preferredSize() {
  return minimumSize();
}


}
```

Sometimes what's needed is multiple instances of the same LayoutManager. For instance, consider the standard Macintosh calculator in Figure 16.6.

On the one hand, this looks like it should be simple to implement in Java. After all, it's just 18 buttons and a TextField. On the other hand, although most of the keys are the same size, two of the keys and the TextField are oversized. You could almost use a GridLayout, but not quite. Panels are one way to solve this problem.

Consider Figure 16.7. First the calculator is broken up into a grid of one column and three rows. Put a Panel in each of those cells.

JAVA DEVELOPER'S RESOURCE

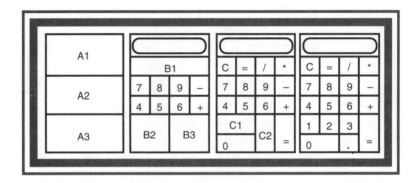

Figure 16.7: *Successive subdivisions via the GridLayout*

Panel A1 will contain the TextField and the top four keys. Panel A2 will contain the middle two rows of keys, and panel A3 will contain the bottom two rows of keys.

The eight keys in the middle panel, A2, are all the same size. Therefore you can use a GridLayout with two rows and four columns in it. However, this isn't true for A1 and A3, so let's continue. Split panel A1 into a grid of two rows and one column. The top cell will be used for the TextField display. However the bottom cell still needs to be split into four pieces so add Panel B1. The bottom is more complex still. Split it into a grid of one row and two columns and put panels B2 and B3 there.

Panel B1 contains four keys, all the same size, so put a grid of one row and four columns there, and add those keys. Next split Panel B2 into two rows and one column. Put the oversized zero key in the second cell and Panel C1 in the first. Next split B3 into two columns and one row. Put a panel in the first cell and the oversized equals key in the second.

Finally split C1 into two columns and one row and put the one and two keys there. Then split C2 into two rows and one column for the three and decimal point keys.

Voilà! A calculator. There is another way to do this which you'll see in the next section. Program 16.4 contains the Java version of the above layout. Figure 16.8 shows the final result.

```java
import java.applet.Applet;
import java.awt.GridLayout;
import java.awt.Button;
import java.awt.TextField;
import java.awt.Insets;
import java.awt.Panel;
import java.awt.Event;

public class Calculator extends Applet {

  TextField screen;

  public void init () {

    setLayout(new GridLayout(3, 1, 3, 3));
    Panel A1 = new Panel();
    this.add(A1);
    Panel A2 = new Panel();
    this.add(A2);
    Panel A3 = new Panel();
    this.add(A3);
    A1.setLayout(new GridLayout(2, 1));
    screen = new TextField(12);
    A1.add(screen);
    Panel B1 = new Panel();
    B1.setLayout(new GridLayout(1, 4, 3, 3));
    B1.add(new Button("C"));
    B1.add(new Button("="));
    B1.add(new Button("/"));
    B1.add(new Button("*"));
    A1.add(B1);
    A2.setLayout(new GridLayout(2, 4, 3, 3));
    A2.add(new Button("7"));
    A2.add(new Button("8"));
    A2.add(new Button("9"));
    A2.add(new Button("-"));
    A2.add(new Button("4"));
    A2.add(new Button("5"));
    A2.add(new Button("6"));
    A2.add(new Button("+"));
    A3.setLayout(new GridLayout(1, 2, 3, 3));
```

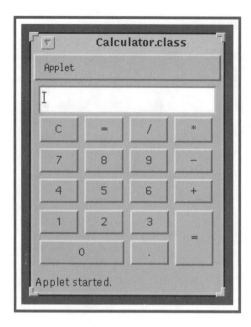

Figure 16.8: *The finished Calculator applet uses one TextField, 18 Buttons, and eight Panels.*

```
// 1, 2 and 0
Panel B2 = new Panel();
B2.setLayout(new GridLayout(2, 1, 3, 3));
// 1 and 2
Panel C1 = new Panel();
C1.setLayout(new GridLayout(1, 2, 3, 3));
C1.add(new Button("1"));
C1.add(new Button("2"));
B2.add(C1);
B2.add(new Button("0"));
// 3, . and =
Panel B3 = new Panel();
B3.setLayout(new GridLayout(1, 2, 3, 3));
// 3 and .
Panel C2 = new Panel();
C2.setLayout(new GridLayout(2, 1, 3, 3));
C2.add(new Button("3"));
C2.add(new Button("."));
B3.add(C2);
B3.add(new Button("="));
A3.add(B2);
A3.add(B3);
```

```
    }

    public Insets insets() {

        return new Insets(5, 5, 5, 5);

    }

    public boolean action(Event e, Object arg) {
        if (e.target instanceof Button) {
            screen.setText((String) arg);
            return true;
        }
        return false;

    }

}
```

The implementation of the functionality of a calculator is left as an exercise for the reader. If you don't worry about operator precedence, it's not particularly difficult.

This applet is on the outer limits of the possibilities of nested Panels and the GridLayout. The 1, 2, 3, and . keys are four panels deep. In the next section, you'll see a different way to implement this applet with only a single LayoutManager.

Insets

The Insets class and method are used to set the gaps around the edges of a Panel. When you set the Insets of your Panel, no Component will get closer to its edge than specified by the Insets.

The Insets class is created by a single constructor:

```
Insets(int top, int left, int bottom, int right)
```

As you probably expect, top is the inset in pixels from the top of the panel. Left is the inset in pixels from the left side of the panel. Bottom is the inset in pixels from the bottom of the panel, and right is the inset in pixels from the right side of the panel.

To set the Insets of your applet (or any other subclass of panel), override its `insets(Insets i)` method like this:

```
public Insets insets() {


    return new Insets(72, 36, 72, 36);


}
```

GridBagLayout

The problem with a GridLayout is that it assumes all objects are the same size. That's often not the case. For instance, in the Calculator applet, the = key and the 0 key were twice as big as the others, and the display at the top of the calculator took up four times as much space. The previous section solved this problem by nesting Panels.

The GridBagLayout is an alternative to nested Panels that allows one element to occupy multiple cells of a grid. Each GridBagLayout uses a rectangular grid of cells, just like a GridLayout. However, the cells are determined and shaped by the Components placed in them rather than the Components being shaped to fit the cells.

The GridBagLayout constructor is trivial: `GridBagLayout()` with no arguments. You use it like this:

```
GridBagLayout gbl = new GridBagLayout();
```

This does not say how many rows or columns there will be. This is determined by the cells your program refers to. If you put a Component in row 8 and column 2, then Java will make sure there are at least nine rows and three columns. (Rows and columns start counting at zero.) If you later put a Component in row 10 and column 4, Java will add the necessary extra rows and columns. You may have a picture in your mind of the finished grid, but Java does not need to know this when you create a GridBagLayout.

Unlike most other LayoutManagers, you should not create a GridBagLayout inside a call to setLayout. You will need access to the GridBagLayout object later in the applet when you add Components to the panel.

GridBagLayout is sufficient to create the Calculator applet without any nested Panels. You do not need to create sub-panels to let Components span multiple cells. Rather you tell each Component which cells it is supposed to occupy.[1] These cells are called the Component's **display area**. You do this by attaching a GridBagConstraints object to the Component.

A GridBagConstraints object specifies the location and area of the Component's display area within the container (normally the applet panel) and how the Component is laid out inside its display area. The GridBagConstraints, in conjunction with the Component's minimum size and the preferred size of the Component's container, determines where the display area is placed within the applet.

The GridBagConstraints constructor is trivial:

```
GridBagConstraints gbc = new GridBagConstraints();
```

There are no arguments. The GridBagConstraints class has only one other method, clone, which clones the object. Your interaction with a GridBagConstraints object takes place through its 11 fields and 15 mnemonic constants.

The use of these variables will be demonstrated by showing how you would lay out different Components of the calculator of the previous section. The discussion assumes that you have imported all the necessary classes, particularly `java.awt.GridBagLayout`, `java.awt.GridBagConstraints`, `java.awt.Button`, and `java.awt.TextField`. It also assumes you have created a GridBagConstraints object `GBC_display` like this:

```
GridBagConstraints GBC_display = new
GridBagConstraints();
```

gridx and gridy

`gridx` and `gridy` specify the x and y coordinates of the cell at the upper left of the Component's display area. The upper-left-most cell has coordinates (0, 0). Figure 16.9 shows a grid for the calculator. The mnemonic constant `GridBagConstraints.RELATIVE` specifies that

---

[1] The display area must consist of a rectangular grid of cells. You can't have a non-contiguous area or a nonrectangular-shaped area. In practice, this limitation is unimportant.

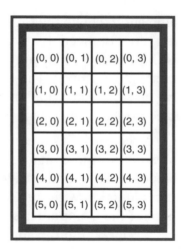

Figure 16.9: *GridBag Coordinates for the calculator*

the Component is placed immediately to the right of (gridx) or immediately below (gridy) the last Component added to this container.

The calculator's display starts at the upper-left-hand corner of the applet. Thus its gridx and gridy members are set like this:

```
GBC_display.gridx = 0;

GBC_display.gridy = 0;
```

The zero key would have

```
GBC_display.gridx = 5;

GBC_display.gridy = 0;
```

gridwidth and gridheight

gridwidth and gridheight specify the number of cells in a row (gridwidth) or column (gridheight) in the Component's display area. The mnemonic constant GridBagConstraints.REMAINDER specifies that the Component should use all remaining cells in its row (for gridwidth) or column (for gridheight). The mnemonic constant GridBagConstraints.RELATIVE specifies that the Component should fill all but the last cell in its row (gridwidth) or column (gridheight).

The calculator's display is four cells wide and one cell high so it's set like this:

```
GBC_display.gridwidth = 4;

GBC_display.gridheight = 1;
```

The equals key is two cells high and one wide so it's set like this:

```
GBC_display.gridwidth = 1;

GBC_display.gridheight = 2;
```

fill

The GridBagConstraints `fill` variable determines whether and how a Component is resized if the Component's display area is larger than the Component itself. The mnemonic constants you use to set this variable are

`GridBagConstraints.NONE`: Don't resize the Component

`GridBagConstraints.HORIZONTAL`: Make the Component wide enough to fill the display area, but don't change its height.

`GridBagConstraints.VERTICAL`: Make the Component tall enough to fill its display area, but don't change its width.

`GridBagConstraints.BOTH`: Resize the Component completely fill its display area both vertically and horizontally.

For the display area of the calculator screen use

```
GBC_display.fill = GridBagConstraints.HORIZONTAL;
```

because you'd like the screen to show as many digits as it can.

ipadx and ipady

Each Component has a minimum width and a minimum height, smaller than which it will not be. If the Component's minimum size is smaller than the Component's display area, then only part of the Component will be shown. `ipadx` and `ipady` let you increase this minimum size by padding the edges of the Component with extra pixels. For instance, setting `ipadx` to two will guarantee that the Component is at least four pixels wider than its normal minimum (`ipadx` adds two pixels to each side). This is not needed for the Calculator applet.

insets

`insets` is an instance of the Insets class which specifies the padding between the Component and the edges of the display area. For all the keys in the Calculator applet, the insets are set like this:

```
GBC_equals.insets = new Insets(3, 3, 3, 3);
```

which provides six pixels of space between each adjacent pair of keys (three from each key).

anchor

When the Component is smaller than its display area, the anchor member variable specifies where to place it. The mnemonic constants you use for this purpose are similar to those used in a BorderLayout, but a little more specific. They are

- `GridBagConstraints.CENTER`
- `GridBagConstraints.NORTH`
- `GridBagConstraints.NORTHEAST`
- `GridBagConstraints.EAST`
- `GridBagConstraints.SOUTHEAST`
- `GridBagConstraints.SOUTH`
- `GridBagConstraints.SOUTHWEST`
- `GridBagConstraints.WEST`
- `GridBagConstraints.NORTHWEST`

The default is `GridBagConstraints.CENTER`. This is not explicitly set in the Calculator applet because the Components are large enough, relative to their display areas, that it really doesn't matter where they go and the default of center is fine.

weightx and weighty

`weightx` and `weighty` determine how the cells are distributed in the container. With weights of zero (the default) the cells all have the minimum size they need, and everything clumps together in the center.

Adding a Component to a GridBagLayout

There are three steps to adding a Component to a GridBagLayout. They are

1. Create a GridBagConstraints object for the Component.
2. Set the GridBagLayout to that GridBagConstraints object.
3. Add the Component to the layout in the usual fashion.

Let's look at this in a little more detail. Here is the start of the init() method from the upcoming GridBagCalculator applet:

```
1.      GridBagLayout gbl = new GridBagLayout();
2.      setLayout(gbl);
3.
4.      // Add the display to the top four cells
5.      GridBagConstraints GBC_display = new
           GridBagConstraints();
6.      GBC_display.gridx = 0;
7.      GBC_display.gridy = 0;
8.      GBC_display.gridwidth = 4;
9.      GBC_display.gridheight = 1;
10.     GBC_display.fill =
           GridBagConstraints.HORIZONTAL;
11.
12.     // add the text field
13.     TextField display = new TextField(12);
14.     gbl.setConstraints(display, GBC_display);
15.     add(display);
```

Let's investigate line by line. Remember that you're working with a grid that's six rows by four columns, counting down and to the right.

Line 1 creates the new GridBagLayout called gbl. Line 2 sets the layout of the applet to gbl. You'll be using gbl's setConstraints method frequently in what follows. Therefore you need the variable that refers to it and cannot combine these two lines with something like

```
setLayout(new GridBagLayout());
```

as you would with many other LayoutManagers.

Line 5 creates a GridBagConstraints object you'll use to set up the layout of the TextField that represents the calculator display.

Line 6 says you start drawing the TextField in the top row.

Line 7 says you start drawing it in the leftmost column.

Line 8 says this TextField will run across four columns.

Line 9 says it will run across one row.

Line 10 says you want the TextField to completely fill these cells across even if it wouldn't normally be large enough to do that.

Line 13 creates the TextField.

Line 14 tells the LayoutManager that it should use the GridBagConstraints object GBC_display which was set up in lines 5 through 10 to lay out this TextField.

Finally Line 15 adds the TextField to the applet panel and you are finished.

The GridBagCalculator applet in the next section shows many more examples of this. They're mostly the same except that you place each Component into different cells.

The GridBagCalculator Applet

Program 16.5 is the complete calculator applet laid out with a GridBagLayout. Although somewhat longer than the version that used a Grid Layout and nested panels, this program is much clearer since you don't have to keep track of different levels of nesting of Panels. Each Component can be placed individually.

Program 16.5: GridbagLayout example

```java
import java.applet.Applet;
import java.awt.GridBagLayout;
import java.awt.GridBagConstraints;
import java.awt.Button;
import java.awt.TextField;
import java.awt.Insets;

public class GridBagCalculator extends Applet {

  public void init () {

    GridBagLayout gbl = new GridBagLayout();
```

```java
setLayout(gbl);

// Add the display to the top four cells
GridBagConstraints GBC_display =
  new GridBagConstraints();
GBC_display.gridx = 0;
GBC_display.gridy = 0;
GBC_display.gridwidth = 4;
GBC_display.gridheight = 1;
GBC_display.fill =
  GridBagConstraints.HORIZONTAL;

// add the text field
TextField display = new TextField(12);
gbl.setConstraints(display, GBC_display);
add(display);

// Add the clear button
GridBagConstraints GBC_clear =
  new GridBagConstraints();
GBC_clear.gridx = 0;
GBC_clear.gridy = 1;
GBC_clear.gridwidth = 1;
GBC_clear.gridheight = 1;
GBC_clear.fill = GridBagConstraints.BOTH;
GBC_clear.insets = new Insets(3, 3, 3, 3);

// add the button
Button clear = new Button("C");
gbl.setConstraints(clear, GBC_clear);
add(clear);

// Add the equals button
GridBagConstraints GBC_equals =
  new GridBagConstraints();
GBC_equals.gridx = 1;
GBC_equals.gridy = 1;
GBC_equals.gridwidth = 1;
GBC_equals.gridheight = 1;
GBC_equals.fill = GridBagConstraints.BOTH;
GBC_equals.insets = new Insets(3, 3, 3, 3);

// add the = button
Button equals = new Button("=");
gbl.setConstraints(equals, GBC_equals);
add(equals);
```

```java
// Add the / button
GridBagConstraints GBC_slash =
  new GridBagConstraints();
GBC_slash.gridx = 2;
GBC_slash.gridy = 1;
GBC_slash.gridwidth = 1;
GBC_slash.gridheight = 1;
GBC_slash.fill = GridBagConstraints.BOTH;
GBC_slash.insets = new Insets(3, 3, 3, 3);

// add the button
Button slash = new Button("/");
gbl.setConstraints(slash, GBC_slash);
add(slash);

// Add the * button
GridBagConstraints GBC_times =
  new GridBagConstraints();
GBC_times.gridx = 3;
GBC_times.gridy = 1;
GBC_times.gridwidth = 1;
GBC_times.gridheight = 1;
GBC_times.fill = GridBagConstraints.BOTH;
GBC_times.insets = new Insets(3, 3, 3, 3);

// add the button
Button star = new Button("*");
gbl.setConstraints(star, GBC_times);
add(star);

// Add the 7 key
GridBagConstraints GBC_7 =
  new GridBagConstraints();
GBC_7.gridx = 0;
GBC_7.gridy = 2;
GBC_7.gridwidth = 1;
GBC_7.gridheight = 1;
GBC_7.fill = GridBagConstraints.BOTH;
GBC_7.insets = new Insets(3, 3, 3, 3);

// add the button
Button b7 = new Button("7");
gbl.setConstraints(b7, GBC_7);
add(b7);
```

```
// Add the 8 key
GridBagConstraints GBC_8 =
  new GridBagConstraints();
GBC_8.gridx = 1;
GBC_8.gridy = 2;
GBC_8.gridwidth = 1;
GBC_8.gridheight = 1;
GBC_8.fill = GridBagConstraints.BOTH;
GBC_8.insets = new Insets(3, 3, 3, 3);

// add the button
Button b8 = new Button("8");
gbl.setConstraints(b8, GBC_8);
add(b8);

// Add the 9 key
GridBagConstraints GBC_9 =
  new GridBagConstraints();
GBC_9.gridx = 2;
GBC_9.gridy = 2;
GBC_9.gridwidth = 1;
GBC_9.gridheight = 1;
GBC_9.fill = GridBagConstraints.BOTH;
GBC_9.insets = new Insets(3, 3, 3, 3);

// add the button
Button b9 = new Button("9");
gbl.setConstraints(b9, GBC_9);
add(b9);

// Add the - key
GridBagConstraints GBC_minus =
  new GridBagConstraints();
GBC_minus.gridx = 3;
GBC_minus.gridy = 2;
GBC_minus.gridwidth = 1;
GBC_minus.gridheight = 1;
GBC_minus.fill = GridBagConstraints.BOTH;
GBC_minus.insets = new Insets(3, 3, 3, 3);

// add the button
Button minus = new Button("-");
gbl.setConstraints(minus, GBC_minus);
add(minus);

// Add the 4 key
```

```
GridBagConstraints GBC_4 =
  new GridBagConstraints();
GBC_4.gridx = 0;
GBC_4.gridy = 3;
GBC_4.gridwidth = 1;
GBC_4.gridheight = 1;
GBC_4.fill = GridBagConstraints.BOTH;
GBC_4.insets = new Insets(3, 3, 3, 3);

// add the button
Button b4 = new Button("4");
gbl.setConstraints(b4, GBC_4);
add(b4);

// Add the 5 key
GridBagConstraints GBC_5 =
  new GridBagConstraints();
GBC_5.gridx = 1;
GBC_5.gridy = 3;
GBC_5.gridwidth = 1;
GBC_5.gridheight = 1;
GBC_5.fill = GridBagConstraints.BOTH;
GBC_5.insets = new Insets(3, 3, 3, 3);

// add the button
Button b5 = new Button("5");
gbl.setConstraints(b5, GBC_5);
add(b5);

// Add the 6 key
GridBagConstraints GBC_6 =
  new GridBagConstraints();
GBC_6.gridx = 2;
GBC_6.gridy = 3;
GBC_6.gridwidth = 1;
GBC_6.gridheight = 1;
GBC_6.fill = GridBagConstraints.BOTH;
GBC_6.insets = new Insets(3, 3, 3, 3);

// add the button
Button b6 = new Button("6");
gbl.setConstraints(b6, GBC_6);
add(b6);

// Add the + key
GridBagConstraints GBC_plus =
```

```
  new GridBagConstraints();
GBC_plus.gridx = 3;
GBC_plus.gridy = 3;
GBC_plus.gridwidth = 1;
GBC_plus.gridheight = 1;
GBC_plus.fill = GridBagConstraints.BOTH;
GBC_plus.insets = new Insets(3, 3, 3, 3);

// add the button
Button plus = new Button("+");
gbl.setConstraints(plus, GBC_plus);
add(plus);

// Add the 1 key
GridBagConstraints GBC_1 =
  new GridBagConstraints();
GBC_1.gridx = 0;
GBC_1.gridy = 4;
GBC_1.gridwidth = 1;
GBC_1.gridheight = 1;
GBC_1.fill = GridBagConstraints.BOTH;
GBC_1.insets = new Insets(3, 3, 3, 3);

// add the button
Button b1 = new Button("1");
gbl.setConstraints(b1, GBC_1);
add(b1);

// Add the 2 key
GridBagConstraints GBC_2 =
  new GridBagConstraints();
GBC_2.gridx = 1;
GBC_2.gridy = 4;
GBC_2.gridwidth = 1;
GBC_2.gridheight = 1;
GBC_2.fill = GridBagConstraints.BOTH;
GBC_2.insets = new Insets(3, 3, 3, 3);

// add the button
Button b2 = new Button("2");
gbl.setConstraints(b2, GBC_2);
add(b2);

// Add the 3 key
GridBagConstraints GBC_3 =
  new GridBagConstraints();
```

```java
GBC_3.gridx = 2;
GBC_3.gridy = 4;
GBC_3.gridwidth = 1;
GBC_3.gridheight = 1;
GBC_3.fill = GridBagConstraints.BOTH;
GBC_3.insets = new Insets(3, 3, 3, 3);

// add the button
Button b3 = new Button("3");
gbl.setConstraints(b3, GBC_3);
add(b3);

// Add the = key
GridBagConstraints GBC_bigequals =
  new GridBagConstraints();
GBC_bigequals.gridx = 3;
GBC_bigequals.gridy = 4;
GBC_bigequals.gridwidth = 1;
GBC_bigequals.gridheight = 2;
GBC_bigequals.fill = GridBagConstraints.BOTH;
GBC_bigequals.insets = new Insets(3, 3, 3, 3);

// add the button
Button bigequals = new Button("=");
gbl.setConstraints(bigequals, GBC_bigequals);
add(bigequals);

// Add the 0 key
GridBagConstraints GBC_0 =
  new GridBagConstraints();
GBC_0.gridx = 0;
GBC_0.gridy = 5;
GBC_0.gridwidth = 2;
GBC_0.gridheight = 1;
GBC_0.fill = GridBagConstraints.BOTH;
GBC_0.insets = new Insets(3, 3, 3, 3);

// add the button
Button b0 = new Button("0");
gbl.setConstraints(b0, GBC_0);
add(b0);

// Add the . key
GridBagConstraints GBC_decimal =
  new GridBagConstraints();
GBC_decimal.gridx = 2;
```

```
    GBC_decimal.gridy = 5;
    GBC_decimal.gridwidth = 1;
    GBC_decimal.gridheight = 1;
    GBC_decimal.fill = GridBagConstraints.BOTH;
    GBC_decimal.insets = new Insets(3, 3, 3, 3);

    // add the button
    Button bdecimal = new Button(".");
    gbl.setConstraints(bdecimal, GBC_decimal);
    add(bdecimal);

    }

public Insets insets() {

    return new Insets(5, 5, 5, 5);

    }

}
```

Going Naked

Now that you've spent an entire chapter learning how to use the various LayoutManagers, you're going to find out that you don't absolutely need them. It is possible to position widgets precisely on the screen using x and y pixel coordinates that are relative to the applet's panel. Before you get the details you should hear why this is a bad idea:

1. Not every instance of your applet will have the same size panel to work with. You should only do this when the applet will run only on your Web pages so you can control the applet's size. Free-standing windows (which are the subject of the next chapter) may even be resized by the user on the fly. If you've used a LayoutManager to position your Components, they'll be adjusted immediately to fit the new window size. This behavior is extremely hard to duplicate if you don't use a LayoutManager.

2. Components use varying amounts of space on different platforms. You should probably only use these techniques when you are writing a single-platform, compiled Java application. You should not use them for applets.

3. Laying out Components manually is a lot of work, especially given the lack of Visual Basic-like interface drawing environments. Don't you have better things to do with your time than moving widgets one pixel to the left, recompiling, and running the applet only to discover the widget was probably better off where it started out?

4. The GridBagLayout and/or nested panels can probably do everything you want to do with manual layout anyway.

If none of those things convince you that you really shouldn't use absolute positioning, I'll let you in on the secret: Pass **null** to setLayout, that is, call

```
setLayout(null);
```

in your init method. Then reshape each of your Components to their desired locations in the paint method. The syntax for the reshape method is

```
reshape(int x, int y, int width, int height)
```

where x and y are the coordinates of the upper-left-hand corner of the bounding box of your Component. width and height are the width and height in pixels of the bounding box of your Component.

Program 16.6 is an applet that puts a button 30 pixels wide by 40 pixels high at (25, 50). Figure 16.10 shows the button.

Program 16.6: Manual layout

```
import java.applet.Applet;
import java.awt.Button;
import java.awt.Graphics;

public class ManualLayout extends Applet {

  private boolean laidOut = false;
  private Button myButton;
```

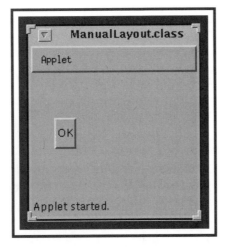

Figure 16.10: *Manual layout*

```
public void init() {

    setLayout(null);
    myButton = new Button("OK");
    add(myButton);
}

public void paint(Graphics g) {
    if (!laidOut) {
        myButton.reshape(25, 50, 30, 40);
        laidOut = true;
    }
}

}
```

Quiz

1. What's the difference between a BorderLayout and a
   FlowLayout?

2. What's the difference between a GridLayout and a
   GridBagLayout?

Exercises

1. Add a Fast Forward Button to Program 16.1.

2. Add a GridLayout to the PaymentMethod applet of the last chapter.

3. Use a CardLayout to provide a complete pizza ordering system. The first card should ask the user about their pizza: how big it is and what toppings they want. The second card should collect payment information, that is how they wish to pay, their name, and their credit card information (name, card number, and expiration date.) The final card should be for the address and delivery instructions.

4. Make the calculator applet behave like a calculator, that is, when you hit the keys 3 + 2 =, the screen should show 5, and so on.

5. Hard: Define a class key which includes both the display as a button and the functionality of the Calculator key. This will require some thought for what the total data structure is which represents the current calculation and how the keys relate to that. This will probably be easier if you do Exercise 1 first.

Summary

In this chapter you learned

- How to use a FlowLayout
- How to use a BorderLayout
- How to use a CardLayout
- How to use a GridLayout
- How to use a GridBagLayout
- How to nest Panels for complex Layouts
- How to position Components exactly

Coming Up

Now that you understand how to make one panel look good using LayoutManagers, in the next chapter you'll learn how to bring up multiple windows simultaneously. The BorderLayout will reappear as the default LayoutManager for Windows.

Further Reading

http://www.javasoft.com/JDK-1.0/api/java.awt.FlowLayout.html

http://www.javasoft.com/JDK-1.0/api/java.awt.BorderLayout.html

http://www.javasoft.com/JDK-1.0/api/java.awt.CardLayout.html

http://www.javasoft.com/JDK-1.0/api/java.awt.GridLayout.html

http://www.javasoft.com/JDK-1.0/api/java.awt.GridBagLayout.html

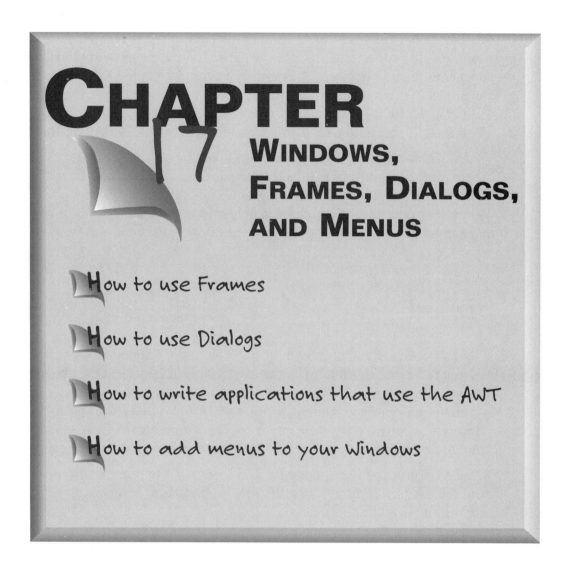

CHAPTER 17

WINDOWS, FRAMES, DIALOGS, AND MENUS

How to use Frames

How to use Dialogs

How to write applications that use the AWT

How to add menus to your Windows

The java.awt.Window class and its subclasses let you create free-standing windows. Stand-alone windows can also be used to build applications that use the AWT instead of the command line or to provide additional space for applets.

A Window is a subclass of java.awt.Container that is independent of other Containers. That is, a Window is self-contained. Since Window is a subclass of java.awt.Container, you can add Components like Buttons and TextFields to Windows. You can arrange the Components you add with a LayoutManager. You can draw directly into a Window in a paint method. Everything you did in an applet panel in the last five chapters can also be done in a Window.

403

Normally you won't use the Window class directly but will access one of its subclasses, either java.awt.Frame or java.awt.Dialog depending on your need. A Frame is what most people think of as a window in their native environment. It can have a menu bar; it can be independently moved and resized; and it will hang around on the screen as long as the user is interested in the content of the window.

A Dialog will not have a menu bar. It can be moved but often can't be resized. Its purpose is to get some particular information from the user (input) or to impart some particularly important information to the user (output). It is normally visible on the screen only until it gets the input or receives acknowledgement from the user about its output.

Frames

Frames are very useful in complex applications. Frames separate different functions or data into different windows. For instance a painting application may have several different pictures in varying states of completion open in different windows. Or it may have only one picture, but a separate window might contain a tool palette to select different brushes or colors. Each of these windows would be a Frame.

Everything you need to create and work with Frames is contained in the java.awt.Frame class. If your applet uses Frames, start by importing this class.

```
import java.awt.Frame;
```

To create a new Frame without a title bar, use the `Frame()` constructor with no arguments.

```
Frame f = new Frame();
```

More commonly, you'll want to name the Frame so pass the constructor a String that specifies the window's title.

```
Frame f = new Frame("My Window");
```

Frames inherit from java.awt.Container so you can add all the Components you learned about in the last three chapters to a Frame. Unlike Panels and applets, the default LayoutManager for a Frame is BorderLayout, not FlowLayout. However, you can change this using the Frame's `setLayout(LayoutManager lm)` method like this:

```
f.setLayout(new FlowLayout());
```

Frames inherit from java.awt.Component so they have paint, update, and user input methods. If you want to draw in the Frame and process events manually as you did in applets in Chapters 11 through 13, create a subclass of Frame and override the appropriate methods. Almost everything you did in those chapters with a user-defined subclass of java.applet.Applet can also be done with a user-defined subclass of java.awt.Frame.[1]

However, most of the time you'll prefer to use Components. To add a Component to a Frame, call the Frame's add method just as you would call an applet's add method. The only difference is that you often call the add method from outside the Frame class so you'll need to prefix add with a variable that points to the Frame and the member operator. In other words, given a Frame f, you need to call

```
f.add(new Button("OK");
```

rather than simply

```
add(new Button("OK"));
```

Of course, this depends on what class you're inside of when you call add. If you're calling add from one of the Frame's own methods you won't need to do this.

Since the default layout for a Frame is BorderLayout, you'll probably need to specify whether you want the component added to the North, South, East, West, or Center. Here's how you'd add a centered label to the center of Frame f:

```
f.add("Center", new Label("This is a frame",
Label.CENTER));
```

The size and position of any given Frame is unpredictable unless you specify it. Specifying the size is easy. Just call the Frame's resize method like this:

```
f.resize(150,150);
```

This size does not include the title bar so you'll need to account for that separately. To determine the height of a Frame's title bar, call its Insets method and look at the top member of the resulting java.awt.Insets object. That will be the height of the title bar. That is,

```
int TitleBarHeight = f.Insets().top;
```

---

[1] The exceptions: The getImage() and getDocumentBase() methods came from java.applet.Applet, not java.awt.Component, so they are not necessarily available in a Frame.

Moving the Frame to the proper place on the screen takes a little more effort. You move a Frame with the `move(int x, int y)` method. However, x and y are relative to the screen, not to the applet. Since different monitors have different display sizes, the first thing you need to do is figure out how big the display is. After all, you don't want to pop up a window in the lower-right-hand corner of a 21-inch monitor if the user is viewing your applet on a 9" compact Mac. The applet's bounds method will give you a Rectangle that encloses the applet so you can position your window relative to that. Similarly the applet's size method will tell you how big the applet is. Using these two quantities, you can make an educated guess about where your Frame should go and how big it should be. For instance, to pop up a window that just covers the applet you would use

```
f.resize(size().width,size().height);

f.move(bounds().x, bounds().y);
```

When a window is first created, it's invisible. Add Components to the Frame while it's still invisible. The effect of Buttons, Labels, and other widgets popping onto a layout in rapid succession while the window jumps around and changes size can be quite disconcerting. When you have finished adding Components, resizing and moving the Frame, make it visible by calling its `show()` method like so:

```
f.show();
```

Program 17.1 is a very simple applet that puts up a window. You can move the window and resize it. The window has a single TextArea component that lets you edit some text. Figure 17.1 shows this window.

Program 17.1: Window Tester

```java
import java.awt.Frame;
import java.applet.Applet;
import java.awt.Event;
import java.awt.TextArea;

public class WindowTester extends Applet {

  public void init() {

    Frame myFrame = new Frame("My Applet Window");
    myFrame.resize(250, 250);
```

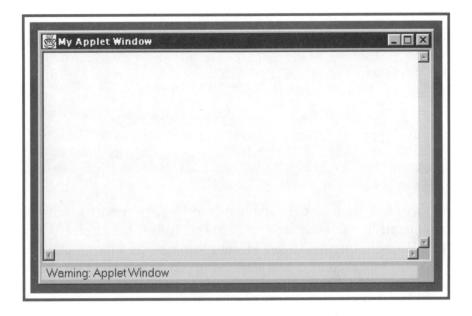

Figure 17.1: *The Window Tester Applet*

```
    myFrame.move(300,200);
    myFrame.add("Center", new TextArea(10, 40));
    myFrame.show();

  }

}
```

Combining Applets and Applications

An applet needs a Frame to run in. Normally, the Web browser or the Applet Viewer provides this. However, you can create instances of your applet inside a Frame of your own creation. This way you can write code that is both an applet and an application.

To convert an applet into an application, import java.awt.Frame and add the following main method to your applet:

```
1. public static void main(String args[]) {
2.
```

```
 3.    myApplet a = new myApplet();
 4.    a.init();
 5.    a.start();
 6.
 7.    Frame appletFrame = new Frame("Applet Window");
 8.    appletFrame.add("Center", a);
 9.    appletFrame.resize(150,150);
10.    appletFrame.move(100,100);
11.    appletFrame.show();
12.
13.  }
```

Line 1 is the standard main method you're used to from all the command-line applications in Chapters 2–9. If the applet is running in a Web browser or Applet Viewer, this method will not be called. It will only be executed if you start the applet as a stand-alone program.

Line 3 creates a new instance of the applet. This assumes that the applet is called myApplet. Change this to match the name of your applet subclass.

After you create the applet, lines 4 and 5 call the applet's init and start methods. Normally, the Web browser or applet viewer does this for you, but you're not running inside such a program so you need to do it yourself.

Once the applet has been created, it's necessary to create a Frame to hold it. Line 7 does this with the normal Frame constructor. You can change the title of the Frame to suit your application.

Line 8 adds the applet to the Frame. Since the default LayoutManager for a Frame is BorderLayout, you add it to the Center. Remember that java.applet.Applet is a subclass of java.awt.Component, so adding an applet to a Frame is kosher.

Line 9 resizes the Frame. Here the size is arbitrarily set to 150 pixels by 150 pixels. If this program were running as an applet, you'd get those numbers from the height and width parameters, but you're not running in an applet so you have to make something up. If you like, you could make it possible to enter the height and width as command-line arguments.

Line 10 moves the Frame to (100, 100). If you don't do this, the exact location of the Frame is unpredictable, but on some machines it has a distressing tendency to show up not only partially off the screen, but also with the title bar completely off the screen so there's no way to move it onto the screen.

Line 11 makes the Frame visible, and the applet is now ready to run, without an Applet Viewer or a Web browser.

Warning | **Even with a Frame, Applets and Applications Are Still Different**

When you convert an applet to an application in this fashion, you need to make sure your program doesn't rely on methods that only make sense in the context of an applet. For instance, you can only read parameters using getParameter in an applet. Conversely, you can only read the command-line arguments in an application. Furthermore, applications have many fewer security restrictions than applets so code that may run well in an application may throw many security-related exceptions in an applet.

Dialogs

Frames are useful for windows that will stick around for awhile, for example, some text that's being edited. Dialogs are more transitory. They're used for simple user input or for quick alerts to the user.

Like Frames, java.awt.Dialog is a subclass of java.awt.Window and hence of java.awt.Container and java.awt.Component. Therefore, a lot of what you learned about Frames applies to Dialogs as well. You move them, resize them, and add to them almost exactly as you do with Frames. There are two differences between Dialogs and Frames:

1. A Frame can have a MenuBar. A Dialog cannot.
2. A Dialog can be modal. A Frame cannot.

MenuBars are covered in the next section of this chapter. Right now, let's talk about modal versus non-modal Dialogs. A modal Dialog blocks all other use of the application until the user responds to it. A modal Dialog cannot be moved and does not allow the user to switch to another window in the same program. On some platforms, the user may not even be able to switch to another program.

In the 1970s, a computer virus worked its way into several early timesharing systems. The computer program would periodically break in on a user's session and say "I WANT A COOKIE." The terminal would then refuse to respond to any user input until the user typed the word "COOKIE", at which point the program would say something like "MMM, MMM, THAT WAS GOOD." and return control to the user.

Modal dialogs are a lot like the cookie monster program. They request input from the user and don't let anything else happen until they get it. Non-modal Dialogs pop up, but they don't prevent the user from doing other things while they're visible. Because modal dialogs inconvenience users by forcing them to respond when the computer wants them to rather than when they want to, their use should be kept to a minimum.

The only methods that are significantly different between a Dialog and a Frame are the constructors. There are two constructors for Dialog which differ in whether or not the Dialog is given a title. This titleless constructor is

```
Dialog d = new Dialog(new Frame(), false);
```

The first argument is a Frame to put the Dialog in. You normally create one right inside the constructor as done here. The second argument is a boolean that specifies whether or not the Dialog should be modal. If it should be, pass `true`. If it shouldn't be, pass `false`.

There are also some common differences between most Frames and most Dialogs, but these are not written in Stone:

1. Most Frames can be moved and resized by the user. Most Dialogs cannot be.
2. Most Frames have title bars. Most Dialogs do not.

You can make a Dialog resizable and movable by calling its setResizable method with a boolean value of true like this:

```
d.setResizable(true);
```

You can give Dialog a title bar by adding the title string to the constructor:

```
Dialog d = new Dialog(new Frame(), false,
"My Dialog Window");
```

All the other methods of the Dialog class are exactly the same as they are for Frames. You resize them the same way. You move them the same way. You make them visible the same way. You add Components to them the same way.

Program 17.2 displays a simple non-modal Dialog with an OK Button and no title bar.

Program 17.2: Dialog tester

```java
import java.applet.Applet;
import java.awt.Dialog;
import java.awt.Frame;
import java.awt.Button;

public class DialogTester extends Applet {

  public void init() {

    Dialog myDialog = new
      Dialog(new Frame(), false);
    myDialog.resize(250, 250);
    myDialog.move(320,240);
    myDialog.add("South", new Button("OK"));
    myDialog.show();

  }

}
```

Figure 17.2 shows this Dialog.

The last two examples are a little artificial. Normally, you create a subclass of Frame or Dialog and instantiate that subclass from the main program. For example, one of the simpler common Dialogs is a notification dialog that gives the user a message to which they can say OK to signify that they've read it. Program 17.3 is such a Dialog class. Program 17.4 is an example of a Program that might use it. Figure 17.3 shows the program running.

Figure 17.2: *A non-modal Dialog with no title bar and an OK Button*

Program 17.3: An Alert Dialog class

```
import java.awt.Panel;
import java.awt.Dialog;
import java.awt.Label;
import java.awt.Frame;
import java.awt.Button;
import java.awt.FlowLayout;
import java.awt.Event;

public class Alert extends Dialog {

  public Alert (String s) {

    super(new Frame(), true);
    add("Center", new Label(s));
    Panel p = new Panel();
    p.setLayout(new FlowLayout());
    p.add(new Button("OK"));
    add("South", p);
    resize(300,100);
    move(100,200);

  }

  public boolean action(Event e, Object o) {

    if(e.target instanceof Button) {
```

Figure 17.3: *An Alert Dialog*

```
      hide();
      return true;
   }
   return false;

   }

}
```

Program 17.4 A simple applet to demonstrate the alert Dialog

```
import java.applet.Applet;


public class AlertExample extends Applet {

  public void init () {

    Alert a = new Alert("Are you sure you want " +
       "to start global thermonuclear war?");
    a.show();

  }

}
```

Figure 17.4: *The Macintosh MenuBar*

Window Events

Since java.awt.Window is a subclass of java.awt.Component, a Window, Frame, or Dialog can receive events. As well as the usual events, java.awt.Event defines five events specially for windows. They are

- WINDOW_DEICONIFY
- WINDOW_DESTROY
- WINDOW_EXPOSE
- WINDOW_ICONIFY
- WINDOW_MOVED

To respond to these events, you need to override handleEvent in your subclass of Window (not in the applet itself—applets are Panels, not Windows) and trap the cases you're interested in. You normally won't want to bother with a WINDOW_EXPOSE or WINDOW_MOVED event. It's better to let the window system handle these for you.

On the other hand, if you get a WINDOW_ICONIFY event, you may want to stop playing an animation or otherwise stop using CPU time since the user won't be looking at your applet. Similarly, you'll want to start again when you get a WINDOW_DEICONIFY message.

Finally, if you get a WINDOW_DESTROY message, then the user is trying to close your window. You should ask the user if they want to save their work, possibly dispose of any data associated with that window, and then hide the window.

Menus

You can add menus to your Frames. (Menus cannot be added to Dialogs.) This is probably overkill for an applet, but it's almost

Figure 17.5: *The Edit Menu*

required for applications. Menus are composed of three hierarchical pieces.

The MenuBar contains the various menus. The MenuBar is at the top of the screen on a Macintosh and in the top of the window in Windows and Motif. Figure 17.4 is a Macintosh MenuBar.

The MenuBar contains a number of menus. The menus are organized topically. File would be one menu. Edit would be another.

Each menu contains one or more menu items. The menu items are the individual actions such as Open, Print, Cut, or Copy. They are not shown except when the menu is active. No more than one menu is active at a time. Figure 17.5 shows an active Edit Menu with a disabled Undo MenuItem followed by a Separator, followed by enabled Cut, Copy, Paste and Clear MenuItems, followed by another separator, followed by an enabled Select All MenuItem.

To use menus in your application, you need to add instances of all three classes, one MenuBar with one or more Menus, each of which has several MenuItems. This functionality is encapsulated in the classes java.awt.Menu, java.awt.MenuBar, and java.awt.MenuItem, so begin by importing them.

```
import java.awt.Menu;
import java.awt.MenuBar;
import java.awt.MenuItem;
```

It's easiest to build the Menus before you display them. A typical order is

1. Create a new MenuBar.
2. Create a new Menu.

3. Add items to the Menu.

4. If necessary, repeat steps 2 and 3.

5. Add the MenuBar to the Frame.

The constructors you need are all simple. To create a new MenuBar, use

```
MenuBar myMenubar = new MenuBar();
```

You almost never need more than one MenuBar in a program.

To create a new Menu, use the `Menu(String Title)` constructor. Pass it the title of the menu you want. For example, this is how you'd create File and Edit Menus,

```
Menu fileMenu = new Menu("File");

Menu editMenu = new Menu("Edit");
```

MenuItems are created similarly with the `MenuItem(String menutext)` constructor. Pass it the title of the menu you want like this

```
MenuItem Cut = new MenuItem("Cut");
```

However most of the time you'll create MenuItems inside the Menus they belong to, just like you created widgets inside their layouts. Menus have add methods that take an instance of MenuItem. This is how you'd build an Edit Menu complete with Undo, Cut, Copy, Paste, Clear and Select All MenuItems:

```
Menu editMenu = new Menu("Edit");

editMenu.add(new MenuItem("Undo"));

editMenu.addSeparator();

editMenu.add(new MenuItem("Cut"));

editMenu.add(new MenuItem("Copy"));

editMenu.add(new MenuItem("Paste"));

editMenu.add(new MenuItem("Clear"));

editMenu.addSeparator();

editMenu.add(new MenuItem("Select All"));
```

The `addSeparator()` method adds a horizontal line across the menu. It's used to separate logically separate functions in one menu.

There's an alternative add method in java.awt.Menu that accepts a String as an argument. This String is just the label of the MenuItem. This method still creates new MenuItems. It just does it behind your back. Here's how it would be used:

```
Menu editMenu = new Menu("Edit");
editMenu.add("Undo");
editMenu.addSeparator();
editMenu.add("Cut");
editMenu.add("Copy");
editMenu.add("Paste");
editMenu.add("Clear");
editMenu.addSeparator();
editMenu.add("Select All");
```

Once the Menus are created, add them to the MenuBar using the MenuBar's `add(Menu m)` method like this:

```
myMenubar.add(fileMenu);
myMenubar.add(editMenu);
```

Finally, when the MenuBar is fully loaded, add the Menu to its Frame using the Frame's `setMenuBar(MenuBar mb)` method. Given a Frame `f`, this is how you would do it:

```
f.setMenuBar(myMenuBar);
```

A particular application may have dozens, even hundreds of MenuItems. Cramming these all into the init() method gets confusing. It's customary to create separate methods that create each individual menu and add each one to the MenuBar. Program 17.5 creates two fairly standard menus: File and Edit.

Program 17.5: Menu tester

```
import java.applet.Applet;
import java.awt.Frame;
import java.awt.Menu;
import java.awt.MenuBar;
import java.awt.MenuItem;
import java.awt.Label;


public class MenuTester extends Applet {

  public void init () {
    Frame f = new Frame("Simple Window");
    f.add("Center", new Label("Look at the Menus",
```

```
            Label.CENTER));
    f.resize(size().width,size().height);
    f.move(320,240);
    MenuBar myMenuBar = new MenuBar();
    makeFileMenu(myMenuBar);
    makeEditMenu(myMenuBar);
    f.setMenuBar(myMenuBar);
    f.show();

  }

  void makeEditMenu(MenuBar mb) {
    Menu editMenu = new Menu("Edit");
    editMenu.add("Undo");
    editMenu.addSeparator();
    editMenu.add("Cut");
    editMenu.add("Copy");
    editMenu.add("Paste");
    editMenu.add("Clear");
    mb.add(editMenu);
  }

  void makeFileMenu(MenuBar mb) {
    Menu fileMenu = new Menu("File");
    fileMenu.add("New");
    fileMenu.add("Open...");
    fileMenu.addSeparator();
    fileMenu.add("Close");
    fileMenu.add("Save");
    fileMenu.add("Save As...");
    fileMenu.addSeparator();
    fileMenu.add("Page Setup...");
    fileMenu.add("Print");
    fileMenu.addSeparator();
    fileMenu.add("Quit");
    mb.add(fileMenu);
  }

}
```

Handling Menu Events

The previous section showed you how to build menus. However the menus you built were dead. Nothing happened when a MenuItem was selected. To make menus do something you need to watch out for their actions. Create an action method for the Frame that contains the MenuBar. Within the action method, check to see if the target of the action is a MenuItem. If it is, get its label and pass it to a handleMenu method. The handleMenu method in Program 17.6 just prints the menu choice on System.out. In a more realistic application, you would take some action that related to the menu choice. Figure 17.6 shows this applet in action.

Program 17.6: Active menu tester

```java
import java.applet.Applet;
import java.awt.Frame;
import java.awt.Menu;
import java.awt.MenuBar;
import java.awt.MenuItem;
import java.awt.TextField;
import java.awt.Event;
import java.awt.Label;

public class MenuTester extends Applet {

  public void init () {
    MenuFrame f = new MenuFrame("Simple Window");
    f.resize(size().width,size().height);
    f.move(300,200);
    f.show();
  }

}

class MenuFrame extends Frame {

  TextField theMenuChoice;

  public MenuFrame(String s) {

    super (s);
    add("North", new Label("The last menu choice was",
      Label.CENTER));
    TextField theMenuChoice = new TextField(
      "Choose a menu item");
    add("Center", theMenuChoice);
    MenuBar myMenuBar = new MenuBar();
    makeFileMenu(myMenuBar);
    makeEditMenu(myMenuBar);
```

```java
      setMenuBar(myMenuBar);
  }

  public boolean action (Event e, Object o) {

    if (e.target instanceof MenuItem) {
      handleMenuChoice((String) o);
      return true;
    }
    else {
      return false;
    }

  }

  private void handleMenuChoice (String s) {
    System.out.println(s);
  }

  void makeEditMenu(MenuBar mb) {
    Menu editMenu = new Menu("Edit");
    editMenu.add("Undo");
    editMenu.addSeparator();
    editMenu.add("Cut");
    editMenu.add("Copy");
    editMenu.add("Paste");
    editMenu.add("Clear");
    mb.add(editMenu);
  }

  void makeFileMenu(MenuBar mb) {
    Menu fileMenu = new Menu("File");
    fileMenu.add("New");
    fileMenu.add("Open...");
    fileMenu.addSeparator();
    fileMenu.add("Close");
    fileMenu.add("Save");
    fileMenu.add("Save As...");
    fileMenu.addSeparator();
    fileMenu.add("Page Setup...");
    fileMenu.add("Print");
    fileMenu.addSeparator();
    fileMenu.add("Quit");
    mb.add(fileMenu);
  }

}
```

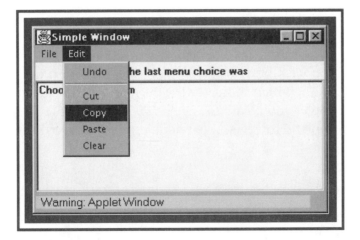

Figure 17.6: Active menu tester

 Warning   ## The Menu Belongs to the Frame

The action method that handles the menu choice belongs to the Frame, **not** to the applet. It's a very common mistake of novices (not to mention authors of books :-) to try to catch the menu choice inside the applet. However, the MenuBar belongs to the Frame, not to the applet and it's the Frame where you need to put an action method that checks for menu choices.

 Q&A

 Q: *A lot of java.awt.Frame's methods like* resize *and* add *seem very similar to the applet methods of the same name. Is there a reason for this?*

A: Yes. add, resize, move, and most of the other methods are inherited from either java.awt.Component or java.awt.Container. java.applet.Applet also inherits from java.awt.Component and java.awt.Container. The apparent difference between the two is that you normally don't prefix a call to an applet's methods with a reference to the applet because the calls occur within the applet's own code. However, a Frame's methods are often called from other classes. Therefore, you need to say `f.resize(145, 124)` rather than simply `resize(145, 124)`. You can, if you wish, refer to the applet's methods with the keyword `this`, which indicates the current object. Thus, inside an applet you'd call `this.resize(145, 124)` to resize the applet. However, most people prefer to avoid the typing.

Quiz

1. What's the difference between a Frame and a Dialog?
2. What's the difference between a Menu and a MenuBar?
3. What's the difference between a Menu and a MenuItem?
4. Why wouldn't you create a Menu inside the MenuBar's add method like you create MenuItems inside a Menu's add method?

Exercises

1. It's a little silly to ask the user if they are sure they want to start global thermonuclear war and then only provide an OK button. Write an OK-Cancel Dialog class that produces a modal dialog with two buttons, OK and Cancel. Make the constructor protected. However, include a static method that creates a new instance of the OKCancel class and handles user input. This method should take a single String as an argument and return a boolean indicating whether the OK or the Cancel button was pressed. The dialog should dismiss itself when a button is pressed. Make sure a long String is handled reasonably (that is, wrap it to fit the box).

2. Create a subclass of the OKCancel dialog that has buttons for "Yes" and "No" instead.

3. Revise Program 17.6 so that instead of printing the Menu Choice on System.out, it pops up an Alert Dialog from Program 17.3 with the MenuChoice.

4. Use Exercise 1 to revise Program 17.6 so that it asks the user to confirm each menu selection.

Summary

In this chapter you learned

- How to create a Frame
- How to put Components in a Frame
- How to create a Dialog
- The difference between modal and non-modal Dialogs
- How to write stand-alone applications that use the AWT
- How to process Window Events
- Menus, MenuBars, and MenuItems
- Handling Menu choices

Coming Up

This chapter concludes your introduction to the AWT. The next chapter returns to Java syntax with a discussion of exceptions and error handling.

In later chapters, you'll learn many other things that are useful in the context of both applets and applications, both graphical and non-graphical, including how to use Threads to produce smooth animation, how to use packages to make useful classes broadly available, and how to use javadoc to document your code.

Further Reading

http://www.javasoft.com/JDK-1.0/api/java.awt.Window.html
http://www.javasoft.com/JDK-1.0/api/java.awt.Frame.html
http://www.javasoft.com/JDK-1.0/api/java.awt.Dialog.html
http://www.javasoft.com/JDK-1.0/api/java.awt.Menu.html
http://www.javasoft.com/JDK-1.0/api/java.awt.MenuItem.html
http://www.javasoft.com/JDK-1.0/api/java.awt.MenuBar.html

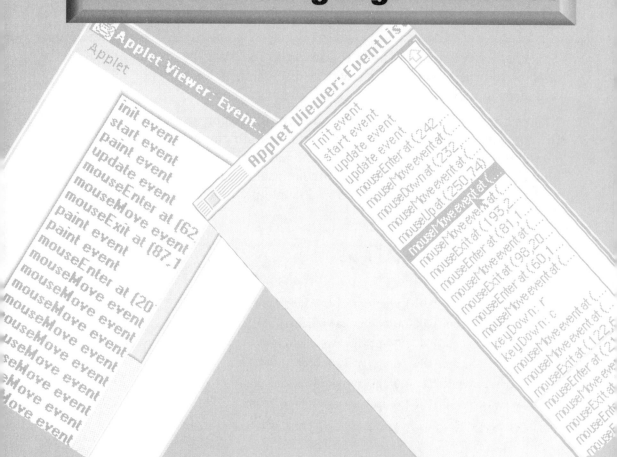

PART THREE

Advanced Language Features

Applet Viewer: EventTutor.clas

Applet

init event
start event
mouseEnter at (171,296)
mouseMove event at (180,289)
mouseMove event at (192,280)
mouseMove event at (198,274)
mouseMove event at (202,268)
mouseMove event at (206,261)
mouseMove event at (216,250)
mouseMove event at (223,240)
mouseMove event at (225,232)
mouseMove event at (226,230)
mouseMove event at (228,229)
mouseMove event at (272,233)

CHAPTER 18

EXCEPTIONS

- What an Exception is, what an Error is, and the difference between them
- How to catch Exceptions
- What to do with Exceptions once you've caught them
- What a RuntimeException is
- How to throw Exceptions of your own devising

When a problem arises in a Java program, for instance when the program tries to write past the end of an array, the program creates and throws an **exception**. Like everything else in Java, exceptions are objects, specifically subclasses of java.lang.Throwable. There are three kinds of Throwable objects built into Java: Errors, Exceptions, and RuntimeExceptions.

Errors represent truly unexpected conditions that the Java compiler and virtual machine guarantee will never occur. Unfortunately, Murphy's Law overrides the guarantees of the Java compiler and virtual machine, and Errors do occur. In general, there's not much you can do about an Error and trying to catch it will only make matters worse. Just let your program crash. Errors aren't very common.

An Exception, on the other hand, violates some form of program logic but does not violate the structure of Java itself. By default, an Exception or Error causes the Thread from which it was thrown to gracefully halt execution while still cleaning up any memory it may have allocated. Depending on how carefully you typed the examples in previous days, you may have already seen an "ArrayIndexOutOfBoundsException" or "NullPointerException." Although less than a perfect solution, this is still preferable to the core dump or General Protection Fault you'd see from a C program that wrote past the end of an array. However, a program doesn't have to stop when an exception is thrown. By judicious use of `try` and `catch` statements, a program can catch the exception and respond accordingly.

Death, Bugs, and Taxes

Human beings have death and taxes. Computer programs have bugs. The bugs may be the result of mistakes in an algorithm, bugs in an operating system or compiler, unexpected user input, variables overflowing the space allocated for them, or any of hundreds of other causes. All but the simplest programs will have some form of bug.

Software bugs range from almost unnoticeable cosmetic bugs like the one that occasionally blinks the cursor when I move it over a particular pixel in a certain dialog box to more serious bugs like the one that led my credit union to overpay interest in my and everyone else's account last January. Even that's small potatoes compared to bugs like the one that crashed the Venus space probe. Computer bugs are so ubiquitous that in modern industrial society "computer error" has become a standard excuse along with "the check is in the mail," and "my answering machine must be broken."

Everyone has seen computers crash because of poorly written software. Many times this could have been avoided if the programmer properly tested for errors and unexpected conditions. Unfortunately, it takes a lot of effort to test every statement for an error condition, to make sure that all methods return values that make sense, that all files are opened as expected, and that all memory allocations succeed. And those are just a few of the more common examples of what a program needs to test for. Testing the result of every statement individually can more than double the size of a program.

Therefore, most programmers do make assumptions in their code they probably shouldn't be making. They assume that memory allocation succeeds, that files are where they're expected to be, that user input makes sense, and that you can represent a year with just two digits. Sometimes these assumptions turn out to be untrue. Many mainframe programs are going to crash spectacularly at midnight on January 1, 2000, precisely because programmers assumed they could always use two digits to represent the current year.

The Java language and runtime environment have been designed to make code errors as limited as possible. Automatic allocation and freeing of memory and garbage collection eliminate as much as 50 percent of the bugs that occur in other languages. Array bounds checking eliminates another ten percent. Boolean variables and strong typing probably eliminate another ten percent.

However, it's still the responsibility of the programmer to test for error conditions and to respond appropriately. What's needed is a way to separate the exceptional cases where the assumptions turn out to be false from the normal cases where memory is successfully allocated, files are where they're expected to be, and arrays are big enough to hold the data. And you need a way to switch from the normal flow of control to the code that handles the exception and back again. Java provides a modern means for programmers to catch and respond to unexpected inputs and events: `try-catch` blocks and exception throwing.

Catching Exceptions

If at first you don't succeed, try, try again. The key to proper exception handling in Java is not to expect that a statement will necessarily succeed. Instead try something, and, if that fails, try something else. Here's how:

```
try {
    // Do something that might fail
}
catch(Exception e) { // Oops. That didn't work.
```

```
        // Respond to the Exception
    }

    // Continue with the rest of the program
```

This is called a **try-catch block**. First you try something. If it fails, the failing statement throws an exception. The exception is caught in the catch block, which responds accordingly. After the exception is caught and any code in the catch block is executed, program flow continues with the first statement after the end of the try-catch block.

Do you remember this program?

Program 3.4 Hello with command-line input

```java
// This is the Hello program in Java
class Hello {

    public static void main (String args[]) {

        /* Now let's say hello */
        System.out.println("Hello " + args[0]);

    }

}
```

Do you remember what happened when you ran the program without giving it any command-line arguments? The runtime system generated an exception:

```
Exception in thread "main"
java.lang.ArrayIndexOutOfBoundsException at
Hello.main(C:\javahtml\Hello.java:7)
```

What happened was that since the program wasn't given any command-line arguments, there wasn't anything in args[0]. Therefore, Java kicked back this not-too-friendly error message about an "ArrayIndexOutOfBoundsException."

In Chapter 3, this problem was fixed by testing the length of the array before an attempt was made to access its first element. This worked well in this simple case, but this is far from the only such potential problem. If you were to check for every possible error condition in each line of code, you would find your code becoming bloated with more error checking than actual code. Moreover, you would then have to start checking for errors in the error conditions. In older languages like C, Basic, and Fortran, sooner or later you find yourself resorting to `goto` or `longjmp` or other such ingredients in the recipe for illegible spaghetti code.

The goal of exception handling is to be able to define the regular flow of the program in one part of the code without worrying about all the special cases. Then, in a separate block of code, you cover the exceptional cases. This produces more legible code since you don't need to interrupt the flow of the algorithm to check and respond to every possible strange condition. The runtime environment is responsible for moving from the regular program flow to the exception handler when an exceptional condition arises.

In practice what you do is write blocks of code that may generate exceptions inside a `try` block. You try the statements that generate the exceptions. Within your `try` block, you are free to act as if nothing has gone wrong or can go wrong. Then, within one or more `catch` blocks that follow the `try` block, you write the code that deals with all the special cases.

Program 18.1 is an example of exception handling in Java using the Hello World program above:

Program 18.1: ExceptionalHello

```java
// This is the Hello program in Java
class ExceptionalHello {

    public static void main (String args[]) {

        /* Now let's say hello */
        try {
            System.out.println("Hello " + args[0]);
        }
        catch (Exception e) {
            System.out.println("Hello whoever you are");
        }
    }

}
```

Some exceptions need to be caught and dealt with while others are generally considered to be so horrific that the runtime system just gives up. The compiler will complain if you write code that doesn't watch out for the not-too-dangerous exceptions, but you'll need to watch out for the really dangerous ones (like ArrayIndexOutOfBoundsException's) yourself.

Sometimes catching an exception can make you feel like a little yippy dog that finally catches a car. Now that it's got hold of the bumper between its teeth, what is it going to do with it? Many times there may not be much you can do. Bad exceptions stop the program by default. This is at least preferable to unhandled exceptions in most programming languages where the entire system can come crashing down around your feet with a core dump or worse.

Other times you may just break out of a loop you were in and continue with the rest of your code. This is most common when an exception isn't really unexpected or when it doesn't badly affect your program logic.

You may or may not print an error message. If you write an exception handler and you don't expect it to be called, then by all means put a

```
System.err.println("Error: " + e);
```

in your exception handler. That way if something does go wrong (and something always does), you'll at least know where it went wrong. However don't put an error message in exception handlers you expect to be exercised in the course of normal program flow. Remember, they're exceptions, not errors.

When a class throws an Exception, it sends an alarm up to all the classes and methods that called it. As the alarm goes out, control begins percolating up the call chain to find the nearest `try-catch` block. If no `try-catch` block is found or if the `try-catch` blocks that are found don't catch the right kind of exceptions, control goes all the way up into the runtime environment. If control reaches the runtime environment, then an error message is printed and the Thread that threw the exception is terminated.

Handling Multiple Exceptions

More than one thing can go wrong with a statement. Thus a single `try` block can have several `catch` blocks, each of which catches its own kind of exception. There are many different exceptions defined by the Java runtime, the Java class library, and even by your own source code. You can catch as many of them as you like. The `try-catch` block is very similar in syntax to an `if-else if` block. There's only one `try`, but there can be as many `catch`'s as necessary. For instance,

```
try {
    // Do something that might fail
}
catch(ArithmeticException e) {
    // Respond to the Exception
}
catch(ArrayIndexOutOfBoundsException e) {
    // Respond to the Exception
}
catch(UserDefinedException e) {
    // Respond to the Exception
}
```

This just catches the exceptions the programmer expects. You can make the code more robust by catching a generic Exception as follows:

```
try {
    // Do something that might fail
}
catch(ArithmeticException e) {
    // Respond to the Exception
}
catch(ArrayIndexOutOfBoundsException e) {
    // Respond to the Exception
}
catch(UserDefinedException e) {
    // Respond to the Exception
}
catch (Exception e) {
    System.err.println("Unexpected Exception: " + e);
}
```

With the addition of the last `catch` statement, any unexpected exceptions will be caught and the code will continue. Since you don't know what other exceptions may occur here, you print out an error message that tells you what the exception is. Then, if you find an additional exceptional condition that you didn't anticipate, you can reproduce the error message and find the cause of the exception. Then you would modify your code to respond more specifically to the particular exception.

Nested Try-Catch Blocks

Even the code that's handling your exceptions can throw exceptions. Fortunately `try-catch` blocks can be nested just like `for` loops or `if-else` statements. The syntax is simple and virtually identical to multiple nested `if-else` blocks. You'd use this when you do non-trivial processing as a result of an exception.

finally

Sometimes there's code that must be executed come hell or high water, no matter what other disasters have occurred, up to and including a complete program crash. For instance, you may have a long CPU-intensive calculation that accumulates a series of numbers (for instance, the prime factors of the numbers between 2 and 2,000,000,000) but doesn't print them out until the calculation is finished. However, if you run out of memory in the middle of the calculation, you may want to stop processing but still print out any numbers that have already been calculated. To do this, add a `finally` statement to the `try-catch` block.

```java
try {
    // Do really long calculation
}
catch (ArithmeticException e) {
    // Bail out
}
catch (Exception e) {
    // Bail out
}
catch (Throwable t) {
    // Bail out
}
finally {
    // Print those numbers you have factored
}
```

The code in a `finally` statement is executed no matter what occurs short of an operating system crash or a hardware failure. It is executed whether or not an Exception is thrown.

Checked and Unchecked Exceptions

What is generically called an "exception" is in Java an instance of a subclass of java.lang.Throwable. java.lang.Throwable has two immediate subclasses: java.lang.Error and java.lang.Exception. Errors are things that aren't supposed to be able to happen, such as a class not having a method it's supposed to have. The Java virtual machine and compiler are supposed to guard against these, but they're not perfect. In general, you shouldn't try to catch an Error since there's very likely nothing you can do about it.

The possible exception to this rule is the most common Error, an OutOfMemoryError. If you're performing an operation that may require scads of memory such as allocating a huge array or performing very deep recursion, you may be able to catch and reasonably respond to an OutOfMemoryError. If you do decide to respond to an OutOfMemoryError, make absolutely certain you test your response before letting your program loose in the world. That is, don't just assume that because the program works on your 128-megabyte development SparcStation with 512 megabytes of virtual memory that never sees an OutOfMemoryError that it will also work on an 8-megabyte PC.

RuntimeExceptions are Exceptions that may be thrown unexpectedly by the Java runtime environment but that can probably be dealt with by an alert programmer. All the examples you've seen so far have been runtime exceptions. These include ArithmeticExceptions, NullPointerExceptions, ArrayIndexOutOfBoundsExceptions, StringIndexOutOfBoundsExceptions, and more. All of these are subclasses of java.lang.RuntimeException. If you have a reasonable expectation that a RuntimeException may be thrown, you should check for it in a `try-catch` block, but this is not enforced by the compiler.

The final kind of Exception is a **checked exception**. Unlike what you'd expect, there is no java.lang.CheckedException class. Rather a subclass of java.lang.Exception that is not also a subclass of java.lang.RuntimeException is a checked exception. Any exception that is not an Error or a RuntimeException is a checked exception. Most user-defined exceptions should be checked exceptions. The compiler requires that statements which throw checked exceptions must be enclosed in a `try-catch` block. Checked exceptions include ClassNotFoundExceptions, IllegalAccessExceptions, and most of the exceptions related to Threads and I/O that you'll encounter in the next two chapters.

There is an alternative to enclosing a statement that throws a checked exception in a `try-catch` block. Instead you can declare that the method `throws` the particular exception. Then it can be caught in another method further up the call chain.

For example, the sleep method of a Thread object can throw the checked exception InterruptedException. The run method from Program 19.6 of the next chapter can be written using a `try-catch` block like this:

```java
public void run() {
  for (int b = -128; b < 128; b++) {
    System.out.println(b);
    try {
      sleep(1000);
    }
    catch (InterruptedException e) {
    }
  }
}
```

However, if you don't want to catch the exception right away, you could instead write that method as

```java
public void run() throws InterruptedException {
  for (int b = -128; b < 128; b++) {
    System.out.println(b);
    sleep(1000);
  }
}
```

Which option you choose is primarily a matter of where it is most convenient to handle the exception. Declaring that your method throws the exception only moves the place where you handle the exception to a different part of the program.

So far you've seen exceptions thrown by the Java runtime and API. However, you can build your own exceptions classes as well. One place you may want to do this is when you need to verify user input.

For instance, suppose you have a system with which users connect to order books. One of the fields in an order form is the number of copies the user wants. You hope that the user will enter a small positive number in this box. However, as anyone who's ever worked with such a system will tell you, only about half the people who use the form will do what you expect. The other half will enter "one," "two," "a few," "1.5," leave it blank, or otherwise enter some value that can't be easily recognized as the number you want. To handle this, you can define a new subclass of Exception called NotANaturalNumberException. Then, when some two-year-old runs his fingers across your keyboard filling your fields with values like "idoaehdoeunth" you can throw a NotANaturalNumberException. The syntax for this is very simple. Here it is:

```
class NotANaturalNumberException extends Exception {
}


...
  public int getANaturalNumber
    throws NotANaturalNumberException (String data) {

    int i = 0;

    try {
      i = Integer.valueOf(data).intValue();
    }
    catch (Exception e) {
    }
    if (i <= 0) throw new NotANaturalNumberException();

    return i;

}
```

getANaturalNumber begins by setting i to an invalid number, zero. Then an attempt is made to convert the data into an integer.

If it succeeds, i is now an integer. If the attempt fails, i is still zero. In either case, you then fall out of the try block and test whether i is a natural number. If it's not, that is, if it's less than or equal to zero, then you throw a new NotANaturalNumberException. If this Exception is thrown then control passes to the nearest enclosing catch block. No value is returned from the getANaturalNumber method.

The NotANaturalNumberException class itself doesn't contain any code or data. It's used purely as a mnemonic for the programmer to know what problem has occurred. You can add code and data to a new Exception. In this example you might want to add the data that was submitted and a toString method with an error message. Program 18.2 is a NotANaturalNumberException with polymorphic constructors and a toString method.

Program 18.2: NotANaturalNumberException

```java
public class NotANaturalNumberException
  extends Exception {

  String errmsg;

  public NotANaturalNumberException() {

    errmsg = "Not a Natural Number";

  }

  public NotANaturalNumberException(String s) {

    errmsg = s + " is not a natural number";

  }

  public String toString() {

    return errmsg;

  }

}
```

You now have all the tools you need to write solid, robust programs that handle errors and unexpected or undesirable conditions gracefully. Let's take some time to plan when and how you should use these tools.

When Should You Use try-catch?

Almost any statement that might conceivably fail for any reason should be wrapped in a `try-catch` block. This includes any statement that allocates a significant amount of memory, accesses an array with a variable defined at runtime, or reads or writes a file. Here are just a few examples of the sorts of things you might want to try and catch:

- Anything that needs access to a file: What if the file isn't there or can't be opened?
- Anything that accesses an array, particularly if it accesses the array with an index to be determined at runtime. What if the access is outside the bounds of the array?
- User input: Did the user type what you expected?
- Anything that connects across a network: What if the other end of the connection is unreachable?

Using `try-catch` is like commenting your code or brushing your teeth after every meal. Everyone knows they should do it more, but no one does it as much as they need to. If you have any doubt at all that some action you're taking may not succeed, then by all means put it in a `try-catch` block.

What Should You Catch?

Since no one ever puts as many `try-catch` blocks in their code as they should, chances are good that you've got a particular potential problem in mind from any code you've blocked out. That would be a good place to start `catching`. For instance, if you're dividing two integers or taking their modulus, you'll want to watch out for an ArithmeticException since one will be thrown if you divide by zero. If you're using arrays, watch for ArrayIndexOutOfBoundsExceptions. Of course, you'll also want to catch any Exceptions you've defined yourself.

Finally, as the final `catch` block in every `try-catch` construct include a generic

```
catch (Exception e) {
    System.err.println("Unexpected Exception: " + e);
}
```

This will catch any exception you've neglected. While it's possible to `catch` a Throwable instead, you generally do not want to `catch` Errors. If an Error happens, there really isn't anything you can do at a programmatic level.

The order in which you catch exceptions is important. The exception will be caught by the first `catch` block that matches it or one of its superclasses. Once an exception is caught, it is not available to `catch` blocks below it. Unlike `switch-case` statements, you do not need to include an explicit `break` statement at the end of each case. Thus if you were to make

```
catch (Exception e)
```

the first of your `catch` blocks, no `catch` blocks after it would ever catch an exception.

What to Do with an Exception Once You've Caught It

Now that you've caught an exception, you need to decide what to do with it. There are a number of choices available to the programmer. They are listed here roughly in order of desirability. Choose the one that has the least impact on the user of your program.

Fix the problem and try again.

It's not always possible to fix the problem that caused the exception, but if you can fix it, do so. For instance, if the exception was thrown because the user entered an invalid value, then throw the bad value away and give the user a chance to try again. Keep in mind, however, that there may have been a reason the user chose the value they did, so be sure to give them a choice to cancel the operation instead.

Patch up any problems as best you can, and continue, but don't try the offending operation again.

Sometimes you can't fix the problem, but you may be able to keep further bad things from happening and plod onward.

If you're in a method that returns a value, calculate an alternative result and return that instead.

For example, if you're dividing and catch an ArithmeticException that indicates a division by zero error, you could return a very large number.

Handle as much of the Exception as you can and then rethrow it to a higher-level method.

Sometimes you have some of the information you need to respond to an Exception, but not all of it. In this case you may want to handle what you can and then throw the same Exception again to let higher-level methods deal with it. The basic syntax is

```
catch (Exception e) {
  // Deal With Exception e…;
  throw e;
}
```

Handle as much of the Exception as you can and throw a new Exception.

Whether you throw the same or a new Exception depends primarily on programmer convenience. If it's possible that try-catch blocks in higher level methods will do the same thing as your lower level method with the same exception, then you should probably create and throw a new exception. The basic syntax is

```
catch (Exception e) {
  // Deal With Exception e…;
  mye = new Exception();
```

```
    throw mye;
}
```

Terminate the Thread

You should only terminate a thread when you're left in an uncertain and unanticipated position. After all, if you anticipated the Exception, you should have been able to deal with it. This is the default behavior if an Exception is thrown and nothing catches it. In addition to terminating the thread, print an error message on `System.err` giving the identity of the exception and as much information about the state of the program as possible.

Terminate the program.

In a single-threaded program, terminating the thread is equivalent to terminating the program. However in a multithreaded program, you should almost never need or want to terminate the entire running program. If you're in doubt because you've encountered an unexpected exception, then terminate the running thread instead. The only time where you might choose to terminate the entire program is if you're running a high-security program where all threads are interdependent and no answer at all is preferable to the wrong one. If you do decide to terminate the program, use the `System.exit` method from the Java class library.

 Q: *What's the difference between an error and an exception?*

 A: An error is a mistake like using < when you need <=. An exception is an unexpected condition that generally occurs at runtime such as running out of memory or disk space. You cannot change the exception by changing the code, but you can make your program exception-resistant. On the other hand, you should strive to make your code error-free.

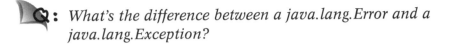

Q: *What's the difference between a java.lang.Error and a java.lang.Exception?*

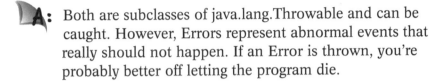

A: Both are subclasses of java.lang.Throwable and can be caught. However, Errors represent abnormal events that really should not happen. If an Error is thrown, you're probably better off letting the program die.

Q: *Couldn't this all be done with* if-then *statements and checks on the return values of methods?*

A: Indeed this is the traditional method of handling errors. However, it has a number of disadvantages compared with try-catch and Exceptions:

- Sometimes all possible return values are legitimate results so nothing is left over to signal an Error condition. (For instance, a function that reads an ASCII character and returns a byte has no extra numbers to use to signal that the user didn't input anything at all.)

- It's easier to put one try-catch block around a large piece of code than to test the return value of every statement in the block individually.

- You don't always have all the information you need to deal with an error where it occurs. The lack of Exceptions has led languages like C to include kludges like goto, setjmp, and longjmp.

Q: *Why raise an exception at all? Why not handle an exception right where it happens?*

A: Sometimes you don't have all the information you need to handle an exception when it occurs. Sometimes you need to handle it at a higher level. For instance, if new produces an OutOfMemoryError, then there may not be anything the runtime can do to produce more memory; but the code that called new may be able to live without the object it was trying to instantiate.

Furthermore, the same exception can happen in multiple places. Exceptions let you unify and reuse the code to handle the errors.

 Q: *What can you do with an Exception's methods?*

 A: If you give a method to an exception, then it can be called from within the block that caught it. A good method to override would be the toString() method. You can make it provide more information about the conditions that caused the Exception to be thrown.

 Quiz

1. Can there be a `try` block without a matching `catch` block?

2. Can there be a `catch` block without a matching `try` block?

3. Can there be a `finally` statement that is not attached to a `try-catch` block?

4. When are Exception objects created?

5. Does an Exception have to be handled by the same `try-catch` block that threw it?

6. How can you make sure you catch every Exception that a statement may throw?

7. If an Exception isn't caught in a user-defined class, where does it go and what does it do?

8. Suppose you've defined an Exception called NotANumberException(). Now suppose that NotAPositiveNumberException extends NotANumberException. Will

```
catch (NotANumberException) {
  System.out.println("Caught a NotANumberException");
}
```

catch a NotAPositiveNumberException? Now suppose you have the following `catch` clause and throw a NotAPositiveNumberException. What happens?

```
catch (NotANumberException) {
  System.out.println("Caught a NotANumberException");
}
catch (NotAPositiveNumberException) {
  System.out.println("Caught a NotANumberException");
}
```

9. In general, which `catch` statement should come first? The one that catches the subclass or the one that catches the superclass? Why?

10. What do you have to do to have an Exception handled by both its own `catch` statement and by its superclass's `catch` statement?

11. What's the difference between `throw` and `throws`?

Exercises

1. Chances are very good that some of the programs you've written before have encountered exceptions. Since you didn't catch the exceptions, they simply halted the execution of your code. Go back to those programs and add exception handling.

2. Write a class that keeps a running total of all characters passed to it (one at a time) and throws an exception if it is passed a non-alphabetic character.

This chapter covered everything you need to know about how Java handles both expected and unexpected Exceptions. The things you learned here included:

- How to anticipate and respond to exceptional conditions
- How your classes can throw exceptions to warn others of exceptional conditions
- How to plan a good exception strategy.

Coming Up

In the next chapter, you'll encounter Threads and then Streams in Chapter 20. You'll find that Exceptions are an integral part of both of those and that try-catch blocks are not just a nice feature but absolutely required to make them work.

Further Reading

Exceptions are covered in Chapter 11 of the *Java Language Specification* and in

http://www.javasoft.com/JDK-1.0/api/java.lang.Throwable.html

http://www.javasoft.com/JDK-1.0/api/java.lang.Exception.html

http://www.javasoft.com/JDK-1.0/api/java.lang.Error.html

http://www.javasoft.com/JDK-1.0/api/java.lang.RuntimeException.html

CHAPTER 19
THREADS AND ANIMATION

▌How to create and control Threads

▌How to use the Runnable interface to thread an existing class

▌How to set Thread priorities

▌How to synchronize Threads

▌How Threads are used to play animations

In this chapter, you'll learn how to make your applications and applets multithreaded to improve user responsiveness and perceived performance. You'll also learn how to use threads to implement timing and animation.

What Are Threads?

The earliest computers did one thing at a time. A computer might calculate detonation waves for a physicist. Next it would calculate mixing ratios for a chemist. All programs were run sequentially, one at a time, and each had full run of the computer. However two programs couldn't be run at once. This is called batch processing, and it's a very efficient way to get maximum usage out of a very expensive computer because almost all the computer's time is spent actually calculating jobs and not switching between one program and another. However batch processing can be very annoying when your differential equation integration program that would take all of two seconds of CPU time gets stuck in line behind the physics department's nuclear structure modeling project that's going run for the next three days.

Time-sharing operating systems were invented to allow multiple people to use one then very expensive computer at the same time. On a time-sharing system many people can run programs at the same time. The operating system is responsible for splitting the time among the different programs that are running. That way you can finish integrating your differential equation while the physics department's nuclear modeling program is still churning away. The physics department nuclear modeling program might take two weeks to run instead of three days, but everyone with the shorter programs was happy (at least until the physicists figured out how to hack the computer so that it only ran their program).

Once systems allowed different users to run programs at the same time, it was a short step to letting the same user run multiple programs simultaneously. And this is where matters stopped for about 20 years. However, it's not just users that want to do different things at the same time. Many programs also need to do several things at once. A Web browser, for instance, can print a file in the background while it downloads a page in one window and formats the page as it downloads. The ability of an individual program to do more than one thing at the same time is most efficiently implemented through threads.

A **thread** can be loosely defined as a separate stream of execution that takes place simultaneously with and independently of everything else that might be happening. A thread is like a classic program that starts at point a and executes until it reaches point b. It does not have an event loop. A thread runs independently of anything else happening in the computer. Without threads an entire program can be held up by one CPU intensive task or one infinite loop, intentional or otherwise. With threads the other tasks that don't get stuck in the loop can continue processing without waiting for the stuck task to finish.

It turns out that implementing threading is harder than implementing multitasking in an operating system. The reason it's relatively easy to implement multitasking is that individual programs are isolated from each other. Individual threads, however, are not. To return to the printing example, suppose that while the printing is happening in one thread, the user deletes a large chunk of text in another thread. What's printed? The document as it was before the deletion? The document as it was after the deletion? The document with some but not all of the deleted text? Or does the whole system go down in flames? Most often in a non-threaded or poorly threaded system it's the latter.

Threaded environments like Java allow a thread to put locks on shared resources so that while one thread is using data, no other thread can touch that data. This is done with **synchronization**. Synchronization should be used sparingly since the purpose of threading is defeated if the entire system gets stopped waiting for a lock to be released. The proper choice of variables and methods to synchronize is one of the more difficult things to learn about threaded programming.

Java applications and applets are naturally threaded. The runtime environment starts execution of the program with the main method in one thread. Garbage collection takes place in another thread. There may be other threads running as well, mostly related to the behavior of the applet viewer or Web browser. All of this happens invisibly to the programmer. Most of the time you're only concerned with what happens in the primary thread, which includes the main method of a program or the event loop of an applet. If this is the case, you don't need to worry about threading at all.

Sometimes, however, you need to add your own threads to an applet or application. The most common reason for adding a separate thread is to perform a long calculation. For instance, if you're trying to find the ten millionth prime number, you probably don't want to make users twiddle their thumbs while you search. Or you may be waiting for a resource that isn't available yet, a large graphic to download from the Internet for example. Once again, you shouldn't make the user wait while your program waits. Any operation that is going to take a noticeable period of time should be placed in its own thread.

The other reason to use threading is to divide the computer's power more evenly among different tasks. If you want to draw random rectangles on the display as Mondrian did in Chapter 12, you would still like the applet to respond to user input. If all the CPU time is spent drawing rectangles, there's nothing left over for the user. On a preemptively multitasking operating system like Solaris or Windows NT, the user may at least be able to kill the application. On a cooperatively multitasking operating system like the MacOS or Windows, the user may have to reboot their machine. This is a bad thing. With threads you can set the priority of different processes, so that user input receives a high priority and drawing pretty pictures receives a low priority. Then the user can stop the applet without flipping the power switch on their machine.

Java has two ways a program can implement threading. One is to create a subclass of java.lang.Thread. However, sometimes you'll want to thread an object that's already a subclass of another class. Then you use the Runnable interface.

Working with Threads

A Thread is a separate, independent flow of execution. When writing a threaded program, you can pretend that you're writing many different programs, each with its own main method. However, instead of main the primary method of the Thread will be called run. Second, instead of extending Object, each Thread must be a subclass of java.lang.Thread. Program 19.1 is a threaded class that prints the numbers between −128 and 127.

Program 19.1: BytePrinter

```java
public class BytePrinter extends Thread {

  public void run() {
    for (int b = -128; b < 128; b++) {
      System.out.println(b);
    }

  }

}
```

You control this Thread from another method using the four methods

- start
- stop
- suspend
- resume

and the **new** operator. To create a Thread, just call the default constructor for your subclass of Thread. For instance,

```
BytePrinter bp = new BytePrinter();
```

This puts the thread at the starting line. The bell goes off and the thread starts running when you call the Thread's start method like this:

```
bp.start();
```

Once the start method is called, program execution splits in two. Some CPU time goes into whatever statements follow `bp.start()` and some goes into the bp thread. It is unpredictable which statements will run first. Most likely they will be intermixed. The bp thread will now continue running until one of three things happens:

1. The run method completes
2. bp's stop method is called
3. bp's suspend method is called.

Once program control reaches the end of bp's run method, the thread dies. This is a fairly short-running thread so this is the most likely result. However, sometimes you have threads that continue for a very long time, even indefinitely. If this is the case, you can stop the thread by calling its stop method like this:

```
bp.stop();
```

However when stop is called, the thread is killed. If you want to restart it, you have to start over from the beginning. If you think you might want to pick up where the thread left off, then use the suspend method instead.

```
bp.suspend();
```

When you're ready to restart the thread call its resume method like this:

```
bp.resume();
```

All these methods are provided by the Thread class. You do not need to create them specifically. Note that you never call run directly; just start, stop, suspend, and resume.

Program 19.2 demonstrates threading in conjunction with the BytePrinter of Program 19.1.

Program 19.2: ThreadTest

```java
public class ThreadTest {

  public static void main(String args[]) {

    BytePrinter bp = new BytePrinter();
    bp.start();
    for (int i = -128; i < 128; i++) {
      System.out.println("Main method: " + i);
    }

  }

}
```

Here's some sample output:

```
%java ThreadTest
Main method: -128
Main method: -127
Main method: -126
Main method: -125
Main method: -124
Main method: -123
Main method: -122
-128
-127
-126
-125
-124
-123
-122
-121
Main method: -121
Main method: -120
Main method: -119
```

```
Main method: -118
Main method: -117
Main method: -116
Main method: -115
-120
-119
-118
-117
-116
-115
-114
-113
-112
-111
-110
-109
-108
Main method: -114
Main method: -113
Main method: -112
Main method: -111
Main method: -110
Main method: -109
```

Note how the output from the main method and the thread's run method is interspersed. The exact interspersion is system dependent and may even vary from one run to the next. This is to be expected. The whole point of threading is that threads run independently of each other.

Multiple Threads

In the previous example there were two Threads running: the default Thread for main and the BytePrinter you created. There's nothing to stop you from creating many more Threads. These may be instances of the same subclass of Thread. They may be instances of different classes, or they may be both. When you do create multiple instances of each Thread, it's often useful to give each Thread a name so you can keep them straight. Do this by passing a String into the Thread's constructor like this:

```
BytePrinter bp1 = new BytePrinter("Frank");
BytePrinter bp2 = new BytePrinter("Mary");
BytePrinter bp3 = new BytePrinter("Chris");
```

Within the Thread you can access the Thread's name with the getName() method. Program 19.3 runs three BytePrinter Threads in parallel. Program 19.4 is a revised BytePrinter that uses the getName() method to specify which Thread is printing the particular line and includes a constructor that sets the name.

Program 19.3: MultiThreadTest

```java
public class MultiThreadTest {

  public static void main(String args[]) {

    BytePrinter bp1 = new BytePrinter("Frank");
    BytePrinter bp2 = new BytePrinter("Mary");
    BytePrinter bp3 = new BytePrinter("Chris");
    bp1.start();
    bp2.start();
    bp3.start();

  }

}
```

Program 19.4: BytePrinter with name printing

```java
public class BytePrinter extends Thread {

  public BytePrinter(String s) {

    super(s);

  }

  public void run() {
    for (int b = -128; b < 128; b++) {
      System.out.println(getName() + ": " + b);
    }

  }

}
```

Priorities

Not all Threads are created equal. Sometimes you want to give one Thread more time than another. Threads that interact with the user should get very high priorities. On the other hand, Threads that calculate in the background should get low priorities.

Thread priorities are defined as integers between one and ten. Ten is the highest priority. One is the lowest. The normal priority is five. Higher priority Threads get more CPU time.

Warning This is exactly opposite to the normal UNIX way of prioritizing processes where the higher the priority number of a process, the less CPU time the process gets.

For your convenience, java.lang.Thread defines three mnemonic constants—Thread.MAX_PRIORITY, Thread.MIN_PRIORITY, and Thread.NORM_PRIORITY—which you can use in place of the numeric values.

You set a Thread's priority with the setPriority(int priority) method. Program 19.5 sets Chris's priority higher than Mary's, whose priority is higher than Frank's. It is therefore likely that even though Chris starts last and Frank starts first, Chris will finish before Mary, who will finish before Frank.

Program 19.5: Mixed Priorities

```
public class MixedPriorityTest {

  public static void main(String args[]) {

    BytePrinter bp1 = new BytePrinter("Frank");
    BytePrinter bp2 = new BytePrinter("Mary");
    BytePrinter bp3 = new BytePrinter("Chris");
    bp1.setPriority(Thread.MIN_PRIORITY);
    bp2.setPriority(Thread.NORM_PRIORITY);
    bp3.setPriority(Thread.MAX_PRIORITY);
    bp1.start();
    bp2.start();
    bp3.start();

  }

}
```

Preemptive and Cooperative Threads

Multitasking computer systems schedule different processes to run in one of two ways, preemptive and cooperative. With preemptive multitasking, the operating system gives each process or Thread slices of time until its complete. The operating system scheduler guarantees that every Thread gets time to run in. This is especially useful for multi-user systems.

In a cooperative multitasking system, each Thread has to voluntarily give up its access to the processor before other Threads get an opportunity to run. This means that a greedy Thread that does not share its time can hold up the entire computer until it's finished. This is especially useful in realtime systems.

Most Java implementations use cooperative multithreading, though this may change in the future. This means that each Java Thread should periodically allow other Threads an opportunity to run. There are several ways to do this. The most common way is to call the Thread's yield method. Typically this is done like this:

```
Thread.currentThread().yield();
```

A Thread can also voluntarily give up time to other Threads by sleeping as you'll learn in the next section.

Sleeping

Sometimes the computer may run too fast for the human beings. If this is the case, you need to slow it down. You can make a particular Thread slow down by interspersing it with calls to the `sleep(long ms)` method. `ms` is the number of milliseconds you want the Thread to wait before proceeding. There are one thousand milliseconds in a second.

The sleep method throws InterruptedExceptions. Therefore when you put a Thread to sleep, you need to catch InterruptedExceptions. Thus every call to sleep should be wrapped in a `try-catch` block like this:

```
try {
```

```
      sleep(1000);
    }
    catch (InterruptedException e) {

    }
```

The sleep method is most commonly called from within the Thread that needs to sleep. If you need to pause a Thread from outside, you'd usually use `suspend` and `resume` instead.

Program 19.6 is revised BytePrinter that sleeps for one second between every byte it prints.

Program 19.6: Sleepy BytePrinter

```java
public class BytePrinter extends Thread {

  public void run() {
    for (int b = -128; b < 128; b++) {
      System.out.println(b);
      try {
        sleep(1000);
      }
      catch (InterruptedException e) {

      }
    }
  }
}
```

Multithreading and Synchronization

So far all the Threads have run independently of each other. One Thread did not need to know what another Thread was doing. Sometimes, however, Threads need to share data. In this case it is important to ensure that one Thread doesn't change the data while the other Thread is executing. The classic example is file access. If one

Thread is writing to a file while another Thread is reading the file, it's likely that the Thread that's reading the file will get corrupt data.[1]

Objects themselves provide the first line of defense against data corruption. Simple objects including most of the ones you've dealt with so far do not require synchronization because different instances of a class do not share data. The x coordinate of one point, for instance, is not the same as the x coordinate of another point.

Problems arise when data is shared between objects. This normally happens in one of three ways:

- When using static variables and methods
- When the Thread is passed as an argument to another object
- When a reference is passed into the Thread

The problem with static variables and methods is that they are shared by different instances of the class. Thus two different objects might try to use a static variable or method at the same time. The problem with object variables is similar though less obvious. Since object variables are references, many different variables in different classes or Threads may refer to the same object.

To prevent data corruption, Java allows you to lock objects and methods using the **synchronized** keyword. Synchronization limits access to a method or object to one Thread at a time. To synchronize a method, just put the keyword synchronized after the access specifier and before the return type like this:

```
public synchronized void print() {
```

Program 19.7 shows a class with a static variable `i` and a `print` method. Since `i` is a static variable, there is a chance that a different instance of this class in a different method might change `i` before you're finished printing. The `synchronized` keyword guarantees that no more than one instance of this method is going to run at once so `i` won't suddenly be changed from 5 to 17 while the `for` loop is executing.

---

[1] Surprisingly, two Threads trying to write the same file at the same time is not as likely to cause problems, because most operating systems will prevent this. Still it's not a good idea to rely on this, and a devilish programmer could sneak around it by opening the file once outside the Threads and passing the same filehandle into both Threads.

```
public class SynchronizedPrinter {

  static int i = 0;

  public synchronized void print() {
    for (i = 1; i <= 10; i++) {
      System.out.println(i);
    }
  }
}
```

Synchronization can also be applied to sections of code smaller than methods, but this is in general a bad idea. If the synchronized method is taking too long to execute and holding up other Threads as a result, then break it into separate methods rather than synchronizing a smaller piece of the method.

Wait, Notify, and Deadlock

Other Threads that want access to a synchronized object must wait for the first Thread to finish running before they can continue. When a Thread is waiting for another Thread to release the lock on an object, it is **blocked**.

Synchronization is a dangerous thing and should be avoided where possible. Two Threads can each lock an object the other needs, and thus prevent both Threads from running. This is called **deadlock**.

To avoid deadlocks, your synchronized sections should include calls to the Thread's wait() method like this:

```
try {
  // execute the code
  wait();
}
catch (InterruptedException e) {
}
```

When `wait` is called, all locks on objects are released. When `wait` returns, the lock on the object is regained. This gives other Threads the chance to finish what they're doing.

You should keep synchronized blocks of code as small as possible. When you only need to read the value of an object, you can synchronize the object, make a private clone of the object, and then release the lock on the object. Then you can continue working with your private copy.

Implementing Runnable

So far all the Threads you've seen have been subclasses of java.lang.Thread. Sometimes, however, you want to add threading to a class that already inherits from a class other than Thread. The most common such occurrence is when you want to add threading to an applet. The easiest way to improve the perceived performance of an applet is to implement the Runnable interface.

The Runnable interface defines just one method, `run`. Your class needs to implement this method just as it would if it were a subclass of Thread and declare that it implements the Runnable interface like this:

```
class myThreadedClass extends someClass implements
   Runnable {
      .
      .

   public void run() {
         .
         .
         .
      }

   }
```

To start the threaded object, create a new Thread and pass the Runnable object to the Thread constructor. Then call the Thread's start method like this:

```
myThreadedClass mtc = new myThreadedClass();
Thread t = new Thread(mtc);
t.start();
```

Animation

Animation is one of the primary uses of the Runnable interface. To animate objects in Java, you create a Thread that calculates successive frames and then calls repaint to paint the screen. You could just stick an infinite loop in your paint method, but that is quite dangerous, especially on non-preemptive systems like the Mac.

Let's begin with a simple animation that bounces a red ball around in a box. The red ball will just be a big red circle. Its coordinates will be stored in a Rectangle field called `ball`. The paint method will do nothing but look at this field and then draw the ball.

The run method of this applet is where the action will take place. Here you'll increment the coordinates of the ball and then check to see if the ball has moved to the edge of the visible area. If it has, reverse the direction of the ball. The applet's really quite simple. Here it is:

Program 19.8 Bounce

```java
import java.awt.Graphics;
import java.applet.Applet;
import java.awt.Rectangle;
import java.awt.Color;


public class Bounce extends Applet
    implements Runnable {

    Rectangle r;
    int x_increment = 1;
    int y_increment = 1;

    public void init () {

        r = new Rectangle( 30, 40, 20, 20);
        Thread t = new Thread(this);
        t.start();

    }
```

```
public void paint (Graphics g) {

    g.setColor(Color.red);
    g.fillOval(r.x, r.y, r.width, r.height);

}

public void run() {

    while (true) {    // infinite loop
        r.x += x_increment;
        r.y += y_increment;
        if (r.x >= size().width || r.x < 0) {
            x_increment *= -1;
        }
        if (r.y >= size().height || r.y < 0) {
            y_increment *= -1;
        }
        repaint();
    }

}
}
```

This ball is a trifle fast. You'll probably want to lower the priority of the Thread, and toss in some sleep time. Here's a revised run method that is somewhat smoother:

```
public void run() {



Thread.currentThread().setPriority(Thread.MIN_PRI-
ORITY);

    while (true) {    // infinite loop
        r.x += x_increment;
        r.y += y_increment;
        if (r.x >= size().width || r.x < 0)
            x_increment *= -1;
        if (r.y >= size().height || r.y < 0)
            y_increment *= -1;
        repaint();
```

```
      try {
        Thread.currentThread().sleep(100);
      }
      catch (Exception e) {

      }
    }

  }
```

Exactly what priority to give the Thread and how long it should sleep is mostly a matter of trial and error, and is regrettably somewhat platform dependent. Faster machines will run animations more quickly. A better applet would add a sleeptime PARAM to let the author of the HTML file set the relative speed of the ball. A truly advanced animation applet would implement a timing engine that looked at the system clock for platform-independent animation, but that's a little beyond the scope of this book.

It's a good idea to give the user a way to stop a Thread from running. With simple animation Threads like this, the custom is that a mouse click stops the animation if it's running and restarts it if it isn't.

To implement this behavior, make the animation Thread a field. Also add a boolean variable bouncing that is true if and only if the Thread is running. Finally, add a mouseUp method that stops the Thread if it's started and starts it if it's stopped. Here's the revised applet:

Program 19.9 Bounce

```
import java.awt.Graphics;
import java.applet.Applet;
import java.awt.Rectangle;
import java.awt.Color;
import java.awt.Event;

public class Bounce extends Applet
  implements Runnable {

  Rectangle r;
  int x_increment = 1;
  int y_increment = 1;
```

```java
Thread t;
boolean bouncing;

public void init () {

   r = new Rectangle( 30, 40, 20, 20);
   t = new Thread(this);
   t.start();
   bouncing = true;

}


public void paint (Graphics g) {
   g.setColor(Color.red);
   g.fillOval(r.x, r.y, r.width, r.height);

}

public boolean mouseUp(Event e, int x, int y) {
   if (bouncing) {
     t.stop();
     bouncing = false;
   }
   else {
     t.start();
     bouncing = true;
   }
   return true;
}

public void run() {

   Thread.currentThread().setPriority(
     Thread.MIN_PRIORITY);

   while (true) {   // infinite loop
     r.x += x_increment;
     r.y += y_increment;
     if (r.x >= size().width || r.x < 0) {
       x_increment *= -1;
     }
     if (r.y >= size().height || r.y < 0) {
       y_increment *= -1;
     }
```

```
        repaint();
        try {
            Thread.currentThread().sleep(100);
        }
        catch (Exception e) {

        }
    }

  }

}
```

This applet shows how to animate a circle. There's nothing special about this though. You could have equally well bounced around a square, a polygon, or, more commonly, an Image. The key to animation is that your paint method knows what it needs to paint and has access to the variables that tell it where to paint. The run method needs to know how to move the objects around. Given these two factors, animation is really quite simple.

Avoiding Flicker

You may or may not have noticed some flickering in the last applet. It's quite common for animation applets to flicker. The problem has to do with a failure to sync between when the computer monitor wants to redraw and when the applet wants to redraw. If they don't match up, there's flicker.

There are two ways to solve this problem. The simplest solution is a clipping region. A clipping region is a rectangular area inside of which you can draw and outside of which you can't. By setting the clipping region you limit the area which is drawn into. This means first of all that nothing outside that region flickers. Second, the smaller area can be drawn more quickly so there's less likelihood of flicker.

To set a clipping rectangle, call `g.clipRect(Rect r)` inside your paint method where `r` is the rectangle you want to clip to. The bounce applet is perfect for this since you have a convenient rectangle to which to clip. Here's a revised paint method for Bounce:

```
public void paint (Graphics g) {
    g.setColor(Color.red);
    g.clipRect(r.x, r.y, r.width, r.height);
    g.fillOval(r.x, r.y, r.width, r.height);
}
```

The second and often more effective method is to use offscreen Images and the update method. The screen isn't actually painted in the paint method. The paint method just sets up an Image to be copied onto the screen. The pixels are actually put on the screen in the update method which most applets don't override. However by overriding the update method, you can do all your painting in an offscreen Image, and then just copy the final Image onto the screen. Copying an image happens much more quickly and evenly than painting individual elements so there's no visible flicker.

The cookbook approach is simple. Add the following update method to your applet. Flicker will magically disappear.

```
public final synchronized void update (Graphics g)
{

    Image offScreenImage = createImage(size().width,
size().height);
    paint(offScreenImage.getGraphics());
    g.drawImage(offScreenImage, 0, 0, null);

}
```

In the first line of the method you create an Image the same size as the applet. In the second line you call paint but pass it your own Image's Graphics object instead of the applet's. Now the painting can take some time, because the user doesn't see each individual thing being drawn. Finally, copy the offScreenImage to the screen in one stroke. There's nothing to stop you from combining both methods. Just include the above update method and call to clipRect in your paint method.

Multiple Independent Animations

There are times when it makes sense to have multiple animations running at once. In this case rather than implementing Runnable, you should subclass Thread. Program 19.10 demonstrates this with an applet that bounces two balls independently of each other.

Program 19.10 Two Balls

```java
import java.awt.Graphics;
import java.applet.Applet;
import java.awt.Rectangle;
import java.awt.Color;
import java.awt.Event;
import java.awt.Dimension;

public class TwoBall extends Applet
  implements Runnable {

  Ball b1, b2;
  boolean bouncing;
  Thread t;

  public void init () {

    b1 = new Ball(10, 32, size());
    b1.start();
    b2 = new Ball(155, 75, size());
    b2.start();
    bouncing = true;
    t = new Thread(this);
    t.start();

  }


  public void paint (Graphics g) {

    g.fillOval(b1.getX(), b1.getY(),
      b1.getWidth(), b1.getHeight());
    g.fillOval(b2.getX(), b2.getY(),
      b2.getWidth(), b2.getHeight());
  }

  public boolean mouseUp(Event e, int x, int y) {
    if (bouncing) {
      b1.stop();
```

```java
      b2.stop();
      t.stop();
      bouncing = false;
    }
    else {
      b1.start();
      b2.start();
      t.start();
      bouncing = true;
    }
    return true;
  }

  public void run() {
    Thread.currentThread().setPriority(
      Thread.MIN_PRIORITY);

    while (true) {    // infinite loop
      repaint();
      try {
        Thread.currentThread().sleep(10);
      }
      catch (Exception e) {

      }
    }

  }

}


class Ball extends Thread {

  private Rectangle r;
  private int x_increment = 1;
  private int y_increment = 1;
  private Dimension bounds;

  public Ball(int x, int y, Dimension d) {
    r = new Rectangle(x, y, 20, 20);
    bounds = d;
  }
```

```java
public int getX() {
  return r.x;
}

public int getY() {
  return r.y;
}

public int getHeight() {
  return r.height;
}

public int getWidth() {
  return r.width;
}

public void run() {

  Thread.currentThread().setPriority(
    Thread.MIN_PRIORITY);

  while (true) {  // infinite loop
    r.x += x_increment;
    r.y += y_increment;

    if (r.x + r.width >= bounds.width || r.x < 0)
    {
      x_increment *= -1;
    }
    if (r.y + r.height >= bounds.height || r.y < 0)
    {
      y_increment *= -1;
    }
    try {
      Thread.currentThread().sleep(10);
    }
    catch (Exception e) {

    }
  }

}

}
```

Q&A

 Q: *In the Threaded Applet example, why don't the applet's start and stop methods override java.lang.Thread's start and stop methods?*

 A: Although java.lang.Thread implements start and stop methods, the Runnable interface only defines the run method. Therefore other methods in java.lang.Thread are not overridden. In fact even the run method of java.lang.Thread isn't really overridden since an Interface can't override a class. However the `Thread(Runnable)` constructor sets the appropriate internal variables and flags in the Thread object such that the Thread's run method will just call the Runnable's run method.

Quiz

1. What's the difference between a Thread created as a subclass of java.lang.Thread and one created as an implementation of Runnable?

2. Why should synchronized blocks of code call `wait()`?

Exercises

1. Add a Color property to the balls.

2. The balls in Program 19.10 always move in 45-degree angles. Allow a broader behavior of the balls.

3. Write a multiball applet where the number of balls is a PARAM that is defined in HTML. You'll probably need to store the balls in a Vector. You should also allow the size, color, starting positions, and directions of each ball to be given in a PARAM.

4. Hard: Allow the balls to bounce off each other as well as the walls.

Summary

In this chapter you learned how to make your applications and applets multithreaded to improve user responsiveness and perceived performance. You also learned how to use Threads to implement timing and animation. Topics covered included

- What Threads are
- How to create Threads as subclasses of java.lang.Thread
- How to create Threads using the Runnable interface
- How to set Thread priorities
- How to synchronize methods
- How to play animations using Threads
- How to avoid flicker with double buffering and clipping regions

Coming Up

You've been using the System.out and System.err streams since Chapter 2. In the next chapter you finally meet the third member of the triad, System.in. You'll also learn just what System.out really is.

Further Reading

The synchronized statement is covered in Chapter 16 of the *Java Language Specification*. You can find more about Threads at

http://www.javasoft.com/JDK-1.0/api/java.lang.Thread.html

http://www.javasoft.com/JDK-1.0/api/java.lang.ThreadDeath.html

http://www.javasoft.com/JDK-1.0/api/java.lang.ThreadGroup.html

http://www.javasoft.com/JDK-1.0/api/java.lang.Runnable.html

CHAPTER 20
STREAMS AND FILES

How to write data onto a stream

How to read data from a stream

How to chain streams together

How to work with files

How to use FileDialogs

Sometimes data is written to a file instead of the computer screen. Under Unix and DOS, you can sometimes do this using the redirection operators < and >. However, sometimes you need a more fine-grained approach that writes only certain data to a file while still putting other data on the screen. Or you may need access to multiple files simultaneously. Or maybe you want to query the user for input rather than accepting it all on the command line. Or maybe you want to read data out of a file that's in a particular format. In Java, all these methods require streams. In fact, the System.out object you've been using since Chapter 2 is a stream.

What Is a Stream?

A **stream** is a sequence of data of undetermined length. It's called a stream because it's like a stream of water that continues to flow. There's no definite end to it.

A better analogy might be a queue of people waiting to get on a ride at an amusement park. As people are processed at the front (i.e., get on the roller coaster), more are added at the back of the line. If it's a slow day the roller coaster may catch up with the end of the line and have to wait for people to board. Other days there may always be people in line until the park closes.

Each person is a discrete individual and must be put on the roller coaster or not put on the roller coaster. There are no half-people. There's always a definite number of people in line though this number may change from moment to moment as people enter at the back of the line and exit from the front of the line. Although all the people are discrete, you'll sometimes have a family that must be put together in the same roller coaster car. Thus although the individuals are discrete, they aren't necessarily unrelated.

In Java, a stream is composed of discrete bytes. The bytes may represent chars or other kinds of data. They may come faster than you can handle them, or your thread may block while waiting for the next one to arrive. It often doesn't matter. The key to processing the stream is a `while` loop that processes each piece of data, until you encounter the end-of-stream character or some other exceptional condition occurs. In Unix end-of-stream is indicated by Control-D. On Windows systems, end-of-stream is Control-Z.

There are two kinds of streams: input streams and output streams. Input streams let you read data into your program. Output streams let you send data from your program to somewhere else.

Since all data is ultimately bytes, any kind of data can be put on a stream for output or read off a stream for input. System.out is an output stream that is normally attached to the main display or command window.

In Java input streams are instances of a subclass of java.io.InputStream. Output streams are instances of a subclass of java.io.OutputStream. InputStreams have methods for reading data. OutputStreams provide methods for writing data.

The constructor for an InputStream attaches the stream to its data source. Think of the data source as a spigot and the stream as a rubber hose. The data is the water that flows out of the spigot and through the hose to your thirsty program at the other end. The data source may be a file, the command line, a pipe, a network connection, another stream, or possibly something more exotic. The constructor for an output stream also connects to a particular data destination which may be a file, a pipe, standard output, the network, another stream, or something more exotic.

Once a stream has been created, you read from it or write to it. Sometimes particular items don't want to be read or written. For instance, you may not have permissions to read a certain file or to open a particular network socket. If this is the case, the attempt to use the stream is likely to throw an IOException. IOExceptions are quite common and any stream operation more complex than `System.out.println()` should be enclosed in a `try-catch` block that looks out for IOExceptions.

java.io.InputStream and java.io.OutputStream are abstract classes so they can't be instantiated. Rather you instantiate one of their subclasses. There are subclasses for special kinds of attachment (File) or special kinds of data. Most commonly you create one of five kinds of stream: FileInputStream, FileOutputStream, DataInputStream, DataOutputStream, and PrintStream.

Each different kind of OutputStream has different functionality. For instance, FileOutputStream sends output to a file. PrintStream gives you access to all the different print and println methods for creating human readable text output. DataOutputStreams write data in a portable, machine-independent fashion for processing by other Java programs. You can chain these Streams together to get a single stream with the functionality of several different ones. To continue with the hose analogy, think of the second stream as a water filter that attaches to the other end of the hose and cleans the water before you drink it. You do this by passing one stream to another stream's constructor like this:

```
FileOutputStream fout = new
  FileOutputStream("test.out");

PrintStream myOutput = new PrintStream(fout);
```

Now `myOutput` can use all the methods of a PrintStream, and its output will be written to a file called test.out. As usual, if you don't intend to access `fout` directly but only through `myOutput`, you can nest the constructors like this:

```
PrintStream myOutput = new PrintStream(new
  FileOutputStream("test.out"));
```

Writing a Text File

System.out and System.err are instances of the PrintStream class. The print and println methods you're used to from the early chapters work for other instances of PrintStream as well, not just for System.out. These methods are used when your output needs to be in ASCII text for eventual reading by human beings.

If you want to send the output of print and println to a file rather than to the screen, you also need to use a FileOutputStream. There are only three things you need to do to write formatted output to a file rather than to the standard output.

First, open a FileOutputStream with the name of the file you want to open like this:

```
FileOutputStream fout = new
  FileOutputStream("test.out");
```

This assumes that a file named test.out already exists. If it does not exist, then an IOException will be thrown. Java does not create a file if it doesn't exist. You'll learn how to create files later in this chapter.

Second, chain the FileOutputStream to a PrintStream like this:

```
PrintStream myOutput = new PrintStream(fout);
```

Third, when you're ready to write data to the file, instead of using `System.out.println` use `myOutput.println`.

System.out and myOutput are just different instances of the PrintStream class. To print to a different PrintStream keep the syntax the same but change the name of the PrintStream. You can have many different Streams open at once.

Program 20.1 demonstrates this via modifications to the Fahrenheit to Celsius conversion program from Chapter 4.

```java
import java.io.PrintStream;
import java.io.FileOutputStream;

class FahrToCelsius   {

  public static void main (String args[]) {

    double fahr, celsius;
    double lower, upper, step;

    // lower limit of temperature table
    lower = 0.0;


    // upper limit of temperature table
    upper = 300.0;

    // step size
    step  = 20.0;
    fahr = lower;

    try {

      FileOutputStream fout = new
        FileOutputStream("test.out");

// Chain the FileOutputStream to a PrintStream
      PrintStream myOutput =
        new PrintStream(fout);

      while (fahr <= upper) {
        celsius = 5.0 * (fahr-32.0) / 9.0;
        myOutput.println(fahr + " " + celsius);
        fahr = fahr + step;
      }

    }
    catch (IOException e) {
      System.err.println("Error: " + e);
      System.exit(1);
    }

  }

}
```

> ### Tip   Applets and Files
>
> Applets will have cause to deal with streams but they will in general have no truck with files. Your applets should never rely on being able to read or write a file on the host system. Security will prevent this. Although the Applet Viewer allows you to weaken security to the point where applets can read and write some files, most users will be unwilling to do so.

Closing Streams

You should close any stream using the stream's close method as soon as you're through with it. Again this isn't very important with a simple program that opens one stream, prints some output, and then exits because garbage collection and finalization will close it for you. However, in more complicated programs, it's possible to lock up a file for some time and prevent other people and Threads from accessing it until garbage collection gets to it. Program 20.2 is a version of FahrToCelsius that closes the output file when it's done.

Program 20.2 Write the Fahrenheit to Celsius table to a file with closing

```java
import java.io.PrintStream;
import java.io.FileOutputStream;

class FahrToCelsius {

  public static void main (String args[]) {

    double fahr, celsius;
    double lower, upper, step;

    // lower limit of temperature table
    lower = 0.0;

    // upper limit of temperature table
    upper = 300.0;

    // step size
    step  = 20.0;
```

```
        fahr = lower;

        try {

            FileOutputStream fout = new
              FileOutputStream("test.out");

        // Chain the FileOutputStream to a PrintStream
            PrintStream myOutput =
              new PrintStream(fout);

            while (fahr <= upper) {
              celsius = 5.0 * (fahr-32.0) / 9.0;
              myOutput.println(fahr + " " + celsius);
              fahr = fahr + step;
            }

            myOutput.close();
            fout.close();
        }
        catch (IOException e) {
            System.err.println("Error: " + e);
            System.exit(1);
        }

    }

}
```

Note that you had to close both the PrintStream and the FileOutputStream.

Reading a Text File

Now that you know how to write a text file, try reading one. Instead of a FileOutputStream, you'll use a FileInputStream. You'll read the data a line at a time, treating each line as a String. In Java, a line is defined as any number of ASCII characters delimited by a carriage return (`'\r'`), a newline (`'\n'`), or both (`"\r\n"`).

Open a file for input just as you open a file for output, only with FileInputStream instead of FileOutputStream:

```
FileOutputStream fin = new
  FileInputStream("test.out");
```

The subclass of InputStream that lets you read data line by line is called a DataInputStream. You'll see a lot more of the DataInputStream class. For now, what you need is its readLine method. Chain the FileInputStream to a DataInputStream like this:

```
DataInputStream myInput = new DataInputStream(fin);
```

Finally when you're ready to read data from the file, call

```
String theInput = myInput.readLine();
```

The readLine method reads every character from the start of the file up to the first \n or \r character and returns that data as a String. It assumes that the data is ASCII text. If it's Unicode text, use readUTF() instead. The second time you call readLine it returns the second line of text in a file. The third time it returns the third line of text, and so forth. This is enough to process a file line by line as you'll see in the next example.

Program 20.3 implements the Unix cat utility through Java. That is, it accepts a series of file names on the command line and prints those files to the standard output in the order they were listed.

Program 20.3 cat

```
import java.io.FileInputStream;
import java.io.DataInputStream;

class cat {

  public static void main (String args[]) {

    String thisLine;

    //Loop across the arguments
    for (int i=0; i < args.length; i++) {

      //Open the file for reading
      try {
        FileInputStream fin =
```

```
          new FileInputStream(args[i]);

        // Chain the FileInputStream to
        // a DataInputStream
        DataInputStream myInput =
          new DataInputStream(fin);
        while ((thisLine = myInput.readLine())
          != null) {
          System.out.println(thisLine);
        }
      }
    catch (IOException e) {
     System.err.println("Error: " + e);
    }
  }
 }

}
```

Command-Line Input

It's a short step from reading data from a file to reading data from the command line. All you have to do is chain System.in to a DataInputStream and call readLine(). Program 20.4 is yet another variation on Hello World. This one asks the user for their name and then prints a personalized greeting.

Program 20.4 A personalized hello

```
1. import java.io.DataInputStream;
2.
3. class PersonalHello {
4.
5.  public static void main (String args[]) {
6.
7.     System.out.println("What is your name?");
8.     try {
9.       DataInputStream myInput =
```

```
10.             new DataInputStream(System.in);
11.        String name = myInput.readLine();
12.        System.out.print("Hello ");
13.        System.out.println(name);
14.      }
15.      catch (IOException e) {
16.        System.out.println(
17.          "I'm Sorry.  I didn't catch your name.");
18.      }
19.
20.  }
21.
22.}
```

Line 1 imports java.io.DataInputStream. Unlike the java.lang classes, the java.io classes are not automatically available and must be imported manually.

Line 3 declares the class and Line 5 declares the main method. There's nothing new here.

Line 7 prints a query requesting the user's name.

Line 8 begins the `try` block. This block ends at line 14. If anything fails between Line 8 and Line 14, the `catch` block in Lines 14 through 16 will be executed. The `catch` block just prints an error message that's appropriate for this program.

Line 9 creates a new DataInputstream from the System.in InputStream. System.in is automatically opened by the runtime so you do not need to open it explicitly.

Line 10 reads one line of input from the user and stores it in a String called name. The program waits here until the user types something and hits the return key on his or her keyboard. The program doesn't see what the user types until he or she types a carriage return. This gives the user the chance to backspace over and delete any mistakes. Once the return key is pressed, everything in the line is placed in name.

Line 11 prints "Hello ." This is print and not println so the line is not broken. Line 12 then prints the value in the name variable and ends the line.

Line 13 ends the `try` block. You've already seen the `catch` block in Lines 14-16. Line 18 ends the main method. Line 20 ends the class and the program.

Often Strings aren't enough. A lot of times you'll want to ask the user for a number as input. All user input comes in as Strings so you just need to convert the String into a number using the methods discussed in Chapter 4.

More Data Input and Output

The readLine method is just one of a number of methods the DataInputStream class provides. The primary purpose of the DataInputStream and DataOutputStream classes is to provide a portable, platform-independent means of reading and writing data.

The DataOutputStream and DataInputStream classes have the following methods which you use to write the different primitive data types onto a stream. Then you use the corresponding read methods from DataInputStream to bring them back into your program.

Output Method	Input Method
`void writeBoolean(boolean)`	`boolean readBoolean()`
`void writeChar(int)`	`char readChar()`
`void writeByte(int)`	`byte readByte()`
`void writeShort(int)`	`short readShort()`
`void writeInt(int)`	`int readInt()`
`void writeLong(long)`	`long readLong()`
`void writeFloat(float)`	`float readFloat()`
`void writeDouble(double)`	`double readDouble()`
`void writeBytes(String)`	`read(byte[])`
`void writeChars(String)`	`read(byte[])`
`void writeUTF(String)`	`String readUTF()`

writeShort, writeByte, and writeChar all take `ints` as arguments. You'd probably expect them to take `short`, `byte`, and `char` respectively but these can all be automatically cast to an `int` as necessary. The data they write onto the stream contains only sufficient information to rebuild a `short`, `byte`, and `char` in any case. When you use the corresponding read method you get back the proper type and value.

You can write Strings onto a DataOutputStream using either writeBytes or writeChars. However, reading them back is more problematic. You need to use `read(byte[])` or `read(byte[], int offset, int max_bytes)`. Then convert the `byte` array back to a String using the appropriate String constructor. This requires you to know how many bytes were written. This will need to be written onto the DataOutputStream separately. The writeUTF method writes a Unicode text format String which can be read back in using readUTF.

The most common use for these methods is in serialization, that is, the saving of state in a data file between runs of a program. You can use a DataOutputStream chained to a FileOutputStream in your class's serialize method and a DataInputStream chained to a FileInputStream to read the data back in. Another potential use is for communication between a client and a server on a network.

Exotics

DataInputStreams, DataOutputStreams, FileInputStreams, FileOutputStreams, and PrintStreams handle 90 percent of your basic I/O needs. However, there are a number of other filter streams for special purposes. Filter streams are attached to one end of the data hose and process the data before it is transferred to its final destination. You've already seen several filters. For instance in the line

```
DataInputStream myInput = new
    DataInputStream(System.in);
```

the data coming in from the raw `System.in` InputStream is filtered through the DataInputStream `myInput`. This means that you can use the methods of DataInputStream like readLine to take data from `System.in`. Using `System.in` alone, your abilities would be sorely constrained. You can chain multiple filters together as well.

Buffered Streams

By default, streams are unbuffered. That is, every byte is read as soon as it comes in and every byte is written as soon as it goes out. This is not always a good idea. For instance, writing data to a disk is often the slowest part of many programs. It's often quicker to write 1000 bytes of data than to write one byte a thousand times. The BufferedInputStream and BufferedOutputStream classes allow you to provide a buffer for your data that is (hopefully) optimized for your system.

For example, to create a BufferedOutputStream that writes to the file foo.txt using the methods of DataOutputStream, you would write.

```
FileOutputStream fout = new
  FileOutputStream("foo.txt")
BufferedOutputStream bos = new
  BufferedOutputStream(fout);
DataOutputStream myOutput = new
  DataOutputStream(bos);
```

You can now write onto `myOutput` using any method of DataOutputStream. However, the data will not actually be written into the file until the buffer is full. The exact size of the buffer is system-dependent.

Data that's sitting around waiting to be written can be forced to be written by calling the stream's flush method like this:

```
myOutput.flush();
```

This isn't necessary with a short program that's just going to run once and be done because when the program ends, the stream is flushed during finalization. However it's very important when you're debugging and using a stream of any kind (including System.out) to track program flow. If you haven't called `flush` when your program crashes, you may think it crashed somewhere before your program really did. Flushing output Streams is also a useful thing to do in the `finally` clause of a `try-catch-finally` block. PrintStreams like `System.out` are buffered by default.

You can also buffer InputStreams. This may result in faster reads, especially from disk. For instance, to create a new BufferedInputStream that reads data from the file foo.txt use

```
FileInputStream fin = new
  FileInputStream("foo.txt")
BufferedInputStream bis = new
  BufferedInputStream(fin);
DataInputStream myInput = new
  DataInputStream(bis);
```

The primary reason to do this is to speed disk access. There is no reason to buffer System.in since users won't type faster than you can read.

Byte Array Streams

Since a stream is just a sequence of bytes, then a sequence of bytes might as well be a stream. At least such is the philosophy of the ByteArrayInputStream and the ByteArrayOutputStream classes.

A ByteArrayInputStream is created by passing the byte array to the ByteArrayInputStream constructor along with optional positions in the array to start and stop reading like this:

```
ByteArrayInputStream bais = new
  ByteArrayInputStream(buf);
ByteArrayInputStream bais = new
  ByteArrayInputStream(buf, offset, len);
```

buf is an array of bytes that will be read from. offset is the position in the array at which to start reading. len is the maximum number of bytes to read.

The ByteArrayOutputStream class is slightly more useful. The constructor creates a buffer that can be used as an OutputStream. The buffer grows as needed when data is written onto the stream. The data can then be turned back into an array of bytes using the toByteArray() method. For example,

```
ByteArrayOutputStream baos = new
  ByteArrayOutputStream();
PrintStream myOutput = new PrintStream(baos);
for (int i = 1; i <= 10; i++) {
  myOutput.print(i);
}
byte[] theBytes = myOutput.toByteArray();
```

LineNumberInputStream

The LineNumberInputStream keeps track of the current line. It also allows you to back up to a marked location in the stream. Other than this it doesn't implement much more than the basic functionality so it's normally used by chaining it to another stream. To add the functionality of a LineNumberInputStream, pass an existing stream into its constructor like this:

```
LineNumberInputStream lnis = new
  LineNumberInputStream(fin);
```

Then when you want to retrieve the current line number, just call `lnis.getLineNumber()`. Program 20.5 is a version of the cat program that numbers lines as it outputs them:

Program 20.5 Print files and line number them

```java
import java.io.FileInputStream;
import java.io.DataInputStream;
import java.io.LineNumberInputStream;


class lcat  {

  public static void main (String args[]) {

    String thisLine;

    //Loop across the arguments
    for (int i=0; i < args.length; i++) {

      //Open the file for reading
      try {
        FileInputStream fin =
          new FileInputStream(args[i]);

        // chain the DataInputStream
        // to a LineNumberInputStream
        LineNumberInputStream lnis =
          new LineNumberInputStream(fin);

        // Chain the FileInputStream
        // to a DataInputStream
        DataInputStream myInput =
          new DataInputStream(lnis);

        while ((thisLine = myInput.readLine())
          != null) {
          System.out.println(lnis.getLineNumber()
```

```
                    + ": " + thisLine);
          }
        }
        catch (IOException e) {
          System.err.println("Error: " + e);
        }

      }

    }

}
```

Here are the first few lines produced when this program is run on itself:

```
% java lcat lcat.java
1: import java.io.FileInputStream;
2: import java.io.DataInputStream;
3: import java.io.LineNumberInputStream;
4:
5:
6: class lcat  {
7:
8:    public static void main (String args[]) {
9:
10:       String thisLine;
11:
12:       //Loop across the arguments
13:       for (int i=0; i < args.length; i++) {
14:
15:          //Open the file for reading
16:          try {
```

Piped Streams

PipedInputStreams and PipedOutputStreams allow you to attach an OutputStream in one thread to an InputStream in another thread. To be useful, you need both. The input of a PipedInputStream can only be chained to a PipedOutputStream and the output of a PipedOutputStream can only be chained to a PipedInputStream. This is one way. That is, data must go into the input of the

PipedOutputStream and then into the PipedInputStream. You cannot chain them in the opposite order. This is most commonly used for interthread communication.

The File Class

The java.io.File class represents file names on the host system.[1] It attempts to abstract system-dependent file name features like the path separator character. Unfortunately not all the necessary functionality is fully implemented in Java 1.0.

There are two ways to reference a file: relative and absolute. Absolute addressing gives a complete path to a file, starting with the disk and working its way down. How this is represented varies from operating system to operating system. Here are some examples:

Unix: `"/home/users/elharo/file1"`

DOS: `"C:\home\users\elharo\file1"`

MacOS: `"Macintosh HD:home:users:elharo:file1"`

All three Strings reference a file called `file1` on the primary hard drive in the `elharo` directory, which is itself in the `users` directory , which is in the `home` directory. One obvious difference is the path separator character. Unix uses a / to separate directories, DOS- and Windows-based file systems use a \. The MacOS uses a :. Other operating systems may use something completely different.

Worse yet, there's no guarantee that the Mac's primary hard drive is called "Macintosh HD" or that it even has such a disk. On Unix, `/home` and `/home/users` may be on completely different disks, perhaps even on different machines. For these and more reasons, absolute pathnames are a royal pain to work with and should be avoided whenever possible.

Relative addressing, which should be used if possible, doesn't give the complete path to the file. Instead, it gives the path relative to some other known file. A relative pathname may point to a file in the same directory as a known file by giving only its name. Other times it may point to a file in a subdirectory of a known directory.

---

[1] java.io.FileName would be a more accurate name for this class.

Generally one directory is set as the current directory. This is where methods that look for files are relative to. Normally this is the directory in which you started running the application.

java.io.File can hold a directory name equally as well as a filename.

Note to C programmers: A File object is not a file handle. Just because you have a File object does not mean that the equivalent file actually exists on the disk. There are methods you can use to determine whether a File object refers to a real file or not (specifically `exists()`).

File Constructors

There are three constructor methods in java.io.File. Each takes some variation of a filename as an argument(s). The simplest is

```
File(String path)
```

`path` is simply a String with either a full or relative pathname to the file which can be understood by the host operating system.

If you like you can separate the path and the filename using the

```
File(String path, String name)
```

constructor. Here name is the filename and path is the name of the directory that contains the file. Finally, there's

```
File(File dir, String name)
```

which is like the previous constructor except that now dir is a File object itself instead of a String.

Some methods return File objects, most notably the FileDialog methods. The File objects returned by these methods will conform to the conventions of the host operating system. For instance, the path separator character will be : on a Mac and \ on Windows.

File Methods

Given that you have a File object in place, there are a number of questions you can ask about it and things you can do with it. What follows assumes that you already have a File object `f` that points to `"/home/users/elharo/file1"` and have imported java.io.File.

String getName0

The most basic question you can ask a file is, "What is your name?" You do this with the getName method which takes no arguments and returns a String. The String returned is just the name of the file. It does not include any piece of the directory or directories that contain this file. In other words, you get back "file1" instead of "/home/users/elharo/file1."

String getPath0

getPath returns a String that contains the path being used for this File. It will be relative or absolute depending on how the File object was created.

String getAbsolutePath0

getAbsolutePath returns the complete, non-relative path to the File.

String getParent0

getParent returns a String that contains the name of the single directory which contains this file in the hierarchy. It does not return a full path all the way back up to the root. If the file is at the top level of the disk, then it has no parent directory and null is returned.

boolean exists0

The `exists()` method indicates whether or not a particular file exists where you expect it to be. You'll normally use this to check for the presence of some file you've created inside your program.

boolean canWrite0

The `canWrite()` method indicates whether you have write access to this file. It's not a bad idea to check `canWrite()` before trying to put data in a file.

boolean canRead()

The `canRead()` method indicates whether you have read access to this file. It's not a bad idea to check `canRead()` before trying to read data out of a file.

boolean isFile()

The `isFile()` method indicates whether this is file exists and is a normal file, in other words not a directory.

boolean isDirectory()

The `isDirectory()` returns true if this file exists and is a directory.

boolean isAbsolute()

`isAbsolute()` returns true if the file name is absolute and `false` if it's relative.

long lastModified()

`lastModified()` returns the last modification time. Since the conversion between this long and a real date is platform dependent, you should only use this to compare modification dates of different files.

long length()

`f.length()` is the length of the file in bytes.

boolean mkdir()

`f.mkdir()` tries to create a directory with the given name. If the directory is created, the method returns `true`. Otherwise it returns `false`.

boolean mkdirs()

`mkdirs()` is a command the author has wanted in other languages for years. Given a filename, it creates not just one but every directory in the path as necessary, permissions permitting. `mkdirs()` returns `true` if all directories in this path are created, and `false` if only some or none of them are created. You may need to manually test the existence of each directory in the path if the method returns `false` because it could have been partially successful.

boolean renameTo(File dest)

`f1.renameTo(f2)` tries to change the name of `f1` to `f2`. This may involve a move to a different directory if the filenames so indicate. If `f2` already exists, then it is overwritten by `f1` (permissions permitting). If `f1` is renamed, the method returns true. Otherwise it returns `false`.

String[] list()

The list method returns an array of Strings initialized to the names of each file in directory `f`. It's useful for processing all the files in a directory.

String[] list(FilenameFilter filter)

This is the same as the previous method except you can use a FilenameFilter object (discussed in the next section) to restrict which files are added to the list.

boolean delete()

`f.delete()` tries to delete the file `f`. This method returns `true` if the file existed and was deleted. (You can't delete a file that doesn't exist). Otherwise it returns `false`.

The File class also contains the usual equals, hashCode, and toString methods, which behave exactly as you would expect. It does not contain a `clone()` method.

Program 20.6 reads a filenames from the command line and returns various information about those files using these methods.

Program 20.6 File info

```
import java.io.File;
import java.io.IOException;

public class FileInfo {
```

```java
public static void main(String[] args) {

  for (int i = 0; i < args.length; i++) {
    File f = new File(args[i]);
    if (f.exists()) {
      System.out.println("getName: " +
        f.getName());
      System.out.println("getPath: " +
        f.getPath());
      System.out.println("getAbsolutePath: " +
        f.getAbsolutePath());
      System.out.println("getParent: " +
        f.getParent());
      if (f.canWrite()) System.out.println(
        f.getName() + " is writable.");
      if (f.canRead()) System.out.println(
        f.getName() + " is readable.");
      if (f.isFile()) {
        System.out.println(f.getName() +
          " is a file.");
      }
      else if (f.isDirectory()) {
        System.out.println(f.getName() +
          " is a directory.");
      }
      else {
        System.out.println("What is this?");
      }
      if (f.isAbsolute()) {
        System.out.println(f.getName() +
          " is an absolute path.");
      }
      else {
        System.out.println(f.getName() +
          " is not an absolute path.");
      }
      try {
        System.out.println("Last Modified" +
          f.lastModified());
        System.out.println(f.getName() + " is " +
          f.length() + " bytes.");
        System.out.println(f.getName() + " is " +
          f.length() + " bytes.");
      }
```

```
        catch (IOException e) {

        }

    }
    else {
        System.out.println(
            "I'm sorry. I can't find the file " +
            args[i]);
    }

    }

  }

}
```

FileDialogs

FileDialogs are a subclass of java.awt.Dialog used for choosing a file to open or save. This class uses the host platform's standard open and save file dialogs. You won't add Components to a FileDialog, or worry about how to handle user interaction. You'll just retrieve the result which will be a File object. Since an applet can't rely on having access to the file system, FileDialogs are primarily useful in applications.

There are four steps to using a FileDialog:

1. Create the FileDialog.
2. Optionally point the FileDialog at a default directory or file.
3. Make the FileDialog visible.
4. Get the directory name and file name of the chosen file.

You create a FileDialog with the constructor

```
FileDialog(Frame parent, String title, int mode)
```

The Frame is the parent of this file dialog. This will normally be the main window of the application, the applet's frame, or the frontmost window of the application. Or you can just create a new Frame. String title is simply the title for the FileDialog, normally something like "Please choose the file to open:". Mode is one of the two mnemonic constants, FileDialog.LOAD or FileDialog.SAVE. Use FileDialog.LOAD if you want the user to choose a file to open. Use FileDialog.SAVE if you want the user to choose a file to save the data into. A typical use of this might look like

```
FileDialog fd = new FileDialog(new Frame(),
    "Please choose the file to open:",
    FileDialog.LOAD);
```

Many times you'll want some control over the FileDialog. You may want to specify that it should start looking in a particular directory, or that only text files should be shown. Java lets you do this. To start the FileDialog off in a particular directory, call the FileDialog's setDirectory(String *dir*) method, where *dir* is the path to the directory. That is

```
fd.setDirectory("/usr/tmp");
```

You can even set the FileDialog to point at a particular file using setFile(String filename). However, if you already know the file-name, why do you need to bring up a FileDialog? More likely you'll want to look for a particular type of file, for instance text files. To make this happen you need to use a FilenameFilter to specify which files you'll accept. FilenameFilters are covered in the next section. The key method is setFilenameFilter(FilenameFilter fnf).

Finally, make the FileDialog visible the same way you make any other window visible. Just call the FileDialog's show method:

```
fd.show();
```

At this point, the operating system takes over and handles user interaction until the user either chooses a file or cancels. Your program stops here and waits for the user to choose a file. When the user does choose a file, the FileDialog disappears from the screen and your program resumes. You then find out what file the user chose by using the FileDialog's getDirectory() and getFile() methods. Use these two Strings to create a new File object. In short,

```
FileDialog fd = new FileDialog(new Frame(),
    "Please choose a file:",
        FileDialog.LOAD);

fd.show();

File f = new File(fd.getDirectory(),
    fd.getFile());
```

The FilenameFilter is an interface with a single method,

boolean accept(File dir, String name)

File dir is a directory and String name is a filename. The method should return true if the file passes through the filter and false if it doesn't.

Since FilenameFilter is an interface, you must subclass it with a class that implements the accept method. Here is an example class that filters out everything that is not a Java source code file.[2]

Program 20.7 A FilenameFilter

```
import java.io.FilenameFilter;
import java.io.File;

public class javaFilter
  implements FilenameFilter {

 public boolean accept(File dir, String name) {

    if (name.endsWith(".java")) return true;
    return false;

 }

}
```

Files do not need to be filtered by filename only. You can test modification date, permissions, file size, and more. For example, this accept method tests whether the file ends with .java and is in a directory to which you have write permission:

public boolean accept(File dir, String name) {

---

[2] More precisely, it filters out everything that does not end in .java. Regrettably, Java has no conception of file types beyond filenames.

```
if (name.endsWith(".java") && dir.canWrite())
    return true;

return false;


}
```

Q & A

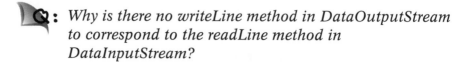

Q: *Why is there no writeLine method in DataOutputStream to correspond to the readLine method in DataInputStream?*

A: PrintStream does a perfectly good job of handling line-oriented output. However, DataInputStream has to do double duty handling the output from both DataOutputStream and PrintStream.

Q: *Why do I need DataInputStreams and DataOutputStreams? Why can't I just write and read text when I want to transmit or save data?*

A: The first reason is efficiency. The number 16542 takes up five bytes as a String and only two as a short. The second reason is roundoff. You don't lose any precision writing a double like 1.25 in its native format.

Q: *Is there a way to create a FolderDialog that allows the user to select a directory instead of a file?*

A: Not in Java 1.0. Perhaps in the future.

Q: *Is there any way to filter based on the type of the file rather than just the filename?*

A: Regrettably no, there is not. Any such method would have to be platform dependent since some operating systems have a very clear idea of file types (the MacOS for one), some have a limited idea of file types (Windows 95) and some have almost no idea at all about the type of a file (Unix).

Quiz

1. What's the difference between a file and a filename? Which is more closely related to the java.io.File class?

Exercises

1. Write a program to recursively list all the files and directories contained in a directory given on the command line.

2. Modify the FileInfo program so that it runs as a GUI application. The user should select a file using a FileDialog and then be presented with a window that shows all the File info.

3. Add a File menu to the above program. It should have functional New..., Open..., Close, Save, and Quit methods. It should allow the user to get information about any file on their hard drive, display that information, and save that information to a text file.

Summary

In this chapter you learned

- How to write data on a stream
- How to read data from a stream
- How to read data from the command line
- How to attach Streams to files
- How to chain Streams together
- How to work with Files
- How to choose a File with a FileDialog

Coming Up

Your introduction to Java is almost complete. The next chapter will cover the final programming topic in this book, data structures.

Further Reading

http://www.javasoft.com/JDK-1.0/api/java.io.DataInput.html

http://www.javasoft.com/JDK-1.0/api/java.io.DataOutput.html

http://www.javasoft.com/JDK-1.0/api/java.io.FilenameFilter.html

http://www.javasoft.com/JDK-1.0/api/java.io.BufferedInputStream.html

http://www.javasoft.com/JDK-1.0/api/java.io.BufferedOutputStream.html

http://www.javasoft.com/JDK-1.0/api/java.io.ByteArrayInputStream.html

http://www.javasoft.com/JDK-1.0/api/java.io.ByteArrayOutputStream.html

http://www.javasoft.com/JDK-1.0/api/java.io.DataInputStream.html

http://www.javasoft.com/JDK-1.0/api/java.io.DataOutputStream.html

http://www.javasoft.com/JDK-1.0/api/java.io.File.html

http://www.javasoft.com/JDK-1.0/api/java.io.FileInputStream.html

http://www.javasoft.com/JDK-1.0/api/java.io.FileOutputStream.html

http://www.javasoft.com/JDK-1.0/api/java.io.FilterInputStream.html

http://www.javasoft.com/JDK-1.0/api/java.io.FilterOutputStream.html

http://www.javasoft.com/JDK-1.0/api/java.io.InputStream.html

http://www.javasoft.com/JDK-1.0/api/java.io.LineNumberInputStream.html

http://www.javasoft.com/JDK-1.0/api/java.io.OutputStream.html

http://www.javasoft.com/JDK-1.0/api/java.io.PipedInputStream.html

http://www.javasoft.com/JDK-1.0/api/java.io.PipedOutputStream.html

http://www.javasoft.com/JDK-1.0/api/java.io.PrintStream.html

http://www.javasoft.com/JDK-1.0/api/java.io.RandomAccessFile.html

http://www.javasoft.com/JDK-1.0/api/java.io.EOFException.html

http://www.javasoft.com/JDK-1.0/api/java.io.FileNotFoundException.html

http://www.javasoft.com/JDK-1.0/api/java.io.IOException.html

http://www.javasoft.com/JDK-1.0/api/java.io.InterruptedIOException.html

http://www.javasoft.com/JDK-1.0/api/java.io.UTFDataFormatException.html

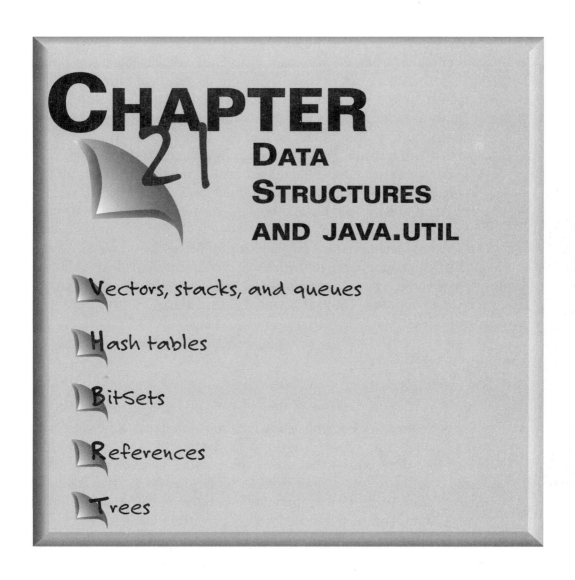

CHAPTER 21

DATA STRUCTURES AND JAVA.UTIL

- Vectors, stacks, and queues

- Hash tables

- Bitsets

- References

- Trees

One common complaint about Java among programmers accustomed to traditional languages like C and Pascal is that the lack of pointers makes the creation of data structures too difficult. What's been removed from Java is not pointers, but rather the ability to do arithmetic with pointers, convert integers into pointers, and other such tricks that cause many bugs in C programs. Pointers themselves are still present, although without pointer arithmetic and explicit memory allocation and deallocation. Pointers without these powers are called **references**. References allow you to create all the data structures you desire without introducing all the bugs common to C code.

Procedural languages like C have great difficulty abstracting data structures. One of the advantages of an OOP language like Java is that the system library can provide highly optimized classes for data structures like linked lists and hash tables with the same ease with which it holds algorithms like sine and cosine. Before creating your own data structure, you should make sure that Java doesn't already provide one that will suit you. The Vector class introduced in this chapter covers almost all uses for linked lists and a number of other things besides. There are also classes to handle stacks, hash tables, and bit sets. All of these would have to be implemented with pointers or multiple arrays in a procedural language like C or Fortran. In Java, they can be implemented once in a highly optimized class, and then used freely by programmers everywhere. This chapter begins with a discussion of these pre-written data structures. Then it shows you how to use references to build your own data structures.

Vectors

Arrays are useful when you know how much data you'll have to hold when you begin writing the program. However, they have trouble when you don't know how many items you'll need to store in the array. They have even greater troubles when your program needs to be able to store something in the middle of an array and not just at the end. For this sort of situation, java.util provides the Vector class.

A Vector is a one-dimensional data structure in which you can store an unspecified number of objects. Unlike an array, you do not need to know the maximum size of a Vector when you create it. It will grow as necessary.

To use Vectors, you must first import java.util.Vector in the usual fashion:

```
import java.util.Vector;
```

A Vector is created like any other object, with the new operator:

```
Vector v = new Vector();
```

If you think you know roughly how many elements the Vector will hold, it is a little more efficient to initialize the Vector to hold that many elements with the following constructor:

```
Vector v = new Vector(1024);
```

This way less resizing needs to be done as elements are added.

Vectors can only contain objects, not primitive data types like `int` or `char`. This makes them slightly less convenient to use, but you can always store a variable in an object of your own creation before putting it in the Vector if necessary.

There are two ways to store an object in a Vector. You can add it to the end of the Vector using `v.addElement(Object)` or you can insert it at a particular position in the Vector using `v.insertElementAt(Object o, int i)`, where `o` is the element you wish to add to the Vector, `i` is the position where you want to add it, and `v` is of course the Vector into which you're inserting the element. All elements past `i` will be pushed back one position.

If you want a particular element of the Vector, you retrieve it using `v.elementAt(int i)` where `i` is the index of the element. This does not remove the element from the Vector.

On the other hand, if, as is more commonly the case, you want to retrieve all the elements of a Vector, one after another, then you can use java.util.Enumeration as follows:

```
for (Enumeration e = v.elements() ;
   e.hasMoreElements() ;) {

   System.out.println(e.nextElement());

}
```

Enumerations are an interface that let you loop through all the components of an object. The `nextElement` method returns successive components of the Vector every time it's called. Hashtables also implement Enumerations.

To remove an Object from a Vector `v`, you use the very straightforward method `v.removeElement(Object o)` where `o` is the Object you wish to remove. You can also remove an element by position using `v.removeElementAt(int i)` where `i` is the location of the element to be removed. As in arrays, locations in Vectors start at 0 and count up to one less than the size of the Vector (which is given by `v.size()`).

You can also replace an element of a Vector using `v.setElementAt(Object o, int i)` where `o` is the new Object to be inserted and `i` is the location of the element to be replaced.

Stacks

Abstractly, stacks are like a tray dispenser in a cafeteria. Trays are put on the top of the stack and they are taken off the top of the stack. The last tray to be put on the stack is at the top of the stack and is therefore the next one to be taken off. A stack can be empty or quite full, but it is always accessed from the top, never from the bottom.

Another way to think about stacks is that they are organized in archaeological order. The most recent items are on top.

Putting an item on the stack is called **pushing**. Taking an item off the stack is called **popping**.

Stacks have the advantage of being very simple. Java.util includes a stack class which has five methods, one constructor, and one Exception. One of the methods, `search(Object o)`, is a Java addition that isn't part of the classical definition of a stack.

Creating a stack is simple. Use the java.util.Stack constructor like this:

```
java.util.Stack myStack = new java.util.Stack() ;
```

Of course you can `import java.util.Stack` or `java.util.*` to avoid prefixing all the methods with java.util, and in the rest of this section it will be assumed that you have done so.

The constructor creates an empty stack. To push an object onto the stack use

```
myStack.push(o);
```

To take an object off the top of the stack use the pop method

```
Object o = myStack.pop();
```

If you want to look at the object on top of the stack without removing it from the stack, you can peek instead:

```
Object o = myStack.peek();
```

The type of the object is lost when it is put on the stack. That is, as far as Java knows, everything on the stack is a generic object, not a String, an Applet, or whatever. You may need to cast it to the appropriate type before using it.

Both `pop` and `peek` throw an EmptyStackException if the stack is empty. This is a RuntimeException, but in many applications you'll want to trap it anyway.

Finally, Java provides the somewhat unusual capability to search a stack for a particular object with

```
int i = myStack.search(Object o);
```

The integer that's returned is the distance of the object from the top of the stack or -1 if the object isn't in the stack. If the object were on top of the stack, the integer returned would be 0; if it were the second object in the stack, it would be 1 and so on.

Stacks in Java are a subclass of java.util.Vector, and they share with Vector the weakness of requiring the objects stored in the stack to be objects. If your application only needs the stack to hold one kind of data, you may wish to subclass stack. For example, Program 21.1 is a subclass of Stack that holds only Strings.

Program 21.1 A String stack

```java
import java.util.Stack

public class StringStack extends {

  public String peek() {
    return (String) super.peek();
  }

  public String pop() {
    return (String) super.pop();
  }

}
```

This isn't absolutely necessary, but it does save one from a lot of confusing casting between generic Objects and Strings in the main body of the program.

This technique is even more useful when you want to fill a data structure with a primitive data type like int or char. However, because you need to replace the methods rather than override them, it takes a little more work. Rather than subclassing java.util.Stack, you embed a java.util.Stack in the class and handle the conversions between primitive data types and type wrapper classes in the individual methods. It's messy, but once you've done it, the rest of your code doesn't need to worry about how you've done it, just that it works. Code reusability is, after all, one of the advantages of object-oriented programming. Program 21.2 demonstrates this with a stack class for `chars`.

Program 21.2 A char stack

```java
import java.util.Stack;

public class charStack {

  private Stack theStack;

  charStack() {
    theStack = new Stack();
  }

  public char peek() {
    Character temp = (Character) theStack.peek();
    return temp.charValue();
  }

  public void push(char c) {
    theStack.push(new Character(c));
  }

  public char pop() {
    Char temp = (Character) theStack.pop();
    return temp.charValue();
  }

  public boolean empty() {
    return theStack.empty();
  }

}
```

Finally you should note that this technique is useful for all the java.util data structures that expect objects, not just for Stacks.

Stacks are last-in, first-out—LIFO for short. Another common data structure is the queue. The queue is like a stack except that elements are put in at the bottom of the list and come off the top of the list. It's first-in, first out, or FIFO. There is no built-in queue data structure in Java, but it's easy to implement one as a subclass of Vector. Program 21.3 is one such implementation.

Program 21.3 A generic Queue class

```java
import java.util.Vector;
import java.util.EmptyStackException;

public class Queue extends Vector {

  public void add(Object o) {
    addElement(o);
  }

  public Object remove() {

    Object o  = peek();
    removeElementAt(0);
    return o;

  }

  public Object peek() {

    if (size() == 0) {
      throw new EmptyStackException();
    }
    return elementAt(0);

  }

  public boolean empty() {
    return size() == 0;
  }

}
```

Hash Tables

Vectors, stacks, arrays, and queues are useful for ordered lists of things. However, sometimes there isn't a natural order. For instance, suppose you want a list of all the people at a company. How do you order them—by last name? by first name? What if there are two John Smith's? or what if sometimes a person goes by the name Elliotte and other times by Rusty? The problems associated with naming generally lead to the use of a key-value system. Every object is assigned a unique key. In personnel applications, this key would probably be the user's Social Security Number, at least in the United States. As long as you know that key you can uniquely identify that person and make sure John Smith, the vice president, doesn't end up with John Smith, the janitor's, paycheck.

Hash tables are a common way to store key-value data. They provide other advantages as well, most notably efficiency. Once you know an object's key, the hash table can generally retrieve the object's value very quickly in an amount of time that doesn't depend on the number of elements in the table. On the other hand, objects stored in an array or Vector take longer to retrieve in proportion to the number of elements.

Hash tables aren't used much in elementary programs because they're a bear to code. However, Java provides a very nice Hashtable class you can use without worrying about implementation details. This class provides the basic functionality of a hash table. A Hashtable has four basic operations:

1. Create a new hash table.
2. Get the value associated with a particular key.
3. Put a key-value pair into the hash table.
4. Remove a value associated with a particular key from the hash table.

Creating a new Hashtable is easy. Simply import `java.util.Hashtable` and use the `Hashtable` constructor like this:

```
Hashtable ht = new Hashtable();
```

Objects are stored in a Hashtable using the `put(Object key, Object value)` method. The value can be any object at all. The key is a little trickier.

Each object you store in the Hashtable must have a unique key. It is the programmer's responsibility to ensure that the key you give a particular object has not been used previously. If you store a new value in the Hashtable using an old key, whatever value previously mapped to that key is overwritten.

Second, the key must be an object that implements the `hashCode()` and `equals(Object o)` methods from java.lang.Object. `hashCode()` is a public method that returns a unique `int` for each object. The same object should always return the same hashcode.

The equals method should determine if two objects are equal. As you might expect it returns a `boolean`.

If you can use a String, Integer, or other System-provided class for your key, then you don't need to worry about implementing these methods. You'll still need to ensure that each different object you store has a unique key.

Once you've put objects in a Hashtable, you retrieve them by requesting them with the `get(Object key)` method. This returns the object or `null` if the key doesn't match any value in the table.

```
Object o = ht.get(mykey);
```

Getting an object does not remove it from the Hashtable. If you want to delete a value, use the `remove(Object key)` method like this:

```
Object o = ht.remove(mykey);
```

This returns the object removed or `null` if the key doesn't match any value in the table.

Java's Hashtable class allows any object to be a value. As with Vectors and Stacks, when an object is removed from a Hashtable, you aren't given any information about its class and will generally need to cast it to the appropriate type.

Additional Hashtable Operations

Java's Hashtable class provides a number of other useful operations beyond the basics. They include

- Getting a list of all the keys in the table
- Removing all elements from the Hashtable.
- Cloning the Hashtable.
- Searching the Hashtable for a specific object.
- Searching the hashtable for a specific key.
- Determining if the Hashtable is empty.
- Finding the number of elements in the Hashtable.
- Converting the Hashtable to a String.

The Hashtable's `elements` method returns an Enumeration of the elements in the Hashtable. Once you have the Enumeration, you can use the same methods you used for an Enumeration of a vector to process every element of the Hashtable.

```
for (Enumeration e = ht.elements();
  ht.hasMoreElements() ;) {
    System.out.println(ht.nextElement());
}
```

You can also get an Enumeration of the keys with the `keys` method.

You make a copy of a Hashtable by calling `Hashtable.clone()` like this:

```
Hashtable ht2 = ht.clone();
```

This only clones the table. It does not clone the individual elements. Therefore, changing the properties of an object in one Hashtable will change the value of the properties of the object in the other Hashtable too.

The clear method empties the Hashtable.

```
ht.clear();
```

The contains method returns true if the requested object is in the HashTable.

```
if (ht.contains("555-8762")) {
```

The `contains` method searches for values. To find out if a particular key is contained use `containsKey`.

```
if (ht.containsKey("555-8762")) {
```

The `isEmpty` method tells you whether or not the Hashtable has any elements.

```
if (ht.isEmpty()) {
    System.out.println("There's nothing in this
        table");
}
```

You can use the size method to find out how many elements are in a Hashtable.

```
if (ht.isEmpty()) {

  System.out.println("There's nothing in this
      table");

}

else {

  System.out.println("There are " + ht.size() +

    " elements in the table");

}
```

The Hashtable class also has a toString method but you really shouldn't use it. The String is way too long for a Hashtable of any size at all.

BitSets

Bit sets are used when dealing with very large data sets about which only one thing needs to be known, and that thing either is or isn't. A bit set is a collection of bits, each one of which may be set or cleared. In Java, a set bit is true and a cleared bit is false. Normally, you think of a bit as being equal to one if it's set and zero if it's not, but this implementation isn't required.

The most common use of a bit set is to determine set membership. Given a collection of objects, each with a unique number, the bit in a bit set is set if a particular object is a member of the set and cleared if the object is not a member of the set.

To create a new BitSet, you can use one of two constructors: BitSet(int num_bits) if you know roughly how many bits you want to keep track of, and BitSet() if you don't. If you don't know or if you underestimate how many bits you'll need, the BitSet will grow to accommodate you. The constructors are used like this:

```
BitSet bs1 = new BitSet();
```

```
BitSet bs2 = new BitSet(256);
```

As usual, it is assumed that you've already imported java.util.BitSet.

To set a bit, use `set(int position)`, where position is the position of the bit you want to turn on. To clear a bit, use `clear(int position)`, where position is the position of the bit you want to turn off. The first bit is at position 0.

To get the value of a bit, use the `get(int position)` method like this:

```
if (bs1.get(7)) {
```

The BitSet class also provides a set of methods for performing bitwise operations on BitSets. These are

```
and(BitSet)
```

that is, logically AND this bit set with the specified set of bits. This is the same as using the bitwise and operator, `&`.

```
or(BitSet)
```

Logically OR this bit set with the specified set of bits. This is the same as using the bitwise or operator, `|`.

```
xor(BitSet)
```

Logically XORs this bit set with the specified set of bits. This is the same as using the bitwise exclusive or operator, `^`.

Interestingly, there is no `not(BitSet bs)` method.

When a BitSet is interpreted to mean set membership, AND is equivalent to the intersection of two sets and OR is equivalent to the union of two sets. For instance, suppose you have a collection of hats. The first BitSet is true for those hats which are made of cotton. The second BitSet is true for those hats which are blue. By ANDing the BitSets, you can find those hats which are both blue and cotton.

References

Although Hashtables, arrays, and Vectors cover about 95 percent of your basic data structure needs, they don't quite do everything. When you need a data structure that isn't built into the standard library, you can create it using references.

Each object in Java takes up a certain amount of memory. This memory exists at a particular place in your computer's memory space. On a machine using virtual memory, this location may or may not be at a particular point in physical RAM, but you don't need to worry about that. What you do need to know is that whenever you declare a variable of a particular object type, that variable doesn't hold the object's data. Instead it holds a number that is the address where that data is stored in memory. Normally the difference won't concern you because the Java runtime handles all the details behind the scenes.

There are two times when this does become important though. The first is with side effects. If you create an object a and then set b equal to a, then changing some property of b changes that property of a also. a and b refer to the same space in memory. For example,

Program 21.4 Side effects

```java
import java.awt.Point;

public class RefTest {

  public static void main(String[] args) {
    Point a = new Point(3, 2);
    Point b = a;
    b.x = 33;
    b.y = -7;
    System.out.println(a);
  }

}
```

And here's the somewhat surprising output:

```
% java RefTest
java.awt.Point[x=33,y=-7]
%
```

This program tried to print a but it looks like you got b instead. That's because a and b are references to the object, not the object itself. When a was assigned to b, b was made to point to the same location as a. Therefore, when the value of the object at that location changes, both a and b change. This is true for any object at all in Java

Language Law: Handles

To be even more precise, the variable actually holds the address a location in memory where the address of the object is stored. This double indirection is called a **handle**. Using handles allows java to move the objects themselves around in memory as it needs to to make efficient use of the memory space.

including arrays. It is not true for primitive data types like int, float, or char.

```
int a = 3;
int b = a;
b = 2;
System.out.println(a);
```

The program still prints 3 because a hasn't changed. This is a crucial difference between primitive and object data types.

If you want to create a copy of a's data in a new object, call a's clone method instead like this:

```
b = a.clone()
```

This has the important implication that multiple copies of Java objects don't take up much space. The first copy of a Java object takes up as much space as the object needs. All subsequent copies take up only as much space as a reference.

Even more importantly, this means that you can create advanced data structures that require multiple references to the same object. This, in fact, is easier in Java than in pointer-based languages like C and C++ because you don't need to concern yourself with the difference between the pointer and the object itself or worry about destroying the object. Garbage collection handles that automatically.

The most commonly requested Java data structure is a linked list. A linked list consists of a series of nodes, each of which contains some data. It also contains a reference to the next node in the list and a means of getting the first node in the list. Finally, methods are provided to insert and remove nodes from the list. This is very simple to implement in Java.

Program 21.5 is a node for a basic linked list.

Program 21.5 A linked list node

```java
public class Node {

   Object data;
   Node next;

   Node(Object o) {
      data = o;
      next = null;
   }

   Node getNext() {

      return next;

   }

   public void setNext(Node n) {

      n.next = next;
      next = n;

   }

}
```

The main thing to notice is that instead of having a pointer to the next node, you just use the next node itself. Of course, it's really just a pointer so nothing is lost and some clarity is gained.

The linked list class itself should have a field `head`, which defines the start of the list, methods for adding elements at particular positions in the list—say first, last, at a particular numeric location, and before or after a given object—methods for traversing the list, and methods for finding a particular object in the list.

The astute may ask what can be accomplished by this class that could not be accomplished by the Vector class. The answer is nothing at all really. The linked list expands more quickly when additional space is needed than the Vector does, and it's quicker to find the nth element of a Vector than a linked list, but the functionality of the two is really the same. The Vector as implemented in Java really does contain all the functionality of a linked list. If java.util.Vector had been called java.util.LinkedList, everyone would be happy.

But what about more complex data structures? In the next section, you'll see a class that really couldn't be implemented as a Vector without great pain—the tree.

Trees

A tree data structure consists of nodes, just like a linked list. Each node contains some data and references to zero or more children. The first node of the tree is called the root and is itself not the child of any other node. All other nodes are the child of exactly one node which is called the parent. Nodes without any children are called leaves. Figure 21.1 demonstrates this.

Many applications only need a tree in which there are at most two children of any given node. This is called a binary tree. The two children of each node are called the left child and the right child. Either or both children may be null. A non-binary tree would include a Vector of nodes as the children.

Binary trees are most often used to store sorted data. Binary trees can sort data as it arrives, rather than having to first wait for all the data to be accumulated as an array or a Vector would. Program 21.6 is a tree that can be used to store a sorted list of doubles. The tree is initialized with a number that's placed at the root. After the construction of the tree, values are added to the tree through its store method.

Program 21.6 shows a treenode class for a binary tree of doubles.

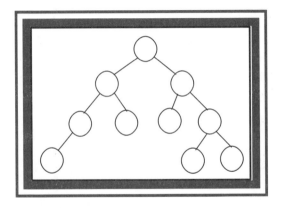

Figure 21.1 *A binary tree*

Program 21.6 A node of a binary tree

```
public class treenode {

   double data;

   treenode left;
   treenode right;

   public treenode (double d) {
      data = d;
      left = null;
      right = null;
   }

   public void store (double d) {
      if (d <= data) {
         if (left == null) left = new treenode(d);
         else left.store(d);
      }
      else {
         if (right == null) right = new treenode(d);
         else right.store(d);
      }
   }

   public void print() {

      if (left != null) left.print();
      System.out.println(data);
```

```
      if (right != null) right.print();

    }


}
```

The store method is the key to the tree. As values are put in the tree, they're compared with the value of the root. If a value is smaller than or equal to the root, it moves down the left-hand side of the tree. Otherwise it moves down the right.

If the child it moves to is null, then a new leaf node is created and the value stored there. Otherwise the value is tested against the value stored in the child and moves to the left or right according to whether it is or isn't larger than the child's value. This process continues recursively until eventually the value is put into a new node.

When values are taken out of the tree in the print method, they are returned in sorted order via the recursive procedure print.

Adding an element to a tree is quite fast. Furthermore, since you generally don't have to process more than a few elements to find any one piece of data, trees can be much faster for random access than Vectors and compare favorably with arrays. It's almost always faster to insert a sorted element in a binary tree than in a Vector or an array. The only exception would be when the data arrives presorted.

Program 21.7 demonstrates the utility of a sorted binary tree by storing ten random numbers into a tree, and then printing them out.

Program 21.7 Tree sort

```java
public class treesort {

  public static void main (String[] args) {

    treenode root = new treenode(Math.random());

    for (int i = 1; i < 10; i++) {
```

```
      root.store(Math.random());
    }

    root.print();

  }

}
```

Q: *Why use BitSets instead of an* `int` *and the bitwise operators?*

A: A BitSet can contain an arbitrary number of bits. BitSets are normally only used when there are very many things to be kept track of, far more than there are bits in an `int`, `float`, or `double`.

Q: *Wouldn't a generic sorted tree class be useful?*

A: It certainly would be. The problem, though, lies in the comparison test used for the sorting. Different sorts of data require different comparison algorithms. What's really needed here is the ability to pass a method as an argument to another method. This is achieved in C with function pointers and in C++ with templates. However, Java doesn't allow this.

Quiz

1. What's the difference between a stack and a queue?

Exercises

1. As written, the StringStack class still allows one to put non-String objects on the stack. Fix this by overriding `push(Object o)` so that it checks for the type of the object. If the object is not an instance of String, push the `o.toString()` on the stack instead. Can you eliminate the check for the type of the object and just always push `o.toString()`? In other words, given that `s` is a String, is `s.toString()` equal to `s`?

2. As written, the StringStack class still allows one to put non-String objects on the stack. Fix this by overriding `push(Object o)` so that it checks for the type of the object. If the object is not an instance of String, throw a user-defined Exception.

3. Modify the `printtree` method in Program 21.6 so that it prints the elements of the tree from largest to smallest.

4. Add two methods to the treenode class, one that returns an Enumeration of the elements in the tree sorted from smallest to largest and another that returns an Enumeration sorted from largest to smallest.

Summary

In this chapter you learned about

- Vectors
- Stacks
- Queues
- Hashtables
- BitSets
- References
- Trees

Coming Up

This chapter completes your introduction to programming in Java. In the next chapter, you'll learn about javadoc, which helps you generate HTML documentation of your source code from your classes.

Further Reading

While there are a number of books about data structures, there aren't many that use object-oriented techniques. The best one I've been able to find is

SEDGEWICK, ROBERT, *Algorithms in C++*, New York: Addison Wesley, 1992

More information about Java data structures can be found at

http://www.javasoft.com/JDK-1.0/api/java.util.Stack.html

http://www.javasoft.com/JDK-1.0/api/java.util.Hashtable.html

http://www.javasoft.com/JDK-1.0/api/java.io.BitSet.html

http://www.javasoft.com/JDK-1.0/api/java.util.Vector.html

http://www.javasoft.com/JDK-1.0/api/java.util.Enumeration.html

CHAPTER 22
JAVADOC

- **D**oc comments
- **V**ersion and author tags
- **C**ross-referencing other classes and methods
- **D**ocumenting parameters and return types

Most of Sun's API documentation has been produced by javadoc, an automated documentation system that uses special comments in source code files to produce HTML documentation. This chapter shows you how you can take advantage of javadoc to document your own packages and classes.

javadoc

javadoc is a command-line program to which you pass either a package name or a list of Java source code files. javadoc then searches the specified package or java source files and produces HTML output that documents the code. It also generates the files packages.html, tree.html, and AllNames.html, which serve as indexes of the collected documentation.

Without any extra work on the part of the programmer, javadoc can produce a detailed listing of the different public and protected fields, constructors and methods in the specified files. Thus, to document the Queue class, you'd use the command line

```
javadoc Queue.java
```

The response looks like this:

```
% javadoc Queue.java

Generating packages.html

generating documentation for class Queue

Generating index

Sorting 5 items . . . done

Generating tree
```

More importantly, the following output is placed in a file called Queue.html. Figure 22.1 shows the first page of the documentation in Netscape.

```
<!--NewPage-->
<html>
<head>
<!-- Generated by javadoc on Sun May 12 14:37:18 EDT 1996 -->
<a name="_top_"></a>
<title>
 Class Queue
</title>
</head>
<body>
<h1>
 Class Queue
</h1>
<pre>
<a href="java.lang.Object.html#_top_">java.lang.Object</a>
```

```
        |
    +--<a href="java.util.Vector.html#_top_">java.util.Vector</a>
          |
          +--Queue
</pre>
<hr>
<dl>
  <dt> public class <b>Queue</b>
  <dt> extends <a href="java.util.Vector.html#_top_">Vector</a>
</dl>
<hr>
<a name="index"></a>
<h2>
  <img src="images/constructor-index.gif" width=275 height=38
alt="Constructor Index">
</h2>
<dl>
  <dt> <img src="images/yellow-ball-small.gif" width=6 height=6 alt=" o
">
      <a href="#Queue()"><b>Queue</b></a>()
  <dd>
</dl>
<h2>
  <img src="images/method-index.gif" width=207 height=38 alt="Method
Index">
</h2>
<dl>
  <dt> <img src="images/red-ball-small.gif" width=6 height=6 alt="o ">
      <a href="#add(java.lang.Object)"><b>add</b></a>(Object)
  <dd>
  <dt> <img src="images/red-ball-small.gif" width=6 height=6 alt="o ">
      <a href="#empty()"><b>empty</b></a>()
  <dd>
  <dt> <img src="images/red-ball-small.gif" width=6 height=6 alt=" o ">
      <a href="#peek()"><b>peek</b></a>()
  <dd>
  <dt> <img src="images/red-ball-small.gif" width=6 height=6 alt="o ">
      <a href="#remove()"><b>remove</b></a>()
  <dd>
</dl>
<a name="constructors"></a>
<h2>
  <img src="images/constructors.gif" width=231 height=38
alt="Constructors">
</h2>
<a name="Queue"></a>
```

```html
<a name="Queue()"><img src="images/yellow-ball.gif" width=12
height=12 alt=" o "></a>
<b>Queue</b>
<pre>
 public Queue()
</pre>
<a name="methods"></a>
<h2>
 <img src="images/methods.gif" width=151 height=38 alt="Methods">
</h2>
<a name="add(java.lang.Object)"><img src="images/red-ball.gif"
width=12 height=12 alt=" o "></a>
<a name="add"><b>add</b></a>
<pre>
 public void add(<a href="java.lang.Object.html#_top_">Object</a> o)
</pre>
<a name="remove()"><img src="images/red-ball.gif" width=12 height=12
alt=" o "></a>
<a name="remove"><b>remove</b></a>
<pre>
 public <a href="java.lang.Object.html#_top_">Object</a> remove()
</pre>
<a name="peek()"><img src="images/red-ball.gif" width=12 height=12
alt=" o "></a>
<a name="peek"><b>peek</b></a>
<pre>
 public <a href="java.lang.Object.html#_top_">Object</a> peek()
</pre>
<a name="empty()"><img src="images/red-ball.gif" width=12 height=12
alt=" o "></a>
<a name="empty"><b>empty</b></a>
<pre>
 public boolean empty()
</pre>
</body>
</html>
```

javadoc relies on the CLASSPATH environment variable to find the packages and source code files to make sure they're located appropriately before producing documentation. It uses .java source code files, not .class byte code files.

You can see from the output that all by itself javadoc finds all public and protected members of a class, all their return types, all public and protected method arguments and their types, and all constructors.

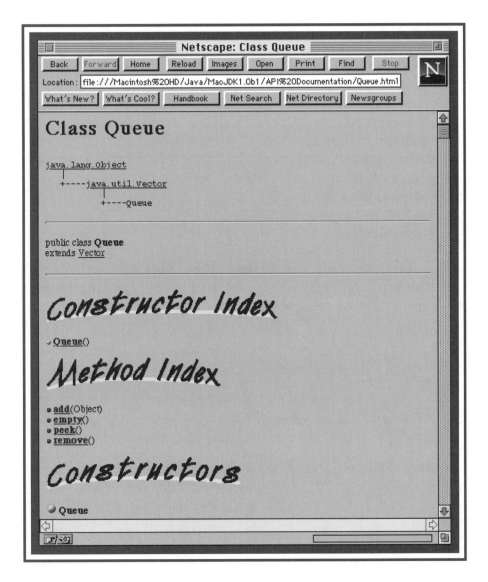

Figure 22.1: *Default documentation for the Queue class*

In short, it finds the contract the class signs with all other classes. javadoc does not document anything that is private or unspecified since a user of this class shouldn't have to know about that anyway.

You should also note that javadoc expects to find several images in a folder called images. The necessary files are

- blue-ball-small.gif
- blue-ball.gif

- class-index.gif
- constructor-index.gif
- constructors.gif
- cyan-ball-small.gif
- cyan-ball.gif
- error-index.gif
- exception-index.gif
- green-ball-small.gif
- green-ball.gif
- interface-index.gif
- magenta-ball-small.gif
- magenta-ball.gif

If you just put your own output in the same folder on your local hard disk where Sun's API documentation is, you shouldn't have any problems. If for some reason you can't do that, just make a directory called images in the same directory where your HTML file is and copy the necessary images into there.

Doc Comments

The documentation produced by source code alone is still a little sparse. Therefore, javadoc recognizes special doc comments which let a programmer add information to the automatically generated documentation.

Doc comments begin with /** and end with */.[1] Any text between the /** and the closing */ will be included in the nearest part of the automatically generated documentation. Doc comments are placed immediately before the item they comment on (a class, method, variable, or Exception). For instance, here is a doc comment which comments on the Queue class:

```
/**

 * This class abstracts a Queue data
 * structure, that is a first-in,
 * first-out or <i>FIFO</i> list of objects.
```

---

[1] The javac compiler does not care about the extra asterisk. To it a doc comment is just another comment that begins with /* and ends with */ and just happens to include an asterisk as the first character of the comment.

```
*/
public class Queue {
```

You can use HTML tags inside a doc comment. The above comment uses the <i> HTML tag to italicize FIFO. However, you should avoid headers (<h1> through <h6>) and horizontal rules (<hr>) since javadoc formats its output based on the assumption that there won't be any of these in the document. You can include links in the tag as well. However, if you're linking to another part of the documentation, you should use @ tags (described below) instead.

The extra asterisks at the beginning of the second and third lines are not technically necessary for a doc comment, but in practice they do seem to help javadoc identify the different parts of the comment, especially the tags of the next section.

javadoc Tags

As well as basic HTML, javadoc lets you include variable tags in your doc comments. Variable tags start with an @ symbol at the beginning of a line. Everything after the @ becomes part of the variable.

Which tags are allowed depends on what you're commenting on. If you're commenting on a public field, you have access to the following three tags:

@see classname

Adds a See Also: hyperlink to this classname. The classname should either be in the current package or fully qualified, for example, java.util.Stack instead of just Stack.

```
/** Compare to the Stack
 * @see java.util.Stack
 */
```

@see fully-qualified-classname#method-name

Adds a See Also: hyperlink to the method method-name of class classname. The classname should be fully specified, for example,

```
/**
```

```
 *    @return The Object at the front of the Queue
 *    @see java.lang.Object
 */
public Object peek() {

    if (size() == 0) throw new EmptyStackException();
    return elementAt(0);

}
```

If you're commenting on a class, you also get version and author tags:

@version version-text

Adds a Version to the documentation. The version must be supplied by the programmer as version-text. Neither Java nor javadoc will track versions for you.

@author your-name

Adds an Author to the documentation. The name is supplied by the programmer.

```
/**
 * This class abstracts a Queue data structure,
 * that is a first-in, first-out or <i>FIFO</i>
 * list of objects.
 * @version 1.0 of March 5, 1996
 * @author Elliotte Rusty Harold
 */
public class Queue {
```

A doc comment for a method can contain all the @see tags as well as tags that describe the arguments, values returned, and Exceptions thrown by a method. These tags are

@param parameter-name description

Use the @param tag to document the parameters a method takes. The parameter-name should be the same as you used in your code. For example,

```
/**
 * This method inserts an object at the back of
 * the Queue.
 * @param o The object to be added to the back
 * of the Queue
 */
public void add(Object o) {
  addElement(o);
}
```

Remember that javadoc can figure out what a parameter is (float, long, String, etc.), but it's up to the programmer to document what a parameter means.

@return description

Use the @return tag to document what a method returns. Remember that javadoc can figure out what the return type is (float, long, String, etc.), but it's up to the programmer to document what a return type means. For example,

```
/**
 * @return the object at the front of the Queue
 */
public Object peek() {

  if (size() == 0) throw new EmptyStackException();
  return elementAt(0);

}
```

@exception fully-qualified-class-name description

Use the @exception tag to document the Exceptions a method throws. You can use this even for methods that do not have a throws clause if they throw RuntimeExceptions. The Exception is linked to its class documentation.

```
/**
 * @throws EmptyStackException if the Queue is
 * empty
 */
```

```
public Object peek() {

    if (size() == 0) throw new EmptyStackException();
    return elementAt(0);

}
```

As convenient as javadoc is, it will not provide good documentation without a lot of effort on the part of the programmer to write that documentation. Although discussed in theory, it is almost unheard of to have too many comments in a source code file.

As a final example, here's a fully documented Queue.java:

Program 22.1: A fully documented Queue class

```java
import java.util.Vector;
import java.util.EmptyStackException;

/**
 * This class abstracts a Queue data structure,
 * that is a first-in, first-out or <i>FIFO</i>
 * list of objects.
 * @version 1.0 of March 5, 1996
 * @author Elliotte Rusty Harold
 */
public class Queue extends Vector {

    /**
     * This method puts an object at the back of
     * the Queue.
     * @param o The object to be added to the back
     * of the Queue
     */
    public void add(Object o) {
        addElement(o);
    }

    /**
     * This method takes the object from the front
     * of the Queue.
     * @return The object at the front of the Queue
     */
    public Object remove() {
```

```java
        Object o  = peek();
        removeElementAt(0);
        return o;

    }

    /**
     * Look at the object at the front of the Queue
     * without removing it
     * @return the object at the front of the Queue
     * @throws EmptyStackException if the Queue is
     * empty
     */
    public Object peek() {

        if (size() == 0) {
            throw new EmptyStackException();
        }
        return elementAt(0);

    }

    /**
     * Tests whether the Queue is empty
     * @return true if the Queue is empty,
     * otherwise return false
     */
    public boolean empty() {
        return size() == 0;
    }

}
```

Here's the HTML output:

```html
<!—NewPage—>
<html>
<head>
<!— Generated by javadoc on Sun May 12 15:57:21 EDT 1996 —>
<a name="_top_"></a>
<title>
 Class Queue
</title>
</head>
```

```
<body>
<h1>
  Class Queue
</h1>
<pre>
<a href="java.lang.Object.html#_top_">java.lang.Object</a>
  |
    +——<a href="java.util.Vector.html#_top_">java.util.Vector</a>
        |
          +——Queue
</pre>
<hr>
<dl>
  <dt> public class <b>Queue</b>
  <dt> extends <a href="java.util.Vector.html#_top_">Vector</a>
</dl>
This class abstracts a Queue data structure, that is a first-in,
first-out or <i>FIFO</i> list of objects.
<hr>
<a name="index"></a>
<h2>
  <img src="images/constructor-index.gif" width=275 height=38
alt="Constructor Index">
</h2>
<dl>
  <dt> <img src="images/yellow-ball-small.gif" width=6 height=6 alt=" o
">
        <a href="#Queue()"><b>Queue</b></a>()
  <dd>
</dl>
<h2>
  <img src="images/method-index.gif" width=207 height=38 alt="Method
Index">
</h2>
<dl>
  <dt> <img src="images/red-ball-small.gif" width=6 height=6 alt=" o ">
        <a href="#add(java.lang.Object)"><b>add</b></a>(Object)
  <dd> This method puts an object at the back of the Queue.
  <dt> <img src="images/red-ball-small.gif" width=6 height=6 alt=" o ">
        <a href="#empty()"><b>empty</b></a>()
  <dd>
Tests whether the Queue is empty
```

```
<dt> <img src="images/red-ball-small.gif" width=6 height=6 alt=" o ">
      <a href="#peek()"><b>peek</b></a>()
<dd>
Look at the object at the front of the queue without removing it

<dt> <img src="images/red-ball-small.gif" width=6 height=6 alt=" o ">
      <a href="#remove()"><b>remove</b></a>()
<dd> This method takes the object from the front of the Queue.
</dl>
<a name="constructors"></a>
<h2>
  <img src="images/constructors.gif" width=231 height=38
alt="Constructors">
</h2>
<a name="Queue"></a>
<a name="Queue()"><img src="images/yellow-ball.gif" width=12
height=12 alt=" o "></a>
<b>Queue</b>
<pre>
  public Queue()
</pre>
<a name="methods"></a>
<h2>
  <img src="images/methods.gif" width=151 height=38 alt="Methods">
</h2>
<a name="add(java.lang.Object)"><img src="images/red-ball.gif"
width=12 height=12 alt=" o "></a>
<a name="add"><b>add</b></a>
<pre>
  public void add(<a href="java.lang.Object.html#_top_">Object</a> o)
</pre>
<dl>
  <dd> This method puts an object at the back of the Queue.
  <dl>
    <dt> <b>Parameters:</b>
    <dd> o - The object to be added to the back of the Queue
  </dl>
</dl>
<a name="remove()"><img src="images/red-ball.gif" width=12 height=12
alt=" o "></a>
<a name="remove"><b>remove</b></a>
```

```html
<pre>
  public <a href="java.lang.Object.html#_top_">Object</a> remove()
</pre>
<dl>
  <dd> This method takes the object from the front of the Queue.
  <dl>
    <dt> <b>Returns:</b>
    <dd> The object at the front of the Queue
  </dl>
</dl>
<a name="peek()"><img src="images/red-ball.gif" width=12 height=12 alt=" o "></a>
<a name="peek"><b>peek</b></a>
<pre>
  public <a href="java.lang.Object.html#_top_">Object</a> peek()
</pre>
<dl>
  <dd> Look at the object at the front of the queue without removing it
  <dl>
    <dt> <b>Returns:</b>
    <dd> the object at the front of the Queue
  </dl>
</dl>
<a name="empty()"><img src="images/red-ball.gif" width=12 height=12 alt=" o "></a>
<a name="empty"><b>empty</b></a>
<pre>
  public boolean empty()
</pre>
<dl>
  <dd> Tests whether the Queue is empty
  <dl>
    <dt> <b>Returns:</b>
    <dd> true if the Queue is empty, otherwise false
  </dl>
</dl>
</body>
</html>
```

Figure 22.2 shows some of the documentation when viewed in Netscape.

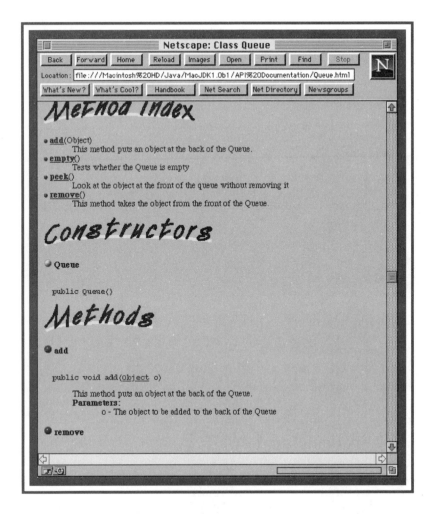

Figure 22.2: *Documentation for the Queue class*

Q&A

Q: *When should I use a doc comment and when should I use a regular comment?*

A: A good rule of thumb is that anything that's public should be documented with doc comments and anything that's private should be documented with regular comments. Interfaces to methods will generally be doc commented. Details of algorithms and data structures will be kept private, as they should be.

Quiz

1. What's the difference between a doc comment and a regular comment?

Exercises

1. Use javadoc to document the treenode class in Program 21.6 of last chapter.

Summary

In this chapter you learned

- What a doc comment is
- How to include version information in your classes
- How to include author information in your classes
- How to cross-reference other classes
- How to cross-reference other methods
- How to document arguments
- How to document return types

Coming Up

In the next chapter, you'll see a non-trivial example of Java programming that generates VRML. Doc comments will be used extensively to explain and document the classes.

Further Reading

FRIENDLY, LISA, "The design of distributed hyperlinked programming documentation," 1995, ftp://ftp.javasoft.com/docs/iwhd.ps

The javadoc man page at

http://java.sun.com/java.sun.com/JDK-1.0/tools/win32/javadoc.html

CHAPTER 23

JAVA AND VRML

- The Virtual Reality Modeling Language 1.0

- Modeling VRML with Java classes

- Using Java to create complex VRML worlds

This chapter is going to take a decidedly different tack. Rather than looking at toy examples that demonstrate specific pieces of Java, this chapter is going to build a fully object-oriented model. This is going to require a lot of pages and a lot of code. You aren't going to learn any new Java syntax or library calls in this chapter, but you will learn something about how real programs come together.

The project this chapter describes is a Java package that handles large parts of VRML 1.0. Of course to model VRML 1.0 in Java, you'll need to understand VRML first, so this chapter begins with a lightning introduction to VRML. Then you'll see how you can abstract the underlying three-dimensional geometry of VRML into Java classes. Finally, you'll see some examples of VRML worlds you can build using Java that would be too difficult to build with VRML alone.

539

What is VRML?

The Virtual Reality Modeling Language, VRML[1] for short, is slightly younger than Java. It was initiated at the World Wide Web Conference in Geneva, Switzerland in October, 1994. Version 1.0 was finalized some months later based on Silicon Graphics' Open Inventor 3-D File Format.

VRML is not a markup language like HTML and it is not a programming language like Java. It is a portable file format for describing three-dimensional scenes in ASCII text. Language primitives include cubes, cylinders, spheres, cones, text, lines, points, and triangles. These objects can be positioned in a three-dimensional Cartesian space and can be stretched, skewed, and rotated into various positions and shapes. Different colors, shading, and textures can be applied to each object. Different lights and cameras can be positioned to provide different views on the three-dimensional space.

VRML 1.0 is a static specification. Although a viewer can move around in a VRML world, the world itself does not change. Objects do not have behaviors, only appearances. This is changing in VRML 2.0, also known as "Moving Worlds." Like Java, VRML is changing very rapidly; and it is likely that by the time you read this some of the information here will be out of date. However in most simple respects, VRML 2.0 will be a superset of VRML 1.0 so most of this material should still be valid.

Java and VRML are made for each other. A VRML world is easy to represent as objects, that is instances of Java classes. This chapter is going to develop a package for creating simple VRML worlds.

Basic VRML for Java Programmers

Example 23.1 shows a very simple VRML file. As with the Java programs of the last 22 chapters, the line numbers are included here only

---

[1] Pronounced "Vee-Are-Em-Ell" or "vermil" (like a cross between vermin and gerbil).

to make referring to them in the text easier. They are not part of the actual VRML file. Type this code into a text file, just like you would with Java source code, and save it in a file called 23.1.wrl or simplecube.wrl. Like Java, VRML is case-sensitive. "Cube" is not the same a "cube," so be sure to type the code exactly as it appears here. Unlike Java files, the name of a VRML file is unimportant as long as it ends with the extension ".wrl"

Example 23.1: A VRML file with one node, a cube

```
1. #VRML V1.0 ascii
2.
3. # Created by Elliotte Rusty Harold
4. # June 17, 1996
5.
6. Cube {
7. }
```

Figure 23.1a shows this file loaded into a VRML viewer. (Here and elsewhere in this chapter the VRML viewer used is Netscape 3.0b4 for the Macintosh. Figures may look slightly different in different viewers.) It appears to be a white square on a green background, the same as could have easily been drawn in a Java applet. However, this is not really a square. Rather it is the projection of a three-dimensional cube onto a two-dimensional computer display. A VRML viewer allows you to move around in the space and look at the figure from different locations and angles. Figure 23.1b shows the exact same cube viewed from a little further away and off-center. To fully understand a VRML scene, you need to move around in the world.

The source code that produces this scene is almost the simplest VRML file imaginable. Line 1 is how all VRML 1.0 files must begin. The version number changes to reflect different versions of VRML. This chapter deals only with VRML 1.0, but in the future you will use later versions of VRML. The ascii keyword signifies that this file contains only 7-bit ASCII text. Future versions of VRML will allow different character sets such as ISO-Latin-1 or Unicode. However VRML 1.0 only supports ASCII.

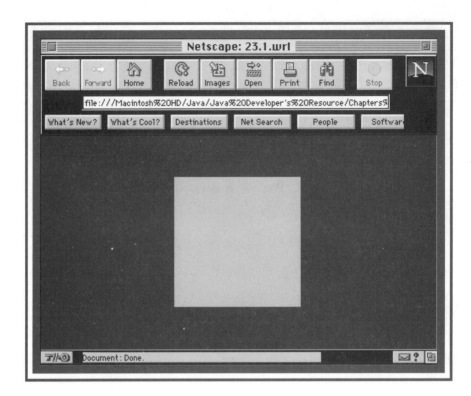

Figure 23.1a: *A VRML cube viewed straight-on*

Line 2 is blank. Just as in Java, blank lines are irrelevant in VRML files. They exist to make the file easier for human beings to read. The VRML viewer does not care.

Lines 3 and 4 begin with a # sign. This signifies a "VRML comment." This is exactly like the // comment in Java. Everything after the # until the end of the line is ignored by the VRML viewer. The purpose of comments in a VRML file is the same as comments in a Java file. It helps to document the source code. Comments do not affect the ultimate appearance of the VRML world in any way.

Line 6 begins a Cube **node**. A node in VRML is very similar to an object in Java. The syntax is much like the syntax for a Java class. That is the name of the node, followed by an open brace, followed by a closing brace. Here the closing brace is on Line 7. In the next example, you'll see that a node can have fields (but not methods) in between the opening and closing braces.

Example 23.1 used only the default Cube. It is possible to change the properties of a node by setting its fields. A Cube has three fields:

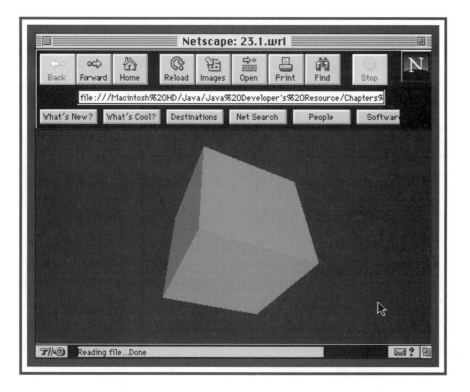

Figure 23.1b: *A VRML cube viewed edge on*

height, width, and depth. Each of these is a floating-point number. To create a cube that is three units high, two units wide, and four units deep, you write

```
Cube {
   height 3.0
   width 2.0
   depth 4.0
}
```

The first thing you should note is that this "Cube" is in fact not a geometric cube, but rather a box. The terminology is a little deceptive.

The second thing to note is that the units are not explicitly specified. However, each is assumed to be given in meters. Thus the above cube is three meters by two meters by four meters. Of course, VRML worlds are not drawn to actual size. You don't need a four-meter-wide display to see the entire cube.

The third thing to note is that lines are not terminated with a semicolon as they are in Java. In fact, these don't even have to be on separate lines. As far as a VRML viewer is concerned, the following is equivalent:

```
Cube { height 3.0 width 2.0 depth 4.0 }
```

The order of the fields is equally unimportant. Depth can come before height or height after width. Similarly extra white space for indentation or line breaks is fine, but is only for humans, not for the VRML parser.

If you don't specify a value for one of these fields, it is assumed to be 2.0. Thus the above example could be written like this with width omitted:

```
Cube {
    height 3.0
    depth 4.0
}
```

Nodes are positioned in a three-dimensional, right-handed Cartesian coordinate space. By default, all objects are drawn centered at the origin, that is, at (0.0, 0.0, 0.0). This is the intersection of the three lines in Figure 23.2. The straight line reaching from the bottom to the top is the y or height axis. The line reaching from the bottom left to the top right is the z or depth axis, and the remaining line drawn from the bottom right to the top left is the x or width axis. Three-dimensional Cartesian coordinates are just like two-dimensional Cartesian coordinates with an extra line running perpendicular to the x-y plane to signify depth. Another way of thinking about it is that from left to right on your computer monitor is the x

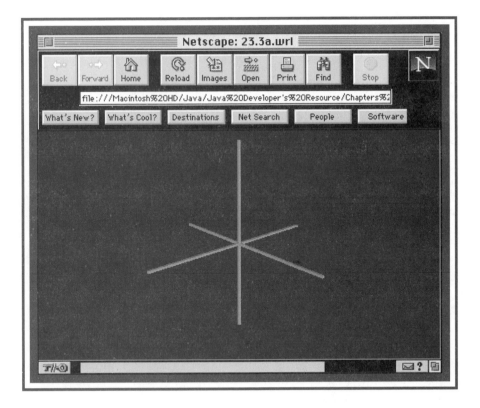

Figure 23.2: *The coordinate axes*

axis. From the bottom to the top of your monitor is the y axis. Then
the line coming out of your computer monitor straight at you is the z
axis. Generally when you enter a VRML scene, you look straight
down on the x-y plane.

Figure 23.2 is itself a VRML file drawn by the code in Example 23.2.
Note how thin Cubes can be used to represent straight lines.

Example 23.2: A VRML file with two cubes

```
#VRML V1.0 ascii

# The y axis
Cube {
  height 40.0
  width 0.5
  depth 0.5
}
```

```
# The x axis
Cube {
  height 0.5
  width 40.0
  depth 0.5
}

# The z axis
Cube {
  height 0.5
  width 0.5
  depth 40.0
}
```

Translation

Height, width, and depth are not the only properties one associates with a cube in three-dimensional space. Other obvious properties include position (x, y, and z), orientation, and color. In VRML, however, these are defined to be properties of a virtual pen that draws nodes rather than properties of each node. The pen is an abstract idea that you can think of as doing the drawing in a VRML scene. The pen reads a VRML file and draws each shape node it encounters. A Cube is one shape node. To change where things are drawn, you change the position of the pen using a Translation node.

Example 23.3 draws a a 1.0-by-1.0-by-1.0 cube at (0.0, 0.0, 0.0) and a 2.0-by-3.0-by-4.0 cube at (1.5, 3.4, 2.6). Figure 23.3 shows the rendered file.

Example 23.3: A VRML file with two cubes

```
#VRML V1.0 ascii

Cube {
  width 1.0
  height 1.0
  depth 1.0
}
```

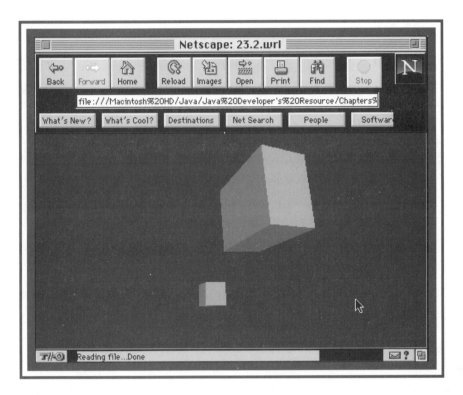

Figure 23.3: *Two Cubes of different sizes at different positions*

```
Translation {
   translation 1.5 3.4 2.6
}

Cube {
   width 2.0
   height 3.0
   depth 4.0
}
```

Translations are cumulative. That is, they are relative rather than absolute. The translation in Example 23.3 moves 1.5 meters in the x direction, 3.4 meters in the y direction, and 2.6 meters in the z direction (up) from wherever the pen was when it started.

Rotation

As well as translating you can rotate objects around the x, y, and z axes. A rotation is accomplished in a Rotation node using the rotation field. The rotation field takes three floating-point numbers that specify the axes of rotation, followed by a single floating-point number that specifies the amount of rotation in radians. For example, to rotate 90 degrees around the x axis, you would write

```
Rotation {
   rotation 1.0 0.0 0.0 1.572646
}
```

To rotate 90 degrees about the y axis, you would write

```
Rotation {
   rotation 0.0 1.0 0.0 1.572646
}
```

Finally, to rotate 90 degrees about the z axis, you would write

```
Rotation {
   rotation 0.0 0.0 1.0 1.572646
}
```

It is possible to rotate about other axes using different combinations of the first three numbers. However, that's beyond the scope of this book. You can rotate into any position you desire by successive rotations about each of these three axes

Like translations, rotations are relative and cumulative. If you rotate an object 90 degrees around the x axis, all shapes you draw from that point on will be rotated 90 degrees around the x axis until you rotate back.

Spheres

Cubes are not the only three-dimensional shapes. VRML includes primitives for cylinders, spheres, and cones as well. A VRML Sphere is defined by a single field, radius. The default value is 1.0. Example 23.4 is a sphere with three meter radius. Figure 23.4 shows this sphere.

Radians vs. Degrees

Most people measure angles in degrees, there being 360 degrees in a circle. This measurement system dates back to ancient Babylon around 1600 B.C.E. However, this is merely a convention and not ordained by nature.[1] The circle could be split into 120 equal units, or 30, or 400.[2]

There is, however, a special number. If you split the circle into approximately 3.14159265358979323846 pieces, certain formulas involving arcs of circles become quite simple. For instance, the length of 30° arc of circle with a two-meter radius is given by the formula

$$\frac{2\pi r\theta}{360°} = \frac{2\pi \times 2m \times 30°}{360°} = 1.047\,m$$

On the other hand, if you convert 30° into 0.52359 radians, then the formula for the length of the arc is the much simpler:

$$r\theta = 2m \times 0.52359 = 1.047m$$

The magic number is, of course, π, and what you've done by choosing to use radians is to scale the dimensions so as to remove π from the equation. It turns out that the formula for arc length is the most minor of formulas that become simpler when they're calculated in radians. There are a number of series expansions that are used to calculate the values of sine and cosine for particular angles. These also work best when calculated in radians:

$$\sin\theta \cong \theta - \frac{\theta^3}{3!} + \frac{\theta^5}{5!} - \frac{\theta^7}{7!} + \frac{\theta^9}{9!} - \cdots$$

$$\cos\theta \cong 1 - \frac{\theta^2}{2!} + \frac{\theta^4}{4!} - \frac{\theta^6}{6!} + \frac{\theta^8}{8!} - \cdots$$

---

[1] Perhaps the choice of 360 has something to do with there being 365 days in a year, since degrees were first used to measure the sky for astrology.

[2] Actually, some engineers do split up the circle into four hundred pieces. These are called grads.

Since Java uses formulas very much like these for its sine and cosine methods behind the scenes, it expects you to pass it all angles in radians. Humans think better in integral degrees than in irrational quantities like most radian measures so you'll find yourself doing a lot of conversion back and forth, especially when doing input and output.

The formulas for conversion are quite simple. Since there are 360 degrees in a circle and 2π radians in the same circle, and if R is the number of radians and D the number of degrees in an angle, then

$$D = \frac{180}{\pi} R$$

$$R = \frac{\pi}{180} D$$

Example 23.4: A VRML file with a sphere of radius three

```
#VRML V1.0 ascii

Sphere {
  radius 3.0
}
```

You can use translation and rotation nodes on spheres just like you use them on cubes. Remember, translation and rotation are properties of the virtual pen, not of an object itself.

Cones

A cone is defined by its height and bottomRadius (the radius of its base). For example,

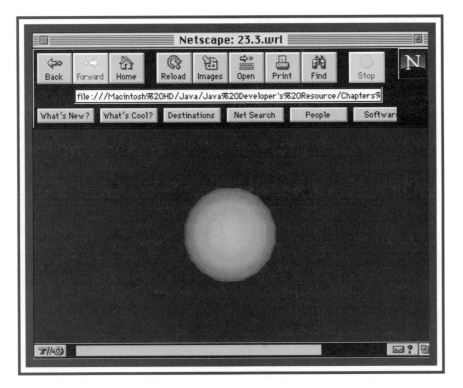

Figure 23.4: *A Sphere*

```
Cone {
    height 3.0
    bottomRadius 3.0
}
```

You also have the option to only draw part of the cone. To do this, set the parts field to a list of the parts you want to be drawn. This list is enclosed in parentheses and list elements are separated by a vertical bar like (BOTTOM|SIDES). A cone has two parts, a BOTTOM and the SIDES. By default, both are drawn. If you only want to draw the sides of the cone but not the bottom, then set the parts field to SIDES. If you only want to draw the bottom and not the sides, then set the parts field to BOTTOM. To draw both, set the parts field to ALL or just leave it unspecified, since this is the default. Example 23.5 draws three cones, the first at (-5.0, 0.0, 0.0) with only a bottom, the second at (0.0, 0.0, 0.0) with only the sides, the third at (5.0, 0.0,0.0) with all its parts. Figure 23.5 shows the rendered image.

Example 23.5: Three cones

```
#VRML V1.0 ascii

Translation {
  translation -5.0 0.0 0.0
}

Cone {
    parts (BOTTOM)
}

Translation {
  translation 5.0 0.0 0.0
}

Cone {
    parts (SIDES)
}

Translation {
  translation 5.0 0.0 0.0
}

Cone {
}
```

Cylinders

A cylinder has three parts: the top, the bottom, and the sides. However, a cylinder is defined by just two fields: its height and its radius. Thus, to create a cylinder that's open at the top, you might write

```
Cylinder {
  radius 3.0
  height 6.0
  parts (SIDES|BOTTOM)
}
```

By default, all parts of the cylinder are drawn. The default height is 2.0 meters and the default radius is 1.0 meter. Long, thin cylinders make nice three-dimensional lines. However, you'll generally need to rotate the coordinate axes to position them. Example 23.6 uses cylinders to draw the coordinate axes.

Example 23.6: Three rotated cylinders along the coordinate axes

```
#VRML V1.0 ascii

# Created by Elliotte Rusty Harold
# June 21, 1996

# Draw a thin cylinder along the y axis

Cylinder {
  radius 0.5
  height 40.0
}

# Rotate around the z axis so the y axis
# moves into the old x axis

Rotation {
  rotation 0.0 0.0 1.0 1.572646
}

Cylinder {
  radius 0.5
  height 40.0
}

# Rotate around the new x axis so the y axis
# moves into the old z axis

Rotation {
  rotation 1.0 0.0 0.0 1.572646
}
```

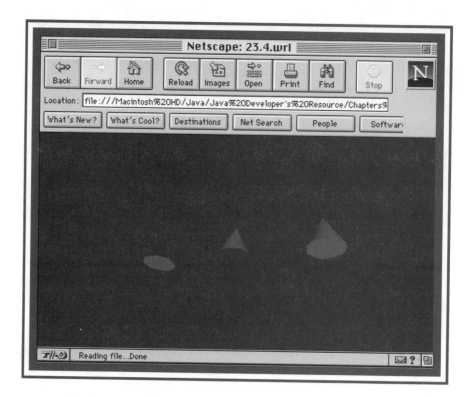

Figure 23.5: *Three cones*

```
Cylinder {
   radius 0.5
   height 40.0
}
```

Strings

You're not limited to three-dimensional shapes. One of the other things you can draw is text. You do this with an AsciiText node with a string field. Example 23.7 is a VRMLized Hello World. Figure 23.6 shows the VRML Hello World viewed straight on.

Example 23.7: Hello World!

```
#VRML V1.0 ascii

AsciiText {
   string "Hello World!"
}
```

Figure 23.6: *Hello World*

Warning VRML does not capitalize the word string, unlike Java. One of the most common errors Java programmers make when writing VRML files is capitalizing the word string. Other common errors include putting an equal sign between a field and its value, and putting a semicolon at the end of a line.

An AsciiText node may contain multiple strings. Each is drawn on a line below the previous one. For example,

```
AsciiText {
    string ["Hello World!", "Goodbye World!"]
}
```

You cannot use Translation nodes to position strings.[4] The first string in a node is always drawn beginning at (0.0, 0.0, 0.0). This is often very inconvenient, but you can use empty strings to push strings down the y axis.

---

[4] At least not until you learn about Separator nodes.

Like most nodes, AsciiText has several fields that can be used to control the appearance of the text. These are justification, width, and spacing. justification has one of the three values LEFT, RIGHT, and CENTER, which signify left-justified, right-justified, and center-justified text respectively.

The width field is a floating-point number that specifies the width for the entire string. The string is compressed or expanded as necessary to fit the width. However, a width of 0.0, the default value, signifies that the string should be exactly as wide as it needs to be, no more and no less.

Finally, the spacing field is a multiplier that specifies the distance in between lines. 1.0 is single-spacing, 2.0 is double-spacing, and so on. Negative spacing tells the pen to draw subsequent lines of text above the previous lines rather than below them. 1.0 is the default value.

However, the most common string attributes–font face, style, and size–are not set by fields. Rather they're set by a FontStyle node that affects all subsequent AsciiText nodes. For example, to make the pen start writing in a 12-unit, bold typewriter font, you would write

```
FontStyle {
    family TYPEWRITER
    style BOLD
    size 12
}
```

The other available choices for font family are SERIF and SANS. The exact font used is system-dependent but TYPEWRITER will always be a monospaced font like Courier, SANS a sans serif font like Helvetica, and SERIF a serif font like Times. SANS is the default.

Possible styles are NONE, BOLD, and ITALIC. The default is NONE, that is, plain text.

The default size for AsciiText is 10 units. These units are the same units used in cubes, spheres, cylinders, and cones. They are not points or any other external measurement.

Example 23.8: Font Tester

```
#VRML V1.0 ascii

FontStyle {
```

```
   family TYPEWRITER
   style BOLD
   size 12
}

AsciiText {
   string "TypeWriter 12 unit BOLD"
}

FontStyle {
   family SANS
   style NORMAL
   size 12
}

AsciiText {
   string ["", "Sans 12 unit NORMAL" ]
   spacing -1
}

FontStyle {
   family Serif
   style ITALIC
   size 12
}

AsciiText {
   string ["", "", "Serif 12 unit ITALIC"]
   spacing -1

}
```

Warning In most viewers, AsciiText nodes are fully three-dimensional. Thus, a single letter can be composed of many different polygons. A simple string like "sans 12 unit normal" can easily be the most complex object in your world. Use strings sparingly and only when absolutely necessary. Worlds that include whole paragraphs or even sentences can bring many viewers to their knees.

Faces, Lines and Points

Not all VRML objects are three-dimensional. VRML also includes the two-dimensional primitive face, the one-dimensional primitive line, and the zero-dimensional primitive point. However, despite their small dimensions, each of these must be located in three-dimensional space.

This is not hard. A point is defined by three floating point coordinates such as (0.0, 0.0, 0.0) or (-1.2, 3.4, 5.0). Two points still define a line segment. It's just that the two points are now three-dimensional points instead of the two-dimensional Point objects you're used to working with in Java. Faces are two-dimensional closed polygons defined by the points on their corners. You can combine faces along edges to create new and unique three-dimensional shapes like pyramids, eggs, and more.

Although faces can theoretically contain an unlimited number of vertices (corners), it's best to work only with triangular faces defined by three points. The reason is that a triangle must lie in a plane, whereas a face with more than three vertices need not. If you create a face with more than three vertices that does not lie in a plane, then the VRML renderer will split it into multiple triangles. However in general, there will be more than one way to split the face into triangles, and the splitting the viewer uses may not be what you envisioned.

All three of these objects—points, lines and faces—are created by selecting vertices from a list of coordinates stored in the point field of a Coordinate3 node. Example 23.9 contains two nodes: a Coordinate3 node that lists a series of points, and a PointSet node that selects points from the Coordinate3 node to be drawn.

Example 23.9: Integrally spaced points

```
#VRML V1.0 ascii

Coordinate3 {
  point [
    -1.000000 -1.000000 -1.000000,  #0
    -1.000000 -1.000000 0.000000,   #1
    -1.000000 -1.000000 1.000000,   #2
    -1.000000 0.000000 -1.000000,   #3
```

```
    -1.000000 0.000000 0.000000,    #4
    -1.000000 0.000000 1.000000,    #5
    -1.000000 1.000000 -1.000000,   #6
    -1.000000 1.000000 0.000000,    #7
    -1.000000 1.000000 1.000000,    #8
    0.000000 -1.000000 -1.000000,   #9
    0.000000 -1.000000 0.000000,    #10
    0.000000 -1.000000 1.000000,    #11
    0.000000 0.000000 -1.000000,    #12
    0.000000 0.000000 0.000000,     #13
    0.000000 0.000000 1.000000,     #14
    0.000000 1.000000 -1.000000,    #15
    0.000000 1.000000 0.000000,     #16
    0.000000 1.000000 1.000000,     #17
    1.000000 -1.000000 -1.000000,   #18
    1.000000 -1.000000 0.000000,    #19
    1.000000 -1.000000 1.000000,    #20
    1.000000 0.000000 -1.000000,    #21
    1.000000 0.000000 0.000000,     #22
    1.000000 0.000000 1.000000,     #23
    1.000000 1.000000 -1.000000,    #24
    1.000000 1.000000 0.000000,     #25
    1.000000 1.000000 1.000000,     #26
    ]
}

PointSet {
   startIndex 0
   numPoints 27
}
```

A Coordinate3 node sets the coordinate list for use by the pen, just like a Translation node sets the position of the pen. These coordinates are then accessed by PointSet, IndexedLineSet, and FaceSet nodes.

To draw points in the space, use a PointSet node and specify the point you want to start drawing with in the startIndex field, and the number of points you want to draw in the numPoints field. Thus, given the above Coordinate3 node to draw points at (-1, 0, 1) and (-1, 1, -1), you would write

```
PointSet {
   startIndex 5
   numPoints 2
}
```

Counting begins at zero. That is, the first point in the Coordinate3 node is the zeroth point. To draw all the points in the set use a startIndex of zero and a numPoints of as many points as there are in the set. Example 23.9 draws all 27 points in the above Coordinate3 node.

The Coordinate3 node in Example 23.9 is the set of all integral coordinates is the two-by-two-by-two cube centered on the origin. The line numbers are included in a comment for later ease of reference. Not so incidentally, this list was produced by the Java program in Example 23.10. Java is perfect for this sort of repetitive work that would be difficult to accomplish either by hand or with a modeling tool.

Example 23.10: A Java program to enumerate coordinates

```java
class origincube {

  public static void main (String[] args) {

    int counter = 0;
    String s1, s2, s3;

    System.out.println("Coordinate3 {");
    System.out.println("  point [");
    for (double x = -1; x <=1; x++) {
      if (x < 0) s1 = "";
      else s1 = " ";
      for (double y = -1; y <=1; y++) {
        if (y < 0) s2 = "";
        else s2 = " ";
        for (double z = -1; z <=1; z++) {
          if (z < 0) s3 = "";
          else s3 = " ";
          System.out.println("      " + x + " " +
            y + " " + z + "," + s1 + s2 + s3 +
            " #" + counter);
          counter++;
        }
      }
```

```
    }
    System.out.println("   ]");
    System.out.println("}");


  }


}
```

The points are a little hard to see in many VRML viewers. After all, they're mathematically infinitesimal and graphically only one pixel, if even that. For a more obvious grid, you can connect these dots with lines. To draw a line, you need a Coordinate3 node and an IndexedLineSet.

An IndexedLineSet has a single coordIndex field that lists the points to be connected in order. Thus to connect the dots in a one-by-one square in the first quadrant of the x-y plane with the above coordinate set, you write

```
IndexedLineSet {
   coordIndex [13, 16, 17, 22, 13]
}
```

This draws a line from coordinate 13, (0, 0, 0), to coordinate 16, (0, 1, 0). Then a line is drawn between point 16 and point 17 (1, 1, 0). Next a line is drawn between point 17 and point 22, (1, 0, 0). Finally the square is closed with a line between point 22 and point 13.

The first point needed to be repeated as the last point to close the square. The order of the points in the Coordinate3 node has no particular relation to the order in which the dots are connected.

Example 23.11 draws a grid using an IndexedLineSet node.

Example 23.11: Integrally spaced points

```
#VRML V1.0 ascii

Coordinate3 {
  point [
     -1.000000 -1.000000 -1.000000, #0
     -1.000000 -1.000000 0.000000,  #1
```

```
      -1.000000 -1.000000 1.000000,    #2
      -1.000000 0.000000 -1.000000,    #3
      -1.000000 0.000000 0.000000,     #4
      -1.000000 0.000000 1.000000,     #5
      -1.000000 1.000000 -1.000000,    #6
      -1.000000 1.000000 0.000000,     #7
      -1.000000 1.000000 1.000000,     #8
      0.000000 -1.000000 -1.000000,    #9
      0.000000 -1.000000 0.000000,     #10
      0.000000 -1.000000 1.000000,     #11
      0.000000 0.000000 -1.000000,     #12
      0.000000 0.000000 0.000000,      #13
      0.000000 0.000000 1.000000,      #14
      0.000000 1.000000 -1.000000,     #15
      0.000000 1.000000 0.000000,      #16
      0.000000 1.000000 1.000000,      #17
      1.000000 -1.000000 -1.000000,    #18
      1.000000 -1.000000 0.000000,     #19
      1.000000 -1.000000 1.000000,     #20
      1.000000 0.000000 -1.000000,     #21
      1.000000 0.000000 0.000000,      #22
      1.000000 0.000000 1.000000,      #23
      1.000000 1.000000 -1.000000,     #24
      1.000000 1.000000 0.000000,      #25
      1.000000 1.000000 1.000000,      #26
    ]
}


IndexedLineSet {
  coordIndex [
    0, 2, -1,
    0, 6, -1,
    0, 18, -1,
    2, 6, -1,
    2, 20, -1,
    6, 24, -1,
    6, 8, -1,
    8, 26, -1,
    18, 24, -1,
```

```
        18, 20, -1,
        20, 26, -1,
        24, 26
    ]
}
```

The Coordinate3 node in Example 23.11 is the same one used in Example 23.9. However, now instead of drawing each point in that set, an IndexedLineSet is used to draw one-dimensional line segments along the edges of the cube. Each line is defined by specifying the successive vertices of the line. When you want to start drawing a new line, insert a -1. In example 23.10, all the lines are single segments but the entire figure could be drawn like this instead:

```
IndexedLineSet {
  coordIndex [
    0, 2, 6, 8, 26, 20, 18, 24, 26, 24, 6, 0, 18,
    -1, 2, 20
  ]
}
```

In other words, a line can have sharp corners and double back on itself.

Finally, an IndexedFaceSet uses a Coordinate3 node to create a face. For example, to draw a square face that colors in a one-by-one square in the first quadrant of the x-y plane with the above coordinate set, write

```
IndexedFaceSet {
  coordIndex [0, 1, 4, 3]
}
```

The coordIndex fields of both IndexedLineSets and IndexedFaceSets use the special value -1 to indicate that a new face or line is starting. For instance, to break up the above square into two triangles you would write

```
IndexedFaceSet {
  coordIndex [0, 1, 4, -1,
    4, 3, 0]
}
```

Example 23.12 uses eight triangles to build an open cube, that is, a box kite. Figure 23.7 shows this object.

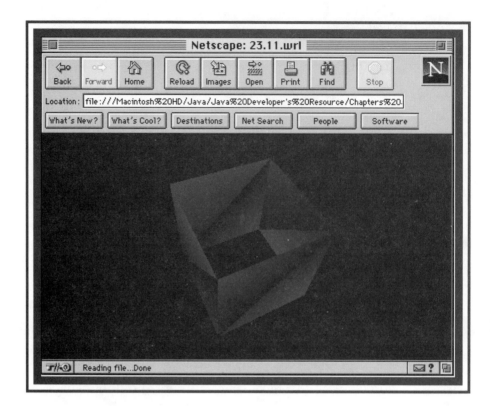

Figure 23.7: *A cube drawn with triangles*

Example 23.12: An open cube

```
#VRML V1.0 ascii

Coordinate3 {
  point [
    -1.000000 -1.000000 -1.000000,  #0
    -1.000000 -1.000000 1.000000,   #1
    -1.000000 1.000000 -1.000000,   #2
    -1.000000 1.000000 1.000000,    #3
    1.000000 -1.000000 -1.000000,   #4
    1.000000 -1.000000 1.000000,    #5
    1.000000 1.000000 -1.000000,    #6
    1.000000 1.000000 1.000000,     #7
  ]
}
```

```
IndexedFaceSet {
  coordIndex [
      # bottom face
      0, 4, 6, -1,
      0, 2, 6, -1,

      #top face
      1, 5, 7, -1,
      1, 3, 7, -1,

      #side faces

      4, 5, 7, -1,
      4, 6, 7, -1,
      0, 1, 3, -1,
      0, 2, 3

  ]
}
```

There's a lot more to VRML, even VRML 1.0, than what's been covered here. There's been no discussion of cameras, shading, grouping,
textures, WWW anchors, and more. Still this gives a basic set of three-
dimensional primitives you can use to build three-dimensional
scenes.

Defining the VRML Package

VRML is great for describing scenes. However, it doesn't provide any
support for building or animating scenes. This is where Java comes in.
With Java, you can algorithmically describe a world and, with an
appropriate package, generate the VRML code for that world.

There is one large choice to be made when constructing a VRML
package. Do you use a shallow wrapping over the VRML nodes that
maps very closely to the VRML syntax, or do you define a higher level,
more abstract three-dimensional structure?

I confess that there's one thing that intensely bothers me about VRML. It does not seem logical to me that location, orientation, color, and the like are parts of the pen rather than parts of a shape node. While it's occasionally useful to put a cube two units to the right of the last cube, I almost always want to locate a cube at a particular point in space. Therefore, this section is going to use the power of objects to create a different way of describing three-dimensional worlds. Each object in the world, which is roughly equivalent to a VRML shape node, will "know" its own position.

Having decided this there are two ways to handle the translation into a VRML world. The simplest is to precede each shape node with a translation node that moves to the object's position from the origin, draws the object, and then moves back. The other alternative is to allow the VRML world object to keep track of where the pen is and adjust the translation accordingly. Either solution is adequate. In fact, the public interface of the package will have no knowledge about which alternative is chosen.[5]

Given that translation will be embedded into shapes, there are two fundamental classes. The first class is an abstract class called shape. The shape class has a position in three-dimensional space, that is, double x, y, and z fields. The moveTo method moves the shape to the specified location. The moveRelative method moves the shape relative to its current location. Thus if a shape is already at (1.0, 2.0, 3.0), moveTo(0.0, 1.0, 0.0) moves it to (0.0, 1.0, 0.0), whereas moveRelative(0.0, 1.0, 0.0) moves it to (1.0, 3.0, 3.0).

Finally, the shape has an abstract draw method that returns a String. This method will be overridden in subclasses to actually print the node and translation and rotation nodes onto an output stream. Example 23.13 is this shape class.

Example 23.13: The abstract shape class

```
package elharo.vrml;

public abstract class shape {
```

---

[5] VRML TransformSeparator nodes allow a third and somewhat more elegant alternative here, but regrettably the margin of this book is too small to contain the details.

```
  double x = 0.0;
  double y = 0.0;
  double z = 0.0;


  public void moveTo(double x, double y, double z) {
    this.x = x;
    this.y = y;
    this.z = z;
  }


  public void moveRelative(double x, double y,
    double z) {
    this.x += x;
    this.y += y;
    this.z += z;
  }

  public abstract String draw() ;


}
```

This class is subclassed to provide implementations for specific shapes like cubes, spheres, and cones. The Cube class needs to add fields that match the fields in the VRML cube node, that is, height, width, and depth. There are three polymorphic constructors: one that takes no arguments and just uses the defaults; one that takes three doubles for height, width, and depth but uses default location; and one that lets the user specify both location and dimension. Methods are also provided to set these fields. Finally, draw must be implemented. Example 23.14 has the code.

Example 23.14: The Cube class

```
package elharo.vrml;

public class Cube extends shape {
```

```java
double width = 1.0;
double height = 1.0;
double depth = 1.0;

public Cube() {
}

public Cube(
 double height, double width, double depth) {

  this.width = width;
  this.height = height;
  this.depth = depth;
}

public Cube(
 double height, double width, double depth,
 double x, double y, double z) {

  this.width = width;
  this.height = height;
  this.depth = depth;
  this.x = x;
  this.y = y;
  this.z = z;
}

public void sizeTo(
  double width,
  double height,
  double depth) {

  this.width = width;
  this.height = height;
  this.depth = depth;
}
```

```
public void sizeRelative(
    double width,
    double height,
    double depth) {

    this.width += width;
    this.height += height;
    this.depth += depth;
}

public String draw() {

    String node1 = "Translation { \n" +
        "translation " + x + " " + y + " " +
        "z + \n}\n\n";

    String node2 = "Cube {\n" +
        "  height " + height +
        "\n  width " + width +
        "\n  depth " + depth +
        "\n}\n\n";

    String node3 = "Translation { \n" +
        "  translation " + -x + " " + -y + " " +
        -z + "\n" + "}\n\n";


    return node1 + node2 + node3;


}

}
```

The next requirement is a class to represent a VRML world. A world will hold various nodes as well as comments and the requisite version string. Example 23.15 is this class.

Example 23.15: The world class

```java
package elharo.vrml;

import java.util.Vector;
import java.util.Enumeration;

public class world {

  String version = "#VRML V1.0 ascii\n\n";

  // a Vector to hold the different objects
  // in the world
  Vector nodes;

  public world() {
    nodes = new Vector();
    nodes.addElement(version);
  }

  public void comment(String s) {

    nodes.addElement("#" + s);

  }

  public void addShape(shape s) {
    nodes.addElement(s.draw());
  }

  public void draw() {

    for (Enumeration e = nodes.elements();
      e.hasMoreElements();) {
      Object o = e.nextElement();
      // There are two possible classes in the
      // Vector, shapes and Strings
      if (o instanceof shape) {
        shape sh = (shape) o;
```

```
      System.out.println(sh.draw());
    }
    else if (o instanceof String) {
      System.out.println((String) o);
    }
  }
}


}
```

In Example 23.15, a VRML world is represented as a Vector that contains shapes and Strings. When the world is drawn, all of these are printed on System.out. This can be stored in a file and served off a web server.

There's a lot still to be added to this package, but first let's see how you might use this package to create a larger VRML world than you could easily do by hand. Example 23.16 fills a section of the x-y plane with a series of cubes ranging in height and width from 1 to 10 and in depth from 1 to 100.

Example 23.16: A large city of cubes

```
import elharo.vrml.*;

public class city {

  public static void main (String[] args) {

    world city = new world();
    int block = 10;

    for (int street = 1; street < 250; street ++) {
      for (int avenue = 1; avenue < 12; avenue++) {
        Cube building = new Cube();
        building.moveTo(street * block,
          avenue * 4 * block, 0);
```

```
      building.sizeTo(street * (block-1),
         avenue*4*(block-1), 30);
      city.addShape(building);
    }
  }


  city.draw();


}
```

As long as you have an algorithmic means of describing your world, it is possible to use Java to create far more complex worlds than would be possible either by writing VRML directly or by using a graphical 3-D modeler like Virtus World Builder. In fact the first worlds the author created using these techniques quickly overwhelmed and crashed his VRML viewer.

Example 23.17, the Cylinder class, is similar to the Cube class except that it has radius and height fields instead of height, width, and depth fields.

Example 23.17: The Cylinder subclass

```
package elharo.vrml;

public class Cylinder extends shape {

  double radius = 1.0;
  double height = 1.0;

  public Cylinder() {
  }

  public Cylinder(
    double radius, double height) {
```

```
    this.radius = radius;
    this.height = height;
}

public Cylinder(
 double radius, double height,
 double x, double y, double z) {

   this.radius = radius;
   this.height = height;
   this.x = x;
   this.y = y;
   this.z = z;
}

public void sizeTo(double radius,
   double height) {

   this.radius = radius;
   this.height = height;

}

public void sizeRelative(double radius,
   double height) {

   this.radius += radius;
   this.height += height;

}

public String draw() {

   String node1 = "Translation { \n" +
      "translation " + x + " " + y + " " + z +
      "\n}\n\n";

   String node2 = "Cylinder {\n" +
      "  radius " + radius +
```

```
        "\n  height " + height +
      "\n}\n\n";

      String node3 = "Translation { \n" +
      " translation " + -x + " " + -y + " " +
      -z + "\n" + "}\n\n";


      return node1 + node2 + node3;

    }


  }
```

By now you should be getting a feel for how these things work. Example 23.18 is a Cone class that has bottomRadius and height fields.

Example 23.18: The Cone subclass

```
package elharo.vrml;

public class Cone extends shape {

  double bottomRadius = 1.0;
  double height = 1.0;

  public Cone() {
  }

  public Cone(
   double bottomRadius, double height) {
    this.bottomRadius = bottomRadius;
    this.height = height;
  }

  public Cone(
   double bottomRadius, double height,
```

```java
   double x, double y, double z) {

  this.bottomRadius = bottomRadius;
  this.height = height;
  this.x = x;
  this.y = y;
  this.z = z;
}

public void sizeTo(double bottomRadius,
  double height) {

  this.bottomRadius = bottomRadius;
  this.height = height;

}

public void sizeRelative(double radius,
  double height) {

  this.bottomRadius += bottomRadius;
  this.height += height;

}

public String draw() {

  String node1 = "Translation { \n" +
    "translation " + x + " " + y + " " + z +
    "\n}\n\n";

  String node2 = "Cylinder {\n" +
    " bottomRadius " + bottomRadius +
    "\n  height " + height +
    "\n}\n\n";

  String node3 = "Translation { \n" +
    " translation " + -x + " " + -y + " " +
    -z + "\n" + "}\n\n";
```

```
    return node1 + node2 + node3;

  }

}
```

Finally, Example 23.19 covers the last predefined shape in VRML, the sphere. This one's a little simpler because spheres are a little simpler. It only has a radius field.

Example 23.19: The Sphere subclass

```
package elharo.vrml;

public class Sphere extends shape {

  double radius = 1.0;

  public Sphere (double radius) {
    this.radius = radius;
  }

  public Sphere ( double x,
   double y, double z, double radius) {
    this.x = x;
    this.y = y;
    this.z = z;
    this.radius = radius;
  }

  public void sizeTo(double radius) {

    this.radius = radius;

  }

  public void sizeRelative(double radius) {
```

```
        this.radius += radius;

    }


    public String draw() {

        String node1 = "Translation { \n" +
            "translation " + x + " " + y + " " + z +
            "\n}\n\n";

        String node2 = "Cylinder {\n" +
            "  radius " + radius +
            "\n}\n\n";

        String node3 = "Translation { \n" +
            "  translation " + -x + " " + -y + " " +
            -z + "\n" + "}\n\n";


        return node1 + node2 + node3;

    }

}
```

You now need classes for the non-three-dimensional shapes, that is, points, lines, and planes. Each of these classes will need its own Coordinate3 node as well as a PointSet, IndexedLineSet, or IndexedFaceSet. There are several design decisions to be made here. Should a point be made into a class? Should a Coordinate3 node be made into a class? Should there be one superclass for all three of these items or should they all be direct subclasses of shape? For that matter, should any of them be subclasses of shape? In VRML terminology, these don't quite meet the definition for shape.

There's no right answer to these questions. There is more than one solution which fits the problem. Which one you pick is primarily a matter of personal preference. In what's gone before we haven't hewn too closely to the VRML way of doing things so I'm not going to start now. Let's define points, lines, and triangles as separate objects, which are subclasses of shape and may thus be drawn. This is the simplest solution and most in keeping with our object model, but it is not the most efficient because many unnecessary nodes will be included in our models, which could be combined if we had an exact equivalent of PointSets, IndexedLineSets, or IndexedFaceSets. However, if this proves to be a real stumbling block in practice, you can return to the world class and modify its draw method to combine the different lines, points, and triangles into PointSets, IndexedLineSets and IndexedFaceSets before outputting them. This would not affect the interface these classes present to the outside world at all. This is, after all, one of the key advantages of object-oriented programming.

Example 23.20 is a point class. A point has position but not much else so all it needs to add to shape is an implementation of draw. For good measure, we'll also throw in a simple constructor that takes the location of the Point. This will be quite useful in many cases, even though it's not absolutely necessary.

Example 23.20: The point subclass

```
package elharo.vrml;

public class Point extends shape {

  public Point(double x, double y, double z) {
    this.x = x;
    this.y = y;
    this.z = z;
  }

  public String draw() {

    String node1 = "Coordinate3 { point [ ";
    String node2 = x + " " + y + " " + z;
    String node3 = "] }\n\n";
    String node4 = "PointSet {\n  " +
       "startIndex 0\n  numPoints 1\n}";

    return node1 + node2 + node3 + node4;

  }

}
```

Example 23.21 is a class that represents a line, or, more precisely, a line segment. The line is stored as two Point objects which represent it endpoints. Notice that the draw method uses the Point class's non-public fields x, y, and z. This is permissible because the Line class and the Point class are in the same package, elharo.vrml.

Example 23.21: The Line class

```java
package elharo.vrml;

public class Line extends shape {

  // a line is defined by two points
  Point p1;
  Point p2;

  public Line(Point p1, Point p2) {
    this.p1 = p1;
    this.p2 = p2;
  }

  public Line(double x1, double y1, double z1,
   double x2, double y2, double z2) {
    p1 = new Point(x1, y1, z1);
    p2 = new Point(x2, y2, z2);
  }

  public String draw() {

    String s1 = "Coordinate3 { point [ ";
    String s2 = p1.x + " " + p1.y + " " + p1.z +
      ",\n";
    String s3 = p2.x + " " + p2.y + " " + p2.z +
      ",\n";
    String s4 = "] }\n\n";
    String s5 = "IndexedLineSet {\n coordIndex [
      " + "0, 1\n] \n}";

    return s1 + s2 + s3 + s4 + s5;

  }

}
```

Example 23.22 is a class that represents a triangle. Although a more general face class would be possible, it's probably better to work with just the triangles out of which other faces are built.

The triangle is stored as three Point objects. As in the Line class, the draw method uses the Point's non-public fields x, y, and z. This is permissible because the Triangle class and the Point class are in the same package, elharo.vrml.

Example 23.22: The Triangle class

```java
package elharo.vrml;

public class Triangle extends shape {

  // a triangle is defined by three points
  Point p1;
  Point p2;
  Point p3;

  public Triangle(Point p1, Point p2, Point p3) {
    this.p1 = p1;
    this.p2 = p2;
    this.p3 = p3;
  }

  public Triangle(double x1, double y1, double z1,
    double x2, double y2, double z2,
    double x3, double y3, double z3) {
    p1 = new Point(x1, y1, z1);
    p2 = new Point(x2, y2, z2);
    p3 = new Point(x3, y3, z3);
  }

  public String draw() {

    String s1 = "Coordinate3 { point [ ";
    String s2 = p1.x + " " + p1.y + " " + p1.z +
      ",\n";
```

```
        String s3 = p2.x + " " + p2.y + " " + p2.z +
          ",\n";
        String s4 = p3.x + " " + p3.y + " " + p3.z +
          ",\n";
        String s5 = "] }\n\"";
        String s6 = "IndexedFaceSet {\n coordIndex [
          " + "0, 1, 2\n] \n}";


        return s1 + s2 + s3 + s4 + s5 + s6;


    }

}
```

Q&A

Q: *What about VRML modeling tools?*

A: There are an increasing number of good graphical tools
for building complex VRML models. However this chapter
focuses on giving you the knowledge and skills to build
your own tools when the existing ones don't suffice.

Quiz

1. Why doesn't the Point class defined in this chapter conflict
   with the Point class in java.awt?

Exercises

1. Add an AsciiText class to the elharo.vrml package. Should this
   be a subclass of shape?

2. Add a two-dimensional rectangle class to the elharo.vrml package. The class should enforce the restriction that all rectangles lie in a plane (that is not be bent).

3. Read the *VRML Language Specification* to learn about TransformSeparator nodes. Use these nodes to provide more efficient draw methods for the Cube, Cylinder, Cone, and Sphere classes.

4. Hard: Add rotation to the VRML package of this chapter. You need to be aware that rotation is in general not a commutative operation. That is, rotating an object by 90 degrees about the z axis followed by a 90-degree rotation about the y axis will not leave it in the same place as a 90-degree rotation about the y axis followed by a 90-degree rotation about the z axis. Hint: The easiest way to handle this is to store all requested rotations in a Vector and output them one at a time. This is hardly the most efficient solution though. For an efficient solution, you'll need a way to describe a shape's orientation in space.

5. The implementation of points, lines, and planes used here is very inefficient.Without changing any of the public signatures, modify the world class so that it uses no more than one Coordinate3 node, one IndexedLineSet Node, and one IndexedFaceSet node. You may need to add additional methods to the Point, Line, and Triangle classes as well. This is fine. Just don't make those methods public.

6. Create a VRML package that more closely maps to the structure of VRML itself, that is do not embed translations into each shape. Instead provide separate commands to move the pen. It may be possible to take an intermediate approach between these two extremes, one where location is part of the pen but the pen is always moved in an absolute sense from (0, 0, 0) rather than from the last location.

Summary

In this chapter you learned

• What VRML is

- How to create cubes, cones, spheres, and cylinders in a VRML world
- How to translate and rotate the virtual pen.
- How to draw points, lines, and faces using the Coordinate3, PointSet, IndexedLineSet, and IndexedFaceSet nodes.
- How to represent VRML objects as Java classes

Although this is the longest chapter in the book, it only begins to cover VRML and its relation to Java. You'll expand on these classes in the exercises.

Coming Up

In the next and final chapter, you'll learn about the many other resources that are available to help you write Java programs.

Further Reading

Only parts of the VRML standard have been even sketched in this chapter. The canonical source of information about VRML 1.0 is

BELL, GAVIN, ANTHONY PARISI and MARK PESCE, *The VRML 1.0C Specification*, http://vag.vrml.org/vrml10c.html

This document, like the *Java Language Specification*, sacrifices readability in favor of precision. A more gentle introduction to VRML can be found in

AMES, ANDREA L, DAVID R. NADEAU, and JOHN L. MORELAND, *The VRML Sourcebook*, New York: John Wiley & Sons, 1996

HARDENBERGH, JAN C., *The VRML FAQ*, http://vag.vrml.org/VRML_FAQ.html

VRML 1.0 is just a beginning. You may also be interested in

BELL, GAVIN, BRIAN BLAU, RIKK CAREY, JAN C. HARDENBERGH, ANTHONY PARISI, MARK PESCE, JON MARBRY, BILL MARTIN, and TOM MEYER, *The VRML 1.1 Specification Draft*, http://vag.vrml.org/vrml-1.1.html

BELL, GAVIN, RIKK CAREY, CHRIS MARRIN, and a cast of thousands, *The VRML 2.0 Specification*, http://vag.vrml.org/VRML2.0/

The following three web sites provide links to much current information about VRML:

The VRML Forum, http://vrml.wired.com/

The VRML Repository, http://sdsc.edu/vrml/

The VRML Architecture Group, http://vag.vrml.org/

Three-dimensional geometry is unfamiliar to many people. For a detailed look at the mathematics of objects in 3-space and the relation to computer graphics, see

FOLEY, JAMES, ANDRIES VAN DAM, STEVEN FEINER, and JOHN HUGHES, *Computer Graphics*, 2nd Edition, New York: Addison-Wesley, 1990

CHAPTER 24

JAVA RESOURCES

- The Java documentation

- Web sites

- Newsgroups and mailing lists

- Products

- User groups

This book has introduced you to Java. Although the book is ending, your journey is just beginning. There is far more you can do with Java and many more resources you can explore. This chapter will serve as your springboard to other Java material.

The Documentation

Twenty years ago computers were big, expensive machines. They cost upwards of a million dollars and required much electricity, special cooling systems and many, many engineers just to keep them running. Today computers are small, cheap easy-to-use (relatively), and do much more. But there are still a lot of the old, million dollar monstrosities deep inside the innards of many large corporations.

The truth is that today's $2000 personal computers are fully capable of doing anything and everything the old million-dollar computers did and doing it better, and the old computers should really be junked. Still, it's hard for a company, even one with billions of dollars of annual revenue, to throw away something they've poured millions of dollars and hundreds of staff-years into. Therefore, they feel obligated to find some use, no matter how ridiculous, for these old dinosaurs until they finally break down completely or get struck by a meteor, whichever happens first.

The typical use these old computers are put to is writing documentation for the new computers. The problem is the old computers aren't very smart so they don't write very well. Furthermore, they're old so sometimes a vacuum tube blows and they spew out a few pages of complete gibberish (as opposed to the usual half-gibberish) before one of the maintenance engineers notices and replaces the vacuum tube.

Therefore, when you're reading the documentation for any computer system, be sure to remember who wrote it (the old expensive, stupid computer) and don't take it too seriously. If it's difficult to understand, just remember that it's not you. The documentation is poorly written because, after all, the computer that wrote it isn't very smart. Sometimes you'll run across a few pages that you can't understand at all. They may seem to be a foreign language, Martian perhaps. When you encounter this, it's almost certainly one of the sections where a vacuum tube blew and the computer started spitting out gibberish. Just skip ahead a few pages and pick up reading at the point where the computer got fixed.

But, above all else, remember that it's not that you're unintelligent. The documentation really just isn't any good.

The Java Language Specification

The Java Language Specification is the official documentation from Sun that explains the Java language syntax. It's available in HTML and PostScript format from Javasoft's ftp site at ftp.javasoft.com in the docs directory. You should definitely print a copy for easy reference. By the time you read this it may also be available as a printed book from Addison-Wesley.

> **Tip** If you don't have a PostScript printer, try to get a copy of ghostscript from any GNU archive such as ftp://prep.ai.mit.edu/pub/gnu/. Ghostscript is available for Macs, Windows, and most popular Unix workstations, and will let you view and print the documentation on whichever printer you do have.

The Java Language Specification concentrates on precision rather than clarity. It's written for compiler designers rather than normal programmers and is thus full of lines like, "THIS specification uses context-free grammars to define the lexical and syntactic structure of a Java program"[1] and "Each constructor parameter (§8.6.1) is initialized to the corresponding argument value provided by an object creation expression (§14.8) or explicit constructor invocation (§8.6.5)."[2] Don't worry too much about lines like this. You can probably make sense out of what you need to know. Assume the rest was just spewed out by a misbehaving Sun-1 with a blown vacuum tube.

The language spec is occasionally invaluable for tracking down a syntax error in a particular line of code. Otherwise, keep a copy in the bathroom and dip into a random section every so often. Most of it is gibberish, but some parts do make sense. And the more work you do with Java, the more parts will make sense. You can learn things by reading the language spec. Just don't expect to learn everything you need to know.

---

[1] *The Java Language Specification*, version 1.0.2 FCS, p.7.

[2] Ibid, p.43

The Java API Documentation

Much of what you learned in this book is part of the Java API rather than the language itself. The Java API is divided into seven packages and the documentation is divided similarly. When you have a question about a particular system supplied method, this is the first place you should look.

There are hundreds of classes and over a thousand different methods in the Java API. A complete printout takes hundreds of pages and is not recommended. Fortunately the API docs are available in HTML format from ftp.javasoft.com and all its mirrors. For ease of reference, you should download a copy to your local hard drive.

Each file in the API documentation is named according to its class. Thus, java.awt.Graphics is documented in the file java.awt.Graphics.html. Most of the time you don't need to worry about this. However if you're using a Macintosh, you'll note that some of the filenames are too long for the Mac to handle. Therefore, there's a special set of files available for the Mac that has renamed the longish filenames to shorter things.

Remember to search for methods and fields in the superclasses of an object as well as in the class itself. This is particularly important for the AWT. Huge amounts of functionality for many classes are hidden in java.awt.Component and java.awt.Container.

Make sure you look in the right class. Many classes have members that are instances of a different class. For example, the Graphics object passed to the paint method of an applet is an instance of java.awt.Graphics, not part of java.applet.Applet. Similarly, most of what you need to know about events is in java.awt.Event.

Another advantage to installing the API documentation on your local hard drive is that you can use grep, BBEdit, or another multifile search tool to search through the entire documentation tree when you absolutely can't find where a particular method is documented.

The API documentation is regrettably short of real examples, and often doesn't say much about what a method does. Thus although it will tell you that java.awt.ACTION_EVENT is a `public static final int` (i.e., a mnemonic constant) and that java.awt.Components have action methods that have two arguments and return a `boolean`, it won't tell you what an action method is or why you should care. Then again, that's why you have this book. :-)

Sun licenses the Java source code for non-commercial use very freely. Essentially as long as you don't ship a program that includes pieces of Sun's source code, you don't need to pay for a license. You can even distribute ports and other derivative works as long as you don't charge for them. You will need to mail or fax Sun a signed piece of paper agreeing to these terms. Email isn't sufficient.

Sun's definition of non-commercial use is quite broad and includes shipping competing products not based on Sun source code as well as shipping any applet or application built with the Java tools. Some other compiler vendors that try to restrict their customers from building competing products through licensing agreements should learn from this. Complete details are available on Javasoft's licensing page at http://www.javasoft.com/license.html.

Much of the source including javac and most of the API is itself written in Java. Other parts including the Java runtime environment are written in C so a knowledge of C will be helpful. However the most common need for source is to explore the inner workings of the API, and this is primarily composed of Java code. At this stage of development of Java and the Java documentation, there are still some things that can only be gleaned by exploring the source.

Web Sites

The key site for Java information is http://www.javasoft.com/. This is Sun's official site for Java, and contains the latest published version of all official Java information. This site has grown quite busy and is mirrored in several places including

United States

    Dimension X   http://java.dnx.com/

    Wayne, Indiana http://www.science.wayne.edu/java/

United Kingdom

      http://sunsite.doc.ic.ac.uk/packages/java-http/

Sweden

      http://www.cdt.luth.se/java/

Singapore

http://sunsite.nus.sg/hotjava/

Korea

http://cair-archive.kaist.ac.kr/java/

Gamelan, http://www.gamelan.com/, maintains a database of applets and other Java resources sorted by category. Source code is available for many of the applets. This is a good place to look to see if someone's already written a particular applet, or just to look for hints about how to code something.

As usual, Yahoo has fairly useful collections of links to Java info at

http://www.yahoo.com/Computers/Languages/Java/

This book hasn't talked about JavaScript which has little relation to Java except for the name. Still if you'd like to learn more, you can start at *The JavaScript Index*,

http://www.c2.org/~andreww/javascript/

Finally, Prentice Hall has put together a web site to support this book with the latest Java news and updates, answers to the exercises, frequently asked questions, special challenge problems, and links to key Java sites. Point your browser to

http://www.prenhall.com/developers_resource_series/

Much of this material is also available at the author's personal site

http://sunsite.unc.edu/javafaq/

Newsgroups and Mailing Lists

comp.lang.java is the key newsgroup for Java. The author of this book reads it regularly and you should too. It's a great place to look for help with simple to advanced Java questions and has so far mostly managed to avoid the various floating flame wars and garbage posts that have rendered so much of Usenet pointless.

Digital Espresso at http://www.io.org/~mentor/J___Notes.html provides a weekly digest of traffic in comp.lang.java. If you don't have time to keep up with that newsgroup, then this site is invaluable.

Natural Intelligence hosts the java-mac mailing list dedicated to platform-specific issues regarding Java on the Macintosh. To subscribe send email to majordomo@natural.com with the words "subscribe java-mac" in the body of your message. There is also a corresponding java-win mailing list for Windows-related Java discussion. You can also use the form at

http://www.roaster.com/submacwin.html

Java-digest is a digested mailing list for anything and everything related to Java. To subscribe, send email to majordomo@shore.net. The body of the email should contain the words "subscribe java-digest" and nothing else.

Products

As this is written, development tools for Java like Integrated Development Environment's (IDE's) and class libraries are just beginning to become available. Many companies have announced products but few have shipped. More will be available by the time you read this.

Sun's Java Workshop is a cross-platform, browser-based IDE written entirely in Java that is in alpha release at the time of this writing. Right now, it is slow to the point of unusability, even on the fastest SparcStations and Pentium Pro's. Future versions may benefit from a just-in-time compiler. Right now, it's little more than a proof-of-concept, though.

Roaster from Natural Intelligence was used to develop many of the applets in this book, primarily because at the time it was the only Java environment that would run on a PowerBook. The source code editor is useful, but otherwise it's buggy, crash-prone, and, at $199, over-priced. I do not recommend it. A less-buggy and more complete version should be available by the time you read this. For more details, see http://www.roaster.com/.

Symantec's Café is an integrated development environment (IDE) for Java that runs on Windows 95, Windows NT, and the Mac. Café includes a syntax-coloring Java source code editor, a debugger, visual design tools, a class editor, a hierarchy editor, a project manager, a native compiler, and the 1.0 Sun Java Development Kit. Café shipped just as this book was completed so I haven't had time to review it yet, but initial reports from the net have been fairly positive. It is subject to the usual bugs of a 1.0 release. Street price is around $100. For more details, see

http://cafe.symantec.com/

Besiex Software is working on FrIJDE (pronounced frigid), a freeware, cross-platform Java IDE. At this writing, it's a very early alpha but it's worth keeping an eye on. See

http://amber.wpi.edu/FrIJDE/

for more details.

TakeFive Software's SNiFF+ is a Solaris-based IDE that can handle multiple languages including Java. It includes the Sun Java Developers Kit, a documentation editor, a project editor, workspace manager, a source code editor, and support for configuration management and version control. Ports are planned to SunOS, HP-UX, IBM AIX, SGI Irix, Digital UNIX, DEC ULTRIX, Novell UnixWare, SCO UNIX, and Linux. The price is close to $3000, which is quite steep. However, if you already own Sniff+, the upgrade to support Java is free. For more information, contact TakeFive Software at (800) 418-2535, (408) 777-1440, email info@takefive.com, or check out the web site at

http://www.takefive.com/snifjava.htm

Rogue Wave's JFactory is a Visual Basic-like visual development environment for creating Java user interfaces. It's available on Windows 95, NT, and Solaris. Pricing is $495. For more information, see

http://www.roguewave.com/rwpav/products/jfactory/jfactory.htm

Kalimantan is a free collection of basic tools for Java development. It includes an inspector, a debugger, and a class browser. For more details, see

http://www.real-time.com/java/kalimantan/index.html

Soft As It Gets' ED supports Java. It includes a hierarchical class and method browser, color syntax highlighting with user-defined keywords, autocorrection, code templates and skeletons, search and replace with regular expressions, visually compare files for differences, and support for 30 programming languages including Java. Visit their web site at

http://www.ozemail.com.au/~saig/ed_java.html

or send email to saig@ozemail.com.au.

Step Ahead Software Pty Ltd publishes JAVelin, a version of their Visual Classworks graphical object oriented development tool for C++ that supports Java. JAVelin costs around $200 and is available for Windows 95 and NT. JAVelin focuses on classes rather than source code files. Classes are represented as icons in a graphical design window. Fields and methods are created and modified from within the design window. Inheritance is implemented via drag and drop in the design window. The source code files are manipulated in the background to reflect the changes made by the programmer through the graphical user interface. For more information, contact Step Ahead at stepsoft@ozemail.com.au or visit their Website at

http://www.ozemail.com.au/~stepsoft/

Quintessential Objects' $79 Diva is a Java IDE for Windows 95 and NT that includes a class browser capabilities, a hierarchy browser, a visual designer, a class wizard to aid Java programmers by generating code to handle Java Events, a code snippet library, and a syntax coloring code and HTML editor. For more information see the Website at http://www.qoi.com/, send email to diva@qoi.com, or call (212) 249-7429.

ModelWorks Software's JPad is a simple $29 Java source code editor integrated with Sun's Java tools so you can compile and run your programs from within your editor. JPad is available for Windows 95 and NT. See

http://www.csn.net/express/

Metrowerks has included Java in Code Warrior 9, their Macintosh-hosted C++ development environment. See

http://www.metrowerks.com/products/java/index.html

Unreleased Products

A number of companies have announced products that may or may not be available by the time you read this.

Borland has promised to integrate Java support into Borland C++ 5.0 for Windows 95 and NT. More details are available at

http://www.borland.com/Product/java/java.html

Microsoft has produced several press releases about Jakarta, their Java environment for Windows. The press releases are certainly impressive and include reference to many features no one else is yet attempting, such as access to the native Windows API and ActiveX controls. However, Microsoft's press releases are always impressive. Their delivery schedule is quite a bit less so. Don't hold your breath waiting for these tools.

Books and Magazines

As of this writing, the available books for Java are rather poor, and all the best documentation is online. That's one reason I decided to write this book. I do expect that by the time you're reading this there will be a host of Java books on the shelves.

There are two magazines worthy of note. First IDG has launched a web-only *JavaWorld* at http://www.javaworld.com/. You'll need to register, but otherwise it's free. Secondly SIGS Publishing produces the bimonthly *The Java Report*. For more details, see http://www.sigs.com/ or send email to subscriptions@sigs.com.

User Groups

One of the best ways to learn more about Java is to join a local user group. Java User Group's (JUG's for short) are popping up all over. If there isn't one in your area, why don't you start one? You don't need much, just a place to meet and a bunch of interested people to talk about what they're doing with Java.

Australia Australian Java User's Group
http://sunsite.anu.edu.au/suninfo/java/

Chicago Chicagoland Java User Group
http://www.gr.com/cjug/cjug.htm

Dallas/Fort Worth Dallas/Fort Worth Java Users' Group
http://www.utdallas.edu/orgs/dfwjava/

Denmark Dansk Java Udvikler Klub

http://sunsite.auc.dk/DJUK/

Denver, Colorado   DAMJUG
http://www.webset.com/jug/

France   Java Cyber Club France
http://www.labri.u-bordeaux.fr/java/

Illinois   I-JUG
http://www.xnet.com/~rudman/java/ijug.html

London   Java Users' Group (Greater London)
http://www.compulink.co.uk/~java/

Lucca, Italy   Mouse Club
http://www.lunet.it/Lucca/ASS_VOL/MOUSE/mouse.htm

DC, Baltimore, Virginia   The Mid-Atlantic Java Users' Group
http://www.rssi.com/info/majug.html

Missouri and Kansas   Midwest Regional Java Users Group Of Missouri & Kansas
http://www.surinam.net/java/mrjug.html

New York City   The Java Study Group
http://www.inch.com/~nyjava/

North Carolina   UNC Java SIG
http://www.cs.unc.edu/Research/javasig/

Oregon   Oregon Java Interest Group
http://www.cs.uoregon.edu/ojig/

Philadelphia   PhillyJUG
http://www.iliad.com/PhillyJUG/

Sacramento   Sacramento Java Users Group
http://www.calweb.com/~statenet/sacjug/

Toronto   Toronto Java Users Group
http://www.jug.org/

United States   Java-SIG
http://www.sug.org/java.html
office@sug.org
(617) 232-0514

Wisconsin   The Wisconsin Java User Group
http://www.hcsinc.com/~rmonson/wjug.htm

Q&A

Q: *Do I need an IDE for Java?*

A: No. You can write and compile Java code just fine with a text editor and a command line compiler.

Exercises

1. Download the *Java Language Specification*. Print it out.
2. Download the JDK API documentation. Install it on your hard drive and add a bookmark to it in your Web browser of choice.
3. Find and read the FAQ list and known bugs page at http://www.javasoft.com/
4. Read comp.lang.java.
5. Join a local user group. If you can't find a local user group, start one.

Summary

In this chapter you learned

- How to read the Java documentation
- Some useful Websites
- That you should read comp.lang.java
- About various third-party products to help you write Java programs
- That you should join a user group.

INDEX

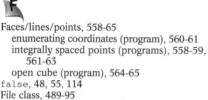

JAVA DEVELOPER'S RESOURCE